THE STATE OF AMERICAN JEWRY

JEWISH STUDIES IN THE TWENTY-FIRST CENTURY

Frederick E. Greenspahn is Gimelstob Eminent Scholar Emeritus in Judaic Studies at Florida Atlantic University. Greenspahn is General Editor of the Jewish Studies in the Twenty-First Century Series, and is the volume editor of the following books in the series:

The Hebrew Bible: New Insights and Scholarship

Women and Judaism: New Insights and Scholarship

Jewish Mysticism and Kabbalah: New Insights and Scholarship

Contemporary Israel: New Insights and Scholarship

Early Judaism: New Insights and Scholarship

The State of American Jewry: New Insights and Scholarship

The State of American Jewry

New Insights and Scholarship

Edited by
Frederick E. Greenspahn

NEW YORK UNIVERSITY PRESS
New York

NEW YORK UNIVERSITY PRESS
New York
www.nyupress.org

© 2025 by New York University
All rights reserved

Please contact the Library of Congress for Cataloging-in-Publication data.

ISBN: 9781479813117 (hardback)
ISBN: 9781479813124 (paperback)
ISBN: 9781479813162 (library ebook)
ISBN: 9781479813179 (consumer ebook)

This book is printed on acid-free paper, and its binding materials are chosen for strength and durability. We strive to use environmentally responsible suppliers and materials to the greatest extent possible in publishing our books.

The manufacturer's authorized representative in the EU for product safety is Mare Nostrum Group B.V., Mauritskade 21D, 1091 GC Amsterdam, The Netherlands.
Email: gpsr@mare-nostrum.co.uk.

Manufactured in the United States of America

10 9 8 7 6 5 4 3 2 1

Also available as an ebook

CONTENTS

Introduction   1
Frederick E. Greenspahn

PART I. PEOPLE

1. Jewish Migration to the United States and the Changing Demographics of American Jewry   9
Steven J. Gold

2. The Gendered Landscape of U.S. Judaism   37
Sarah Imhoff

3. The Changing Face of Jewish America in the Twenty-First Century   58
Bruce Haynes

4. Non-Jews in Jewish Communities   85
Jennifer A. Thompson

PART II. JEWS' PLACE IN AMERICAN SOCIETY

5. Jewish Americans through a Socioeconomic Lens   115
Ilana M. Horwitz

6. The Liminal Place of Jews in American Society   131
Marc Dollinger

7. The Changing American Jewish Relationship with Israel   162
Dov Waxman

PART III. CHANGING STRUCTURES WITHIN THE JEWISH COMMUNITY

8. American Judaism in the Twenty-First Century   185
Ari Y. Kelman

9. Orthodox Judaism in the United States   210
Zev Eleff

10. Continuity and Change in the American Jewish
    Organizational Ecosystem   242
    Theodore Sasson

Conclusion: The Ever-Changing People   271
    Hasia Diner

About the Contributors   281

Index   285

Introduction

FREDERICK E. GREENSPAHN

Although there were Jews in North America more than a hundred years before the Revolutionary War, most of what characterizes the contemporary American Jewish community took shape a century later, when huge numbers of immigrants arrived from eastern Europe at the end of the nineteenth century, following an earlier wave from the center of that continent. It was then that most of the organizations that would provide the infrastructure for American Jewish life were created, including the Reform, Conservative, and Orthodox denominations; Jewish community centers; and local federations, as well as the Jewish Publication Society, the American Jewish Historical Society, the National Council of Jewish Women, the American Jewish Committee, Hadassah, the Anti-Defamation League, the Jewish Welfare Board, the American Jewish Congress, Hillel, and the United Jewish Appeal.

Decades later, the 1961 trial of Adolf Eichmann, a leading figure in the Nazi effort to exterminate Jews, and the Six-Day War between Israel and a coalition of its Arab neighbors in 1967, along with America's growing emphasis on ethnicity, brought the Holocaust and Zionism to the center of American Jewish identity, a dramatic change from the Reform and Orthodox communities' previous opposition to the creation of a Jewish state. Today, however, much of what has characterized American Jewry for several decades—an emphasis on remembering the Holocaust, supporting the state of Israel, and maintaining long-standing institutions that mediate community and philanthropic life while emphasizing east European Ashkenazi Jewish heritage—is changing, as aging baby boomers (those born in the mid-1940s to the mid-1960s) give way to younger cohorts. The Reform and Conservative movements are shrinking while alternative entities are emerging, including nondenominational seminaries and Orthodox groups that welcome nonobservant followers. At the same time, many Iranian, Israeli, and Russian Jews have come to the United States, dramatically affecting the tenor of Jewish communities, where synagogue pews now include Asian, African American, and Latinx faces, challenging long-standing assumptions as to what it means to be a Jew in the United States.[1] Meanwhile, women have assumed leadership positions, including rabbinical ordination. These phenomena were epitomized by a nationally televised public service announcement showing an Asian American woman proclaiming, "People sometimes ask me if I like being the first Korean American rabbi. Are they meshuggah? What's not to like?"[2] Even non-Jews have found a place within the American Jewish community, as exemplified by one rabbi, who invited those in her congregation to come forward on the holiest day of the year and be blessed for casting their "lot with the Jewish people by becoming part of this congregation, and . . . raising your sons and daughters as Jews."[3] Meanwhile, Israel has become an increasingly divisive element in American Jewish life, with some groups openly criticizing the actions of its government while others "double down" on their support. At the same time, those century-old organizations which for so long occupied an uncontested place at the heart of American Jewish life have experienced declining membership, even as new organizations with varying missions have emerged. As tempting as it would be to focus on contemporary societal factors, such as intermarriage, adoption, and political changes in both Israel and the United States, as contributing to these developments, it is important to remember that change is as old as Judaism itself. Moreover, almost every development in American Jewish life has parallels in other ethnic and religious groups, as long-established denominations and their institutions weaken while nondenominational conservative movements grow, women assume leadership positions, and the wealthy wield ever-increasing power at the expense of less advantaged groups.[4]

At the same time that these changes have taken place, a growing number of Jews have reached the highest levels of American society. While Louis Brandeis's appointment to the U.S. Supreme Court in the early part of the twentieth century set the precedent for a "Jewish seat," subsequently occupied by Benjamin Cardozo, Felix Frankfurter, Arthur Goldberg, and Abe Fortas, by the century's end there were three Jews, Ruth Bader Ginsburg, Stephen Breyer, and Elena Kagan, serving simultaneously, following the remarkable ascent of a Jewish candidate for the vice presidency, Joseph Lieberman, in 2000, and multiple Jews in Congress and even within the first families of both political parties.[5] However, these signs of acceptance were followed by evidence of growing antisemitism, as expressed at a 2017 march in Charlottesville, Virginia, in which marchers chanted "Jews will not replace us" and shootings at synagogues in Pittsburgh, Pennsylvania (2018), and Poway, California (2019), followed by a similar attempt in Colleyville, Texas, in 2022.

This book explores the nature of these changes within American Jewry over the past few decades and charts their impact on its composition, structure, and behavior as well as its attitude towards a host of issues, ranging from gender to politics and international affairs. It offers a comprehensive overview of how American Jewish life and community have evolved in the new millennium. The extent of these developments is readily apparent at synagogue events, where many of the pews are filled with worshippers of various skin tones. As Bruce Haynes describes in his chapter, these shifts in the composition of the Jewish community seem to contradict the premise of Karen Brodkin's book *How Jews Became White Folks and What That Says about Race in America*.[6] Equally visible is the prevalence of women, described here by Sarah Imhoff, who notes in her chapter how women often bring different styles of leadership from those of men. Less conspicuous is the presence of converts and even non-Jews in Jewish organizations, including synagogues; Jennifer Thompson's chapter explores the profound ways in which their backgrounds can affect the tenor and even focus of these settings. Similarly, Jewish immigrants, most extensively from Israel, the former Soviet Union, and Latin America, are changing the ethnic profile of American Jewry, and, as Steven Gold points out in his chapter, the community's focus and direction. Collectively, these shifts in gender, ethnicity, and national background signal the likelihood of different priorities, styles, and emphases coming to the fore within American Jewish communities.

Against this backdrop it is no wonder that the organizational structure of the American Jewish community is also taking on new forms, with long-established entities weakening and newer ones emerging, as explained by Theodore Sasson in his chapter, reflecting a more diverse agenda from that of the past. While the established Jewish leadership often laments these developments, Sasson argues that they are actually signs of vitality, albeit ones that can be discomfiting for those accustomed to the familiar order.

The demographic and institutional changes described above have inevitably affected the nature of religious practice, which, as Ari Kelman's chapter notes, is ultimately as much a social phenomenon as it is theological. Even the Orthodox community has changed in ways described here by Zev Eleff. Moreover, as Ilana Horwitz demonstrates in her chapter, American Jewry is more economically diverse than many (including Jews themselves) often assume, with some highly successful and others left behind. However, among the most conspicuous phenomena are the visible shifts in attitudes toward Israel, which is evolving as well, becoming now a polarizing element within American Jewry, as explored by Dov Waxman.[7]

As we attempt to absorb and even make sense of all these changes, it is worth remembering that none of the underlying dynamics is completely new.[8] Judaism has been diverse from the days of the Bible, when Israelites constituted two kingdoms that were often at odds with one another. Centuries later, communities in Jerusalem and Babylon produced two separate Talmuds, while the Shulḥan Aruch, the definitive code of Jewish practice, notes often different practices for Jews in Central and Eastern Europe as opposed to those of Spanish (Sephardic) ancestry.

As a result of these developments, Jews' place in America is now more complicated than it once was. Whereas there were three Jews on the Supreme Court at the turn of the twenty-first century, twenty years later there was again only one, while antisemitism had become increasingly visible and, perhaps, widespread. Collectively, these developments reflect Marc Dollinger's observation in this book about American Jews' liminality. In sum, the state of American Jewry, religiously, socially, and politically in the twenty-first century has changed significantly from the immigration era and even from the era during and immediately following the world wars.

The chapters in this volume describe this reality, which differs both from the contours of the Jewish community a generation ago and from what it is still widely thought to be. The contributors explore these developments under the rubric of dramatic change, a phenomenon they also reflect. Significant scholars within the larger realm of Jewish Studies, they were mostly trained within and teach at secular universities, where Jewish Studies has exploded over the past generation, rather than being confined to the Jewish settings that prevailed in decades past, with ramifications that merit careful consideration.[9] Moreover, the Association for Jewish Studies, the professional society for Jewish Studies scholars, is now similar in size to the rabbinic organizations in each of the major Jewish movements—Reform, Conservative, and Orthodox—with attendance at its annual conference far exceeding that of those rabbinical associations. The heightened status of Jewish Studies professors was confirmed in 2018, when Williams College, which was founded in the late eighteenth century in Williamstown, Massachusetts, appointed Jewish Studies professor Maud Mandel as its president, another reflection of the growth and acceptance of both Jewish Studies and Judaism within American culture. This phenomenon had been evident already in references to America's "Judeo-Christian" tradition in contrast to earlier references to the United States as a "Christian country," thereby marking the acceptance of Judaism as part of the American religious/cultural fabric, though it also highlighted the weakened hold that the Jewish community has on its own development.[10] It is the goal of this book to explore the various dimensions of these developments and what they can tell us about the current state of American Jewry.

This volume would have been inconceivable without the guidance and support of Jeanne Abrams, Annie Jollymore, Bruce Phillips, Shari Rabin, Adam Rovner, Elias Sacks, Jonathan Sarna, Jack Wertheimer, Stephen Whitfield, and Gary Zola. As always, at New York University Press, Jennifer Hammer's confidence and encouragement contributed greatly to its realization. And, of course, Barbara Pearl's suggestions and observations were instrumental in helping me recognize and contemplate the significance of a profoundly changing environment. For all that and much more, I am deeply grateful.

NOTES

1 See also Laura Limonic, *Kugel and Frijoles: Latino Jews in the United States* (Detroit: Wayne State University Press, 2019); Helen Kim and Noah Samuel Leavitt, *JewAsian: Race, Religion, and Identity for America's Newest Jews* (Lincoln: University of Nebraska Press, 2016); and Saba Soomekh, *From the Shahs to Los Angeles: Three Generations of Iranian Jewish Women between Religion and Culture* (Albany: State University of New York Press, 2012).

2 "CBS Cares Diversity PSA—Rabbi Buchdahl," YouTube video, 0:10, www.youtube.com.
3 Lauren Markoe, "At Yom Kippur, a Blessing for the Congregation's Non-Jews," *Washington Post*, September 17, 2015.
4 Jonathan Sarna cites numerous parallels between developments in American Jewry and American Christendom. See *American Judaism: A History*, 2nd ed. (New Haven: Yale University Press, 2019), 17, 18, 21, 41, 44, 48, 54, 59, 72, 80, 81, 84, 86, 91, 103, 106, 108, 123, 127, 142, 145, 148, 151, 176, 180, 181, 186, 194, 195, 212, 246, 248, 268, 272, 274, 278, 279, 280, 281, 286, 299, 300, 309, 314, 219, 320, 326, 327, 328, 340, 345, 347, 352, 353, 357, 362, 373, and 386. See also Ryan P. Burge, *The Nones: Where They Came From, Who They Are, and Where They Are Going*, 2nd ed. (Minneapolis: Fortress, 2021); Jim Davis and Michael Graham, *The Great Dechurching: Who's Leaving, Why Are They Going, and What Will It Take to Bring Them Back?* (Grand Rapids, MI: Zondervan, 2023); and Lila Corwin Berman, *The American Jewish Philanthropic Complex: The History of a Multibillion-Dollar Institution* (Princeton, NJ: Princeton University Press, 2020).
5 David G. Dalin, *Jewish Justices of the Supreme Court, from Brandeis to Kagan* (Waltham: Brandeis University Press, 2017).
6 Karen Brodkin, *How Jews Became White Folks and What That Says about Race in America* New Brunswick, NJ:(Rutgers University Press, 1998).
7 See also Andrew Lapin, "American Rabbis, Wrestling with Israel's Behavior, Weigh Different Approaches from the Pulpit," *Forward*, www.forward.com.
8 See also Robert Goldenberg's description of the "the vigorous diversity in ways of life that different groups of Jews have adopted" 2000 years ago, suggesting that "perhaps . . . plurality, not consensus, is the natural Jewish configuration." "In the Beginning Is My End," in *Early Judaism*, ed. Frederick E. Greenspahn (New York: New York University Press, 2018), 233.
9 See also Frederick E. Greenspahn, "Have We Arrived? The Case of Jewish Studies in U.S. Universities," *Midstream* 52, no. 5 (September–October, 2006): 16–19.
10 Robert Handy, *A Christian America: Protestant Hopes and Historical Reality*, 2nd ed. (New York: Oxford University Press, 1984). See also Will Herberg, *Protestant, Catholic, Jew: An Essay in American Religious Sociology*, rev. ed. (New York: Anchor Books, 1960); and Mark Silk, "Notes on the Judeo-Christian Tradition in America," *American Quarterly* 36 (1984): 65–85.

PART I

People

1

Jewish Migration to the United States and the Changing Demographics of American Jewry

STEVEN J. GOLD

The current era of international migration is marked not only by unprecedented numbers of migrants, but also by an especially varied range of origins and characteristics. Globally, a wide variety of social, political, economic, and environmental events have prompted human beings to cross international borders in search of survival, physical security, economic opportunity, and broader horizons. These numerous and diverse migrants travel under a host of legal statuses, including undocumented, temporary laborers, refugees, students, tourists, skilled workers, and investors, and as family unification migrants.

Jews, a group known for their high levels of education and geographic dispersion and for their multiple engagements in social, political, cultural, economic, and religious life, are involved in many of these processes. The Pew Research Center notes that while only 5 percent of Christians and 3 percent of Muslims globally have migrated internationally during their lifetime, 25 percent of living Jews no longer reside in their country of birth.[1]

Applying world system theory, Sergio DellaPergola showed that the post–World War II migration of Jews has followed a pattern of movement from less developed areas of the world to more economically central, advanced regions, demonstrating that economic improvement ranks with nationalism as a major force behind Jewish migration.[2] Since the United States is among the most economically developed countries globally, migration from the Former Soviet Union (FSU), Iran, Latin America, South Africa, and Israel is consistent with this general trend.

While most migrants to the U.S. prior to the mid-twentieth century were from Europe, the recent era encompasses a much larger fraction from Asia, Africa, Latin America, and the Middle East. That same pattern is evident among Jewish migrants, who increasingly come from the Middle East, Latin America, and elsewhere. Contemporary Jewish migrants to the U.S. are diverse in language, culture, religious outlook, and occupational profile. They maintain extensive contacts with their countries of origin, with Israel, and with coworkers, friends, and relatives worldwide. Finally, like migrants globally, their numbers include a broad array of legal statuses. New Jewish immigrants bring energy, diversity, imagination, youth, and numbers to the American Jewish community, while allowing another generation of Jews born abroad to partake of an environment that has been conducive to Jews' achievements and well-being.

At the same time, it is important to note that the meeting of minds, cultures, and communities required for Jewish immigrants, U.S. Jews, and the larger American population to develop constructive and salutary relations is not an easy endeavor. Rather, this process is challenging for newcomers, hosts, and, in some cases, bystanders as well.

This chapter reviews recent Jewish migrants' motives for migration and also outlines their social and demographic characteristics, models of economic adaptation, community formation, social and religious practices, and integration into the American Jewish community. In addition, it explores patterns of contention and collaboration between host communities and newly arrived Jewish groups. A review of American history suggests that the appearance and partial resolution of such intragroup conflicts—like those occurring between German and Yiddish-speaking Jews during the late nineteenth and early twentieth century—are near universal aspects of the history of American ethnic groups (Jewish and non-Jewish) and informs us about the processes of growth and accommodation that are central features of life in a diverse and dynamic society.[3]

Jewish Migrants to the U.S. during the Late Nineteenth and Early Twentieth Century

From the mid-nineteenth century until the formation of Israel in 1948, the U.S. was the primary destination for Jewish migrants globally. From

1881 to 1928, 2,414,989 Jews entered the U.S. During those same years, 112,611 Jews (5 percent) departed, yielding a net increase in population of 2,302,378.[4] The overwhelming majority originated from Russia and other areas of Eastern Europe. According to Thomas Archdeacon's statistics, the 1.8 million "Hebrews" were the second largest immigrant group to enter the U.S. from 1899 to 1924, their numbers surpassed only by Italians.[5]

Even those entering the U.S. from other locations (Germany, France, the United Kingdom, Canada, and Africa) were largely "transmigrants from Eastern Europe."[6] Hailing from the "Pale of Settlement," they shared many commonalties in culture, religious practice, diet, and language (Yiddish). These similarities acknowledged, this group was also stratified by considerable differences in terms of urban experience, political outlook, religiosity, work experience, cultural orientation, and time of arrival.

Between 1924 and 1965, immigration to the U.S. from regions outside of Western Europe was heavily restricted by the Johnson–Reed Act. Nevertheless, approximately 500,000 Jews were able to enter the country during that time. Many were admitted as refugees and, as such, were exempt from the Johnson–Reed Act's restrictions.[7] From 1954 through 1995, the Hebrew Immigration Aid Society (HIAS) assisted 519,750 Jewish arrivals. The largest numbers were from the Former Soviet Union (FSU, 367,021), North Africa (61,430), Iran (10,803), and other countries (80,496). Finally, substantial numbers of Jewish migrants from other nations were not assisted by HIAS and hence do not appear in their counts. The largest of these, Israelis, comprise something on the order of 175,000 to 250,000 persons.[8]

Latin American Jews are the fastest growing recent Jewish immigrant group in the U.S. and have been the subject of an expanding body of research. While they have a presence in several U.S. locations, their largest settlement is in Miami, the major American city with the largest fraction of foreign-born persons as well as the largest fraction of foreign-born Jews. Israelis and FSU Jews, together with Latin Americans and immigrants from other locations account for about one-third of adults in Miami's Jewish population—a fraction slightly larger than New York's 29 percent,[9] and more than twice that of the national percentage of foreign-born Jews, which is about 15 percent.[10]

Data Sources

Studying Jews and Jewish immigrants in the U.S. presents a significant challenge, due to definitional matters and the cost of obtaining large, high-quality data sets. The first obstacle is definitional, since both "Jew" and "immigrant" have multiple meanings that vary depending on context and location, and self-reported definitions are unreliable.[11] Since much of the data used in this chapter is from secondary sources, the best we can do is to be aware of the definitions originally used and cognizant of when they are contradictory.

A second challenge involves the constitutional prohibition on collecting data about religiously defined populations. Demographers and students of migration commonly rely on government sources such as the U.S. Census as the basis for their enumerations of migrant nationalities. However, the Establishment Clause of the First Amendment to the U.S. Constitution precludes this. Accordingly, government statistics are of limited utility for identifying Jews. Several alternative sources have been developed to overcome these challenges. They include community-level Jewish population studies that enumerate migrants as well as the National Jewish Population Studies conducted in 1990 and 2000–2001.[12]

Academic studies provide another source of information about Jewish immigrants. These vary in size, sophistication, and attention. While few offer large representative samples of immigrant communities, they do provide detailed information about migrant groups' history, identity, patterns of social and economic adaptation, collective concerns, politics, and other topics.[13] Finally, a wide variety of additional sources including official statistics, communal reports, and journalistic accounts supply data on Jewish migrants.

Migrant Populations

The following section discusses the experience and social characteristics of the three largest and best documented recent Jewish immigrant groups: Russian-speaking Jews, Israelis, and Cuban/Latin American Jews.

Jews from the Former Soviet Union (FSU)

From 1975 until 2007, 605,100 refugees (including Jews and non-Jews) from the FSU arrived in the U.S., making them the second largest refugee nationality to enter the country (after the Vietnamese) during the last quarter of the twentieth century. The peak year of arrival was 1992, when HIAS resettled 45,871 refugees from the FSU, and the U.S. Office of Refugee Resettlement reported the arrival of 61,397 persons from the same location.[14] Since 2000, about 7,500 refugees have come into the U.S. annually from the FSU, but only a small fraction of these have been Jewish.

Soviet Jews' exit was motivated by blocked mobility and antisemitism as well as the desire for family unification and free religious and cultural expression. Following the fall of the Soviet Union, Jews continued to leave the FSU in record numbers, fleeing a hostile and unstable environment. Most had refugee status that was conferred as a consequence of the Cold War.[15] This made them eligible for permanent resident status as well as citizenship and entitled them to cash assistance and social benefits, such as housing, job training, and health care. Such benefits, which varied considerably according to migrants' time and place of arrival in the U.S., were often supplemented by services from Jewish and other communal organizations.

RUSSIAN SPEAKING JEWS' FAMILY AND GENDER PATTERNS

Patterns of family composition that have their roots in the FSU reinforce intimacy and mutual involvement among Russian émigrés in the U.S. Because of Soviet housing shortages and the desire to maximize available resources for promoting children's mobility, family size was typically small. Families rarely had more than one or, at the most, two offspring. Soviet grandparents retired early (women at age fifty-five, men at age sixty) and were often extensively involved in the lives of their children and grandchildren, with whom they lived. Russian families often migrated with their aged members to remain intact, care for children, and access an environment more secure than that in their country of origin. Women outnumber men and are significantly older, indicating their greater life expectancy as well as the effects of World War II.¹⁶

According to the 2000 U.S. Census, the early age of marriage and childbearing in FSU households was sustained in the U.S. The fraction of women born in the FSU and residing in the U.S. who are unmarried by age forty (4 percent) is less than one-third of that for all U.S. women (14 percent) and substantially lower than that for other migrant populations, including women born in China and Latin America.¹⁷

Jews from the FSU who have relocated to the U.S. tend to feel satisfied with their life here. Although they retain cultural and linguistic patterns associated with their country of origin and enjoy interacting in coethnic settings, they are generally content to fit into the widely accepted pattern of "hyphenated American" ethnic membership. Their white skin, legal status, and high educational profile grant them a privileged position in the new setting, which contrasts quite favorably with the centuries of oppression that their group had endured in their country of origin.

ADAPTATION OF RUSSIAN-SPEAKING JEWISH CHILDREN

Reflecting their access to family and community resources, Russian-speaking Jewish immigrant children and the children of Russian-speaking Jewish immigrants who have entered the U.S. since the 1970s generally have a strong educational background and do well in American schools. For example, in a 1991 comparison of the twelve largest immigrant groups attending New York City public schools, grades 3–12, who had been in the country three years or less, students from the FSU ranked first in reading scores, second in math, and fifth in English. Their reading and math scores were much higher than the average for all students, including the native born. In addition, their mean increase in score over the previous year in both reading and English was the highest of all groups and among the highest in math.¹⁸

Russian immigrants' educational accomplishments make sense because many described America's educational opportunities as a major reason for their families' immigration.¹⁹ (They also have high rates of attending college. Over 70 percent of a sample of New York residents between age eighteen and thirty-two who had been in the U.S. at least six years attended.)

ECONOMIC ADJUSTMENT

Russian-speaking Jews who have entered the U.S. since 1970 have had very high levels of education, often in technical and professional fields. As such, their economic progress has been impressive. According to the 2000 Census, 59.9 percent of FSU-born persons residing in the U.S. age twenty-five to sixty-five had a bachelor's degree or higher. Thus, they are much better educated than all foreign born, of whom 26 percent have a bachelor's degree or higher. Their educational achievements also outstrip those of the native-born population.

Reflecting their high levels of education, recent Russian immigrants experience rapid economic mobility. Data from the 2000 census found that their earnings exceeded those of the average income for native and foreign-born workers. According to the 2000 U.S. census, 73 percent of immigrants from the FSU age twenty-five to sixty-four and in the labor force were employed as managers, administrators, sales, professionals, or technical specialists, compared to 54 percent of all foreign-born persons in the U.S. age twenty-five to sixty-four and in the labor force.[20]

One economic asset of recent Russian immigrants over natives and other migrant groups is the high proportion of women with professional and technical skills—a product of the FSU's egalitarian educational system. As of 1981, 67 percent of Soviet women in the U.S. were engineers, technicians, or other kinds of professionals prior to migration, whereas only 17 percent of American women worked in these occupations. According to the 2000 Census, 31 percent of women from the FSU in the U.S. were college graduates. This is more than double the 15.1 percent figure of college graduation for all foreign-born women in the U.S. in 2000.[21]

A recent summary of this group's economic adaptation found that while Russian adults had relatively low levels of English skill and earnings upon arrival, they experienced rapid improvement over time and obtained parity more rapidly than other immigrants. In fact, "they appear to obtain greater earnings (compared to other immigrants) in the U.S. labor market from their schooling, their time in the United States, and their English proficiency."[22]

RELATIONS WITH AMERICAN JEWS

The migration and resettlement of several hundred thousand Jews from the FSU to the U.S. during the late twentieth century was an impressive undertaking. The American Jewish community and U.S. government provided prized refugee status and a generous package of services and benefits for rebuilding émigrés' lives.[23] The resettlement is notable not only for its size, but also for the rapid adjustment made by a population that included a particularly large fraction of elderly persons.

Despite its general success, the migration and resettlement of Soviet Jews to the U.S. also involved certain forms of conflict and contention among the migrants, the host community, and other interested parties. The most significant issues concerned the extent to which Soviet Jews were expected to conform to the broader Jewish community's perspective on where and how they should live their lives.

The international Soviet Jewry movement, which began in the early 1960s, sought to permit members of this group to leave the oppressive and atheistic Soviet Union so that they could escape antisemitism, move to the Jewish homeland, and freely practice their religion. From the late 1960s until the mid-1970s, the majority of Soviet Jews granted exit visas did settle in Israel. However, between 1976 and 1989, at least half opted instead to move to the U.S., and by the late 1980s fewer than 10 percent each year chose Israel.[24]

Émigrés' desire to live in the U.S. caused considerable consternation among Soviet Jewry activists, as they appeared to be favoring material comfort and affluence over religion and Zionism. In response, there was a growing call to deny Soviet Jews refugee status in the U.S., thus directing their resettlement exclusively to Israel.[25] According to journalist J. J. Goldberg, "The first Soviet Jewry activists in the 1960s hardly intended their work to result in Jewish immigration to the U.S. The movement was from the start a Zionist enterprise, conceived by Israelis and driven by activists who wanted the world's second largest Jewish community 'repatriated'—brought en masse 'back' to Israel, their ancestral homeland."[26]

Following the loosening of emigration restrictions by the U.S.S.R. in late 1989, a middle ground position was adopted. The Bush administration revoked Soviet Jews' universal refugee status and instead provided U.S. resettlement on a case-by-case basis, favoring those with relatives already here.[27] By the 1990s, Israel had received far more Soviet Jewish arrivals than the U.S., ultimately equalling one million persons, even as the U.S. resettled several thousand.[28] Despite this compromise, conflicts over Soviet Jews' place of resettlement continued to disrupt relations between the émigrés, American Jews, and Israel.[29]

Members of the Russian-speaking Jewish community in the U.S. resented efforts to compel their resettlement in Israel, which they described as a source of their own alienation from American coreligionists. Saying "Let my people go, indeed," they pointed out the hypocrisy of Jews who enjoy the wealth, freedom, and security of the U.S. while telling others to live in Israel.

A second major source of conflict between Soviet Jews and their American hosts involved disagreement about the ways that Russian Jews should express their Jewish identity. Primed by decades of anti-Soviet/Russian propaganda and having heard numerous tales about religion-seeking Soviet Jewish refuseniks from the Soviet Jewry movement, American Jews assumed that Russian speakers came to the U.S. to reestablish their religious identities and would graciously accept their instructions on how to become American Jews, as well as rapidly repudiate their linguistic, cultural, and sentimental attachments to the FSU.

Russian-speaking Jewish immigrants were grateful for the benefits and services they received from American Jews. However, they had very different outlooks and life experiences than their hosts. Accordingly, they sometimes locked horns with members of the host community with regard to the nature of group identity, religious involvement, social and political behavior, and location of settlement. American Jews were often taken aback to find that the newcomers were more interested in finding jobs and attending to their children's futures than frequenting synagogues or keeping kosher; had their own ideas about religious and national identity; prized the Russian language, culture, and landscape; took pride in the accomplishments of the FSU; and retained elements of Russian identity in the U.S.[30] According to anthropologist Fran Markowitz, "As American Jews found some of the ways that Soviet Jews act to be alien, they came to label these behaviors and the individuals associated with them not 'Jewish' but 'Russian.'"[31]

By the late 1980s, professional and lay members of the American Jewish community finally began to acknowledge that most Soviet Jews in the U.S. were not interested in becoming religious in the manner planned by their hosts. Initial hopes for rapid religious assimilation were replaced by a more realistic acknowledgment of Soviet émigrés' secular and ethnic (rather than religious) identification.[32]

COMMUNAL LIVES

Russian and American Jews maintain distinct attitudes and social habits. Accordingly, emigrés gravitate toward their own enclaves, where they can interact in a familiar environment and maintain a measure of control over their adaptation to the U.S. This tendency is enhanced by the fact that the population includes many elderly people who are limited in their ability to adjust to American life and speak English and, hence, are highly dependent on coethnic settings.

Because Russian immigrants have relatively high rates of self-employment, their neighborhoods feature numerous ethnically oriented shops, restaurants, service providers, and media industries that present a venue for socializing, maintaining Russian cultural practices and identity reconstruction. While these communities have geographic, cultural, religious, and economic links with those of American Jews, the conational preference often predominates.

Coming from large cities, accustomed to living in apartment buildings, and being dependent on public transport and coethnic shops and services that assist the elderly, Russian-speaking Jews are much more attached to urban locations than are native-born Jews and other Jewish immigrants like Israelis, who often gravitate toward suburban communities.[33] Russian Jews' shared discomfort with American values and cultural patterns is one reason some turn away from their American coreligionists. Even those born in the U.S. often maintain a preference for those with Russian origins as friends and marriage partners.

The political affiliation of most American Jews tends to be Democratic.[34] In contrast, having been admitted to the U.S. with refugee status from the discredited and now defunct FSU, many Russian-speaking immigrants are politically conservative and, when they become naturalized citizens, identify with the Republican Party. A New York–based survey of Russian-speaking Jews' voting patterns in the election of 2004 found that 77 percent favored George W. Bush, and many supported Donald Trump for president in 2016 and 2020.[35]

Some of the greatest differences between American Jews and Russian Jewish immigrants are found in their patterns of religious and ethnic identification—apparent commonalities that would seem to bring these groups together. This is because, for most American Jews, Judaism is rooted in religious knowledge and practice. In contrast, Judaism was regarded as a nationality in the atheistic FSU.

Further separating American Jews from Russian immigrants is the fact that the latter are not comfortable with the Western denominations with which the vast majority of American Jews associate. Only 28 percent of New York Russian Jews identify with Reform, Conservative, or Orthodox Judaism, in contrast to 55 percent of non-Russian Jewish New Yorkers.[36] Instead, many Russian-speaking Jewish migrants affiliate with Chabad, an ultra-Orthodox, Ḥasidic sect that provides an array of outreach programs for disaffiliated Jews and supports conservative Republican politicians.

Despite Russian immigrants' feelings of distance from American Jews, most see their eventual amalgamation with coethnic hosts as both positive and inevitable. They are also more strongly attached to Israel than American Jews.[37]

Israeli Emigrants

Since the 1960s, approximately 200,000 Israelis have entered the United States as voluntary immigrants. They came in search of economic and educational opportunities, to broaden their horizons, and because of their disenchantment with Israeli society. Few planned to stay permanently, and a significant fraction does eventually return.

DEMOGRAPHICS

The number of Israelis in the U.S. has been a subject of intense controversy. Estimates drawing from the 2000 U.S. census, the Israeli census, and Israeli Border Police data suggest that approximately 153,000 to 175,000 Israelis (including those born both in Israel and elsewhere) reside in the U.S. Rebhun and Lev-Ari estimate the total population of Israelis, including their U.S.-born children and American spouses, to be 250,000.[38]

Israelis in the U.S. tend to be relatively young. Of the 21,661 persons born in Israel age eighteen and over who became naturalized in the U.S. between 2003 and 2010, fewer than 27 percent were age forty-five and over. The proportion of Israelis living in the U.S. who are married is quite high. Of the 21,661 persons born in Israel age eighteen and over who became naturalized in the U.S. between 2003 and 2010, 74 percent were married and 56 percent were male.[39]

PATTERNS OF GENDER AND FAMILY ADAPTATION

In nearly every study of Israelis in the U.S., we find that while migration was a "family decision," and the family as a whole enjoys economic benefits as a result of migration, the decision to migrate was generally made by the men for the expanded educational and occupational opportunities available in the U.S.[40] Once in the U.S., men often enjoy the benefits of such expanded opportunities and, consequently, feel more comfortable with the new country.

Women, however, especially those with children and established careers, have more negative views of migration. Even when Israeli women work in the U.S., they have less of a professional identity than men and would prefer to return home. In reflecting on their experience in the U.S., Israelis contrast the nation's positive economic and occupational environment to its communal and cultural liabilities: immigrants almost universally regard Israel as a better place for children. In Israel, Jews are the culturally and religiously dominant group. The institutions of the larger society teach children Hebrew and instruct them in basic national, ethnic, and religious identity as well as Jewish history. In the U.S., however, Israelis become a minority group and find it more difficult to maintain communal networks based upon family, friendship, institutional participation, and neighborhood, which provide a social life and assistance in raising children. Consequently, the presence of young or school-age children in Israeli immigrant families often heightens their ambivalence about being in the U.S.

ECONOMIC ADAPTATION

The 2000 census shows that Israelis in the U.S. are relatively well educated. Forty-three percent have a bachelor's degree or higher. Half the population age twenty-four to sixty-four are employed as managers or professionals, while 31.4 percent are in technical/sales or administrative occupations. About 6.7 percent are in service, and 11.9 percent are operators or laborers.[41] Of employed Israel-born persons age eighteen and over who became naturalized between 2006 and 2010, almost 24 percent are in management, professional, and related occupations.[42]

Israeli Americans' rate of self-employment—33.4 percent—is among the highest of all nationality groups recorded in the 2000 U.S. Census. The earnings of Israelis in the U.S. are considerable. While men attain high rates of labor force participation, a surprisingly large fraction of Israeli women are not in the labor market. Despite their relatively high educational profiles, their labor force participation rate (about 54 percent) is below that of all foreign-born women in the U.S. (59 percent).[43]

RELATIONS WITH AMERICAN JEWS

Soviet Jews' resettlement in the U.S. provoked conflicts within the global Jewish community about where Jews should live. Debates regarding Israelis' settlement abroad were even more heated. From Israel's formation in 1948 until the 1980s, the country explicitly condemned emigration as a personal failing and a threat to its military, economic, and demographic survival.[44] While emigration was illegal for only a brief time, it remained heavily stigmatized, and, until recently, emigrants were often depicted in political discourse, social science research, journalism, and popular culture as disillusioned, lonely, and impoverished, subject to family breakdown and a loss of Jewish identity, and alienated from coreligionists in places of settlement.[45] As a consequence, they were condemned as *yordim*—a stigmatizing Hebrew term that describes those who "descend" from the "higher" place of Israel to the diaspora, as opposed to immigrants, the *olim*, who "ascend" from the diaspora to Israel.[46]

By the late 1980s, however, the country's increased involvement in the worldwide economy—much of it a product of links established by Israeli emigrants in global centers of innovation and commerce—made Israel more tolerant of its citizens living abroad. Having changed its views regarding emigration, the Israeli government endorsed and financed various services for them, including outreach programs, cultural activities, and communal celebrations. Summer-in-Israel experiences for emigrant youth allowed Israeli parents living overseas to provide children with forms of Israeli socialization. Following the lead of Israel, American

Jewish organizations also created outreach and integration activities for Israeli immigrants in the U.S.

The decision of the Israeli government and the American Jewish community to encourage rather than prohibit affiliation and outreach between American Jews and Israeli immigrants resulted in the creation of a variety of programs and activities and improved relations among the two groups. Nevertheless, American Jews and Israelis remained dissimilar in many of their attitudes, behaviors, cultural and religious activities, language use, patterns of socialization, and identities.

While both populations share the same religion and a sizable fraction have common ancestral origins in Eastern Europe, Israeli and American Jewish notions of group membership often contrast because the basic group identities associated with being either Israeli or American Jewish are rooted in distinct cultural and national contexts. For many Israelis, ethnic identity is secular and national. While they are knowledgeable about Jewish holidays and speak Hebrew, they often connect these behaviors to "Israeliness" rather than Jewishness.

A significant fraction of Israelis do not actively participate in organized religious activities and are accustomed to relying on the larger society and public institutions to socialize their children, free of charge. Hence, they often complain about paying fees to join a synagogue or attend holiday services.[47] Moreover, Reform and Conservative Judaism, with which the great majority of American Jews affiliate, are infrequently practiced in Israel. Finally, while American Jews are accustomed to life as a minority group in a religiously pluralistic society, Jewish Israelis were raised in an environment where religion and nationality were one and the same.

Observers contend that Israeli emigrants are able to actively participate in American Jewish life while simultaneously maintaining links to Israel. They note that Israelis speak Hebrew, are involved in a variety of Jewish institutions, and visit Israel frequently. A growing body of survey data on Israeli immigrants in the U.S. reveals that they engage in many religious and cultural Jewish behaviors at higher rates than native-born Jews and are also more likely to live in neighborhoods characterized by high Jewish population density.[48] Enhanced rates of ritual practice may reflect the efforts of these Jewish migrants to retain their religious identity within a predominantly non-Jewish country.[49]

COMMUNAL PATTERNS

Most Jews who entered the U.S. during the past three hundred years have been de jure or de facto refugees, with few opportunities for reverting to their countries of origin. By contrast, Israelis retain the real possibility of returning to Israel. Indeed, American Jews, Israel, and even the immigrants themselves generally agree that they should return. This distinguishes Israelis from most other Jewish entrants in U.S. history.

Despite their ambivalence about living in the U.S., however, Israelis have been active in building a life for themselves and in becoming U.S. citizens. In fact, Israeli immigrants have developed many organizations to resolve their misgivings about being abroad. Community activities include socializing with other Israelis, living near coethnics (and within Jewish communities), consuming Hebrew-language media (produced in both the U.S. and Israel), frequenting Israeli restaurants and nightclubs, attending coethnic social events and celebrations, joining Israeli associations, working with other Israelis, consuming goods and services provided by Israeli professionals and entrepreneurs, keeping funds in Israeli banks, sending children to Israeli-oriented activities, raising money for Israeli causes, calling family and friends in Israel, and hosting Israeli visitors.

Prior to the late 1980s, American Jewish organizations delivered few (if any) resources to Israeli emigrants. More recently, these organizations have come to view Israelis as providing a vital, new, Jewish-identified population to an otherwise shrinking and aging community. The Israeli presence is especially appreciated in older urban neighborhoods, where large numbers of local Jews have recently departed for more family-friendly suburban locations or retirement communities. Accordingly, American Jewish organizations now supply Israeli newcomers with various services. Jewish population studies in New York (1991, 2002, 2011), Los Angeles (1997), Miami (2004, 2014), and elsewhere enumerate Israelis and note their presence as one of the few positive tendencies in a general trend of shrinking Jewish demographics and lessening religious identification.[50]

TRANSNATIONALISM

Israelis are more likely to engage in transnational lifestyles associated with frequent international travel than are Russian-speaking Jews. They often have access to networks in both countries that can provide a broad variety of resources ranging from pretravel information to job opportunities, childcare, housing, and social life. While some Israelis in the U.S. lack legal resident status, as a group they are very likely to become naturalized.

A whole series of factors surrounding Israelis makes their movement to the U.S. relatively easy. Well educated, they possess occupational and cultural skills useful in both countries. Even prior to migration, many Israelis feel familiar with American society from their exposure to popular culture, American visitors, and intergovernmental relations.

We have already noted a variety of Israeli-oriented activities that allow migrants to maintain a semblance of Israeli life in the U.S. Travel between the two nations is easily arranged. Israeli immigrants often report making frequent trips from the U.S. to Israel, and it is not uncommon for children to return to Israel to spend summer vacations with relatives or to perform military service.

Despite national, ideological, and religious differences between Israeli and American Jews, Israelis do feel connections to other Jews and see themselves, Jewish migrants from other countries, and native-born Jews in settlement countries, as members of the same ethnic and religious group. It would appear that the whole notion of being an Israeli versus an American is not nearly as clear-cut a distinction as the literature on international migration suggests. Instead, such factors as flexible notions of ethnic and national identity, access to and participation in social and occupational networks, and the ability of people to sustain cultural competence and legal status in more than a single society allow Israelis to maintain meaningful forms of involvement in multiple national settings.

Cuban and Latin American Jews in the U.S.

Approximately 10,000 Jews arrived in Miami between 1959 and 1962 as part of the Cuban exodus of 120,000 who entered the U.S. following the establishment of the Castro regime.[51] Cuban Jews' departure is attributed to ideological and financial concerns, not antisemitism. Because nearly the entire Jewish population was self-employed in Cuba, they believed that life in a society that banned private enterprise would be intolerable.[52]

Regardless of their religion, first-wave Cuban entrants to the U.S. benefited from a series of fortuitous circumstances that facilitated their rapid and positive adjustment. Fleeing a Communist revolution during the height of the Cold War, they received legal status, government assistance, service from voluntary organizations, and the support of powerful allies and benefactors. As the elite of Cuban society, they were highly educated, entrepreneurial, and racially White.

In addition, their shared class origins, political commitments, and dislike of Castro's polices contributed to the group's political mobilization and economic collaboration, which, according to Cuban-born sociologist Alejandro Portes, facilitated their development of an extensive array of coethnic businesses that generated both income and jobs.[53] Reflecting their high rates of premigration involvement in manufacturing, banking, and commerce and their ties with established coreligionists in Miami, Cuban Jews played important roles in the Cuban community's economic adjustment to the U.S.

As refugees who planned to return home following Castro's hoped-for demise, Cubans had a strong commitment to preserving their national cultural and linguistic traditions. At the same time, they also quickly mastered U.S. culture and English. This reinforced in-group solidarity while also enhancing their ability to function in the larger society. The bilingual and business-savvy Cuban community's financial achievements were accelerated by beneficial economic trends during the 1960s and 1970s, including growing commerce with Latin America and the demographic and industrial expansion of the Sun Belt region of the U.S.

Immersed in this array of growth-fostering circumstances, a sizable fraction of Jewish and Catholic Cubans, who had arrived without assets and worked odd jobs just to survive, quickly became successful in banking, manufacturing, the professions, and other endeavors. The long period of their migration, from 1959 to the present, also provided benefits. Among these were increasing population size, retained involvement in the culture of origin, and links with a new generation of immigrant workers who helped to sustain the Cuban American economy.[54]

Currently, about 40 percent of all persons of Cuban ancestry in the U.S. are U.S.-born. Suggesting Cuban Americans' security and mobility, the group reveals higher standing than other Latin American nationalities on a wide variety of socioeconomic measures, including education, income, and home ownership. Cuban adults born in the U.S. have social characteristics close to those of native-born Whites.[55]

CUBAN JEWS AND THE ESTABLISHED JEWISH COMMUNITY

The economic and political adjustment of Cuban Jews reflects the success and mobility of the larger first-wave Cuban American population of which they were part. However, Cuban Jews' experience of joining the American Jewish community was generally more challenging than their economic adaptation. During the 1960s, Cuban Jews received little assistance from the local Jewish American population in building a life in America. Indeed, veterans of that migration still remember their reception with resentment a half century later.

The literature offers several explanations for the host community's chilly welcome. First, research describing the period of their arrival suggests that U.S. Jews felt little connection with the newly arrived Cuban Jews, whose language, culture, diet, and social patterns were unlike their own. According to Margalit Bejarano, "For the English-speaking Jews, it was almost inconceivable that Hispanics could also be Jews."[56]

The local community's indifference is further indicated in its efforts to avoid the financial burden of assisting Cubans. As a case in point, Arthur Rosichan, executive director of the Greater Miami Jewish Federation (GMJF), issued a 1961 statement to the U.S. Senate committee that addressed Cuban refugee problems, contending that Cuban Jews, like Cubans more generally, were ill suited for surviving in Miami. Accordingly, he argued that Cuban resettlement needed to be financed through the allocation of extensive federal government resources (rather than Jewish communal philanthropy) and should involve the Cubans' relocation to other parts of the U.S.[57]

In fact, many Cuban Jewish refugees were in poor financial straits, as they were unable to transfer assets and even professional diplomas to Florida. Historical accounts and more recent interviews describe how Miami synagogues and day schools were unwilling to reduce their membership fees so that the newly arrived could participate. Cuban Jews remember with bitterness their encounters with the host community and emphasize that they had been rejected from synagogues because they were unable to pay membership fees.

Having access to conationals with whom they developed an array of entrepreneurial activities, Cuban Jews were able to survive. As Margalit Bejarano writes,"Nevertheless, the indifferent welcome of their coreligionists and the uninviting attitude of most religious institutions have not been forgotten."[58] American Jews' lack of empathy for their Cuban coreligionists' plight is surprising, given that only a few years later, they would be mobilized for a decades-long movement to liberate and resettle Soviet Jews.[59]

The Cuban community in Miami adapted rapidly in the U.S., establishing significant political and economic power as well as a variety of communal organizations. As a consequence, the mushrooming Spanish-speaking population became a magnet for other migrant groups, especially those from Latin America.[60] As the immigrant and Latin American population increased in Miami, non-Hispanic Whites—including English-speaking Jews—shrank by nearly 23 percent between 1990 and 2012.[61] As Whites left, Cuban and other Latin American Jews became major players in the local Jewish population.

THE ARRIVAL OF LATIN AMERICAN JEWS

The first wave of Latin American Jewish migrants entered the U.S. in the 1970s, a decade after the Cuban Jewish settlement, as a consequence of political and economic crises in their countries of origin. Bokser Liwerant estimated that between the 1970s and 2012, approximately 150,000 Latin American Jews lived in the U.S.[62]

Speaking the same language, hailing from a common region, and having arrived in the U.S. relatively recently, Cuban and Latin American Jews have much in common. Even prior to their settlement in the U.S., both groups were accustomed to travelling internationally for business, family visits, or vacations. Further, they often obtain a higher level of education outside of their country of birth and retain ties to Jewish groups with whom they share pre–Latin American origins (in Europe or the Middle East).

Latin American Jews often maintain links with non-Jewish conationals and are socially, politically, economically, and culturally involved with the flourishing Latino population in the U.S. Finally, in contrast to most U.S. Jews, their community exhibits significant ties with, and recurring travel to, Israel.[63] At the same time, Cuban and Latin American Jews also have distinct outlooks, reflecting their disparate national origins and times of arrival. These shape their patterns of adaptation to the U.S., their interactions with each other, and their connections to their countries of origin.

Latin American Jews' entry to Miami is seen as part of a more general multidirectional movement of members of the Latin American middle classes to other locations in search of secure, Spanish-speaking surroundings.[64] Popular stereotypes depict Latin American migrants as a low-skilled population. However, thousands of skilled and educated Latin Americans have also traveled abroad. As a group, Latin American Jews can be considered as part of this migration.[65] As of 2014, 14,730 Hispanic Jewish adults lived in Miami, their numbers having increased by approximately 54 percent since 2004.[66] Twenty-three-and one-half percent were Cuban, followed by 18.4 percent Argentinean, 16.1 percent Venezuelan, 14 percent Columbian, 6.1 percent Peruvian, 4.4 percent Spanish, 3.6 percent Mexican, 2.7 percent Honduran, and 1.9 percent Panamanian.[67]

OUTREACH AND INCORPORATION OF LATINO JEWISH MIGRANTS INTO THE MIAMI JEWISH COMMUNITY

By the 1990s, the American Jewish community's awareness of high rates of assimilation, intermarriage, and aging among the native Jewish population made its leaders appreciate the social, economic, and demographic significance of recent Jewish immigrants. In this light, they understood that the Greater Miami Jewish Federation's Cuban/Latin Division was a promising venue for fundraising, community building, and promoting pro-Israel activities.[68] Accordingly, just as user-friendly outreach programs were directed toward the incorporation of Russian-speaking Jews and Israelis living in the U.S. since the 1980s, so too were endeavors devoted to integrating Latin American Jewish migrants.[69]

As they adjusted to the U.S., Cuban and Latin American women contributed to Jewish activism and continuity as they established social and philanthropic organizations that resembled those in their countries of origin. As a case in point, the Latin American Migration Program

(LAMP) was created by Jewish Community Services of South Florida to provide support and assistance to both recently arrived and established members of the Latin Jewish community. High on its agenda was helping persons with tourist visas to obtain legal permission to work in the U.S.

In addition, Jewish day schools, such as the Reform-focused Sinai Academy in North Miami Beach, have cultivated Latin American constituencies. As recently as 1990, its student body included only a handful of Latin American students, and speaking Spanish was discouraged by assimilation-oriented administrators. Currently, however, the school offers a Spanish immersion preschool class where both English- and Spanish-speaking children are exposed to Spanish at an early age. Sinai Academy's student body is currently estimated to be 75 percent Latin American, and despite tuition in excess of $16,000 per year, it has a waiting list of fifty. School administrators and Latin American families have ambitious plans for the institution's growth, including the creation of the only Reform Jewish senior high school in the U.S.[70]

The number of Latin American Jewish migrants continues to increase in Miami as well as in Los Angeles, San Diego, New York, and other locations. Consequently, the youthful, energetic, and recently arrived Latin American Jewish population is now ascendant among Miami Jews and increasingly influential elsewhere.

Conflict and Amalgamation among Immigrant and Host

As the case studies of Russian-speaking, Israeli, and Cuban/Latin American Jewish migrants suggest, a significant record of contention exists between Jewish immigrant groups and the host community. Similar patterns were observed during the early twentieth century in the U.S., France, and England.[71] Indeed, disputes between the established and recently arrived have been documented among a wide range of religious and ethnic groups throughout U.S. history.[72]

In retrospect, we see that conflicts among Jewish immigrants of Russian, Israeli, and Cuban/Latin American origins with the U.S. Jewish community were linguistic, cultural, political, economic, religious, and identificational. Soviet Jews were condemned for settling in the U.S. rather than Israel as well as for expressing their Jewish identity in ways that members of the host community found to be inappropriate. Israelis' presence outside of Israel and their secular and nationalistic notions of identity were disturbing to many American Jews. Finally, Latin American Jews were denounced because of their linguistic and cultural orientation as well as the expenses entailed in resettling first-wave Cuban Jews in South Florida.

Despite these significant disputes, relations between migrant populations and the host Jewish community improved with the passage of time. Drawing on relatively high levels of education and economic mobility, newcomers obtained social and political resources, established their own institutions, and began to enjoy a degree of assurance and respect within the larger community. Their contributions—demographic, economic, religious, and philanthropic—are increasingly valued by their hosts, who have become concerned about communal decline due to locals' assimilation, intermarriage, aging, fragmentation, and weakening attachment to Israel.

The growing diversity in American Jewish life facilitates the adaptation of immigrant groups by allowing them to establish organizations and activities of their own choosing. In addition, a wide range of Jewish institutions and synagogues—ranging from Jewish Federations, Jewish Community Centers and Reform Jewish day schools to Chabad—offer cultural, linguistic, social, religious, and culinary activities that appeal to immigrants.

Differences related to language, culture, religious outlook, politics, philanthropy, gender, and many other factors continue to divide the American Jewish community. At the same time, relations between the different ethnicities, nationalities, and lifestyles of American Judaism are increasingly addressed in communal planning and accepted as part of the status quo.[73] In this, the increasing diversity of the U.S. Jewish population mirrors the cultural multiplicity of the larger society. While certainly difficult to mobilize and coordinate, such variety fosters self-determination and equality.

Conclusions

These observations suggest that a welcoming and tolerant approach by the American Jewish community toward new Jewish immigrants will foster their smooth adaptation to U.S. society and their development of positive relations with American-born Jews while also retaining ties to the world Jewish community and with conationals, regardless of their religious identification. The diverse and resource-rich American Jewish community is well positioned to encourage this practice, which would maximize new immigrants' feelings of comfort and foster their contribution to the host society while allowing them to retain established ties and outlooks.

NOTES

1. *A Portrait of Jewish Americans: Findings from a Pew Research Center Survey of U.S. Jews* (Washington DC: Pew Research Center, 2013).
2. Sergio DellaPergola, "Israel and World Jewish Population: A Core-Periphery Perspective," in *Population and Social Change in Israel*, ed. Calvin Goldscheider (Boulder, CO: Westview, 1992) 39–63; Sergio DellaPergola, "World Jewish Migration System in Historical Perspective," paper presented at the International Conference on Human Migration in a Global Framework, University of Calgary, Alberta, Canada, June 9–12, 1994.
3. Calvin Goldscheider and Alan S. Zuckerman, *The Transformation of the Jews* (Chicago: University of Chicago Press, 1984) 7; Irving Howe, *World of Our Fathers* (New York: Harcourt Brace Jovanovich, 1976); Stephen H. DeHass Castles and Mark J. Miller, *The Age of Migration*, 5th ed. (New York: Guilford, 2014).
4. *American Jewish Year Book, 5690*, vol. 31 (Philadelphia: Jewish Publication Society of America, 1929), 326–27.
5. Thomas Archdeacon, "Immigration, 1899–1924," www.wisc.edu.
6. Moses Rischin, *The Promised City* (Cambridge, MA: Harvard University Press, 1970), 270.
7. Immigration restrictions from the 1920s through 1940s did exclude thousands of European Jews seeking refuge from the Nazis. Richard Breitman and Alan Kraut, *American Refugee Policy and European Jewry, 1933–1945* (Bloomington: Indiana University Press, 1987), 9; Goldscheider and Zuckerman, *Transformation of the Jews*, 174.
8. Yinon Cohen, "Migration Patterns to and from Israel," *Contemporary Jewry* 29 (2009): 115–25.
9. *Jewish Community Study of New York* (UJA-Federation of New York: 2011).
10. *National Jewish Population Survey 2000–2001: Strength, Challenge, and Diversity in the American Jewish Population, United Jewish Communities Report 2003* (New York: United Jewish Communities in Cooperation with the Mandel L. Berman Institute—North American Jewish Data Bank, 2003); *A Portrait of Jewish Americans: Finding from a Pew Research Center Survey of U.S. Jews* (Washington, DC: Pew Research Center, 2013).

11 "Portrait of Jewish Americans"; Barry Kosmin, "Highlights of the CJF 1990 National Jewish Population Survey," (New York: Council of Jewish Federations, New York, 1991).
12 Kosmin, "Highlights"; *National Jewish Population Survey, 2000–2001*.
13 Steven J. Gold, *Refugee Communities: A Comparative Field Study* (Newbury Park, CA: Sage, 1992); Steven J. Gold and Bruce A. Phillips, "Israelis in the United States," *American Jewish Year Book* 96 (1996) 51–101; Steven J. Gold, *The Israeli Diaspora* (Seattle: Routledge/University of Washington Press, 2002).
14 Office of Refugee Resettlement, "Report to Congress Administration for Children and Families" (Washington, DC: U.S. Department of Health and Human Services, 2007), 71.
15 Geoffrey Cameron, *Send Them Here: Religion, Politics, and Refugee Resettlement in North America* (Montreal: McGill-Queen's University Press, 2021).
16 Vladimir Shlapentokh, *Love, Marriage, and Friendship in the Soviet Union: Ideals and Practices* (New York: Praeger, 1984).
17 U.S. Bureau of the Census, 2000 Census of Population, 5 Percent Public Use Microsample.
18 Test Scores of Recent Immigrants and Other Students, Grades 3–12, New York City Public Schools, Office of Research, Evaluation and Assessment, 1991.
19 Philip Kasinitz, John H. Mollenkopf, Mary C. Waters, and Jennifer Holdaway, *Inheriting the City* (New York: Russell Sage Foundation, 2009).
20 This paper relies on census data from 2000 because U.S. Census stopped collecting data sufficiently detailed to describe migrant groups' characteristics after that year. Barry R. Chiswick and Nicholas Larsen, "Russian Jewish Immigrants in the United States: The Adjustment of their English Language Proficiency and Earnings in the American Community Survey," *Contemporary Jewry* 35 (2015): 191–209.
21 U.S. Bureau of the Census, 2000 Census of Population, 5% Public Use Microsample.
22 Chiswick and Larsen, "Russian Jewish Immigrants."
23 Timothy J. Eckles, Lawrence J. Lewin, David S. North, and Dangole J. Spakevicius, "A Portrait in Diversity: Voluntary Agencies and the Office of Refugee Resettlement Matching Grant Program" (report produced by Lewin and Associates for the Office of Refugee Resettlement, Washington DC, 1982); Steven J. Gold, "Enhanced Agency for Recent Jewish Migrants to U.S.," *Contemporary Jewry* 33 (2013): 145–67.
24 Zvi Y. Gitelman, *Jewish Identities in Postcommunist Russia and Ukraine: An Uncertain Ethnicity* (New York: Cambridge University Press, 2012), 245–47.
25 Steven J. Gold, *From the Workers' State to the Golden State: Jews from the Former Soviet Union in California* (Boston: Allyn & Bacon, 1995); Annelise Orleck, *The Soviet Jewish Americans* (Westport, CT: Greenwood, 1999).
26 J. J. Goldberg, *Jewish Power: Inside the American Jewish Establishment* (Reading, MA: Addison-Wesley, 1996), 180.

27 S. J. Ungar, "Freedom's Door Shut in Face of Soviet Jews," *Los Angeles Times*, November 12, 1989) pp. M2 and M8; E. Woo, "Anticipated Reunion Turns into a Nightmare for Soviet Émigré," *Los Angeles Times*, November 24, 1989; Madeleine Tress, "United States Policy Toward Soviet Emigration," *Migration*, nos. 3–4 (November–December, 1991): 93–106.
28 Steven J. Gold, "Soviet Jews in the United States," in *American Jewish Year Book* (1994), 3–57.
29 Frederick A. Lazin, *The Struggle for Soviet Jewry in American Politics: Israel versus the American Jewish Establishment* (Lanham, MD: Rowman & Littlefield, 2005).
30 Larissa I. Remennick, *Russian Jews on Three Continents* (New Brunswick, NJ: Transaction, 2007).
31 Fran Markowitz, "Jewish in U.S.S.R., Russian in U.S.A," in *Persistence and Flexibility: Anthropological Perspectives on the American Jewish Experience*, ed. Walter P. Zenner (Albany: State University of New York Press, 1988), 84.
32 Joel M. Carp, "Absorbing Jews Jewishly: Professional Responsibility for Jewishly Absorbing Immigrants in Their New Communities," *Journal of Jewish Communal Service* 66, no. 4 (1990): 366–74.
33 Gold, *Israeli Diaspora*.
34 Uzi Rebhun and Lilach Lev-Ari, *American Israelis: Migration, Transnationalism and Diasporic Identity* (Leiden: Brill, 2010), 148.
35 Sam Kliger, "Russian-Jewish Opinion Survey 2004," Research Institute for New Americans, New York, 2004); "Explaining Trump's Popularity Among Russian Speakers in America," Eurasianet, April 19, 2019, eurasianet.org.
36 UJA-Federation of New York, Jewish Community Study of New York, 2011, 236.
37 Paul Ritterband, "Jewish Identity among Russian Immigrants in the U.S.," in *Russian Jews on Three Continents: Migration and Resettlement*, ed. N. Lewin-Epstein, Y. Ro'i, and P. Ritterband (London: Frank Cass, 1997), 333; Ira M. Sheskin, Jewish Community Study of New York, 2011 and "Assimilation of Jews from the Former Soviet Union," presentation at Ruppin Academic Center, February 2010, available from isheskin@miami.edu.
38 Yinon Cohen, "Migration Patterns to and from Israel," *Contemporary Jewry* 29 (2009) 115–25; Uzi Rebhun and Lilach Lev Ari, *American Israelis: Migration, Transnationalism, and Diasporic Identity*, (Leiden: Brill, 2010), 15.
39 U.S. Department of Homeland Security, "Profiles on Naturalized Citizens," www.dhs.gov.
40 Mirra Rosenthal and Charles Auerbach, "Cultural and Social Assimilation of Israeli Immigrants in the United States," *International Migration Review* 26 (1992): 982–91; Lilach Lev-Ari, *The American Dream: For Men Only? Gender, Immigration, and the Assimilation of Israelis in the United States* (El Paso, TX: LFB Scholarly, 2008).
41 U.S. Bureau of the Census, 2000 Census of Population.
42 U.S. Department of Homeland Security, "Profiles on Naturalized Citizens," www.dhs.gov..

43 U.S. Bureau of the Census, 2000 Census of Population.
44 Calvin Goldscheider, *Israel's Changing Society: Population, Ethnicity, and Development* (Boulder: Westview, 1996).
45 Moshe Shokeid, *Children of Circumstances: Israeli Emigrants in New York* (Ithaca, NY: Cornell University Press, 1988); Zvi Sobel, *Migrants from the Promised Land* (New Brunswick, NJ: Transaction, 1986), 55; Naama Sabar, *Kibbutzniks in the Diaspora* (Albany: State University of New York Press, 2000); Nir Cohen, "From Legalism to Symbolism: Anti-mobility and National Identity in Israel, 1948–1958," *Journal of Historical Geography* 36 (2010): 19–28.
46 Sherry Rosen, "The Israeli Corner of the American Jewish Community" (New York: American Jewish Committee, Issue Series No. 3, Institute on American Jewish-Israeli Relations, New York, 1993.
47 Gold, *Israeli Diaspora*.
48 Pini Herman, "Jewish-Israeli Migration to the United States since 1948," paper presented at the Annual Meeting of the Association of Israel Studies, New York, June 7, 1988; Steven M. Cohen and Judith Veinstein, "Israeli Jews in Greater New York: Their Numbers, Characteristics and Patterns of Jewish Engagement," (New York: UJA Federation of New York Report, March 2009; Uzi Rebhun, "The Israeli Jewish Diaspora in the United States: Socio-cultural Mobility and Attachment in the Homeland," (Jerusalem: Division of Jewish Demography and Statistics, A. Harman Institute of Contemporary Jewry, Hebrew University of Jerusalem, 2009.
49 Gold and Phillips, "Israelis in the United States"; Pini Herman, "Los Angeles Jewish Population Survey '97," Jewish Federation of Los Angeles, 1998; Cohen and Veinstein, "Israelis Jews in Greater New York"; Lilach Lev-Ari, "Jews Residing in Three Cities in France and Belgium: Patterns of Ethnic Identity and Identification 2020," in *Wandering Jews: Global Jewish Migration*, ed. Steven J. Gold (West Lafayette, IN: Purdue University Press, 2020), 81–117.
50 Nir Cohen, "State, Migrants, and the Negotiation of Second-Generation Citizenship in the Israeli Diaspora," *Diaspora: A Journal of Transnational Studies* 16 (2007): 133–58.
51 U.S. Bureau of the Census, Census of Population 2000; Silvia Pedraza, *Political Disaffection in Cuba's Revolution and Exodus* (New York: Cambridge University Press, 2007), 6.
52 Robert M. Levine, *Tropical Diaspora: The Jewish Experience in Cuba* (Princeton, NJ: Marcus Weiner, 2010), 236.
53 Alejandro Portes, "The Social Origins of the Cuban Enclave Economy of Miami," *Sociological Perspectives* 30 (1987): 340–72.
54 Alejandro Portes, *Economic Sociology: A Systematic Inquiry* (Princeton, NJ: Princeton University Press, 2010).
55 "Cubans in the United States," Pew Hispanic Center, 2006, pewhispanic.org.
56 Margalit Bejarano, "Ethnicity and Transnationalism: Latino Jews in Miami," in *Reconsidering Israel-Diaspora Relations*, ed. Eliezer Ben Rafael, Judit Bokser de Liwerant, and Yosef Gorny (Leiden: Brill, 2014), 172.

57 Bejarano, "Ethnicity and Transnationalism," 169–84; Caroline Bettinger-López, *Cuban-Jewish Journeys: Searching for Identity, Home, and History in Miami* (Knoxville: University of Tennessee Press, 2000).
58 Margalit Bejarano, "From Turkey to the United States: The Trajectory of Cuban Sephardim in Miami" in *Contemporary Sephardic Identity in the Americas: An Interdisciplinary Approach*, ed. Margalit Bejarano and Edna Aizenberg (Syracuse, NY: Syracuse University Press, 2012), 151; Alejandro Portes, "The Social Origins of the Cuban Enclave Economy of Miami," *Sociological Perspectives* 30 (1987): 340–72.
59 Gold, *From the Workers' State*; Gal Beckerman, *When They Come For Us, We'll Be Gone: The Epic Struggle to Save Soviet Jewry* (New York: Houghton Mifflin, 2010).
60 Elizabeth M. Aranda, Sallie Hughes, and Elena Sabogal, *Making a Life in Multiethnic Miami: Immigration and the Rise of a Global City* (Boulder, CO: Rienner, 2014).
61 Aranda et al., *Making a Life in Multiethnic Miami*, 22.
62 Judit Bokser Liwerant, "Transnational Expansions of Latin American Jewish Life in Times of Migration: A Mosaic of Experiences in the United States," in *Research in Jewish Demography and Identity*, ed. Eli Lederhendler and Uzi Rebhun (Brookline, MA: Academic Studies Press, 2015), 205.
63 Sergio DellaPergola, "Israel and World Jewish Population: A Core-Periphery Perspective," in *Population and Social Change in Israel*, ed. Calvin Goldscheider (Boulder, CO: Westview, 1992), 39–63.
64 Liwerant, "Transnational Expansions," 198–240; Bejarano, "Ethnicity and Transnationalism," 169–84.
65 Liwerant; Bejarano.
66 Ira M. Sheskin, *The 2014 Greater Miami Jewish Federation Population Study: A Portrait of the Miami Jewish Community* (Miami, FL: Greater Miami Jewish Federation, 2015).
67 The population of Latin American Jews has recently grown in several U.S. cities including New York, the San Francisco Bay Area, Los Angeles, and San Diego. However, the Jewish Federation of Greater Miami has conducted Jewish communal surveys with greater detail than other settlements, producing more comprehensive data about the Latin American Jewish population of Miami than is available for other communities.
68 Liwerant, "Transnational Expansions," 198–240.
69 Gold, "Enhanced Agency."
70 Uriel Heilman, "Reform Judaism with Latin Flavor Takes Root in Miami: Sinai Academy Is a Very Unusual Jewish School," *Forward*, February 1, 2014, forward.com.
71 Harold Pollins, "The Development of Jewish Business in the United Kingdom," in *Ethnic Communities in Business: Strategies for Economic Survival*, ed. Robin Ward and Richard Jenkins (Cambridge: Cambridge University Press, 1984), 73–88;

Paula E. Hyman, *The Jews of Modern France* (Berkeley: University of California Press, 1998).

72 Pedraza, *Political Disaffection in Cuba's Revolution*; Steven J. Gold, *Refugee Communities: A Comparative Field Study* (Newbury Park, CA: Sage, 1992); Pyong Gap Min, *Ethnic Solidarity for Economic Survival: Korean Greengrocers in New York City* (New York: Russell Sage Foundation, 2008); Gary Ross Mormino, *Immigrants on the Hill: Italian Americans in St. Louis, 1882–1982* (Urbana: University of Illinois Press, 1986); Val Colic-Peisker, *Migration, Class, and Transnational Identities: Croatians in Australia and America* (University of Illinois Press) 2008.

73 David Shneer and Caryn Aviv, *New Jews: The End of the Jewish Diaspora* (New York: New York University Press, 2005).

2

The Gendered Landscape of U.S. Judaism

SARAH IMHOFF

In the past two decades, Orthodox Jews in the United States have fought over whether women could be rabbis, the Conservative movement's Rabbinical Assembly issued a resolution affirming transgender and gender nonconforming Jews as full participants in Jewish life, and Jews from all religious affiliations, including none at all, have reassessed what a good and healthy masculinity should look like. Gender, it is fair to say, matters to American Jews.

Demographically, Jews in the U.S. often mirror wider trends with respect to gender. For example, Jewish women in the U.S. participate in Jewish activities, including synagogue attendance, at a higher rate than men do.[1] In the Christian world, "church ladies" are a well-known type in a way that "church men" are not, and this is reflected in attendance and participation in many communities. Across religious affiliations, of those who attend services at least once a week, 57 percent are women, and 42 percent are men.[2] (Jews of all genders, however, attend synagogue less frequently than others attend houses of worship: 19 percent of U.S. Jews reported they attend services at least once a week as compared to 36 percent of U.S. Americans as a whole.)[3]

Yet there is a twist: Orthodox men are more likely to attend services frequently than Orthodox women. Even though women are more likely to be "joiners" or participants in Jewish activities, when it comes to synagogue services, the numbers for men and women are almost equal (20 percent of men and 19 percent of women attend weekly or more frequently).[4] Perhaps this is in part because most Orthodox services and theologies place a greater importance on men's public participation than on women's. Although interpretations vary, almost all Orthodox Jews believe that women and men have different religious obligations, roles, and responsibilities. For example, most count only adult men in a prayer quorum, and most have only men read publicly from the Torah. Even physical spaces reflect the importance of gender in religious practice: Many Orthodox religious spaces use a *mechitza*, or a divider between men and women. Ḥasidic, and Ḥaredi, or "ultra-Orthodox" spaces often use a balcony for women and reserve the main area for men. Reform, Reconstructionist, and Conservative services and theologies more commonly provide equal opportunities and expectations of people of different genders, though this does not always mean they are identical. Observing these dynamics—Jewish women's greater participation in social and religious organizations in general as well as the particular theological dynamics privileging men's participation in Orthodox Judaism—demonstrates the importance of looking both at what Jews share with others as well as what is distinctive in Jewish contexts.

Discussing the gendered landscape of Judaism in the U.S. requires looking in a variety of locations—including beyond synagogues. Many Jews think of themselves as religious or spiritual, but they do religious practices at home or in other spaces. In fact, many of Judaism's most commonly practiced rituals do not take place in synagogues: Passover seders, for example, are the most commonly practiced ritual for U.S. Jews, and they typically take place in the home. Study groups, whether institutional ones like SVARA (a queer yeshiva), structured-yet do-it-yourself ones like Daf Yomi (a "page-a-day" approach to the Talmud), or informal partnerships, have grown in popularity and begun to expand what was typically a male enterprise.

As the expansion of Talmud study suggests, ideas about gender underpin many aspects of Jewish life, and these aspects are not just those that affect women. Historians often attend to women's changing gender roles, but men's gender roles change too. In recent decades, masculinity in the United States has become a prominent topic of discussion, and Jewish communities are no exception. Especially following prominent instances of sexual assault and the #MeToo movement, questions about male expressions of power, dominance, and sexuality have animated conversations about ethics and ideals.

Another significant development has been the visibility of trans, genderqueer, and nonbinary members of Jewish communities. Trans people are those who do not identify with the gender they were assigned at birth. The terms "genderqueer" and "nonbinary" both refer to people who do not identify as simply male or simply female. Non-binary specifically refers to those who identify outside of a male-female gender binary, while genderqueer may refer to those whose gender is fluid as well as those whose gender includes both male and female, or neither. While all branches of Judaism have trans or nonbinary Jews, the halakhic and social approaches to their inclusion (or exclusion) differ. Orthodox Jewish opinions on gender tend to uphold a gender binary in which there is a bright line between male and female. Those who do not fit easily on one side or the other are often seen as tragic or as a medical problem. Although some individual rabbis offer different opinions, leaders generally do not see a halakhic space for trans Jews. Liberal Jews, on the other hand, often point to talmudic categories of sexes beyond male and female, such as the *androginos* and the *tumtum*, to celebrate the progressiveness of Judaism. And yet nonbinary and genderqueer people still often face discrimination or confusion about their presence in Jewish spaces.

This chapter sketches the gendered landscape in contemporary U.S. American Judaism, paying particular attention to newer developments. It considers women's leadership, feminist interpretations of tradition, and other ways women engage Judaism as women. Next, as the #MeToo movement's critique of toxic masculinity has shown, the way men enact gender matters deeply, and so the chapter describes the relationship of Judaism and masculinity.[5] Finally, it discusses the way that religious Jews of different affiliations interact with trans or nonbinary Jews.

Women's Leadership

Rabbis and cantors occupy the most visible form of Jewish leadership, and these positions have undergone substantial gendered changes in the past several decades. The first woman in the U.S. to be ordained as a rabbi was Sally Priesand in 1972. In the half-century since, many U.S. Jewish communities have moved from a landscape of women's opportunity characterized by Shuly Rubin Schwartz's article on *rebbitzens* (rabbis' wives) as "They Married What They Wanted to Be" to a situation where women make up more than half of newly ordained non-Orthodox rabbis in the U.S. each year.[6] This does not mean they constitute the majority of practicing rabbis—in 2020, 24 percent of

Conservative rabbis identified as female, for example—but numbers are growing.[7]

The increasing number and percentage of women rabbis has subtly reshaped both the position of the rabbinate as well as the dynamics between clergy and laypeople. The gender of the leaders shapes how they lead as well as how congregants and others respond to them. Increasing gender diversity in Jewish religious leadership has corresponded with changes in Jewish religious life. In an early study of women rabbis, almost all said they "carry out the rabbinical role" differently than male rabbis. They saw themselves as "less formal, more approachable, more egalitarian," less invested in their own prominence, and more committed to having people interpret and experience rituals through their own perspectives.[8] Rabbi Laura Geller asserts that this has changed the face of Judaism in the U.S.: women rabbis' "success has led to a breakdown of hierarchy between rabbis and congregation. It has led to a more inclusive Judaism." She also emphasizes that leadership models have changed, moving toward "partnership instead of hierarchy, empowerment instead of 'power over'—and [the presence of women rabbis] has changed the culture and structure of synagogues and other Jewish institutions to become more participatory and less focused on one leader."[9]

Cooperation, listening, counselling, and cocreation might all be considered feminine modes of leadership, and that may mean that women are more likely to use them, as Geller suggests. But it is also true that others may employ them, and that congregants may grow to like and expect these modes of leadership, even from rabbis who are not women. This story of changing non-Orthodox leadership is not just a story about women, then; it is also a story about gender.

A survey of employment advertising for rabbinic positions emphasized skill sets that more closely fit with interpersonal modes of interaction than with top-down modes of leadership. Reform and Conservative congregations were looking for someone to "lead innovative and meaningful participatory worship experiences,"[10] and bring "congregational engagement skills."[11] Many emphasized cultivating interpersonal relationships, such as those who wanted a rabbi to "relate to, attract and teach children," "build relationships with adults," "create an inviting atmosphere," and be "outgoing, approachable, non-judgmental, and genuinely interested in all persons of any sexual preference and ability."[12]

Even an independent, previously Orthodox synagogue wanted a rabbi to "create a warm, welcoming and accepting prayer environment."[13] These synagogues' lists of desires suggest that their ideal rabbis do not conform to stereotypes of male leadership. These Jewish communities seek collaborative rather than hierarchical leadership and emphasize the importance of relationships over independence. This does not mean that women face equal prospects for hiring and pay; in Jewish communities, as in others, sexism can still hold women back. (In fact, there is evidence that gender gaps in pay are larger in Jewish communal organizations than in society at large.)[14] And one might also argue that decreases in independence, hierarchy, and prestige also mean that when women entered the rabbinate, the rabbinate became a less powerful position.

Orthodox communities still have stricter divisions between gender roles, especially in religious spaces. Yet the recent past has seen an efflorescence of women's learning and leadership. Open Orthodoxy, a small, more inclusive segment of the U.S. Orthodox Jewish community, now ordains women. In 2009, the Orthodox rabbis Avi Weiss and Daniel Sperber ordained Sara Hurwitz. Some groups expressed their support vocally. The Jewish Orthodox Feminist Alliance, for example, circulated an online petition that declared, "We believe individual communities and all of Klal Yisrael can only benefit from the inclusion of the voices and ideas of highly trained and committed women in positions of communal authority."[15] Because of the controversy around women rabbis, as well as the acknowledgement that women rabbis would not be halakhically authorized to do all the same things as men rabbis, the movement often gave ordained women the title *maharat*, an acronym for *manhiga hilkhatit rukhanit Toranit* (female leader of law, spirituality, and Torah). Those who affiliate with Open Orthodoxy still disagree about the proper title of an ordained woman—should it be rabbi, rabba, rabbanit, maharat, or something else?

Orthodox organizations outside of Open Orthodoxy objected not only to rabbinical titles, but more generally to ordaining women at all. When Yeshivat Maharat, a seminary founded by Weiss and Hurwitz to educate and ordain women, opened in 2010, Orthodoxy's Rabbinical Council of America (RCA) issued a statement about the proper role of women in Jewish religious leadership. It said: "The RCA reaffirms its commitment to women's Torah education and scholarship at the highest levels, and to the assumption of appropriate leadership roles within the Jewish community." Rabbinical leadership, it decreed, was still exclusively male. "Appropriate leadership roles" included those of teachers (outside of rabbinical schools) or community leaders. The RCA reaffirmed its stance in 2013 and again in 2015, doubling down on its view of appropriateness and going beyond to declare that Orthodox institutions may not hire, ordain, or give title to a woman in a rabbinical role.[16] Shortly after Hurwitz began using the title *rabba* (a neologism), Agudath Israel of America, an umbrella organization that represents many Haredi Jews, declared that Open Orthodoxy was a "radical and dangerous departure" that meant it was no longer even Orthodox Judaism because of its ordination of women.[17]

The women who have graduated from Yeshiva Maharat since its opening in 2010 have taken different positions, from pulpit rabbis to communal leaders, and use different titles. For some, their learning, leadership, and presence has become routine, but, for others, it is controversial or even heretical. In that time, people have looked to Sara Hurwitz as an example, while others have accused her of "destroying the Orthodox community."[18] Very little of the controversy has to do with her as an individual; it is about the relationship of gender, leadership, and Jewish law.

Women have been at the forefront of other halakhic developments, even as they are still excluded from some halakhic obligations within Orthodoxy. While women have long played unofficial roles as halakhic advisors to other women on issues of the body, menstruation, and sex, in the past three decades official education, credentials, and titles have created a new halakhic category: that of the *yoetzet halakhah*, or halakhic advisor.

Nishmat, a Jerusalem-based modern Orthodox educational institution for women, has been training yoatzot since 1997.[19] They undergo two years of training in traditional sources, overseen by male Orthodox rabbis and culminating in an examination process. Then they are credentialed as yoatzot. Some Orthodox synagogues have a yoetzet halakhah on staff, but their most significant impact has been through the internet and the Women's Halakhic Hotline, a telephone service.

Typically, women consult yoatzot over email, telephone, or video chat. Yoetzot.org, run by Nishmat, offers a way for halakhically observant women to consult an expert on intimate matters relating to sex, menstruation, fertility, breastfeeding, postpartum depression, medical procedures, and women's bodies—removing the potential embarrassment or shame of having to speak to and be directed by a male rabbi. In this way, the cycle of halakhic questions and answers about women's bodies actually circumvents male authorities, though in particularly ambiguous situations yoatzot are told to bring the matter to a male rabbi. In the first decade, the hotline and website had received about twenty-five thousand distinct questions.[20] The ethnographer Michal Raucher has shown how these women's actions and expertise both "affirm and challenge Orthodox rabbinic authority" not only on the internet, but also offline. In addition to consultation, the website provides videos featuring learned women as well as classes designed for halakhically observant women to educate themselves. These remain limited to particular areas of Jewish law that are seen as appropriate to women, but nevertheless they increase women's visible halakhic authority. And, lastly, as Raucher observes, the advice of the yoatzot "alter[s] the practice of Judaism for halakhically observant women."[21] These yoatzot, then, have not only changed the gendered face of halakhic expertise, but also subtly affected the practices of halakhically observant women.

In Ḥasidic communities, gender segregation characterizes much of Jewish ritual life as well as social life. In Ḥasidic interpretations, both halakhah and modesty require separation or single-sex spaces. Women often occupy domestic spaces and while men can operate in the public sphere. Men provide the only bodies and voices of public leadership. Women's photographs do not appear in newspapers, and men are prohibited from hearing women singing. Women function as public speakers only when the audience is all women.[22] But, of course, these distinctions are not absolute. Girls' education often includes more English-language instruction and preparation in "secular" subjects, which can better equip women to function in public settings beyond the Ḥasidic community.

If some other Jewish communities are moving toward greater inclusion and leadership of women, many Ḥasidic groups are moving toward greater separation and distinction. For most Satmar married women, hats on top of wigs are now the norm, as are Palm brand tights, named after the rebbe Joel Teitelbaum (whose name means "palm tree" in Yiddish) and manufactured in-house to ensure the appropriate thickness and opacity. Ḥasidic women's leadership, then, appears in proscribed forms and contexts: as lecturers to audiences of other women, for example. But new technology such as WhatsApp has allowed the virtual sharing of women's lectures to surge, which makes it much easier for men to listen to women speakers.[23]

Religious leadership, however, can take many forms and need not be in the context of denominational life. Feminist interpretations of Jewish tradition have flourished beyond institutional bounds. The first wave of self-declared feminist readings of Judaism are now decades old, but they still compel readers.[24] Judith Plaskow's critique of women's exclusion from textual interpretations and communal traditions still resonates for many women,[25] and Rachel Adler's concerns about halakhah and women remain at center stage for many halakhically observant Jewish women.[26] New feminist readings have also emerged from scholarly circles as well as religious ones and from intimate memoirs of spiritual searches to a new feminist commentary on the Babylonian Talmud.[27] New histories focusing on women and feminism have served as centerpieces of synagogue book discussion groups, and feminist theology continues to be a vibrant genre.[28]

Although, traditionally, women have been halakhically exempt from Torah study, most legal interpreters do not take this to mean they are prohibited. And over the last two decades Talmud study programs for women have become increasingly popular in both liberal and Orthodox circles.[29] Not all Talmud study programs for women emphasize feminist rereadings, but in-person study groups are now supplemented by groups on Facebook and other websites, as well as podcasts. Svara, which brands itself as a "traditionally radical yeshiva," includes Jews of all genders and explicitly encourages queer and feminist readings of the Talmud in online events and courses as well as its signature summer residential camp.

New feminist ritual has also emerged. Small woman-centered group celebrations of Rosh Hodesh originated in the 1980s and are still practiced today. More formal institutions have also begun to change the ritual possibilities. The Kohenet Hebrew Priestess Institute serves women and genderqueer people "not only as a clergy-training program but also as a Sisterhood," as ethnographer Cara Rock-Singer explains.[30] By drawing on biblical texts and other traditions, it "reclaims and innovates embodied, earth-based feminist Judaism," including temple-based ideas and practices.[31] In her writing and teaching, the institute's founder, Rabbi Jill Hammer, who was ordained at the Jewish Theological Seminary in 2001 and then cofounded Kohenet in 2006, explores themes of incorporating a feminine divine into Jewish practice.[32]

Jewish women also create feminist art to engage, represent, and even dispute the Judaism they encounter in their lives.[33] To take just one example, an Orthodox artist's painting addressed two ironies about halakhic interpretations of women and tallitot (prayer shawls). First, it asks the viewer to consider the irony that a woman cannot wear a tallit, but mothers often teach their sons how to do the practice correctly. Second, it "addressed an additional debate on whether men must tuck the fringes on their tallit in the presence of deceased women (while at a cemetery or during a funeral), as is required in the presence of deceased men, to avoid mocking the dead for no longer being able to follow God's commandments." The artist "spoke to the absurdity of this debate by highlighting how women are, in fact, already mocked while alive by tallitot they are forbidden from wearing."[34] This art illustrates women's deep knowledge of but also frustration with Jewish religious traditions and interpretations.

Jewish women have also led cultural and political movements beyond religious spheres. Women CEOs head Jewish hospitals, museums, and other agencies. And, beyond Jewish communities, they also occupy prominent places in education, philanthropy, medicine, politics, law, and entertainment. Ruth Bader Ginsburg and Elena Kagan served on the U.S. Supreme Court together, a fact in which many U.S. Jews took pride. Jewish publications print lists of "powerful," "influential," and "trailblazing" Jewish women.[35] Even though men still outrank women in terms of pay and prestige, gaps to which Jewish organizations and businesses are no exception, Jewish women's prominence is often celebrated by Jewish communities.

Masculinity

In 2017, the growing #MeToo movement brought new attention to women's stories of sexual assault. But it also brought new attention to masculinity. It sparked discussions that take masculinity not as a given or a historical constant, but as shaped by society. "Boys will be boys" could no longer explain why men did what they did; social images and expectations rewarded boys and men for behaving in some ways while shaming them for behaving in others. Some masculinities might even be "toxic" and require change. Moreover, proponents of the movement insisted, dealing with these destructive forms of masculinity should no longer take place only behind closed doors but also in public—in families, communities, and even, when necessary, courtrooms. Even those who defended what they saw as traditional forms of masculinity participated in public debates about what men are and how they should behave.

Jewish communities participated in #MeToo conversations, in part because many women had been victims of sexual harassment or assault, and in part because prominent Jewish men had acted inappropriately. Harvey Weinstein, a prominent Hollywood producer, assaulted multiple women, facts that came forward as part of one of the first cases in a public reckoning. Although the assaults did not particularly target Jewish women or take place in Jewish religious spaces, many U.S. Jews started conversations about how sexual assault and a culture that allowed men to get away with it was a Jewish problem too. #GamAni, Hebrew for #MeToo, circulated as an identifier for those sharing stories. Jane Eisner, editor-in-chief of the *Forward*, called for a response "as individuals and as a Jewish community."[36] Weinstein's acts did not characterize Jewish communities as a whole, but many felt called to respond by exploring their own expectations for men.

While they also participated in the larger cultural reckoning, Jewish communities in the U.S. had distinctive conversations about masculinity. Many people, both historically and in the present, hold gendered assumptions about Jewish men that are different from those they hold about other men.[37] For example, many believe that Jewish men are gentle and family oriented, and do not abuse spouses or children.[38] One rabbi explained: "Like most Ashkenazi men, [I] grew up spoon-fed on the following pride-inducing factoids: Jewish men were superior to other men when it came to winning Nobel Prizes, writing comedy, accounting, making money on the stock market, and pressing lawsuits."[39] But these largely positive stereotypes were not the whole story—and sometimes they could even make gendered problems more difficult to see. For example, stereotypes about kind and gentle family men made domestic violence within Jewish communities seem unlikely, even though we now know it takes place at rates similar to those in other communities, and many abusive husbands use Jewish laws or observance to reinforce abusive behavior.[40]

Sexual assault and harassment also take place within religious contexts. Although sexual abuse cases in the Catholic church may be the most prominent stories of clergy abuse, Judaism also had to wrestle with the abuse by religious leaders. The Reform movement's Hebrew Union College commissioned a study of sexual harassment and discrimination at its four campuses and found a history of repeated offenders and frequent administrative inaction.[41] Ḥasidim in New York witness sexual abuse of children but hesitate to involve authorities.[42] A powerful cantor in New York sexually abused girls and women for years.[43]

Perhaps the single most prominent case within Jewish religious contexts is not one of the present, but one of the past. The "singing rabbi" Shlomo Carlebach, who had attracted Jews from all walks of life and across the spectrum of observance, had long been revered as loving, inclusive, and inspiring. His stories and music have appeared in synagogues across the world, and some Jews even identify themselves as "Carlebachian."[44] Yet, since his death in 1994, more and more women have come forward to tell stories of his unwanted sexual touching, late-night phone calls, rubbing up against women and girls, and worse. Although an article in *Lilith* magazine brought many of these women's stories to the public's attention in 1998, the most widespread communal reckoning with Carlebach's legacy did not take place until more than a decade later.[45] At that time, some synagogues decided not to include any of Carlebach's music, either for a time or permanently.[46] Others used the occasion to have larger discussions about confronting sexual abuse or harassment within their communities.

Some who responded to the problem of sexual harassment and assault explained that the right response was to increase gender separation and modesty, which they believe benefits women. The television star Mayim Bialik wrote in a *New York Times* essay:

> I still make choices every day as a 41-year-old actress that I think of as self-protecting and wise. I have decided that my sexual self is best reserved for

private situations with those I am most intimate with. I dress modestly. I don't act flirtatiously with men as a policy.... In a perfect world, women should be free to act however they want... But our world isn't perfect... Nothing—absolutely nothing—excuses men for assaulting or abusing women... But we can't be naïve about the culture we live in.[47]

While some people agreed, many also pushed back, worrying that Bialik's solution put the onus of response to the social acceptance and frequency of men's bad behavior on women. Other responses focused explicitly on how Jewish law could help women. For example, "How Modesty Laws Can Help Us Reclaim Our Personal Space" used a woman's Orthodox upbringing to recommend strategies for women: "And the moment I was in a situation with a male colleague that could turn secluded, no matter where I was, that yeshiva education came back into my mind, the letters of Hebrew texts flashing before me: Get out of here... Open the door... Move the meeting elsewhere... Those narrow escapes stopped harassment from turning into anything more... Tools like these should be used to help in particular Orthodox young women, who are often particularly vulnerable in the face of male authority."[48] Framing a response to #MeToo in this way made the problem one of what women should do to protect themselves. Of course, conversations about what women should do to protect themselves from men raping or assaulting them are nothing new.

What was new was the breadth of the conversation about what *men* should and should not do. Research and conversations took place across the Jewish community, including questions about how men are encouraged to be and behave in Jewish spaces, by Jewish communities, by Jewish tradition. A Union for Reform Judaism discussion included rabbinical voices emphasizing "accepting that your (male) experience is not the only one, or the default one, or the correct one, and that if and when [someone of a different gender] shares their differing experience with you, to actually consider taking it seriously as another truth," the importance of self-reflection, respect because each human is created in the image of God, and the ways that patriarchy hurts men too.[49] Groups from synagogues to Jewish family service organizations held lectures, and conversations discussed how conventional ideas about masculinity could create unhealthy attitudes and behaviors with respect to power, dominance, consent, and emotional limitations.[50]

Many Jewish communities considered how gender ideals and stereotypes are created and saw a need to change the messages that tweens and teens receive. Jewish camps set up structured conversations about masculinity for campers. One resource for an hour-and-a-half long exercise explained that participants would come away with the following four understandings:

> Masculinity should not be confined by reductive definitions (e.g. "All men like sports."), shallow criteria for male expression (e.g. "Real men don't show emotion.") or outdated value judgements (e.g. "Gay men are less male than straight men.") My identity, and the way that I relate to men, manhood and masculinity are bound up in the relationships I've had with boys and men in my life. Masculinity, like most identifiers is, at face value, neither good nor bad. Camp is a place where we come to explore our inner life alongside others in order to become our highest selves.[51]

This particular activity set up Jewish summer camp as a central place for all campers, but especially boys and men, to create a nontoxic masculinity. It used Jewish themes, such as Shabbat and the yetzer hara (sometimes called the "evil inclination") to focus campers' attention on choosing and creating "positive" masculinities rather than identifying negative ones. Partly spurred by issues of sexual harassment and assault, then, Jewish communities also took the opportunity to explore and sometimes even redefine ideals of masculinity.

Beyond the Gender Binary

Although there have always been people with bodies that do not neatly fit a male-female gender binary, their number and visibility has increased in the past several decades.[52] Some identify themselves not as male or female but as gender nonbinary, gender nonconforming, genderqueer, or other terms. Trans identity, often also called "transgender identity," has also increased in visibility. Trans individuals do not identify with the gender they were assigned at birth. Furthermore, not all trans people want to fit neatly into a gender binary even if they could "pass" as male or female.[53] As trans and nonbinary people have become more visible in the U.S. in general, Jewish communities have confronted questions about how to understand them; trans and nonbinary Jews in communities have raised their own voices as part of these discussions.

Many Jews have turned to textual traditions that emphasize both the presence and the inclusion within the Jewish community of bodies that are sexed and gendered beyond just male and female. Trans and nonbinary Jews themselves have been at the forefront of many of these interpretations. One often cited passage from the Babylonian Talmud discusses the *androginos*, a category of person with dual genitalia: "An *androginos* is in some ways equivalent to men, is in some ways equivalent to women, is in some ways equivalent to both men and women, and is in some ways not equivalent to either men or women" (*Tosefta Bikkurim* 2:3). The androginos and the ṭumṭum (a person with ambiguous genitalia) appear in rabbinic texts as legal questions, but also as unquestioned members of the Jewish community. Their gender is under discussion, but their belonging is not. Scholar Max Strassfeld explains that, although there is not a one-to-one equivalence of the rabbinic androginos and the trans person today, contemporary readings present meaningful articulations of what kinds of gendered bodies get recognized as human.[54] As Rabbi Elliot Kukla puts it, "Jewish gender diversity provides anyone who can't or won't conform to modern binary gender, a solid connection to another time, space and community—a spiritual home."[55] In these views, rabbinic texts' inclusion of a diversity of sexed bodies authorizes, or even demands, that contemporary Jews do the same.

Kukla also describes a trans theology that sees all Jews as cocreators with God. He sees the inclusion of the androginos and ṭumṭum as "a proclamation that God creates a diversity of bodies and an abundance of desires that is far too complex for human beings to understand. It conveys an understanding that all people are created . . . by the hand of heaven; and that every divine creation is entitled to be seen, loved, and desired."[56] This trans theology of gender cocreation has implications for all Jews, not just trans or nonbinary people.

Trans Jews have also adapted and created liturgy and ritual, especially but not exclusively related to transitioning. For some, this means reciting a blessing when receiving hormone therapy; for others, reinterpreting existing rituals to resonate with their experiences.[57] Trans rabbi Emily Aviva Kapor, for example, has reframed immersion in a mikveh as a method of cleansing the body of the anti-trans cultural assumptions: "[After] I'd actually changed my name about a week had gone by without me needing to say my old name out loud and then I had to for some reason or other. . . . I had to do it, and I felt dirty afterwards like I needed to take a shower, and that got me thinking about mikveh."[58] Kapoor partnered with an egalitarian mikveh, Mayyim Ḥayyim, to create a space and experience that was inclusive of people of all genders.

The recent institutional direction of Judaism in the U.S. seems to be moving toward greater recognition of gender diversity and inclusion. The first LGBTQ synagogues—though at the time most were gay and lesbian synagogues—were founded in the 1970s: Beth Chayim Chadashim in Los Angeles in 1972, Congregation Beit Simchat Torah in New York in 1973,[59] and Am Tikva in Boston in 1976.[60] Ameinu, a national organization for gay, lesbian, and bisexual rabbis, cantors, rabbinical students, and cantorial students, operated for several years in the early 1980s.[61] The Reform movement declared lesbian and gay Jews equal members and eligible for ordination in 1990, and in 2003 it expanded the same policies to apply to trans and bisexual Jews. Since 2006, Conservative Judaism has allowed individual congregations to decide their positions on gay and lesbian marriage as well as ordination, and it recognizes the gender of trans Jews who have undergone "sexual reassignment surgery."[62] For the leaders and many of the members of these more liberal Jewish communities, these moves signal greater inclusion in terms of gender and sexuality.

And yet trans, nonbinary, and genderqueer people still often face discrimination, stigma, or confusion about their presence in Jewish spaces. Even spaces that see themselves as inclusive are not always experienced that way by LGBT Jews.[63] (Though we often group those alphabetic letters together and calls for political change often make use of a solidarity among these groups, the lived experiences of people in different categories are hardly uniform.)[64] Claiming that sexuality or trans identity is not an issue, as some congregations do, can make people feel like they do not belong, or that they are not affirmed in the fullness of their person. They may feel as if they are expected to leave their gender or sexuality at the door. To be "welcoming" still implies that "our" community welcomes a "you" who is outside it; it leaves heterosexual norms in place and simply invites others to join in. This can be all the more pronounced for trans Jews because most U.S. Judaism still operates with a normative gender binary and the assumption of cisgender bodies—that is, bodies that are not trans and continue to identify with the gender they were assigned at birth.

Orthodox spaces make this abundantly clear with the meḥitza, or divider between men and women, as well as halakhic reasoning that roots itself in a gender binary. Individual rabbis may grant permission for, say, gender confirming surgery or a romantic relationship between men as long as it does not include anal sex, but gay, lesbian, bisexual, and trans people are often seen as suffering from mental illnesses. The vast majority of Orthodox halakhic rulings about trans Jews still seek to fit individuals into either male or female categories, though some are moving in more innovative directions while staying inside that binary.[65]

Same-sex sexuality remains a halakhic as well as a social issue for most Orthodox communities. The ordination of out gay male rabbis remains a contentious issue, and the bounds of halakhah around male-male and female-female sex are anything but settled. Orthodox Jews, however, have created organizations such as Orthodykes and Eshel that focus on community and advocacy for lesbian, gay, or bisexual observant Jews.[66] "Off the derech" groups for those who leave the Ḥaredi world are often also supportive because gender and sexual identity can contribute to a person's departure from that community.

Conclusion

This brief description of the gendered landscape of U.S. Judaism shows both Jews' similarities to their non-Jewish neighbors as well as ideas and dynamics that are specific to Jewish spaces. It shows historical continuity, such as the ongoing increase in women's leadership both in and beyond religious spaces, and the way that U.S. Jewry remains diverse with respect to halakhic, theological, and sociological approaches to gender. Yet there are also new developments, such as the increasing interest in Jewish articulations of healthy masculinity or investments in including LGBTQ Jews in ways that recognize them fully.

NOTES

1. Sergio DellaPergola, "Demography," Jewish Women's Archive, July 15, 2021, jwa.org.
2. "Religious Landscape Study," Pew Forum, May 12, 2015, www.pewforum.org.
3. "U.S. Public Becoming Less Religious," Pew Forum, November 3, 2015. www.pewforum.org.
4. "Gender Composition Among Jews," Pew Forum, www.pewforum.org.
5. The idea that gender is performed rather than, say, biologically determined has a robust theoretical literature; most prominent is Judith Butler, *Gender Trouble* (New York: Routledge, 1999).
6. Shuly Rubin Schwartz, "They Married What They Wanted to Be: Rebbetzins and Their Unconventional Paths to Power," in *Gender and Religious Leadership: Women Rabbis, Pastors, and Ministers*, ed. Hartmut Bomhoff, Denise L. Eger, Kathy Ehrensperger, and Walter Hamolka (Lanham, MD: Lexington, 2019), 183–202.
7. Shuly Rubin Schwartz and Helene Herman Krupnick, "Conservative Judaism in the United States," Jewish Women's Archive, June 23, 2021, jwa.org.
8. Rita J. Simon and Pamela Nadell, "Teachers, Preachers, and Feminists in America: Women Rabbis," *Shofar: An Interdisciplinary Journal of Jewish Studies* 10 (1991): 7.
9. Laura Geller, "What the Success of Women Rabbis Means for Judaism," HuffPost, December 6, 2017, www.huffpost.com.
10. "Rabbi/Hazzan," Rabbi Careers, rabbicareers.com.
11. "Seeking Part-Time Rabbi for NW Ohio Reform Congregation," Rabbi Careers, rabbicareers.com.
12. "rabbi or cantor," Rabbi Careers, rabbicareers.com.
13. "Congregation Kneseth Israel in Annapolis, Maryland," Rabbi Careers, rabbicareers.com.
14. Kate Bigam, "Reality Check: Wage Gap for Jewish Professionals Worse than National Average," Jewish Women's Archive, December 16, 2010, jwa.org; Jill Jacobs, "Making Jewish Paychecks Fair," Forward, December 1, 2010, forward.com.
15. Hannah Dreyfus, "RCA Bans Female Rabbis, Again; Agudath Goes Further," Jewish Week, November 4, 2015, jewishweek.timesofisrael.com.
16. "Rabbinical Council of America Officially Bans Ordination and Hiring of Women Rabbis," Jewish Telegraphic Agency, November 15, 2015, www.jta.org; "2015 Resolution: RCA Policy Concerning Women Rabbis," Rabbinical Council of America, October 31, 2015, rabbis.org.
17. Rori Picker Neiss, "A New Reality," in Renee Edelman, Sally J. Priesand, and Jacqueline Koch Ellenson, *The Sacred Calling: Four Decades of Women in the Rabbinate* (New York: CCAR, 2016), jewishweek.timesofisrael.com.

18 Sara Hurwitz, "The Tide Has Turned," *Times of Israel* Blogs, July 12, 2021, blogs.timesofisrael.com.
19 Michal Raucher, "Yoatzot Halacha: Ruling the Internet, One Question at a Time," in *Digital Judaism*, ed. Heidi A. Campbell (New York: Routledge, 2015), 65–82.
20 Tova Ganzel and Deena Rachel Zimmerman, "Women as Halakhic Professionals: The Role of the Yo'atzot Halakhah," *Nashim: A Journal of Jewish Women's Studies & Gender Issues* 22 (2011): 162–71.
21 Raucher, "Yoatzot Halacha," 58.
22 Rose Waldman, "Women's Voices in Contemporary Ḥasidic Communities," *Shofar* 38 (2020): 35–60.
23 Ayala Fader, "Nonliberal Jewish Women's Audiocassette Lectures in Brooklyn: A Crisis of Faith and Morality," *American Anthropologist* 115 (2013): 72–84.
24 This is not to say there was nothing before then, but the 1970s through the 1990s saw the first widespread published feminist critiques or interpretations of Judaism.
25 Judith Plaskow, *Standing Again at Sinai: Judaism from a Feminist Perspective* (New York: Harper & Row, 1990).
26 Rachel Adler, "The Jew Who Wasn't There: Halacha and the Jewish Woman," *Off Our Backs* 2, no. 6 (1972): 16–17.
27 Ṭal Ilan, Tamara Or, Dorothea M. Salzer, Christiane Steuer, Irina Wandrey, Monika Brockhaus, Tanja Hidde et al., eds., *A Feminist Commentary on the Babylonian Talmud* (Tübingen: Mohr Siebeck, 2007); Rivkah Slonim, ed., *Bread and Fire: Jewish Women Find God in the Everyday* (New York: Urim, 2008).
28 Pamela Nadell, *America's Jewish Women: A History from Colonial Times to Today* (New York: W. W. Norton, 2019); Joyce Antler, *Jewish Radical Feminism* (New York: New York University Press, 2018). For examples of feminist theology, see Mara H. Benjamin, *The Obligated Self: Maternal Subjectivity and Jewish Thought* (Bloomington: Indiana University Press, 2018); and Tamar Ross, *Expanding the Palace of Torah: Orthodoxy and Feminism*. (Hanover, NH: University Press of New England, 2004). For more on these and additional trends, see also the essays in Riv-Ellen Prell, ed., *Women Remaking American Judaism* (Detroit, MI: Wayne State University Press, 2007).
29 Caroline M. Block, "Rabbis, Rabbas, and Maharats: Aspiration, Innovation, and Orthodoxy in American Women's Talmud Programs" (PhD diss., Johns Hopkins University, 2017). There are also popular books centered on this; see, for example, the award winning Ilana Kurshan, *If All the Seas Were Ink: A Memoir* (New York: St. Martin's, 2017).
30 Cara Rock-Singer, "Milk Sisters: Forging Sisterhood At Kohenet's Hebrew Priestess Institute," *Nashim* 37 (2020): 87–114.
31 "Mission," Kohenet, kohenet.org.
32 Jill Hammer, "Wedding the Dragon: The Powerful Feminine as Seen in Jewish Women's Dreams," *Journal of Lesbian Studies* 23 (2019): 105–18.

33. Thuy Anh Tran and Chaya Halberstam, "'I Think God Is a Feminist': Art and Action by Orthodox Jewish Women," *Journal of Feminist Studies in Religion* 37 (2021): 5–24.
34. Tran and Halberstam, "'I Think God Is a Feminist,'" 17–18.
35. Laura Adkins, "The World's Most Powerful Jewish Women," *Forward*, June 15, 2016, forward.com; Elana Sztokman, "50 Most Influential Jewish Women," Jewish Women's Archive, May 21, 2010, jwa.org; "Listen to 10 Trailblazing Jewish Women on AJC's People of the Pod," American Jewish Committee, March 7, 2021, www.ajc.org.
36. Jane Eisner, "How the Jewish Community Can Make #MeToo into #WeToo," *Forward*, November 20, 2017, forward.com.
37. Sarah Imhoff, *Masculinity and the Making of American Judaism* (Bloomington: Indiana University Press, 2017).
38. Carol Kaufman, *Sins of Omission: The Jewish Community's Reaction to Domestic Violence* (New York: Basic Books, 2003).
39. Daniel Brenner, "Are Jewish Men Pigs?," Medium, January 19, 2018, medium.com.
40. Lisa Gelber, "The Power of the Rabbinate: Opportunities for Education and Awareness in Combating Domestic Violence in the Jewish Community," in *Domestic Abuse and the Jewish Community: Perspectives from the First International Conference*, ed. Cindy Enger and Diane Gardsbane (New York: Haworth Pastoral, 2004), 149–53; Lynn Gottlieb, "Women's Right to a World Free of Violence," in *The New Jewish Feminism: Probing the Past, Forging the Future*, ed. Elise Goldstein (Woodstock, VT: Jewish Lights, 2009), 369–81; Alison Cares and Gretchen Cusick, "Risks and Opportunities of Faith and Culture: The Case of Abused Jewish Women," *Journal of Family Violence* 27 (2012): 427–35.
41. Grace E. Speights, Sharon P. Masling, Martha B. Stolley, Jocelyn R. Cuttino, and Ira G. Rosenstein, "Report of Investigation into Misconduct at Hebrew Union College-Jewish Institute of Religion," November 3, 2021, huc.edu.
42. For an excellent review of the scholarly literature on abuse in Ḥaredi communities, see Efrat Lusky-Weisrose, Amitai Marmor, and Dafna Tener. "Sexual Abuse in the Orthodox Jewish Community: A Literature Review," *Trauma, Violence & Abuse* (2020), doi: 10.1177/1524838020906548.
43. Rahel Musleah, "Childhood Abuse, Adult Reckoning," *Hadassah Magazine*, May 2021, www.hadassahmagazine.org.
44. Natan Ophir (Offenbacher), "Evaluating Rabbi Shlomo Carlebach's Place in Jewish History," *American Jewish History* 100 (2016): 541–46.
45. Sarah Blustain, "A Paradoxical Legacy: Rabbi Shlomo Carlebach's Shadow Side," *Lilith* 45, no. 23 (Spring 1998): 10–17. For a call to hear these women's stories, see Sarah Imhoff, "Carlebach and the Unheard Stories," *American Jewish History* 100 (2016): 555–60.
46. See, for example, Angela Warnick Buchdahl, "Why My Synagogue Is Taking a Break from Singing Carlebach," *Forward*, January 31, 2018, forward.com.

47 Mayim Bialik, "Being a Feminist in Harvey Weinstein's World," *New York Times*, October 13, 2017, www.nytimes.com.
48 Avital Chizhik-Goldschmidt, "How Modesty Laws Can Help Us Reclaim Our Personal Space," *Forward*, December 2017, forward.com.
49 Chaim Ezra Harrison, "Healthy Masculinity: The Best a Mensch Can Be," ReformJudaism.org, March 28, 2019, reformjudaism.org.
50 For just one example, see Jewish Family Service of Metropolitan Detroit's program "Toxic Masculinity," April 24, 2018, www.jfsdetroit.org.
51 Adam Allenberg and Catherine Rothstein, "Cornerstone 2019 Resource: Detoxifying Masculinity," Foundation for Jewish Camp, jewishcamp.org.
52 Michael Goodman, Noah Adams, Trevor Corneil, Baudewijntje Kreukels, Joz Motmans, and Eli Coleman, "Size and Distribution of Transgender and Gender Nonconforming Populations: A Narrative Review," *Endocrinology and Metabolism Clinics* 48 (2019): 303–21.
53 S.J. Crasnow, "'I Want to Look Transgender': Anti-Assimilation, Gender Self-Determination, and Confronting White Supremacy in the Creation of a Just Judaism," *Journal of the American Academy of Religion* 88 (2020): 1026–48.
54 Max Strassfeld, "Translating the Human: the *Androginos* in Tosefta Bikurim," *Transgender Studies Quarterly* 3 (2016): 587–604.
55 Elliot Kukla, "A Created Being of Its Own: Toward a Jewish Liberation Theology for Men, Women and Everyone Else" TransTorah, 2006, www.transtorah.org.
56 Elliot Kukla, "Created by the Hand of Heaven: Sex, Love, and the Androgynous," in *Sacred Encounter: Jewish Perspectives on Sexuality*, ed. Lisa J. Grushcow (New York: CCAR Press, 2014), 145–56. S. J. Crasnow also has an excellent discussion of theologies of cocreation in their dissertation, "From the Gay Synagogue to the Queer Shtetl: Normativity, Innovation, and Utopian Imagining in the Lived Religion of Queer and Transgender Jews" (University of California, Riverside, 2017).
57 S. J. Crasnow, "On Transition: Normative Judaism and Trans Innovation," *Journal of Contemporary Religion* 32 (2017): 403–15.
58 Emily Aviva Kapoor, interview with S. J. Crasnow, in Crasnow, "On Transition," 408.
59 Beit Simchat Torah's origins may be traced to a community forming in 1972–73 or a more formal founding in 1975. The House of David and Jonathan, a Brooklyn-based institution, pre-dated even these gay synagogues, but it lasted less than two months. See Gregg Drinkwater, "Creating an Embodied Queer Judaism: Liturgy, Ritual, and Sexuality at San Francisco's Congregation Sha'ar Zahav, 1977–1987," *Journal of Modern Jewish Studies* 18 (2019): 177–93.
60 See Carol Conaway, "On My Own Terms," *Journal of Lesbian Studies* 23 (2019): 68–82.
61 Julie Greenberg, "My Piece of Truth," in *Lesbian Rabbis: The First Generation*, ed. Rebecca T. Alpert, Sue Levi Elwell, and Shirley Idelson (Piscataway, NJ: Rutgers University Press, 2001), 181–89.

62 Elliot N. Dorff, Daniel S. Nevins, and Avram I. Reisner, "Homosexuality, Human Dignity, and Halakhah: A Combined Responsum for the Committee on Jewish Law and Standards," Rabbinical Assembly, www.rabbinicalassembly.org; Noach Dzmura, *Balancing on the Mechitza: Transgender in Jewish Community* (Berkeley, CA: North Atlantic, 2010) 12.
63 Caryn Aviv, Gregg Drinkwater, and David Shneer, *We Are You: An Exploration of Lesbian, Gay, Bisexual, and Transgender Issues in Colorado's Jewish Community* (Denver, CO: Mosaic–National Jewish Center for Sexual and Gender Diversity, 2006), 2.
64 See Crasnow, *From the Gay Synagogue*, 28, for an excellent example of how gay and trans identities and needs can be quite distinct.
65 For excellent examples and analysis, see Hillel Gray, "The Transitioning of Jewish Biomedical Law: Rhetorical and Practical Shifts in Halakhic Discourse on Sex-Change Surgery," *Nashim* 29 (2015): 81–107.
66 See Marla Brettschneider, "Jewish Lesbians: New Work in the Field," *Journal of Lesbian Studies* 23 (2019): 2–20.

3

The Changing Face of Jewish America in the Twenty-First Century

BRUCE HAYNES

More than two decades ago, sociologist R. Stephen Warner noted that "American Christians, Buddhists, and Muslims come in all colors and speak a babel of languages."[1] The fact that Jews were excluded from this list reflects the myopic construction of American Judaism that we had long embraced, one that presumed White and Ashkenazi (of East European descent) normativity. Yet sweeping changes to race-based immigration policy, laws governing both naturalization and interracial marriage, and the ways that Americans have come to view racial identity and multiracial people have made it increasingly difficult to rely on conventional signifiers like skin color to determine what "looking Jewish" looks like. This chapter lays out the legal context, demographic changes, and societal forces shaping perceptions of Jews and race in America. It also explores the distinction between political Whiteness and White social identity and the shift in Jewish Studies scholarship toward a more critical exploration of race, color, and culture in Jewish life.

Political Whiteness and the Courts

In America, the documents that first established the nation also established white skin (color) as a key condition of becoming a citizen. Whiteness was not an inherent characteristic of a person so much as a "social fact" about one's ascribed legal and economic status in society. The "natal alienation" and stigma of slavery under the American Constitution made Africans into nonpersons, devoid of honor or the means to achieve honor, and the ultimate signifier of low status, even below that of other non-White peoples, including indigenous Indians.[2] Millions of Africans were sold at profit to work on plantations in North America, building the nation's wealth, while an additional six million perished in the hunt for slaves.

The first census recognized only free White males, free White females, all other free persons, and slaves. Slaves were presumed to be people of African descent, and free persons were presumed to be White people who owned slaves. Legal scholars have theorized how the formation of race and race identity, along with the development and protection of White property rights, have been deeply interrelated within American law.[3] Limiting citizenship and property rights to White folks was essential in establishing a racial hierarchy and White racial and economic domination. As professor Charyl Harris has pointed out, "In protecting the property interest in Whiteness, property is assumed to be no more than the right to prohibit infringement on settled expectations, ignoring countervailing equitable claims that are predicated on a right to inclusion."[4] Thus, Whiteness is defined by the exclusion of non-Whites and is itself a form of property possessed by all White people. American jurisprudence presumed the White status of American Jews.

Jewish Whiteness was a kind of self-evident truth from the first days when persecuted Portuguese and Iberian Jews (Levantine Sephardim) fled to New Amsterdam, where they secured special privileges of residence and rights to trade.[5] By the eighteenth century, they were followed by Jews from Poland and Germany (Ashkenazim) as well as Jews from northern Africa (Mizraḥim), groups that also laid claim to White status in the courts and were granted the formal political and economic privileges that came with that recognition. In America, traditional distinctions embedded in culture and religious practice among Jews were superseded by an embrace of American White status. Three legal clauses are key to establishing the link between race, color, and social status. First, slavery was the only constitutional provision that came with an expiration date: Article 1, Section 9, Clause 1 legalized the importation of "bonded persons" until 1808. Second, under the Three-fifths Clause, these enslaved Africans were counted as only three-fifths of a human being for purposes of apportioning political power among the states. Lastly, the Fugitive Slave Acts of 1793 and 1850, which required every state, including those that forbade slavery, to capture and return runaway slaves to their owners, further reinforced White privilege. Together, these clauses made slavery a foundational institution in the production of American wealth and the organization of the social order. These constitutional provisions for slavery were buttressed by anti-miscegenation laws extending back into the late 1690s.

To ensure that race would determine the right to citizenship, the first Continental Congress established the 1790 Naturalization Act to limit citizenship to "free white persons," while constitutional protections for people of African and other racialized non-White groups would remain uncertain for generations. In succeeding years, numerous states like Alabama, Oregon, Utah, and Nebraska adopted miscegenation laws and other racial restrictions barring Black or Colored people formally into their state constitutions.

The status of Jews as White folk was implicit in their immigration status. Under the 1790 Naturalization Act, Jews from eastern and central Europe and the Iberian Peninsula were considered legally White, not as a corporal body per se but as individuals eligible for American citizenship as well as the right to vote, run for office, or serve on juries. Buttressed by the passage of an additional amendment in 1795, called the "declaration of intent to naturalize," Jews were granted political and economic privileges under federal law immediately upon arrival, while those designated as non-White were denied.[6]

Legal scholars have shown how the "free white persons" clause acted as a "super-statute" that "established a fundamental principle of racism in American law" by denying access to citizenship to non-Whites.[7] While Congress amended the Naturalization Act numerous times from its original passage in 1790, there is no evidence that the "free white person" clause was ever called into question in congressional testimony. Congress agreed sub silentio that, regardless of station, Europeans were to be afforded Whiteness and access to naturalization and property ownership. Across the decades, congressional representatives even spoke favorably of extending naturalization specifically to Jews and Catholics without mention of non-White groups.[8] Whiteness is what political philosopher Charles W. Mills calls a "racial contract" that defines one's relationship to the state.[9] His work illustrates how White supremacy underpinned Western democratic societies across the modern world. Race and color moved to the forefront of both politics and social identity.

In combination with federal law, many states helped to make Whiteness, White space, and White supremacy normative. On arrival,

Europeans by the tens of thousands were instantly eligible to claim land as White citizens through policies like the Homestead Act of 1862. This was likely the single greatest stimulus to the formation of White wealth ever enacted during the nineteenth century. For a small filing fee, new Americans could make claims to 160-acre plots on public land. The act significantly impacted the development of the West and Northwest territories as largely White settlements, especially in Montana, North Dakota, Colorado, and Nebraska.

Between the 1870s and 1930s, the courts ruled that persons from Japan, the Philippines, Burma, Hawaii, and India could not become U.S. citizens. Meanwhile, states and federal courts developed a set of principles and legislative rules toward Jews as White individuals, granting recognition of their voluntary religious, charitable, and educational organizations. Jews have nearly always been presumed to be White within the American legal system, which recognizes religiously based "voluntary adherence to a creed, a certain pattern of observance or particular association."[10] As a result, the courts have granted specific powers to Jewish clergy over marriage, family, divorce, the Bet Din, Sabbath, and kashrut ritual observance, while at the same time validating claims to their political privilege as White people.[11] In this highly color-conscious world where skin tone substituted for race, Jewish Whiteness solidified. Being classified as White was a "valuable asset that whites sought to protect"—Jews included.[12]

People of African descent had a unique role to play because the definition of Blackness served as an asymmetrical anchor to define the boundaries of Whiteness. While the offspring of an Indian and a White person was considered White, as was true for the offspring of all other groups mixing with Whites, the offspring of a Negro and a White person remained a Negro. This was true for mixed (White? European?) Jews and Africans across the New World. This status transcended slave status itself. It was not unfree status that was passed from parent to child; it was the taint of race embedded in Negro blood. This "one-drop rule" for Negro blood was also known as "hypodescent" or the "traceable amount rule." The rule deemed anyone with known African ancestry as a "Negro" or Black. Across America, designating who was Black and who was White in practice varied from state to state. Most mixed-ancestry European Jews and Africans were classified as Negroes, making any mixture with African lineage automatically Negro regardless of color.¹³

The 1896 *Plessy v. Ferguson* decision upheld the constitutionality of Jim Crow racial segregation through the "separate but equal" doctrine while at the same time hardening the White/non-White. Although Homer Plessy claimed seventh-eighths White ancestry, the Supreme Court ruled that he was still a Negro. Legal scholar Thomas J. Davis has argued that the *Plessy v. Ferguson* decision reached far beyond the "separate but equal" doctrine it is most often associated with because it affirmed states' authority over personal agency in deciding questions of identity. Plessy rejected the binary racial distinctions of the state. "He was not claiming to be white," Davis writes. "He rejected that box. Nor was he claiming to be colored. He rejected that box too. He asserted autonomy, claiming self-identification as a right beyond state encroachment."¹⁴

This landmark federal decision was based upon two centuries of legal precedent that had been crafted at the state level. The new term "colored" was often used as a substitution for Negro, though it sometimes referred to other non-White persons and was reflected in a growing body of state law that relegated "Colored" people (translated as people of African descent) to second class citizenship. In 1911, for example, the state of Arkansas passed a bill that defined as "Negro" anyone "who has . . . any negro blood whatever."

By the twentieth century, American Jews were increasingly viewed as White people, as well as America's first model minority. Yet their path to Whiteness might be traced back to the eighteenth century, when Lamarckian scientists distinguished between historical races—groups with heterogeneous origins that consolidated over time into a common blood line—and natural racial groups, which corresponded to large geographic regions and were signified primarily by color. Africans were understood to be a natural race, unchanged by time or environment, while Jews were favored as a historical race. But it was the German scientist Johann Friedrich Blumenbach who reduced humanity to "five principal varieties" and distinguished between Africans north of the Sahara Desert as "Caucasian" and "white" as the "most handsome and becoming," while labeling the remainder of the African continent as "Ethiopian," "black," and "bandy-legged" inferiors.¹⁵ It was during the eighteenth century that many Jews also deployed racial language to defend their uniquely

Jewish experience. Linguistic typologies were constructed using ideas about racial types, and scientific racial classifications were based on linguistic definitions, creating a circular racial logic. Thus, the linguistic term "Semite" came to be used to denote Jews and Arabs, linking them to the Caucasian family and White status while severing their connection to Black Africans like the semitic speaking Ethiopians.

As America entered the early twentieth century, ethnologists, sociologists, and anthropologists debated over whether Jews belonged to the Caucasian race or were perhaps a "preindustrial" race.[16] New Jewish immigrants from eastern Europe were often viewed through an Orientalist lens as inferior to both German Jews and old-world Protestants. In the European theater, the rise of scientific racism, Social Darwinism, and the emerging fields of eugenics and ethnology raised questions about Jews and their White status. Jews in Europe were often considered to be a racially distinct group, and the Nazi Nuremberg Laws in fact mirrored American naturalization and anti-miscegenation policy. But, in America, Jews made a conscious effort to cross the American color line and claim Caucasian status, despite facing routine antisemitic vandalism.

American Pluralism Hides Jewish Whiteness

While Jews had at times used racial rhetoric to negotiate their place, by the 1950s most Jews had abandoned the racial language of an earlier generation along with racialized terms like "Hebrew."[17] They adopted a new terminology fashioned within the context of American pluralism and an emerging Black/White racial binary. Cultural pluralism provided a way for Jews to conceal their cultural distinctiveness while reconciling anxieties and questions about their Whiteness by reimagining America "as a nation of hyphenated identities." Jewish intellectuals helped construct a bridge between Jewish otherness and Whiteness.[18] It was the scholars at the University of Chicago's Department of Sociology that most shaped future generations of thinking about Jews and other European immigrants. The German-born American sociologist Louis Wirth along with the German-born American philosopher Horace M. Kallen, aided by Black intellectuals like Alain Locke and his Harlem Renaissance cultural project, helped develop a distinctive vocabulary around American cultural pluralism. Jews used this pluralism to claim a "right to be different" while also retaining White privilege.[19] This new framework challenged the melting-pot model and ideas about assimilation and racial amalgamation, yet all the while rendering racial Whiteness invisible.[20] Jews could be both "different" culturally and religiously, yet remain White.

The birth of ethnicity and the solidification of racial distinctions in America had profound implications for Jews from Europe. Whiteness served as both a legal strategy for citizenship and a racial project led by Jewish intellectuals who used pluralism to claim both political and civic equality with other White Americans.[21] Mythical ideas about the unity of the Caucasian race helped to "reconsolidate" groups once seen as outsiders to Europe into White folks in America.[22] At the same time, Kallen's cultural pluralism provided a space for Jews to retain their distinctive cultures while protecting themselves from racial marginalization and exclusion.[23] Rather than disappearing into Whiteness, Jews even used racial rhetoric to inhabit a liminal position between Whiteness and racial otherness.[24]

So, while many Jews secured and valued a political status as White people, many also maintained distinctly Jewish identities that rejected identification with Christian Whites. Nevertheless, being White in America is more than identifying as a White person; it involves being treated as a White person.[25] Consequently, Jews from Europe could enjoy the privilege of political Whiteness while preserving their distinct personal identities embedded in their experiences as Jews.

Many postwar Jews, on the other hand, expressed anxieties about rising interfaith marriage rates and an erosion of Jewish culture and identity. By the 1960s, numerous sociologists had become prominent for their role in providing data tracking Jewish intermarriage to stakeholders like Jewish communal institutions. Several Jewish leaders expressed concern that high out-marriage rates might threaten the future of the Jewish community itself; Jews might become so successful at becoming anglicized White people that they would disappear altogether. As sociologist Lila Corwin Berman put it, "An intimate affair between Jews and sociologists was consummated by the 1970s around their common interest in—and, for some, deep fear of—Jewish intermarriage."[26] Nevertheless, many Jews continued to marry non-Jews.

By the 1980s, most American Jews had gained both the privileges of White status and a "possessive investment in Whiteness."[27] Despite their successful assimilation into the White mainstream, many continued to see themselves as distinct from other White Americans. Some still hold essentialist notions of Jewishness.[28] Indeed, new advances in genetic research have only bolstered biological understandings of Jews. Sociologists Shelly Tennenbaum and Lynn Davidman have found the trend more pronounced among nonreligious, unaffiliated Jews, with many claiming that, despite their lack of observance or religious belief, "their biology was enough to make them feel essentially Jewish for life" and even leading some to question "whether or not a person could convert and become 'really' Jewish."[29] It's also true that Jews have held a variety of social identities in their day-to-day lives in ways that do not prioritize Whiteness. In fact, scholars have long noted that Jewish identity has been variable across the centuries.[30]

Since the postwar era, American Jews have used a mix of culture, religion, the rules of membership in various institutional frameworks, and even biology (race) to define who is Jewish. European Yiddishkeit culture, the Holocaust, and the State of Israel have often served as anchors to American Jewish identity as well as indicators of one's Jewishness.[31] But today many scholars contend that these traditional cultural and institutional measures of Jewish identity have been "transformed by a postmodern, individualistic, multicultural society."[32] People are no longer relying on these "objective measures" to determine Jewish identity but turn to more subjective indicators like social identity. But the racial typing of European Jews as White has often obfuscated our ability to even see the challenges faced by non-White American Jews.

As American Jewry celebrates its cultural, national, and even racial diversity in the twenty-first century, Yiddishkeit, the Holocaust, the State of Israel, and presumptions of Whiteness are insufficient anchors to contemporary American Jewish identity.

Multiheritage and Multiracial Jews and the Future of Jewish Scholarship

The face of American Jewry has been changing along with the nation. The abolishment of racial restrictions in naturalization (1952) and the passage of the Immigration Act of 1965 led to population increases from the Global South. This may have signaled the first demographic change to the face of American Jewry. Mizraḥim from northern Africa along with Jews from other corners of Africa, Asia, and various islands were steadily immigrating to America. This development brought heightened attention to questions of mixed heritage Jews, color, and race in Jewish Studies not long after many scholars had declared that postwar "Jewish Whiteness" had become "American Whiteness," and that Jews were White folks.[33] Growth in the non-European immigrant population and the expansion of civil rights discourse that no longer included references to Jews as a discriminated American minority have contributed to major changes in the way Americans think about race in the twenty-first century.

Just two years following sweeping changes to immigration policy, the Supreme Court ruled in the 1967 landmark *Loving v. Virginia* case, which declared anti-miscegenation statutes to be unconstitutional. During the following two decades, interracial marriage rates steadily climbed, as did the numbers of mixed-heritage children. At the beginning of the twentieth century, most mixed-ancestry European Jews and Africans were classified as Negroes, making any mixture with African lineage automatically "Negro" regardless of color.[34] But by the 1990s America was experiencing a veritable "biracial baby boom," as observers declared that the "New Face of America" was multicultural and multiracial, and that a "new American melting pot" was underway.[35]

Today, more than 33.8 million American self-identify as more than one race, according to the 2020 U.S. Census. In 2018, the Pew Research Center reported that the American immigrant population had reached 13.7 percent, at a record 44.8 million people, of whom an unknown number were in fact Jews.[36] According to Pew's 2013 data, first- or second-generation Israelis account for about 5 percent of American Jews, and as many as three hundred thousand were either born in Israel or born to an Israeli parent. These diverse groups have contributed to a rather dramatic shift in the racial and cultural composition of American Jewry. Questions about Jewish identity, which once centered on ethnicity, institutional association, and cultural assimilation, now pivoted toward investigating the "social construction of race" and its impact on Jewish identity and life.

Complicating these changes was Israel's Six-Day War, in 1967, which altered the political landscape and changed the relationship of American

Jews to Israel, civil rights, and Zionism, while transforming the public discourse surrounding Jews, Jewish identity, and Whiteness.[37] Ironically, the emphasis on Jewish Whiteness had also been reinforced in other disciplines and academic circles and may have contributed to the tendency to exclude Jews from discussions of racial bias, multicultural curriculum, and, more recently, diversity, equity, and inclusion.

The wave of Whiteness studies that took off in the 1980s explored how European groups like the Irish, Slavs, Italians, Germans, French, and Jews all became accepted as White people in America. That was juxtaposed with a right-wing shift in American politics among the White working classes and often reflected their concerns with working class politics. Scholars like David Roediger, Ruth Frankenberg, Cheryl Harris, Theodore W. Allen, Karen Brodkin (Sacks), Noel Ignatiev, Mathew Frye Jacobson, and George Lipsitz helped to move "Whiteness" to the foreground of the critical investigation of the European immigrant experience.[38] The scholarship of W. E. B. Du Bois took on renewed significance as an academic consensus began to emerge that posited the idea that the political and economic privileges afforded to different ethnic groups were commensurate with their level of acceptance as White folk.[39] Mobility into the American middle class was both cause and effect of Jewish acceptance within the White American mainstream.[40] So, with few obstacles ahead, most academicians agreed that Jews were not a minority group but had incorporated, much like other Europeans, despite often remaining outside of the dominant Christian culture.[41]

Meanwhile, the visibility of non-White, non-Ashkenazi normativity Jews was also growing, and presumptions of Jewish Whiteness were brought into the spotlight anew. In 1988, the Black scholar and former civil rights activist Julius Lester published his memoir, *Lovesong: Becoming a Jew*.[42] Winner of the National Jewish Book Award, it chronicled Lester's Orthodox conversion to Judaism, traced his Jewish roots back to American slavery, and opened new conversations regarding Jews of African descent.

Meanwhile, the plight of Ethiopian Jews had also reached the American press. Media accounts of Operations Solomon and Moses, which brought these Jews to Israel between 1980 and 1994, placed the spotlight on these "Black Jews." In January 1985, the *New York Times* reported that Israel had airlifted ten thousand Ethiopians. By 2002, there were some eighty-five thousand Ethiopian Jews concentrated in the cities of Netanya, Rehovot, Haifa, Hadera, and Ashdod.[43] The number of new works by historians and anthropologists was also growing, including Tudor Parfitt's *The Thirteenth Gate: Travels Among the Lost Tribes of Israel*, Steven Kaplan's *The Beta Israel (Falasha) in Ethiopia: From Earliest Times to the Twentieth Century*, and James Quirin's *The Evolution of the Ethiopian Jews: A History of the Beta Israel (Falasha) to 1920*, which began to change the conversation about Jews and race in the African context.[44] After all, Israel came into existence as a people during a forty-year exile in Africa's Egypt.

While the Beta Israel of Ethiopia are perhaps the most well-known African Jews, numerous groups in Africa were also laying claim to Jewish identities and Jewish practices. Some self-identified African Jews, like the Tutsis of Rwanda, began seeking recognition as Jews. Among the Igbo of Nigeria, some 30,000 practice some form of Judaism, while another 1500–2000 practice normative Orthodox or rabbinic Judaism.[45] Parfitt refers to these developments as Judaizing movements. Others, like the Abayudaya of Uganda, underwent formal conversion to Conservative Judaism after having practiced an informal Judaism for decades.[46]

In America, people began to take notice of rising numbers of self-identified Black Jews and other non-Ashkenazi Jews. Soon a few began to organize. One of the first events devoted to Black Jews took place in 1993 at the Los Angeles African American Museum. There, the Bridges and Boundaries Conference presented the panel "Where Worlds Collide: The Souls of African American Jews." Although the event drew little media attention, it was significant for bringing together an international cadre of Jews of African descent. The next two years saw the founding of the Alliance of Black Jews, the first voluntary social advocacy group organized by and for Jews of African descent. The Alliance was soon followed by Bechol Lashon (1997) and the Jewish Multiracial Network (1997), groups that organized in support of multiracial and multicultural Jews and their families.[47] The Alliance of Black Jews has since been superseded by the Black Jewish Liberation Collective. According to its website, the collective seeks to create "space for community building and strategizing to support Black people who are working towards liberation and dismantling White supremacist patriarchy, racialized capitalism, and antisemitic violence."[48]

The Bay Area Multicultural Jewish Family Connection was founded at Bechol Lashon to provide space for families to explore their ethnic and racial identities within a Jewish context. The rise of the internet in the late 1990s provided the first spaces for non-White Jews to connect with one another and explore their Jewishness as indigenous Jews, Latinx Jews, Asian American Jews, Black Jews, Mizraḥi Jews, Sephardic Jews, and Jews of Color.[49] As people made new connections and allies and talked to one another about their experiences, new venues for Jews of Color to express themselves was a logical next step. The Yahoo! Group Aframjews billed itself as the "premier online community for Jews of African descent" in 1998.[50]

The year 2001 is when the idea that Jews really do come in all colors began to spill into the mainstream media. In January 2001, Yavilah McCoy began running her own listserv on Yahoo! Groups for "born and converted Jews of Color." McCoy founded the Ayecha Recource Center (2001–2008) for "Jews of color" and "Jewish diversity." Also in 2001, the Brooklyn-brewed culture magazine *Heeb* began publishing articles about multiracial people with Jewish identities. The magazine claims to have been "the highest circulated Jewish culture magazine in the world" between 2002 and 2010, reaching what it describes as "the Jewish community's most elusive demographic": 18 to 34 year-olds unaffiliated with a Jewish organization but in search of ways to express their Jewish identities with meaning. The same year, the feminist Jewish journal *Bridges: A Journal for Jewish Feminists and Our Friends* put out a special issue titled "Writing and Art by and for Jewish Women of Color," which included Puerto Rican, indigenous, Ethiopian, Yemenite, Arab, Indian, Peruvian, Mizraḥi, Ashkenazi, Jews by Choice, and mixed-heritage Jewish women. Scholars identified culture and racial ascription as central to understanding social identity. Since the 1990s, *Bridges* had mixed the Jewish values of social justice and *tikkun olam* ("healing the world") with insights drawn from Black, feminist, gay, and lesbian social movement activism.

A critical turn in scholarship was taking place across multiple disciplines, and Jewish Studies was no different. By the first decades of the twenty-first century, scholars studying the Jewish experience were influenced by new critical ideas entering the academy through the rise of Marxism, feminism, queer theory, critical race studies, critical

Whiteness studies, postcolonial studies, and even the Black radical tradition. As some scholarship challenged presumptions of Jewish Whiteness, Jewish communal and synagogue institutions began to respond to the changing demography and to growing pressure from groups like the Bay Area–based Jews of Color Initiative. Founded in the City of Berkeley in 1997 as the Jews of Color Field Building Initiative, much like Be'chol Lashon, the Initiative generates structural and communal support for Jews of Color while educating the public about their presence.[51] It has received generous support from the Charles and Lynn Schusterman Family Philanthropies, the Jim Joseph Foundation, the San Francisco–based Jewish Community Federation, and other donors.[52] Today, it seems likely that the common institutional arenas of Jewish life—Jewish day schools, Jewish community centers, synagogues, and college Hillel houses—will continue to witness growing numbers of Jews who identify as non-White.

Questions about the color of Jews and whether they should be considered a distinct race have impacted Jewish identity since at least the eighteenth century.[53] Yet, today, the ways in which Jews of European descent perceive themselves as insiders or outsiders in America can collide with how many perceive them as White. Jews continue to negotiate "their place in a complex racial world where Jewishness, whiteness, and blackness have all made significant claims on them."[54]

The investigations into culture, color, and the race of Jews have been further enriched by the work of Black and multiracial Jewish scholars who emerged on the scene during the 1990s. The feminist philosopher Naomi Zack wrote intimately about mixed-race Jewish identity in America. She was joined by Laurence M. Thomas, the author of *Vessels of Evil: American Slavery and the Holocaust*; Lewis R. Gordon, author of *Fanon and the Crisis of European Man* (1995) and *Bad Faith and Anti-Black Racism* (1995); and Katya Gibel Mevorach (formerly Azoulay), who wrote *Black, Jewish, and Interracial: It's Not the Color of Her Skin but the Race of Your Kin, and Other Myths of Identity*.[55]

Recent scholarship has generated new narratives and raised questions about the role of race, culture, and color in shaping Jewish identity. In 2013, Efraim Sicher brought together an interdisciplinary group of scholars including Edith Bruder, Sander L. Gilman, Cheryl Greenberg, Bruce D. Haynes, Steven Kaplan, Fran Markowitz, Glynis Cousin, and

Robert Fine and published the volume *Race, Color, Identity: Rethinking Discourses about "Jews" in the Twenty-First Century*.[56] In 2016, the journal *American Jewish History* published a special issue titled "Jews, Race, and Color." University programming also began to appear as partnerships between universities and private foundations and has led to the creation of new programming infrastructures.[57]

Rising Visibility of Non-White Jews

The rising visibility of what many now call "Jews of Color" has brought new attention and insights to the role race has played in shaping the American Jewish experience. In *The Soul of Judaism*, I argue that just as American Jews made claims to European roots and Whiteness, there have also been many Africans and African Americans who have also found religious expression in Judaism and Judaic practice. While many are aware of Mizraḥi Jews from the Middle East and North Africa, Sephardic Jews from Spain, Cochin Jews from India, Chinese Jews from Shanghai, and even Ethiopian Jews from Africa, the popular image of Jews in Israel and in America remains overwhelmingly White and European. While individual Jews of African descent have existed in the Caribbean, Curacao, and the Americas for decades, if not centuries, until recently they were largely dismissed as either insignificant or not halachically Jewish.[58]

Over centuries of colonialism, millions of Africans and African Americans believed that they were descended from the ancient Hebrews. Consequently, a wide variety of Hebrew Israelite groups (often simplified under the umbrella term "Black Hebrew Israelite") have gained visibility. But the term conflates many different groups that hold a variety of beliefs. Some of these groups have origins in Kansas and Philadelphia in the early nineteenth century while others had their roots in urban Black communities like New York's Harlem and Chicago's South Side. Organized groups of nonrabbinic Black Jews began to emerge during the exodus of Southern migrants to Arkansas, Kansas, Missouri, Philadelphia, Chicago, and New York City.[59] Historian James Landing traces the early foundations of a variety of groups that, for various ideological reasons, have preferred to call themselves "Hebrews" or "Israelites."[60] Some choose to embrace their European coreligionists as brethren and often have strong halachic leanings, while others are labeled "Radical Hebrew Israelites" by the Southern Poverty Law Center. And while there are also groups indigenous to Africa who make claims to primeval ties with the ancient Israelites, some groups even claim that all Black African peoples are Jews.

There are still others, like Rabbi Capers Funnye, who cross between boundaries. While Funnye has formally converted to traditional (rabbinic) Judaism, he identifies as Hebrew Israelite. Some religiously observant Hebrew Israelites fall outside of halachic definitions, but many consider themselves to be Jews returning to Judaism (*ba'alei teshuvah*) and often cite family ancestry in order to call themselves "reverts" as opposed to converts.[61]

The latest scholarship has begun to explore centuries of African-Jewish contact in the New World and the influence of Judaism and Jewish culture on transatlantic Black populations. Jacob Dorman's *Chosen People: The Rise of American Black Israelite Religions* traces the cultural evolution of African American engagement with Judaism and shows ideational connections between Pentecostal Christianity, the ancient Hebrews, Israelites, Black Jews, and Anglo-Israelite traditions.[62] Judith Weisenfeld's, award winning *New World A-Coming: Black Religion and Racial Identity During the Great Migration* challenges the stock narrative that Black religion in America is either the Black Church or Islam.[63] And my own work, *The Soul of Judaism: Jews of African Descent in America*, outlines the history of Jews of African descent in the United States and challenges the dominant Western paradigm of Jews as White and of European descent.[64]

Anecdotal evidence suggests that increased access to social media and technology in the United States and Africa has combined with a long-held belief of ancestral ties to the ancient Hebrews to generate a growth in Israelite identities that vary across practice, perspectives, and origins. These reports overlap with provocative academic studies on African Judaism like Tudor Parfitt's *Black Jews in Africa and the Americas* and John L. Jackson's *Thin Description: Ethnography and the African Hebrew Israelites of Jerusalem*.[65] We have only just begun to explore what filmmaker and urban anthropologist John L. Jackson calls "the eclectic and fascinating landscape of groups, histories, and ideologies that animate the nexus of blackness and Jewishness."[66]

Many people are surprised by the growth of rabbinic Jews of Color and Jews of non-Ashkenazi-normative backgrounds who identify as non-White today. Dozens of organizations focus on the experiences of American non-White Jews. One such group is Jews Indigenous to the Middle East and North Africa (JIMENA). Based in San Francisco, the organization is dedicated to celebrating and sharing the rich and vibrant culture of Sephardic and Mizraḥi Jewry. On the other side of the country, Rabbi "Manny" Viñas, a bilingual Cuban-born Jew (JuBan), has served as the rabbi of El Centro de Estudios Judios Torat Emet, which is dedicated to outreach and Jewish education for those descending from the *anusim*—a Hebrew term meaning "forced ones" that refers to Spanish and Portuguese Jews who were forcibly converted to Christianity during the Inquisition. For years, Rabbi Manny has held classes on Judaism over the internet in Spanish with over six thousand weekly attendees. Other organizations have sprung up that serve both Orthodox and non-Orthodox Jews of Color: The Ayecha Resource Organization, Be'chol Lashon, Jews in All Hues, Jewtina y Co., the Jewish Multiracial Network, AMMUD Jews of Color Torah Academy, Kamochah, Kulanu, Olamim, the LUNAR Collective, and the Jews of Color Initiative. With support from the Jewish Federation and $200,000 from Stephen Spielberg, the Jews of Color Initiative, led by Ilana Kaufman, may be the largest and most financially endowed of all organizations advocating for Jews of Color.

Conversion among non-White Americans to Judaism seems to be on the rise in recent decades, while some unknown numbers of Jews have also adopted non-White children and chosen to raise them with Jewish culture and identities. Several Jews of Color have chosen to pursue a life in the rabbinate, including Alysa Stanton (ordained in 2009), who grew up in a Pentecostal family in Cleveland, and Angela Buchdahl (ordained in 2001), the first Asian American rabbi and the senior rabbi at New York's two-thousand-member Central Synagogue. Rabbi Sandra Lawson, one of the first African American queer female rabbis in the world, joined Reconstructing Judaism, the central organization of the Reconstructionist movement, as the inaugural director of racial diversity, equity, and inclusion in January 2021. Her vision goes beyond discussing racial justice issues with the congregation. "I'm more interested in changing the culture," she said in an issue of the *Forward*.[67]

In recent years, a new generation of self-identified Black Jews—including Tiffany Haddish, Nissim Black, Rabbi Sandra Lawson, and Michael Twitty—have become celebrities on social media. Rabbi Shais Rishon, also known by the pen name MaNishtana, is a New York–born African American Orthodox rabbi, blogger, writer, and activist. In 2014, he made the *Jewish Week*'s annual "36 to Watch" list of influential Jewish New Yorkers under the age of 36. Across the continent is Rabbi Yonason Perry, a biracial Chabad-Lubavitch rabbi based in Los Angeles. Perry teamed up with Rabbi Isaiah Robinson, a Black Jew recently ordained at New York's Yeshiva University, to help found Kamochah, an organization that supports Black Orthodox Jews. With chapters in Los Angeles, Baltimore, and New York City, Kamochah hopes to expand to cities across the nation with programming that targets all Black Jewish youth, Orthodox or not. And then there is Rabbi Gershom Sizomu, ordained in 2007 at the Ziegler School of Rabbinic Studies, the Conservative movement's seminary in Los Angeles, as the first Conservative sub-Saharan Black rabbi. He was also the first Jew elected to the Ugandan parliament.

Counting Jews of Color

Rabbi Capers Funnye, a cousin to Michelle Obama, is the spiritual leader of the Beth Shalom B'nai Zaken Ethiopian Hebrew Congregation of Chicago, one of the largest Black synagogues in America. In June 2015, he was elected as chief rabbi of the International Israelite Board of Rabbis of the Ethiopian Hebrews. While Funnye's roots are in the Hebrew Israelite movement, he and his family converted to Conservative Judaism and maintain ties to both communities. On Martin Luther King Jr. Day in 2008, Funnye was invited to speak at New York's Stephen Wise Free Synagogue, a historically Ashkenazi synagogue. Some seven hundred New York Jews across the Reform and Hebrew Israelite traditions came together for the occasion. The *New York Times Magazine* columnist Zev Chafets reported, "But even with your eyes closed you could tell who was who: the black Jews and the white Jews clapped to the music on different beats."[68]

Such alliances between Black and White Jews are unique but not unprecedented. Hatza'ad Harishon (First Step) was a New York–based, cross-racial Jewish organization that briefly emerged in the wake of the Civil Rights Act of 1964. Its mission was to create a bridge between Hebrew Israelite groups, like Harlem's Commandment Keepers, and mainstream rabbinic Judaism, as extensively documented in Janice W. Fernheimer's *Stepping into Zion: Hatzaad Harishon, Black Jews, and the Remaking of Jewish Identity*.[69]

Traditionally, rabbinic Judaism has recognized only Jews of matrilineal descent or those who have formally converted under the auspices of a bet din, while demographers and Jewish communal organizations have tended to operationalize and quantify "Jewishness" based on a combination of behavioral and attitudinal indicators, along with religious affiliation, institutional and organizational participation, and cultural identification. But recent changes in the social and racial demography of the American Jewish population mandate more nuanced strategies to count Jews and study Jewish identity. Still, there are several challenges in measuring the number of Jews of Color: First, since the 1980s most community population studies have been organized and funded by local Jewish federations, and numerous survey sampling designs rely on organizational lists, distinctive Jewish names, or geography to identify the Jewish population.[70] Second, until recently most surveys excluded questions about race. Scholars Aaron Hahn Tapper, Ari Y. Kelman, and Aliya Sapperstein's analysis of surveys used in 175 American Jewish population studies and community portraits since 1970 shows that the majority failed to look at questions of racial and ethnic diversity, a practice that resulted in undercounting Jews of Color (JOCs) while contributing to the presumption that American Jews are White.[71] Third, there is no single definition of the category "Jews of Color." Are Hispanic Jews also Jews of Color? Do all Jews of Latin heritage consider themselves to be Jews of Color? What about those who identify as Sephardic and Mizraḥi? When do people of Iranian, Syrian, Indian, or other non-Western backgrounds choose to identify as non-White? Should these Jews be identified as Jews of Color even if they do not identify as such?[72] Fourth, given America's history of racial segregation and housing, an unequal distribution of Jews of Color (interreligious and interracial marriages are highest in the western states) could lead to lower estimates. And, finally, not all non-White Jews may choose to self-identify as non-White, making population estimates more problematic.[73]

Survey research has tended to produce more conservative estimates based on how the sample of Jews is selected. The first comprehensive study of the American Jewish population was conducted in 1970 by the National Jewish Population Survey, and in 1990 the NJPS conducted the first pure probability sample to calculate a statistical estimate of the size of the American Jewish community. It sampled 2,441 households in which at least one member self-identified as Jewish, and found that 2.4 percent of the sample, or an estimated 125,000 individuals, also identified as Black. By the turn of the millennium, no respectable survey of Jewish Americans could avoid a racial identity question. But scholarly estimates varied as to the total number of Jews in America as well as the total number of "Jews of Color," a term that activists and social demographers were increasingly adopting.

The 2013 Pew Research Center study—heralded by many as the gold standard in Jewish population surveys—reported that only 6 percent of roughly 5.3 million Jewish adults in the U.S. identified as non-White. (A year earlier, Brandeis University conducted its own national survey and found that a significantly higher number of Jewish adults—12 percent—were non-White.) Bruce Phillips cautions about potentially low estimates, agreeing with Ari Kelman and colleagues that younger cohorts of Jews are more likely to self-identify as non-White,[74] and that more inclusive definitions of Jews lead to larger estimates of Jews of Color, while more restrictive definitions lead to lower estimates.[75] Jews from Spain, Portugal, Algeria, Egypt, Iraq, Iran, Lebanon, Libya, Morocco, Syria, Tunisia, or Yemen have traditionally identified as Mizraḥim or Sephardim, but, today, depending on the context, people originating in those countries may also consider themselves Jews of Color right alongside Jews from Ethiopia.

In a special issue of the journal *Contemporary Jewry*, Steven Cohen argued that those Jewish population studies that have moved away from using random digit dialing often paint a "deficient and distorted" picture by overlooking important population groups.[76] According to Brandeis University's 2021 Study of Jewish Los Angeles, 6 percent of Jews self-identify as people of color, and 9 percent of Jewish children are considered people of color by their parent.

The latest Pew Research survey, conducted in 2020, identified 8 percent of self-identified Jews who also identified as non-White, and concluded that American Jews are "culturally engaged, increasingly diverse, politically polarized and worried about anti-Semitism." These numbers appear consistent with other national population sample surveys. More important are the trends recent surveys identify. According to the Pew Research Center's 2020 survey, 15 percent of Jewish adults ages eighteen to twenty-nine identify as Black, Hispanic, Asian, other race, or multiracial, compared with only 3 percent of Jews ages sixty-five and older.[77]

It is also important to keep in mind that local surveys of targeted populations also reveal variation by city and that locations like New York City, the San Francisco Bay Area, and selected western states may have higher rates of Jews of Color.[78] In fact, variation exists across locations for synagogue membership, age profiles, and other kinds of demographic data, so counting Jews is never simple or straightforward. Still, there is strong evidence that the number of Jews of Color is rising among younger cohorts and may exceed 15 percent among younger adults. The advocacy group the Jews of Color Initiative sponsored a study in which they estimated the percentage of Jews of Color to be between 12 percent and 15 percent.[79] The Jews of Color Initiative Report claimed to be "the first national survey of Jews of Color and the largest dataset of interviews with self-identified Jews of Color to date," but it was not a statically representative sample survey of non-White Jews. Controversy erupted when Ira Sheskin and Arnold Dashefsky concluded in the 2019 *American Jewish Year Book* that the report probably overinflated their estimates.[80] Since then, the Pew Research Center published its 2020 report, which has tended to settle tensions with their updated estimate of 8 percent Jews of Color.

Soon after, the Jews of Color Initiative did the largest comprehensive nonstatistical qualitative survey of Jews of Color ever conducted: *Beyond the Count: Perspectives and Lived Experiences of Jews of Color*, published in 2021.[81] Led by Stanford University researcher Tobin Belzer, the study surveyed 1018 self-identified Jews of Color, supplemented by sixty-one in-depth interviews. Their major finding was that a majority of their sample (80 percent) reported experiencing discrimination in Jewish settings. This finding is consistent with my research, which showed that

Black Jews experienced both racial discrimination from Jews and antisemitism from non-Jews.[82]

According to the Southern Poverty Law Center, a group that has tracked extremist groups for more than three decades, today's "antisemitic hate groups seek to racialize Jewish people and vilify them as the manipulative puppet masters behind an economic, political, and social scheme to undermine white people."[83] Non-White Jews may experience either racism or antisemitism or both. Nevertheless, many of the concerns surrounding the term "Jews of Color" and how best to count them cannot be disentangled from the ongoing debate over Jewish Whiteness.

Conclusion

Jewish identities are ever shifting, contextual, and intersectional. In Israel, for instance, where Jews make up 80 percent of the population, Jewish identities are more nationalistic, religious, and cultural and far less embedded in the idea of Whiteness. Nevertheless, on today's global stage, Israel has been labeled a "white colonial-settler state" in some activist circles, while in America, where Jews make up just 2 percent of the population, most Jews of European descent lay claim to a White identity even as they maintain distinctly Jewish identities in their personal lives. Yet, despite the "White" label and comfortable economic status in recent years, American Jews have experienced rising vandalism, physical assault, and racist stereotyping in social media. In fact, America entered the most violently anti-Jewish period ever recorded in American history with the murder of eleven people by a White supremacist at the Tree of Life synagogue in the Squirrel Hill neighborhood of Pittsburgh in 2018. Hate crime against Jews, Sikhs, and Muslims have been increasing for decades, but attacks against Jews reached unprecedented highs over the past two years. According to the most recent audits by the Anti-Defamation League, antisemitic acts of online harassment and hate speech, as well as attacks on Jewish Americans and their property set record highs in 2022. And, following the October 7, 2023, attacks in Israel, hate crimes against Jews in America are on track to set a new record for 2024.

At the same time, Jews face increased scrutiny for having crossed the color line as White folk. The tension is particularly salient in conversations surrounding the consideration of Jewish Americans for "multicultural" spaces and diversity, equity, and inclusion initiatives. For example, should Jews be included in ethnic studies curricula focused on racism in the United States?

Far-reaching changes to American law in the post–civil rights era have brought a new legitimacy to interracial people that has combined with a major shift in immigration to transform the racial landscape of the American Jewish population. Movement activists, many born Jews who also call themselves "Jews of Color," have emerged on the scene and pushed for institutional recognition. Jewish federations, communal leaders, and national organizations have begun to think seriously about how best to reconcile the challenge posed by racial and cultural diversity within the Jewish community.

It was nearly sixty years ago, in May 1964, that *Look* magazine ran a cover story that predicted "The Vanishing American Jew." Yet the dire projection did not bear out. Not only did American Jews not disappear, but the population is larger and more diverse than ever before. Of course, Jewish diversity raises important questions surrounding how best to count American Jews while considering race. Should Jews be racially identified as White in the first place if race classification and racism most often lead towards racial states and racial nationalism?

The 2017 *American Jewish Yearbook* aggregated over 900 local surveys from across the nation to come up with its own estimate of the Jewish population. The number, about 6.85 million, had climbed more than 10 percent from 6.06 million estimated in 1971. Ira Sheskin estimates that the Jewish population growth likely peaked during the 2010s, when "three different estimates derived using three different procedures suggest that the American Jewish population ranged from 6.7 to 7.1 million."[84] Meanwhile, scholars have engaged in lively debates about the numbers of Jews of Color and how best to count them. Afro-Jewish scholar Lewis Gordon recently talked to me about how terms like "mainstream Jewish community" invariably mean to most people Ashkenazi or "White" Jews. So, while methodological challenges to assigning neat categories to Jews who consider themselves to be either "White" or "non-White" persist, it is certain that the increasing diversity of Jews has only just begun to shore up the whole and defy those grim forecasts of a "vanishing American Jew."

NOTES

1. R. S. Warner, "Religion and New (Post-1965) Immigrants: Some Principles Drawn from Field Research," *American Studies* 41 (2000): 267–86.
2. Orlando Patterson, *Slavery and Social Death: A Comparative Study* (Cambridge, MA: Harvard University Press, 1982).
3. Cheryl I. Harris, "Whiteness as Property," *Harvard Law Review* 106 (1993): 1707–91.
4. Harris, "Whiteness as Property," 1791.
5. Clifton Harby Levy, "The First Jewish Colony on Manhattan Island: One of the Most Important Events in Israel's History Will Be Celebrated This Thanksgiving Day—How the Jewish Population of New York Has Swelled from 23 Persons to 500,000," *New York Times*, November 26, 1905, F6.
6. Gabriel J. Chin and Paul Finkelman, "The 'Free White Persons' Clause of the Naturalization Act of 1790 as Super-Statute," *William & Mary Law Review* (forthcoming).
7. Chin and Finkelman, "'Free White Persons' Clause."
8. Chin and Finkelman.
9. Charles W. Mills, *The Racial Contract* (Ithaca, NY: Cornell University Press, 1997).
10. Annalise Glauz-Todrank, *Judging Jewish Identity in the United States* (London: Rowman & Littlefield, 2023).
11. Daniel J. Elazar and Stephen R. Goldstein, "The Legal Status of the American Jewish Community," *American Jewish Yearbook* 73 (1972): 3–94.
12. Harris, "Whiteness as Property," 1713.
13. F. James Davis, *Who Is Black? One Nation's Definition* (University Park, PA: Pennsylvania State University Press, 1991); Bruce D. Haynes, *The Soul of Judaism: Jews of African Descent in America* (New York: New York University Press, 2018).
14. Thomas J. Davis, "Who Gets to Say Who's Who? Plessy's Insidious Legacy," *Russell Sage Foundation Journal of the Social Sciences* 7 (February, 2021): 32–49.
15. Haynes, *Soul of Judaism*.
16. Eric L. Goldstein, *The Price of Whiteness: Jews, Race, and American Identity* (Princeton, NJ: Princeton University Press, 2006).
17. Goldstein, *Price of Whiteness*.
18. Haynes, *Soul of Judaism*, 40.
19. David Weinfeld, *The American Friendship: Horace Kallen, Alain Locke, and the Development of Cultural Pluralism* (Ithaca, NY: Cornell University Press, 2022).
20. Weinfeld, *American Friendship*; Haynes, *Soul of Judaism*.
21. Haynes, 10.
22. Matthew Frye Jacobson, *Whiteness of a Different Color: European Immigrants and the Alchemy of Race* (Cambridge, MA: Harvard University Press 1998) p. 8.

23 Haynes, *Soul of Judaism*, 40.
24 Haynes, 40.
25 Kwame Anthony Appiah, "I'm Jewish and Don't Identify as White. Why Must I Check That Box?," *New York Times Magazine*, October 18, 2020, 14.
26 Lila Corwin Berman, "Sociology, Jews, and Intermarriage in Twentieth-Century America," *Jewish Social Studies* n.s. 14 (2008): 32–60.
27 George Lipsitz, *The Possessive Investment in Whiteness: How White People Profit from Identity Politics* (Philadelphia: Temple University Press, 1998).
28 Haynes, *Soul of Judaism*, 44.
29 Shelly Tennenbaum and Lynn Davidman, "It's in My Genes: Biological Discourse and Essentialist Views of Identity among Contemporary American Jews," *Sociological Quarterly* 48 (2007): 435–50.
30 Haynes, *Soul of Judaism*, 19, 111.
31 Haynes; David Biale, Michael Galchinsky, and Susannah Heschel, *Insider/Outsider: American Jews and Mujlticulturalism* (Berkeley, CA: University of California Press, 1998).
32 Arnold Dashefsky, Bernard Lazerwitz, and Ephraim Tabory, "A Journey of the 'Straight Way' or the 'Roundabout Path': Jewish Identity in the United States and Israel," in *A Handbook of the Sociology of Religion*, ed. Michele Dillon (Cambridge: Cambridge University Press, 2003), 246.
33 Karen Brodkin, *How Jews Became White Folks and What That Says about Race in America* (New Brunswick, NJ: Rutgers University Press, 1998).
34 F. James Davis, *Who Is Black: One Nation's Definition* (State Park, PA: Penn State University Press, 1991); Haynes, *Soul of Judaism*.
35 See G. Reginald Daniel, *More than Black? Multiracial Identity and the New Racial Order.* (Philadelphia: Temple University Press, 2001); G. Reginald Daniel and Jasmine Kelekay, "From *Loving v. Virginia* to Barack Obama: The Symbolic Tie That Binds," *Creighton Law Review* 50 (2017): 641–68; and *Time Magazine's* feature issue "The New Face of America," November 18, 1993.
36 See Abby Budiman, Christine Tamir, Lauren Mora, and Luis Noe-Bustamante, "Facts on U.S. Immigrants, 2018, Statistical Portrait of the Foreign-Born Population in the United States," Pew Research Center, August 20, 2020, www.pewresearch.org.
37 Eric Alterman, *We Are Not One: A History of America's Fight Over Israel* (New York: Basic Books, 2022).
38 See David Roediger, *The Wages of Whiteness: Race and the Making of the American Working Class* (London: Verso, 1991); Ruth Frankenberg, *White Women, Race Matters: The Social Construction of Whiteness* (Minneapolis: University of Minnesota Press, 1993); Harris, "Whiteness as Property"; Theodore W. Allen, *The Invention of the White Race* (London: Verso, 1994–97); Karen B. Brodkin, *How Jews Became White Folks and What That Says About Race in America*; Noel Ignatiev, *How the Irish Became White* (New York: Routledge, 1995); Matthew Frye Jacobson, *Whiteness of a Different Color: European Immigrants and the Alchemy of*

Race (Cambridge, MA: Harvard University Press, 1998); Lipsitz, *Possessive Investment in Whiteness*.

39 Brodkin, *How Jews Became White Folks*.
40 Karen B. Sacks, "How Did Jews Become White Folks?," *Jewish Currents*, June 1992; *How Jews Became White Folks*.
41 Ian Daniel Rubin, "Still Wandering: The Exclusion of Jews From Issues of Social Justice and Multicultural Thought," *Multicultural Perspectives* 15 (2013): 213–19.
42 Julius Lester, *Lovesong: Becoming a Jew* (New York: Henry Holt, 1988).
43 Haynes, *Soul of Judaism*.
44 Tudor Parfitt, *The Thirteenth Gate: Travels Among the Lost Tribes of Israel* (Bethseda, MD: Adler & Adler, 1987); Steven Kaplan, *The Beta Israel (Falasha) in Ethiopia: From Earliest Times to the Twentieth Century* (New York: New York University Press, 1992); James Quirin, *The Evolution of the Ethiopian Jews: A History of the Beta Israel (Falasha) to 1920* (Philadelphia: University of Pennsylvania Press, 1992).
45 Remy Ilona, "Nigeria's 'Igbo Jews' Returning to Their Roots," *Israel National News*, August 25, 2015.
46 Haynes, *Soul of Judaism*.
47 Haynes.
48 Black Jewish Liberation Collective, www.blackjewishliberation.org.
49 Helen Kiyong Kim and Noah Samuel Leavitt, *JewAsian: Race, Religion, and Identity for America's Newest Jews* (Lincoln: University of Nebraska Press, 2016); Melanie Kaye/Kantrowitz, *The Colors of Jews: Racial Politics and Radical Diasporism*. (Bloomington: Indiana University Press, 2007); Michael Scott Alexander and Bruce D. Haynes, "The Color Issue: An Introduction," *American Jewish History* 100 (2016): ix–x; Haynes, *Soul of Judaism*.
50 Haynes, *Soul of Judaism*, 15.
51 Diane Tobin, Gary A. Tobin, and Scott Rubin, *In Every Tongue: The Racial and Ethnic Diversity of the Jewish People* (San Francisco: Institute for Jewish and Community Research, 2005); Haynes, *Soul of Judaism*.
52 J. Staff, "The Jews of Color Initiative Is Now Its Own Independent Nonprofit Organization," *Jewish News of Northern California*, June 20, 2022.
53 Haynes, *Soul of Judaism*.
54 Goldstein, *Price of Whiteness*, 5.
55 Laurence M. Thomas, *Vessels of Evil: American Slavery and the Holocaust* (Philadelphia: Temple University Press, 1993); Lewis R. Gordon, *Fanon and the Crisis of European Man* (1995) and *Bad Faith and Anti-Black Racism* (Atlantic Highlands, NJ: Humanities Press, 1995); Katya Gibel Mevorach, *Black, Jewish, and Interracial: It's Not the Color of Her Skin but the Race of Your Kin, and Other Myths of Identity* (Durham, NC: Duke University Press, 1997). Lewis Gordon has been including reference to "Afro-Jews" and "Black Jews" since his first book, *Bad Faith and Antiblack Racism* (Atlantic Highlands, NJ: Humanities, 1995) as well as in *Fanon and the Crisis of European Man* (New York: Routledge, 1995); *Existentia Africana* (New

York:Routledge, 2000); and *An Introduction to Africana Philosophy* (New York: Cambridge University Press, 2008).
56 Efraim Sicher, *Race, Color, Identity: Rethinking Discourses about the "Jews" in the 21st Century* (New York: Berghahn, 2013).
57 Michael Scott Alexander and Bruce D. Haynes, "The Color Issue: An Introduction," *American Jewish History* 100 (2016): ix–x.
58 Alexander and Haynes, "Color Issue"; see also Haynes, *Soul of Judaism*.
59 James Landing, *Black Judaism: Story of an American Movement* (University of North Durham, NC: Carolina Press, 2002); Haynes, *Soul of Judaism*, 13.
60 Landing, *Black Judaism*.
61 Haynes, *Soul of Judaism*.
62 Jacob Dorman, *Chosen People: The Rise of American Black Israelite Religions* (New York: Oxford University Press, 2013).
63 Judith Weisenfeld, *New World A-Coming: Black Religion and Racial Identity during the Great Migration* (New York: New York University Press, 2017).
64 Haynes, *Soul of Judaism. Chosen People, New World-A-Coming*, and *The Soul of Judaism* were awarded the Albert J. Raboteau Prize for the best book in Africana religions in 2014, 2017, and 2018, respectively.
65 Both books were published in Cambridge, Massachusetts, by Harvard University Press in 2013.
66 John L. Jackson, review of *The Soul of Judaism* in the *American Journal of Sociology* 125 (2019): 873–75.
67 TaRessa Sovall, "How One Trailblazing Rabbi Is Fighting Racism in the Reconstructionist Movement," *Forward*, April 6, 2022, forward.com.
68 Zev Chafets "Obama's Rabbi," *New York Times*, April 2, 2009, www.nytimes.com.
69 Janice W. Fernheimer, *Stepping into Zion: Hatzaad Harishon, Black Jews, and the Remaking of Jewish Identity* (Tuscaloosa: University of Alabama Press, 2014); see also Janice W. Fernheimer, "'Hatzaad Harishon' Broke Barriers—Until Race, Identity Questions Proved Too Much," *Forward*, February 7, 2022, forward.com.
70 Ira M. Sheskin, *How Jewish Communities Differ: Variations in the Findings of Local Jewish Population Studies* (Hartford CT: North American Jewish Data Bank, 2001).
71 Aaron Hahn Tapper, Ari Y. Kelman, and Aliya Sapperstein, "Counting on Whiteness: Religion, Race, Ethnicity, and the Politics of Jewish Demography," *Journal for the Scientific Study of Religion* (2022): 1–21.
72 Ari Y. Kelman, Aaron Hahn Tapper, Izabel Fonseca, and Aliya Saperstein, "Counting Inconsistencies: An Analysis of American Jewish Population Studies with a Focus on Jews of Color," 2019, jewsofcolorinitiative.org.
73 Bruce A. Phillips, "Complicating Jewish Whiteness: Jews of Color in the American West," in *Jewish Identities in the American West: Relational Perspectives*, ed. Ellen Eisenberg (Waltham, MA: Brandeis University Press, 2022), 326–65.
74 Phillips, "Complicating Jewish Whiteness"; Aaron Hahn Tapper, Ari Y. Kelman, and Aliya Sapperstein, "Counting on Whiteness: Religion, Race, Ethnicity, and

the Politics of Jewish Demography," *Journal for the Scientific Study of Religion* (2022): 1–21.
75 Haynes, *Soul of Judaism*; Phillips, "Complicating Jewish Whiteness."
76 Steven M. Cohen, "Deficient, If Not Distorted: Jewish Community Studies That Totally Rely on Known Jewish Households," *Contemporary Jewry* 36 (2016): 359.
77 Pew Research Center, "Jewish Americans in 2020," May 11, 2021, www.pewresearch.org.
78 Phillips, "Complicating Jewish Whiteness."
79 Ari Kelman et al., "Counting Inconsistencies."
80 Ira M. Sheskin and Arnold Dashefsky, "United States Jewish Population, 2019," in *American Jewish Year Book* 2019 (Cham: Springer, 2019) 135–231; Ira M. Sheskin and Arnold Dashefsky, "An Open Letter to the Jewish Community: We Stand with Jews of Color," eJewishPhilanthropy, May 2020, www.ejewishphilanthropy.com; "How Many Jews of Color Are There?," www.ejewishphilanthropy.com, May 2020, reprinted in *Forward*.
81 I served on the advisory committee along with Amy Born, Valerie Feldman, Tamara Fish, and Eric Greene.
82 Haynes, *Soul of Judaism*.
83 "Ideologies," Southern Poverty Law Center, www.splcenter.org.
84 Ira M. Sheskin and Arnold Dashefsky, "United States Jewish Population, 2017," *American Jewish Yearbook* 117 (2017): 180.

4

Non-Jews in Jewish Communities

JENNIFER A. THOMPSON

On a Shabbat (Sabbath) morning, proud parents stand together in their synagogue listening to their child read from the Torah for the first time as he becomes bar mitzvah. Family members and friends sit in the congregation, some following along in the *chumash* (Torah in book form) while others review the booklet they received as they entered the sanctuary. Regular members of the congregation also participate; some are called to the *bimah* (the platform where the Torah is read) to be given honors while others remain in the pews. Occasions like this one happen regularly in synagogues across the United States. Bar and bat mitzvahs are just one example of ways that Jews and non-Jews may come together in Jewish spaces. Other examples of non-Jews' involvement in Jewish spaces include non-Jewish students and scholars of Yiddish who devote themselves to learning and sharing in Yiddish culture, and people who are neither born Jews nor converts but who nevertheless feel Jewish because of their social and/or familial relationships with Jews.[1]

What is interesting about ritual occasions like the bar mitzvah described above is the variety of ways non-Jews are included in them. The proud parents may well be an interfaith or intermarried couple, meaning that one of the parents on the bimah is not Jewish, and the couple's extended family may include both Jews and non-Jews.[2] If the Jewish parent in the interfaith marriage is a convert to Judaism, all of the extended family members may be non-Jews. And, within any congregation, there may be non-Jews who are in the process of converting to Judaism, since the conversion process takes months, if not years.

This is just one way non-Jews engage in Jewish life in Jewish spaces. The 2020 Pew study of Jewish Americans found that 62 percent of all U.S. Jews "at least sometimes share Jewish culture and holidays with non-Jewish friends."[3] Non-Jews may visit Jewish spaces in support of a friend's ritual occasion or celebration, or for the purpose of interfaith learning or a religious studies class assignment. They may also engage in a more extended way because of marriage into a Jewish family, having a relative who converts to Judaism, being the biological parent of a child adopted into a Jewish family, or discovering that they have Jewish heritage through DNA analysis by 23 and Me or another company.

These forms of engagement can improve relations between Jews and non-Jews. Political scientists Robert D. Putnam and David E. Campbell explain that "religiously diverse social network[s]" provide regular, sustained, and positive contact across religious lines, which improves religious tolerance and acceptance. "When birds of different feathers flock together, they come to trust one another," they write.[4] Surveys of Americans consistently find that Jews are among the most liked religious groups in the U.S., as Jews have become increasingly well integrated into non-Jewish society.[5] Sociologists Alex Pomson and Randal F. Schnoor note that Jews' non-Jewish friends and family members frequently participate in Shabbat dinners and Passover seders, in contrast to earlier generations, when this "would have been inconceivable."[6] Inclusion of non-Jews in Jewish life happens regularly, on a casual basis as guests as well as in synagogues and other Jewish organizations with guidance from written institutional policies.

The most common way for non-Jews to become involved with the Jewish community is through inclusion in an interfaith family. There are diverse ways such families may seek to engage in Jewish communities, if they do so at all. In a 1997 study, sociologist Bruce A. Phillips outlined a typology of interfaith families that displayed the numerous possibilities for their identities: Judaic Mixed Marriages, Dual Religion, Interfaithless, Christo-Centric, Judaeo-Christian, and Christian. Judaic Mixed Marriages observe Jewish ritual practices but tend not to observe Christian ones; Dual Religion households observe both. (Households with religions other than Christianity were not reported.) Interfaithless marriages are secular, generally observing neither religion's rituals. Families in the Christo-Centric, Judaeo-Christian, and Christian categories also observe some Jewish rituals, though they lean more heavily toward Christian ones. Nevertheless, families in all of these categories engage with Jewish communities in different ways.[7]

In the case of non-Jews with an ongoing relationship to a Jewish community, questions of boundaries and belonging—topics of extensive scholarly investigation to date—inevitably arise: Who may belong to a Jewish community and under what conditions? What are the responsibilities and privileges of membership and who may hold them? But equally important, although less frequently investigated, are questions of recognition and shared fate: What does it mean to be a non-Jewish member of a Jewish community? In what ways do Jewish communities recognize non-Jewish members? To what degree do non-Jewish members feel that their fate is tied to that of the Jewish community? In some Jewish communities non-Jews occupy a liminal space, what some cultural studies researchers have called "a cultural/spiritual state of being betwixt and between," where they are neither fully part of the community nor fully *not* part of the community.[8] In others their membership is well defined and celebrated.

Liminal Jews

The same social forces that have led to non-Jews' presence in Jewish communities have also led to controversy over who "counts" as Jewish, leaving some Jewish community members in a liminal status where they are recognized by some but not others as Jews. Going back to the beginning of the Enlightenment, when the Western embrace of rationality and science supported the tentative admission of Jews into non-Jewish society, Jews in the West have experienced increasing integration into non-Jewish society as well as increased religious diversity within Judaism. Increased integration means that Jews have interacted and intermarried with non-Jews more, and increased religious diversity has resulted in different ways for Jewish communities to adapt to and recognize the stream of non-Jews who are entering Jewish communities.

In the twenty-first century, Jewish religious diversity in the U.S. spans numerous denominations or movements as well as a significant proportion of Jews who do not affiliate with any movement. Across these movements one may find a variety of attitudes toward *halakhah* (Jewish religious law), which undergirds the movements' assessments of how one comes to be Jewish. Halakhah sets out a definition, but movements that don't see halakhah as binding have developed their own definitions as well.

The Reform Movement, the Reconstructionist Movement, and many Jewish communities and individual Jews who do not affiliate with any movement do not see Jewish law as binding. Rather, they see Jewish law as an important part of Jewish civilization but individual Jews as the locus of religious authority. They believe individuals choose religious practice, meaning, and experience for themselves rather than following Jewish law because it is the law. In contrast, the Conservative Movement, all varieties of Orthodoxy, and some Jewish communities and individual Jews who do not affiliate with any movement do see Jewish law as binding. For them, Jewish law is the expression and enactment of Jews' collective and individual relationships with God. These groups and individuals vary in their understanding of how Jewish law may change over time, but they agree that Jews must uphold the Jewish covenant with God by living according to Jewish law.

Different understandings of the authority of Jewish law underlie differing assessments of who is a Jew. Rabbinic law stipulates who counts as a Jew: one who is born from a Jewish woman, or one who converts according to Jewish law. Conversion requires a period of instruction, *brit milah* or *brit dam* (actual or symbolic circumcision) for males, an interview with a *beit din* (rabbinic court), acceptance of the yoke of the law, and immersion in a *mikveh* (ritual bath). These remain the requirements for halakhic Jews, who together with those who do not adhere to Jewish law recognize those who arrive at their Jewishness in these ways. However, non-halakhic Jews also recognize as Jews those who have a Jewish father and non-Jewish mother and those who undergo conversions that do not adhere to the rabbinic standard by, for example, omitting immersion in a mikveh, while halakhah-abiding Jews do not. Additionally, Orthodox Jews generally do not recognize conversions done under Conservative auspices, even though both movements are halakhic, because Orthodox Jews often suspect that the notion of "accepting the yoke of the law" is not the same in both movements. Even some Orthodox conversions are not accepted in all Orthodox communities.

These disagreements mean that a person may be considered a Jew in one place and a non-Jew in another. For example, if a person is a Jew by patrilineal descent, Reform and Reconstructionist communities will regard them as Jewish. But when the same person goes to a Conservative or Orthodox community, they will be regarded as a non-Jew because these communities accept only halakhic conversion or matrilineal descent as establishing Jewishness. Similarly, a convert whose conversion was done under Reform, Reconstructionist, or Conservative auspices will be considered Jewish in their own movement and most likely within each of the others listed here, but not in most Orthodox communities. Additionally, there is significant variation in how and when the State of Israel recognizes conversions as valid: for purposes of immigration under the Law of Return, non-Orthodox conversions may count, but, for purposes of personal status matters such as marriage, Jews converted under non-Orthodox auspices are considered non-Jews.[9]

People who are most likely to find themselves in a liminal or "betwixt and between" category of Jewishness are converts, including adoptees who are converted, children of converts, and children of intermarried parents. The people in these categories are a small percentage of the U.S. Jewish population: 27 percent of U.S. Jews are of mixed ancestry, meaning they have a non-Jewish parent and a Jewish parent;[10] about 5 percent of Jewish families have adopted a child;[11] about 2 percent of the U.S. Jewish community have converted formally; and 1 percent consider themselves as having converted to Judaism informally.[12] The liminal category is growing, however: Jews of mixed ancestry make up 49 percent of the U.S. Jewish population between eighteen and twenty-nine years old and 41 percent of the thirty-to-forty-nine population. Forty-six percent of all children in U.S. Jewish households have intermarried parents, compared with 39 percent who have two Jewish parents (and 15 percent with single parents).[13]

This liminality is exacerbated by assumptions made about Jewishness based on people's appearances and names. Jews who are part of the majority— White, Ashkenazi, with recognizably Ashkenazi names— frequently ask people in these liminal categories to explain how it is that they are Jewish. Although Jews are an ethnically and racially diverse people, the vast majority of those in the United States are White and Ashkenazi. Converts and non-Jewish spouses of Jews may be of any ethnic or racial background, and often they increase the diversity of their communities. Adoptees, for example, are highly likely to be people of color. Only 34 percent of adoptees in the Jewish community were White according to the 2000–2001 National Jewish Population Survey. Adopted children are likely to have been converted to Judaism, since only 4 percent of adoptees had Jewish mothers and 3 percent a Jewish father.[14] People of color in Jewish communities report being routinely asked about their backgrounds, which can only add to an unwelcome sense of liminality at these times, particularly for those whose background includes conversion.

Jews in these liminal categories do not generally experience problems with having their Jewishness recognized within their own communities, where their Jewish practice is most likely centered on a day-to-day basis. Issues are more likely to arise when going outside the local community— for example, receiving synagogue honors, finding a rabbi to officiate at a wedding or b'nei mitzvah, or finding a mohel (Jew who performs ritual circumcisions) to circumcise a newborn son. In some big cities, non-halakhic movements have built their own Jewish infrastructure, including kosher restaurants, mikvaot, and mohels, which treat Jews in liminal categories the same as all other Jews. In smaller towns, these resources may not be as readily available.

As the existence of these liminal categories demonstrates, there is a whole range of lived experience between "Jewish" and "non-Jewish." The incomplete reciprocity among communities means that non-Jews and people whose Jewishness is disputed are more likely to be concentrated in non-Orthodox communities. Because of this uneven concentration, Jewish communities' experience with non-Jews in Jewish spaces is bifurcated. Both liberal and Orthodox communities have experience with non-Jews studying for conversion, but liberal communities generally have a lot of experience with non-Jews who are not seeking conversion, while Orthodox ones have less. That being said, converts are a different category from other non-Jews in Jewish communities, as they intend to identify as and remain in the community as Jews. Even if some Jewish communities do not accept their conversions as valid, that is different from the experience of a non-Jew who wants to participate in Jewish spaces without being recognized as a Jew.

At the same time, non-Jews participate in Jewish communities in a range of ways, with an array of motivations and meanings. The most ephemeral forms of participation include visits to synagogues in search of interfaith knowledge but no intention to return. Slightly less ephemeral are guests at Shabbat dinners, seders, or life cycle events. Those whose participation is longer term can have different motivations, interests, and desires. Someone who is in the conversion process, for example, participates as a non-Jew but with the intention to participate as a Jew in the future. Someone who is dating or engaged to a Jew may be exploring what it means to be part of a Jewish community but not yet sure of the kind of role they wish to have. And non-Jews who have already married Jews have differing desires for participation and belonging.

Non-Jews married to Jews sometimes have negative experiences in Jewish communities that shape their interest, or lack of interest, in being part of Jewish life. One rabbi told me, "Non-Jewish people who come into our community are made to feel like they are an enemy, or at very best that we have to put up with them." He described an interfaith couple in which one partner was a seemingly unflappable military man: "I thought literally he was going to cry because of how he'd been treated." The man was "shocked" when the rabbi told him, "I just want to connect to you as a person." He explained that he found the treatment this man had experienced upsetting: "The Talmud says humiliating somebody is like murdering them. So what makes it okay in these instances?" Because of his awareness of what some non-Jewish partners of Jews have experienced, he tries to provide context to non-Jews for why such behavior happens in synagogues while also trying hard to welcome them to make up for what they've gone through.[15]

Non-Jewish women specifically may experience being called "shiksa," a Yiddish word for a non-Jewish woman. It usually carries connotations of sexual desirability and availability as well as the suggestion that a shiksa lures Jewish men away from Jewish women and Judaism. Sometimes the word is used in an intentionally derogatory way, as historian Keren McGinity explains: "In an explanation of why her son was the only child not included under the ḥuppah (wedding canopy) at an Orthodox relative's wedding, a Christian woman was told, 'It's because you're a shiksa!'" The word "shiksa" can sometimes be neutral, meaning only "non-Jewish woman," but it always connotes conspicuous non-Jewishness.[16]

Despite such negative interactions, some non-Jews remain engaged with Jewish communities, but many become and remain engaged because the community welcomes them and supports them and their families. Some Jewish leaders have suggested that these people be called *gerei toshav* after the biblical concept of the non-Jew who resides with the Jewish community.[17] In a 2019 oral history, Rabbi Yitz Husbands-Hankin describes his colleague Rabbi Myron Kinberg's use of this concept at interfaith weddings in the 1980s: "*Ger toshav* is a Biblical term and it's a resident, somebody who lives within the community but doesn't take on the personal covenant of Judaism, but they live within the community and respect the community, work for its well-being.... It's someone who's inside the community but not fully a covenanted member of the community."[18] Rabbi Amichai Lau-Lavie suggests that people in this category be called "Joy," a title chosen by a non-Jewish friend married to a Jew who explained, "I'm a Jew who's also a goy [non-Jew]."[19] Another title suggested by Rabbi Geela Rayzel Raphael in 1992 is "fellow traveler."[20] Whatever they may be called, the biblical concept of ger toshav describes someone who is and will continue being part of a Jewish community but will not be converting.

The Limits of Religious Participation

Disagreements over who counts as a Jew can make participation in Jewish ritual fraught for both Jews and non-Jews, but they don't always have to. Whether out of their own convictions or at the behest of their congregations, Jewish religious leaders often devise modes of participation and recognition for non-Jews while still maintaining the boundaries that their understandings of religious law require.

Sociologist Patricia Munro explores these modes of participation and recognition in b'nai mitzvah ceremonies. At stake for religious leaders is the essence of Jewishness itself, as expressed through rituals recognizing the attainment of Jewish adulthood by children with intermarried parents. Munro summarizes the issues religious leaders struggle with: "To what degree can a non-Jew participate in a Jewish ritual before that Jewish ritual loses its meaning? And to what degree can or should supportive parents—though not Jewish—be excluded from their children's ritual?" Munro points out that such questions about how inclusion and exclusion from ritual practices and other activities shape group boundaries are fundamental sociological questions and are not limited to Jews.

As Munro describes, congregational rabbis in liberal denominations who oversee b'nai mitzvah services for children in interfaith families weigh the non-Jewish parent's "status as a non-Jew with [their] role as a community member and the parent of a Jew."[21]

Different Jewish communities answer these questions in their own ways. In liberal Jewish contexts, clergy and laypeople frequently agree in principle about the inclusion of non-Jews in congregational life, although there may be differences about details; in cases of larger disagreements, there may be significant push and pull.[22] In an Orthodox context, there is no expectation that non-Jews will be accommodated. Orthodox communities define and organize themselves around adherence to Jewish practices that in large part are available only to Jews. Non-Jews may be welcomed to participate in the community on the community's own terms in some ways and in some communities, but without any special measures to ensure that non-Jews participate or feel included. However, Orthodox communities are not free from the push-and-pull factors that liberal ones may experience between clergy and laypeople: Munro highlights pressure for greater gender equality from congregations as one way Orthodox leaders do have to negotiate boundaries.

In communities that do seek to include non-Jews, the specifics of how these questions are answered often revolve around participation in synagogue ritual: What can non-Jews do, say, or use?[23] English readings that are extraneous to the required parts of the service and religious or folk innovations like blessings for non-Jewish family members or passing the tallit (prayer shawl) or Torah are more likely to be done by non-Jews. Rabbis tend to prohibit non-Jews from holding any leadership positions or doing or saying or using things "that are incumbent on Jews but not on non-Jews"—that is, things that Jewish law obligates only Jews to do, like having an *aliyah* (the honor of being called to the Torah when it is read publicly), reading texts, or leading services. It is notable that the motivation for establishing these boundaries has generally arisen not from non-Jews' requests or interest in participating in rituals incumbent only on Jews, but instead from their Jewish spouses who want their non-Jewish spouses to participate.[24]

While it is unremarkable if non-Jews do not participate in everyday congregational life, life-cycle events have specific roles for parents, raising the question of how non-Jews may participate.[25] For example, during a bar or bat mitzvah, the child's parents usually receive an aliyah. This honor is typically reserved for Jews. In synagogues where the non-Jewish parent participates, a distinction is made in the language of the blessing "to signal that the inclusion is partial," or the non-Jewish parent recites a different blessing in English. However, some synagogues do not allow the non-Jewish parent on the bimah at all.[26] Beyond the parents, non-Jewish relatives and friends sometimes are given ways to participate in the event, such as reading an English poem or handing out programs and greeting guests at the door, that do not impinge on activities reserved for Jews.[27] "No matter what the denomination, the rabbi interprets what is and is not allowed . . . result[ing] in changes to the bar or bat mitzvah ritual as rabbis work to accommodate the needs of non-Jewish parents. . . . These changes, in turn, affect the congregation's composition as stricter or more open attitudes attract different types of members," Munro writes.[28] In other words, there is bidirectional influence on the congregation's boundaries.

Interfaith weddings also raise questions about modes of participation and recognition, primarily in Reform, Reconstructionist, and unaffiliated contexts. Often, Jews who marry non-Jews prefer to have a rabbi or cantor officiate at the wedding ceremony and wish to include Jewish elements such as a ketubah (marriage contract), ḥuppah (wedding canopy), and the breaking of a glass at the end. Sometimes the marrying couple wishes to have the rabbi co-officiate with a clergy member of a different religion. Like b'nai mitzvah ceremonies that include non-Jews, interfaith weddings also raise questions about what makes a ritual Jewish, who may participate in a Jewish ritual, and what non-Jewish participants may do, say, or touch in such rituals.

These questions are most relevant for clergy in liberal Jewish movements because rabbis and cantors in halakhic movements like Orthodoxy and Conservative Judaism are not permitted to officiate at such weddings.[29] Orthodox and Conservative clergy operate within the framework of Jewish law, and Jewish law does not allow for marriage of a Jew to a non-Jew. The Conservative Movement's organization of rabbis, the Rabbinical Assembly (RA), treats officiating at an interfaith wedding ceremony as an extremely serious matter—along with sexual and financial misconduct, it can be sanctioned by expulsion.[30] Some Conservative rabbis have chosen to officiate anyway, and some of them have resigned or been expelled from the RA.[31] A 2015 survey by Big Tent Judaism found that 38 percent of Conservative rabbis were willing to officiate if the RA prohibition on doing so were lifted.[32]

Although Conservative and Orthodox rabbis generally do not officiate at interfaith weddings, the 2020 Pew survey of Jewish Americans found that 64 percent of U.S. Jews want rabbis to officiate at interfaith weddings, 25 percent want officiation in some cases, and only 9 percent want rabbis not to officiate at all.[33] Sixty-one percent of marriages of Jews since 2010 have been intermarriages,[34] which aligns with the larger U.S. trend of adults marrying across religious boundaries.[35] For same-sex couples, the interfaith marriage rate is even higher. The 2020 Pew study reports that 3 percent of Jews who are married or living with a partner are in same-sex relationships. While a 2009 study found that only about 11 percent of long-term same-sex relationships were between two Jews, and that same-sex relationships involving Jews were much more likely than not to be interfaith, sociologist Bruce Phillips found that the 2020 Pew data shows that same-sex and heterosexual marriages now have roughly parallel intermarriage rates.[36] In contrast to Conservative and Orthodox rabbis, 88 percent of Reconstructionist and 84 percent of Reform rabbis were willing to officiate, according to a 2017 survey by Interfaithfamily.com.[37] A majority (59 percent) require that the marrying couple commit to raising their children as Jews within a Jewish household.[38] Congregational rabbis may require that the marrying couple be members of the synagogue. Some rabbis who officiate at interfaith weddings are freelancers who do not have to worry about the demands of congregations or rabbinical associations.

Marrying couples often construct their wedding ceremonies to be expressions of their identities and heritages, including religious backgrounds. While there are many parallels between interfaith weddings and b'nai mitzvah ceremonies involving non-Jews, it would be rare to encounter a request to include elements from religions other than Judaism in the latter context whereas this is quite common in wedding ceremonies. Marrying couples may wish to engage a Christian or other clergy member to co-officiate their weddings, to include readings from the New Testament or other non-Jewish religious scriptures, and to use songs from non-Jewish religions. The website 18Doors.org features stories of interfaith weddings. One described a co-officiated "Jewish,

Christian, and Nigerian" wedding in Massachusetts that highlighted their "Jewish roots and ... Jamaican ancestry and African American culture." The wedding combined Jewish, Jamaican, and West African cultural customs, music, clothing, and food, Christian prayer and practices such as foot washing, and was co-officiated by the groom's mother, a Christian minister, and a rabbi the couple found through 18Doors who was amenable to this plan. The couple's wedding included an interfaith ketubah signed by Christian witnesses and a ḥuppah that the couple built.[39] A different couple chose not to mix their traditions and instead held two separate ceremonies, one Hindu and one Jewish: "By combining traditions, it's possible to accidentally omit something that might be meaningful; by separating the wedding into two sections, each partner's heritage was equally celebrated as they began married life."[40] A "visibly LGBTQ+" and "interfaith/multicultural" couple went in a different direction, seeking a Jewish wedding that would be "accessible" to the non-Jewish partner's family and officiated by a rabbi or cantor "who could respectfully and accurately honor our marriage." The couple and the cantor officiating their wedding developed a ceremony together that, the Jewish partner wrote, was "meaningful ... for my Jewish soul."[41]

Jewish clergy also recognize the identity-constructing elements of wedding ceremonies. The late rabbi Myron Kinberg had the non-Jewish partner in interfaith couples sign a "Brit Ger Toshav" (Covenant of a Resident Stranger) to that effect. The contract commits the signer to be "unreservedly committed to the perpetuation of Judaism in [their] personal home life," to exclude non-Jewish religious traditions from the home, to raise any children as Jews, and to participate in Jewish life. The couple also enacts a Brit Nissuin (Covenant of Marriage) that emphasizes the couple's choice to "establish a Jewish home according to the traditions of Moses and Israel," echoing but not directly using the language of the Jewish marriage ceremony.[42] To assert the Jewish character of the weddings they officiate, most rabbis decline to co-officiate with a clergy member from another religion.[43] They may work with the marrying couple to include non-Jewish religious readings and songs, but often resist statements concerning the divinity or salvific power of Jesus. Such statements seem contradictory in a Jewish context given supersessionist theology that holds that Christianity has surpassed and replaced Judaism as well as the long history of Christian proselytizing and persecution of Jews. The Jewish ceremony is meant to signal the couple's commitment to a Jewish identity as a family unit, and many rabbis insist that the couple agree to raise their children as Jews as a condition of officiating. Rabbis often insist that Jewish ritual and symbols need to be understood in a coherent and internally consistent way. In this view, mixing them with non-Jewish symbols, particularly supersessionist ones that contradict Jewishness, creates an incoherent and inconsistent family identity.[44] Beyond officiating, some rabbis use blessings specifically written for non-Jewish partners who participate in creating Jewish homes.

Inclusion and Appreciation of Non-Jews

Despite their qualms about the potential for non-Jews to change the nature of Jewish community, Jewish leaders have remarked on non-Jews' capacity to energize Jews' appreciation and knowledge of Jewish ritual, practice, belief, and culture. Reform rabbi Alexander Schindler made this point by quoting Rabbi Harold Schulweis: "Something happens to the student who is called upon to teach, something happens to the Jew who is asked to explain the character of his tradition to one outside the inner circle"—it sparks a self-consciousness or recognition that would otherwise not have been present. Thus the goal of "Outreach" programs that Schindler established in the 1970s was to encourage non-Jews in intermarriages to convert and to encourage couples to raise their children as Jews: "The non-Jewish spouse . . . sees our religion through fresh eyes and revives the Jewish partner's interest in Judaism."[45]

Such outreach efforts have generated numerous resources to explain Jewish practice and how to engage in it. It is common to find handouts that explain what to do, especially at life-cycle rituals where non-Jews will be present. Along the same lines, the book *How To Be a Perfect Stranger*, edited by Stuart M. Matlins and Arthur J. Magida, explains not only how to act in Jewish contexts but also in numerous other religious contexts, from what not to wear to whether it's permissible to leave early from an event.[46] The book was first published in 1999, with a sixth edition in 2015, a testament to its long-lasting popularity. The idea that these texts convey is that non-Jewish participants are welcome when they attend in a spirit of community and respect.

Congregations and umbrella organizations also offer Introduction to Judaism and prayerbook Hebrew courses for all kinds of people, including gerei toshav. Many outreach efforts that include non-Jews are responding to the perception that intermarried families want and need specialized support and instruction. Among the organizations that provide such support and instruction are Interfaithfamily.com, 18Doors, Mothers Circle, and Big Tent Judaism. The website of 18Doors includes portals for clergy, institutions, and intermarried people. These resources can also be helpful for the non-Jewish extended family members of Jews who have converted to Judaism or non-Jews who have married into Jewish families.

The 18Doors website includes personal narratives that model different ways Jewish life may include non-Jews. For example, one narrative explains how a Jew by choice mourned her Lutheran father with Jewish rituals.[47] Rose Costa's conversion story, "Jew by Choice," relates her surprise when her non-Jewish father died and her congregation and rabbis came together to support her. Congregants sent food and flowers, and the rabbis and some of the staff at the temple attended his funeral. "The temple offices must have almost completely shut down for my father's funeral," she writes.[48]

Despite Jewish institutions' efforts to create inclusive environments, many Jews cling to the notion that Jewishness resides solely within one's blood or genes. This biological determinism is often hurtful to converts and adoptees in Jewish communities. In his memoir, *Lovesong: Becoming a Jew*, Julius Lester recounts a conversation in which a woman told him after he had converted that he wasn't really Jewish. Lester said that it was the more secular Jews who would say such things to him; more religious and learned Jews did not.[49] In her conversion story, "My Soul Was Standing at Sinai," Barbara Oleinick reports that Jews generally were less supportive of her conversion than non-Jewish friends and family. She notes that if she had converted to any denomination of Christianity, her fellow congregants "would have ... celebrated" her, but Jews made rude comments to her like "I would never understand the feelings Jews have for Israel and that I would never really be accepted as a Jew."[50]

Non-Jewish family members also have varying responses to converts to Judaism. Conversion can mean the new Jew and their Christian families of origin no longer understand each other as well as they once had because the contexts in which they live have changed so much.⁵¹ In her memoir describing her and her husband's conversion to Judaism, Shannon Gonyou writes, "One of the hardest aspects of conversion is that your family doesn't convert with you. Family members might want neat and tidy explanations for the conversions that don't reflect the complexity of the decision. . . . I don't think my mom had ever met a Jew other than our family physician, so it's unsurprising that she wouldn't know anything about Judaism."⁵² While none of Gonyou and her husband's extended family on either side were familiar with Judaism, they were open to learning about Jewish customs and participating in Jewish holiday and life-cycle event celebrations. Regarding her daughter's naming ceremony, Gonyou writes, "I tell Christians that it's like a baptism with no water. That doesn't really capture the nature of a baby naming, but sometimes a simple explanation works best."⁵³ Such explanations are needed regularly as the newly Jewish family member integrates their Christian family members into their new practices and contexts. Sometimes these explanations generate considerable enthusiasm. In her conversion story, Barbara Oleinick reported that her non-Jewish family members supported her in her practice of the dietary laws: "My brothers and sister can recognize most hechshers (symbols certifying that a product is kosher). They carefully make vegetarian spaghetti sauce and buy kosher hot dogs with parveh (neither dairy nor meat) buns! My sister shopped in the kosher market for Passover items. I couldn't ask for more."⁵⁴

Yet, whether intended or not, a certain distance can remain between Jewish and non-Jewish family members. Erika Davis, a Jew by choice, wrote of mourning her non-Jewish sister, "while I did find slight comfort in reading Tehillim [Psalms] to her in English and in saying the Sh'ma and Mourner's Kaddish when we turned off her machines, I continued to wonder how a Jew-by-choice goes about honoring a dead loved one in a way that doesn't offend non-Jewish relatives and honors my adopted Jewish traditions."⁵⁵ She found common ground in that Psalms were familiar to her Christian family members, but also observed Jewish mourning rituals on her own and with her Jewish community. In other cases, non-Jewish family members of intermarried couples can sometimes be overtly antisemitic, employing Christian anti-Jewish theological claims about Jews having "killed Christ" and being legalistic rather than ethical.[56] Encountering these statements can be profoundly alienating for Jewish family members.

Beyond inclusion of non-Jews in existing Jewish practice, new rituals and blessings have been created to respond to the consistent presence and participation of non-Jews in Jewish communities. These blessings often highlight non-Jews' assistance in the project of Jewish continuity. Such blessings sometimes acknowledge non-Jews' sacrifice of their own religious traditions in favor of Jewish ones and recognize non-Jews as a part of the Jewish community. These blessings have become so common in liberal Jewish communities that they attracted the attention of the *Washington Post* in 2015. And, earlier, journalist Lauren Markoe for Religion News Service recounted Rabbi Janet Marder's blessing for non-Jews as part of Yom Kippur services at Congregation Beth Am in Los Altos Hills, California, in 2004. Rabbi Marder summoned the approximately one hundred non-Jews in her congregation to rise for a blessing, which read, in part, "What we want to thank you for today is your decision to cast your lot with the Jewish people by becoming part of this congregation, and the love and support you give to your Jewish partner. Most of all, we want to offer our deepest thanks to those of you who are parents, and who are raising your sons and daughters as Jews.... In our generation, which saw one-third of the world's Jewish population destroyed ... every Jewish boy and girl is a gift to the Jewish future." As word of the blessing spread, other rabbis expressed interest in doing the same. While Marder did not make a regular practice of bestowing this blessing on Yom Kippur, the Union for Reform Judaism circulated the text of the blessing, and it went into broad use in Reform synagogues.[57] One non-Jewish man who is an active part of his Jewish family's synagogue's life commented on receiving such a blessing, "It was awesome.... It kind of gave you goose bumps. Not anything had happened like this before."[58]

Just as Marder's blessing highlights that non-Jews are an integral part of the community, a blessing for non-Jews to say as part of the Torah service at Rabbi Toba Spitzer's Congregation Dorshei Tzedek in West Newton, Massachusetts, does as well. Before the reading of the Torah, the non-Jewish community member recites, "Blessed is the Source of Life, who has brought me into loving relationship with the Jewish people and the Torah. Blessed is the Source of Torah," followed by a Jewish community member's recitation of the standard blessing. After the reading and the standard blessing by a Jew, the non-Jewish person recites, "Bless us as one, Source of Life, by the light of your Presence and Teaching."[59] This blessing and its linkage to the standard blessing recited by a Jew highlight the non-Jewish person's membership in the Jewish community and highlights their collective orientation toward the Torah as well as their different relationships to the Torah. The congregation's website explains, "Because the language of the Hebrew blessing assumes that the person saying the blessing is Jewish, we have created a blessing in English that reflects the special role and connection of a non-Jewish parent to their child's Jewish journey, and to the Jewish community in general. In so doing, we are hoping to affirm the integrity of the blessings, and to honor the decisions our members who were not raised Jewish have made, some of whom have decided to convert to Judaism, others who have chosen to remain allies and fellow travellers."[60] The diversity of relationships to God within a Jewish community are also expressed in a prayer for the sick. Rabbis Maurice Harris and Yitzhak Husbands-Hankin created a "Mi Sheberakh Blessing of Appreciation for People of Different Identities" that makes the same points that Marder and Spitzer do in their blessings, along with prayers for the welfare of non-Jewish community members themselves. The second half of the prayer reads, "Holy One, please bless them to find acceptance, appreciation, and joy here in this synagogue. And during life's sorrows may they know they can take refuge among us, under the Wings of your Protection. May they know that they are immeasurably valued just as they are. May the works of their hands be blessed with much success, and may they walk the paths of peace along with their sisters and brothers in the Household of Israel and the wider human family. And let us say, Amen."[61] These blessings emphasize that people within the community may have different identities and be part of the community in different ways. They envision Jewish community as a mosaic rather than a uniform entity.

Foregrounding the wholeness of the non-Jewish community members' identities matters especially for those from non-White and/or non-Christian backgrounds. Religious studies scholar Samira Mehta highlights the racial power dynamics that may affect interfaith families' interactions with Jewish communities. As she explains, the most salient power dynamic in interfaith couples involving a White Christian and a White Jew is often that of the long and continuing history of Christian oppression of Jews and Judaism. In such cases, the Jewish partner may feel that Jewish traditions should take precedence over Christian ones in their home given the historical and cultural context that makes it harder for Judaism than for Christianity to thrive. In interfaith couples involving a White Jew and a non-Jew who is not White, the most salient power dynamic is more likely to be racial.[62] One family, a White Jewish woman and an African American Baptist man and their child, attends to these dynamics to ensure that their child feels completely part of his extended family's Baptist traditions and that their Christian family members feel welcome and respected when they attend Jewish life cycle celebrations.[63] Mehta points out that research on intermarriage often focuses only on the need of Jews to push back against Christian hegemony, but in some cases the power dynamic of Whiteness for White Jews versus minoritized racial identities for non-Jews is more salient.[64]

Institutional Policies about Non-Jews

Synagogues' lay leadership and rabbis sometimes establish formal policies concerning non-Jews' involvement in congregational life, and these policies signal to intermarried families and non-Jews in the process of conversion how the institution regards them and their place in the congregation. Through these policies, the belonging of non-Jews in Jewish communities is formalized and recognized at a permanent, institutional level and not handled on an ad hoc basis. Synagogue membership can be financially daunting, and intermarried families may not choose to affiliate if they are unsure if they will be fully welcomed.[65] Sylvia Fishman notes that intermarried couples in her 2004 study often avoided bad experiences in Jewish communities by having the Jewish partner find the policies of synagogues and Jewish schools toward intermarried families and filter out ones that might treat them poorly.[66]

The organization 18Doors offers "Recommendations for Creating a Welcoming Policy Document," with examples from Reform, Reconstructionist, and Conservative synagogue policies. 18Doors recommends an inclusive opening statement to convey that interfaith families are welcome. Beyond that, the document should tactfully describe how the congregation defines who is a Jew as well as non-Jews' eligibility for synagogue membership, leadership positions, and ritual participation.

The document should also make clear that all members of the family are welcome to attend services, explain the congregation's perspective on conversion to Judaism, and state whether clergy are available to officiate at intermarriages as well as mourning, funeral, and burial services for non-Jewish family members.[67]

Individual synagogues may set their own policies in many cases, but are informed by guidance from rabbinical organizations. This guidance has become substantially more inclusive over the years as non-Jews have become increasingly integrated into congregations. Responsa from the Reform movement's Central Conference of American Rabbis (CCAR) concerning non-Jews in Jewish congregations go back at least as far as 1914, when it addressed the question of whether non-Jewish wives could be buried in Jewish cemeteries.[68] Since that time, the CCAR has issued additional responsa on questions of mourning, funerals, and burial of non-Jews as well as rabbinic officiation at interfaith weddings, co-officiation, the status of children of mixed marriages and Gentile children who are adopted by Jews, the conditions under which someone may or must convert to Judaism, whether intermarried families and non-Jewish spouses specifically may be synagogue members, whether non-Jews can serve on committees in congregations, and in what ways non-Jews may participate in Jewish rituals.[69] The Reform movement has devoted a great deal of attention and thought to questions of how non-Jews may be integrated into Jewish communities. The Rabbinical Assembly has issued fewer policies and halakhic rulings concerning non-Jews in Jewish communities than the CCAR and has emphasized stigmatization of intermarriage until quite recently. Its responsa generally address the same questions that the CCAR has addressed: whether intermarried Jews and their families may be synagogue members, whether rabbis may officiate at intermarriages, in what ways non-Jews may participate in religious services, and under what conditions someone may convert to Judaism.[70] But additional RA responsa focus specifically on methods for stigmatizing intermarriage by forbidding rabbis to attend interfaith weddings, advising synagogues not to publicly acknowledge or congratulate intermarried couples upon their weddings or the birth of their children if the mother is not Jewish and there is not a clear intention to convert the child to Judaism very soon after birth, and not to accept donations in honor of these occasions, and holding that Conservative congregations and day schools may not employ intermarried people as clergy, teachers, or executive directors because they would be bad Jewish role models.[71] More recently, a 2014 statement by the Rabbinical Assembly and the United Synagogue of Conservative Judaism encouraged acceptance and welcoming of intermarried families while reserving "certain Jewish rituals" for Jews alone,[72] and in 2017 the United Synagogue formally permitted individual Conservative synagogues to decide whether non-Jews could be members.[73] Some Conservative rabbis have continued to press for greater acceptance and engagement of interfaith couples, and these specific rabbis' congregations may be quite welcoming to interfaith families, but the history of the movement as a whole has not emphasized such welcoming.[74] The Reconstructionist Rabbinical Association (RRA) has issued few resolutions about intermarriage or non-Jews,[75] but its comprehensive 1980 resolution on intermarriage asserts that Reconstructionist rabbis should "help [intermarried couples] find their place in the Jewish community," with special emphasis on creating programming to help people create a Jewish home and engage in "the life of the Jewish people."[76] The resolution addresses many of the same issues as the Conservative and Reform responsa, including the status of children of intermarriages, rabbinic officiation at intermarriages, and whether non-Jews may be synagogue members. But it also holds that laity and clergy should make these policy decisions jointly. Another 1980 resolution affirms the RRA's earlier acceptance of patrilineal descent as well as encouragement of conversion of interested non-Jews whether they are intermarried or not.[77] A 2000 resolution establishes a policy against co-officiation with non-Jewish clergy at weddings.[78]

On the matter of synagogue membership for non-Jews, as Munro notes, different denominations have handled this question in different ways.[79] In some situations, only the Jew may be a member and have a vote. In others, the membership unit is the family itself, so all family members are synagogue members, and, in still others, individual adults who are Jews, in the process of conversion, or immediate family members of Jews, may be voting members. Synagogues define "Jew" and "non-Jew" in different ways; in some, only those who are Jewish by matrilineal descent or formal conversion are considered Jews while, in others, both matrilineal and patrilineal descent and conversion are accepted. Other definitions may also exist.

Membership entails what Reconstructionist congregation Dorshei Tzedek in West Newton, Massachusetts, terms "civic participation" and "ritual participation." Civic participation is being an active part of the community's life, while ritual participation involves carrying out obligations of Jews who are part of the Jewish covenant. Other synagogues' policies use the same distinction without using this terminology. A range of definitions and limitations within each category exists among U.S. synagogues.[80]

Few restrictions pertain to civic participation, although there are some. The Reconstructionist congregation Kol HaLev in Cleveland, Ohio, permits non-Jews to be on the Board of Trustees but not in leadership roles that entail representing the congregation or supervising religious life and education.[81] Dorshei Tzedek lists a number of ways non-Jewish members participate: "serving on the CDT Board, welcoming new members, editing the newsletter, taking part in adult education classes, coordinating child care during Shabbat and High Holydays services, serving as class parents in the religious school and as members of the Education Committee, participating in Shabbat morning services and other celebrations, taking action through our Tikkun Olam committee, and more."

In all instances that I examined, limitations on ritual participation concern the Torah service, public leadership of prayers or blessings that represent the leader as part of the Jewish covenant with God, and public leadership of worship services and blessings that Jews are commanded to perform. Reconstructionist congregation Dorshei Tzedek explains that "the language of the Hebrew blessing assumes that the person saying the blessing is Jewish," so permitting only Jews to say such blessings is "to affirm the integrity of the blessings, and to honor the decisions our members who were not raised Jewish have made, some of whom have decided to convert to Judaism, others who have chosen to remain allies and fellow travellers." This statement emphasizes that the policy is intended to respect the individual identities of each community member. Likewise, only Jews may participate in the Torah service because

> the Torah is the symbolic center of our understanding of ourselves as a people. Judaism as . . . traditionally understood . . . is a covenantal relationship between and among the Jewish people and the Divine. These

covenantal commitments include a whole set of responsibilities (traditionally understood as mitzvot [commandments]), that devolve solely on Jews. In this understanding, Jewish status confers obligations upon a Jewish member of the community, such as the obligation to help make a minyan (quorum for prayer) for someone in mourning, to enable them to say Kaddish.

"Understood another way, to be a Jew is to locate oneself within the mythic narrative of the Jewish people: to say, 'I came out of bondage in Egypt' at the Passover seder, or to bless the Source of Life as 'the One who has given us the Torah' during the Shabbat morning service. In these moments, a Jew—whether born or converted into the covenant—affirms their particular commitments and connections."[82]

Reform congregation Beth Hillel Temple in Kenosha, Wisconsin, lists specific prayers, categories of prayers, and blessings that are reserved for Jews only, including "any prayer which identifies the reader as a Jew" or "links the reader with the Jewish covenant concept or implies that the reader has formally taken on the commandments of Judaism as part of his/her life."[83] The egalitarian, halakhic, independent minyan Altshul in Brooklyn, New York, limits the Torah and ritual leadership roles in the same way, although it adds that non-Jews can "deliver a drash."[84] This difference may have to do with Altshul's status as an independent minyan where individual members perform this role as opposed to congregations led by rabbis who usually deliver sermons. In contrast to Dorshei Tzedek's explanation that restrictions on ritual participation are needed to "affirm the integrity" of the rituals, Altshul's concern is "balanc[ing] our core value of inclusion with the halacha surrounding requirements that certain service roles be fulfilled by the halachically Jewish."[85]

While there is general consensus among synagogues as to why there are limits on ritual participation for non-Jews, the way these synagogues frame the limitations does vary. Reform congregation Beth Hillel Temple repeatedly points out that they respect the desire of some non-Jewish members not to participate in Jewish ritual and explains that their policy, "Opportunities for Non-Jewish Members," is for "those who are unable, for whatever reason, to make that commitment [conversion to Judaism] and still choose to worship among us."[86] The Reconstructionist community Kol HaLev's document "The Role of Non-Jews in Kol

HaLev" highlights its inclusivity as part of its identity from the start: "Our founders in 1992 included intermarried couples, and we have always been open to a diverse membership."[87] The language in these two examples demonstrates openness to and inclusion of non-Jews, while nevertheless maintaining some distance from non-Jews. This framing emphasizes non-Jews' separate status within the community.

In contrast, two other examples insist that non-Jews are integral to the community. In its February 2017 document "Involvement of Non-Jews in Davening," the egalitarian halakhic independent minyan Altshul states, "We are . . . a community that is comprised of both Jews and non-Jews."[88] Dorshei Tzedek's document "Non-Jewish Members at Dorshei Tzedek" is emphatic in its inclusion of non-Jews, stating that its purpose is "to help clarify what it means to be a non-Jewish member of a caring and inclusive congregation that is dedicated to Jewish practice and learning."[89] It is impossible to say whether these differences in framing are reflected in the feelings of warmth and conviviality that non-Jews may experience in these congregations. However, these documents reflect a range of attitudes present across congregations.

Conclusion: Recognition and Belonging

Non-Jews arrive in Jewish communities in numerous ways, frequently through intermarriage or connection to someone who has converted to Judaism. Just as Jews have varied levels of interest in connecting to Jewish communities, so too do non-Jews have diverse types of connection, from the most minimal possible to formal acceptance of an identity as a *ger toshav*. Jewish communities respond to non-Jews in their midst in varied ways as well, denominational as well as local, formal as well as informal. They develop formal policies and create blessings. They describe what it means to be a non-Jewish member of a Jewish community, what to emphasize, what to encourage, what to forbid. They may also recognize non-Jewish members specifically for what they bring to the community as individuals and not only as tools for the project of Jewish continuity.

Non-Jews who engage in Jewish communities on an ongoing basis negotiate together with those communities their sense of shared fate as well as ethical commitments to the Jewish people. Although it has been common for Jewish leaders to view non-Jews married to Jews as the biggest threat to Jewish continuity, many non-Jews in this position consider themselves responsible for helping to repopulate the Jewish community after the Holocaust. One woman explained, "My husband's father is a Holocaust survivor, and I wanted to add to the Jewish population, not take away from it."[90] Likewise, some non-Jewish family members of Jews have made it their mission to combat antisemitism, in part out of their own convictions and in part because their Jewish family members have sought their understanding and support.[91]

The anxiety in Jewish communities about how exactly to integrate non-Jewish community members comes largely from the Jewish members and leaders, rather than from the non-Jews themselves. Sociologist Patricia Munro notes that in life-cycle ceremonies for interfaith couples, it is the Jewish partners, not the non-Jewish ones, who are most invested in ensuring that their partners may participate in Jewish ritual. In many cases, non-Jewish community members appreciate simply being recognized for who they are and for their contributions to their Jewish communities.

NOTES

1. "Non-Jews Studying Yiddish Compilation" (interviews for the Wexler Oral History Project, Yiddish Book Center), YouTube video, 8:12, January 29, 2013, www.youtube.com; Alex Pomson and Randal F. Schnoor, *Jewish Family: Identity and Self-Formation at Home* (Bloomington: Indiana University Press, 2018), 12.
2. "Interfaith" implies that each partner has a religion, which is not always true; "intermarried" simply means that the partners are each from a different background.
3. Jonathan Magonet, "Who Is a Jew? Conversion and Jewish Identity Today"; Jonathan Wittenberg, "The Significance of Motivation in the Halachah of Conversion"; and John D. Rayner, "Counting the Commandments," in *Not by Birth Alone: Conversion to Judaism*, ed. Walter Homolka, Walter Jacob, and Esther Seidel (London: Cassell, 1997), 55–73, 89–97, and 98–100.
4. Robert D. Putnam and David E. Campbell, *American Grace: How Religion Divides and Unites Us* (New York: Simon & Schuster, 2010), 526–27.
5. Pew Research Center, "What Americans Know about Religion," July 23, 2019, www.pewresearch.org, 60; Pew Research Center, "Jewish Americans in 2020," 134n19; Bruce A. Phillips, "Re-Examining Intermarriage: Trends, Textures, and Strategies" (Boston: Susan & David Wilstein Institute of Jewish Policy, 1997), 4.
6. Pomson and Schnoor, *Jewish Family*, 66.
7. Phillips, "Re-Examining Intermarriage," 44–48.
8. Ian R. Lamond and Jonathan Moss, "Introduction," in *Liminality and Critical Event Studies: Borders, Boundaries, and Contestation*, ed. Ian R. Lamond and Jonathan Moss (Cham: Springer, 2020), 1–13.

9   Magonet, "Who Is a Jew?"; Wittenberg, "Significance of Motivation"; Rayner, "Counting the Commandments."
10 This figure was calculated by Bruce A. Phillips (Hebrew Union College) from the 2020 Pew study of Jewish Americans data (personal communication).
11 Jennifer Sartori and Jayne K. Guberman, "Boundaries of Identity," *Journal of Jewish Communal Service* 89 (Fall 2014): 48.
12 These figures are reported in Pew Research Center, "A Portrait of Jewish Americans," October 1, 2013, www.pewforum.org, calculations run by Bruce A. Phillips using the data from the 2020 Pew study aligned with the 2013 findings: 1.6 percent of Jewish Americans have converted formally to Judaism, and 0.9 percent have informally done so (personal communication).
13 Phillips, personal communication.
14 Harriet Hartman, "The Jewish Family," in *American Jewish Year Book 2016: The Annual Record of North American Jewish Communities*, ed. Arnold Dashefsky and Ira M. Sheskin (Cham: Springer International, 2017) 90.
15 Jennifer A. Thompson, *Jewish on Their Own Terms: How Intermarried Couples Are Changing American Judaism* (New Brunswick, NJ: Rutgers University Press, 2014), 148–49.
16 Keren R. McGinity, *Marrying Out: Jewish Men, Intermarriage, and Fatherhood* (Bloomington: Indiana University Press, 2014), 103–9.
17 See extended discussion in chapter 3 of Amichai Lau-Lavie, "Joy: A Proposal," June 2017, labshul.org.
18 "Rabbi Yitz Husbands-Hankin, b. 1947," Oregon Jewish Museum and Center for Holocaust Education, 2019, www.ojmche.org.
19 Lau-Lavie, "Joy," 31.
20 Lau-Lavie, 18.
21 Patricia Keer Munro, *Coming of Age in Jewish America: Bar and Bat Mitzvah Reinterpreted* (New Brunswick, NJ: Rutgers University Press, 2016), 103–4.
22 Munro, *Coming of Age in Jewish America*, 105.
23 Munro, 108.
24 Munro, 110, 112, 122.
25 Munro, 113.
26 Munro, 115.
27 Munro, 114.
28 Munro, 121.
29 "Finding a Rabbi or Cantor to Officiate at an Interfaith Wedding," 18Doors, January 12, 2009, 18doors.org.
30 "In a Shift, Conservative Movement Publicly Lists the Rabbis It Has Expelled and Suspended," Jewish Telegraphic Agency, www.jta.org.
31 Debra Nussbaum Cohen, "More Conservative Rabbis Struggle with Interfaith Marriage Ban-and Some Are Flouting It," *Forward*, May 10, 2022, forward.com; Seymour Rosenbloom, "I Performed an Intermarriage. And Then I Got Expelled," *Washington Post*, April 24, 2017, www.washingtonpost.com.

32 Lauren Markoe, "Controversial Study: Many Conservative Rabbis Open to Officiating at Intermarriage," Religion News Service, October 21, 2015, religionnews.com.
33 Pew Research Center, "Jewish Americans in 2020," 47.
34 Pew Research Center, "Jewish Americans in 2020," 93.
35 Pew Research Center, "Jewish Americans in 2020," 22.
36 Steven M. Cohen, Caryn Aviv, and Ari Y. Kelman, "Gay, Jewish, or Both?," *Journal of Jewish Communal Service* 84 (2009) 154–66; Phillips, personal communication.
37 "Nearly All Reform Rabbis Perform Intermarriages—but Not with Non-Jewish Clergy, Study Finds," Jewish Telegraphic Agency, August 8, 2018, www.jta.org.
38 "Rabbi Officiation Survey Results," 18Doors, August 2, 2017, 18doors.org.
39 Kimberly Sara Kabonga, "How We Did Our Jewish, Nigerian, and Christian Wedding," 18Doors, November 9, 2021, 18doors.org.
40 Ezra Kiers, "One Day, Two Ceremonies: Hindu and Jewish," 18Doors, August 8, 2021, 18doors.org.
41 Ezra Kiers, "Here's What We Didn't Know about Finding a Jewish Wedding Officiant," 18Doors, July 23, 2021, 18doors.org.
42 Myron Kinberg, "Brit Ger Toshav (Covenant of a Resident Stranger) and Brit Nisuin (Covenant of Marriage)," Ritualwell: Tradition & Innovation, www.ritualwell.org.
43 "Nearly All Reform Rabbis Perform Intermarriages."
44 See Thompson, *Jewish on Their Own Terms*, 144.
45 Alexander M. Schindler, "Introduction: Not by Birth Alone," in Homolka et al., *Not by Birth Alone*, 3–5.
46 Stuart M. Matlins and Arthur J. Magida, eds., *How to Be a Perfect Stranger: A Guide to Etiquette in Other People's Religious Ceremonies* (Woodstock, VT: SkyLight Paths, 1999).
47 Tara Worthey Segal, "Having a Yahrzeit For My Lutheran Dad," 18Doors, 18doors.org.
48 Rose Coste, "Jew By Choice" in Homolka et al., *Not by Birth Alone*, 185.
49 Julius Lester, *Lovesong: Becoming a Jew* (New York: Henry Holt, 1988), 240.
50 Barbara Oleinick, "My Soul Was Standing at Sinai," in *Not by Birth Alone*, ed. Walter Homolka, Walter Jacob, and Esther Seidel, p. 199.
51 McGinity, *Marrying Out*, 123.
52 Shannon Gonyou, *Since Sinai: A Convert's Path to Judaism* (Hollister, CA: MSI, 2022), 30.
53 Gonyou, *Since Sinai*, 261, 270f.
54 Oleinick, "My Soul Was Standing at Sinai," 201.
55 Erika Davis, "Jewish Grieving for a Non-Jewish Relative," Ritualwell: Tradition & Innovation, July 20, 2015, ritualwell.org.
56 Sylvia Barack Fishman, *Double or Nothing?: Jewish Families and Mixed Marriage* (Waltham, MA: Brandeis University Press, 2004), 37, 89; Keren R. McGinity, *Still*

Jewish: A History of Women and Intermarriage in America (New York: New York University Press, 2009), 145.
57 Lauren Markoe, "At Yom Kippur, A Blessing for the Congregation's Non-Jews," *Washington Post*, September 17, 2015, www.washingtonpost.com; "The Blessing of Jewish Adjacent Members," Temple Shalom, www.templeshalom.net/.
58 Markoe, "At Yom Kippur."
59 Toba Spitzer, "Torah Blessings for Interfaith Partners," Ritualwell: Tradition & Innovation, ritualwell.org.
60 "Non-Jewish Members." Congregation Dorshei Tzedek," www.dorsheitzedek.org.
61 "Mi Sheberakh Blessing of Appreciation for People of Different Identities—Jewish Ritual," Ritualwell: Tradition & Innovation, ritualwell.org.
62 Samira K. Mehta, *Beyond Chrismukkah: The Christian-Jewish Interfaith Family in the United States* (Chapel Hill, NC: University of North Carolina Press, 2018), 133.
63 Mehta, *Beyond Chrismukkah*, 123–25.
64 Mehta, 120, 133; Samira K. Mehta, "Asian American Jews, Race, and Religious Identity," *Journal of the American Academy of Religion* 89 (2021): 978–1005.
65 Munro, *Coming of Age in Jewish America*, 42.
66 Fishman, *Double or Nothing?*, 89.
67 Karen Kushner, "Recommendations for Creating a Welcoming Policy Document," 18Doors, December 5, 2011, 18doors.org.
68 Walter Jacob, ed., "Burial of Non-Jewish Wives in Jewish Cemeteries (1914, 1916, 1919, 1936)," in *American Reform Responsa: Collected Responsa of the Central Conference of American Rabbis* (New York: Central Conference of American Rabbis, 1983), 323–35.
69 For example, "The Funeral of a Non-Jewish Spouse of a Member" (1989); "Rabbi Officiating at Mixed Marriages" (1919, 1982); "Reform Judaism and Mixed Marriage" (1980); "Dual Wedding Ceremonies" (1982); "Patrilineal and Matrilineal Descent" (1983); "Children of Mixed Marriages" (1919); "Status of Children" (1980); "Report of the Committee on Patrilineal Descent on the Status of Children of Mixed Marriages Adopted by the Central Conference of American Rabbis at Its 94th Annual Convention, March 15, 1983" (1983); "The Status of a Gentile-Born Child Adopted into a Jewish Family" (1956),; "Adoption and Adopted Children" (1978); "Jewishness of an Adopted Child" (1989): "A Black Jew, Falashas, and Conversion" (1988); "Teenagers and Gerut" (1984); "Forfeiture of Congregational Membership by Intermarriage" (1916); "Synagogue Membership of a Mixed Couple" (1982); "Congregational Membership for a Non-Jewish Spouse" (1982); "Gentile Members in Congregational Committees" (1983); "May a Non-Jew Light the *Shabbat* Eve Candles" (1984); "Non-Jewish Participation in Bar/Bat Mitzvah Service" (1983); and "Participation of Non-Jews in a Jewish Public Service" (1979), published in *American Reform Responsa* (New York: Central Conference of American Rabbis, 1983); *Contemporary American Reform Responsa* (Central Conference of American Rabbis, 1987); and *Questions and Reform Jewish Answers: New American Reform Responsa* (New York: Central Conference of American

Rabbis, 1992), www.ccarnet.orgccar-responsa. Numerous additional chapters addressing questions about conversion appear in *Contemporary American Reform Responsa* and *American Reform Responsa*.

70 See Epstein, "Congratulations to Mixed Married Families"; Booth, "Non-Jews Opening the Ark"; Alexander, "Concurring Opinion"; Miriam Berkowitz et al., "Dissonance of a Non-Jew"; Jerome Epstein, "Role of the Non-Jewish Parent"; and Ben Zion Bergman, "The Case of the Unconverted Spouse," at www.rabbinicalassembly, *Even HaEzer* 16.1989, 16.2013a, 16.2013b, 16.2013c, 16.1993, and *Yoreh Deah* 268.1993.

71 These are all discussed in Epstein, "Congratulations to Mixed Married Families" and "Issues Regarding Employment of an Intermarried Jew by a Synagogue or Solomon Schechter Day School," in *Even HaEzer*, 16.1989 and 16.1997.

72 Rabbinical Assembly, "RA and USCJ Statement on Keruv and Intermarriage," Rabbinical Assembly, December 19, 2014, www.rabbinicalassembly.org.

73 Lauren Markoe, "Conservative Synagogues Can Now Officially Accept Non-Jews as Members," Religion News Service, March 7, 2017, religionnews.com.

74 Charles Arian et al., "As Rabbis, We Believe a New Intermarriage Narrative Can Strengthen Conservative Judaism—EJewish Philanthropy," EJewish Philanthropy, April 5, 2022, ejewishphilanthropy.com.

75 "A Word about Resolutions," Reconstructionist Rabbinical Association, 2022, therra.org.

76 "Reconstructionist Rabbinical Association Resolution: Committee on Intermarriage," 1980, therra.org.

77 Reconstructionist Rabbinical Association, "Resolution: The Children of Mixed Marriages, Jews by Choice and Proselytism," 1980, therra.org.

78 Reconstructionist Rabbinical Association, "Resolution: Co-Officiation," 2000, therra.org.

79 Munro, *Coming of Age in Jewish America*, 11, 42, 107.

80 Statements on the websites of synagogues discussed in this chapter were chosen out of convenience, not as a representative sample.

81 "The Role of Non-Jews in Kol HaLev," Kol HaLev—Cleveland's Reconstructionist Jewish Community, July 19, 2004, kolhalev.net.

82 "Non-Jewish Members."

83 "Opportunities for Non-Jewish Members," Beth Hillel Temple, www.bethhillel.net.

84 "Involvement of Non-Jews in Davening," Altshul, February 2017, www.altshul.org.

85 "Involvement of Non-Jews in Davening."

86 "Opportunities for Non-Jewish Members."

87 "Role of Non-Jews in Kol HaLev."

88 "Involvement of Non-Jews in Davening."

89 "Non-Jewish Members."

90 Thompson, *Jewish on Their Own Terms*, 116; see also McGinity, *Marrying Out*, 131.

91 McGinity, *Still Jewish*, 144–45.

PART II

Jews' Place in American Society

5

Jewish Americans through a Socioeconomic Lens

ILANA M. HORWITZ

In the United States, people's socioeconomic status plays a powerful role in how they perceive the world and how they behave. Broadly speaking, socioeconomic status is a measure of a person's or household's economic and social position in society based on income and education level.[1] It influences a range of behaviors, including how people raise their children, what food they eat, and how they talk as well as their attitudes, values, and preferences about politics, religion, and life in general.[2]

Over recent decades, American Jews have emerged as one of the most socioeconomically advantaged religious and ethnic groups in the U.S., a stark contrast to their status in the first half of the twentieth century.[3] Initially, many Jewish immigrants were low-wage, blue-collar workers. In 1910, a time when the U.S. economy was heavily reliant on manual labor and production, 75 percent of Jewish men were engaged in crafts and other blue-collar jobs, with only a small fraction in professional or managerial roles.

However, from 1910 to 1970, as the U.S. economy evolved significantly toward office work and managerial roles, American Jews ascended the occupational ladder more rapidly than many other ethnic and religious groups.[4] By 1990, a significant portion, 65 percent, occupied high-level occupations, including half as professionals and 17 percent in management positions. By the end of the twentieth century, the American Jewish community was predominantly an upper-middle-class, highly educated group characterized by a prevalence of dual-career couples across various professional fields. Into the third generation, the educational attainment of Jewish women nearly matched that of men, with many pursuing professional careers, making dual-career households common among young Jewish families.[5]

This chapter delves into the current socioeconomic landscape of American Jewry, examining various subgroups within the community. It explores educational and income disparities among different Jewish denominations, the financial perceptions of Jews in different age groups amid rising living costs, gender dynamics in educational and professional achievements, regional economic variations, and the impact of increasing racial and ethnic diversity within the community.

Data for this analysis comes from the comprehensive, nationally representative 2020 Pew Research Center survey of Jewish Americans.[6] This study includes "Jews by religion"—those who identify religiously as Jewish—and "Jews not by religion," those who are culturally or ethnically Jewish, or Jewish based on their family background.[7]

This chapter primarily analyzes data from respondents aged thirty and above. This age group is chosen because most individuals over thirty are likely to have completed their bachelor's degrees, providing a more stable foundation for assessing socioeconomic factors. In contrast, I exclude data concerning individuals aged eighteen to twenty-nine from detailed analysis.[8] This younger demographic typically experiences significant fluctuations in education levels, income, and financial security, largely because many are still in the process of completing their education and may not yet be fully financially independent. Additionally, the financial data for many college students can be skewed by partial or full parental support, which may not accurately reflect their true economic status. This consideration ensures the data analyzed provides a clearer, more accurate picture of socioeconomic conditions among more settled adult populations.

The data are weighted using Pew's constructed weights, which ensures that the sample more accurately mirrors the broader population. This is crucial for drawing reliable and generalizable conclusions from the survey data. In the results section, I present weighted cross-tabulations to explore the relationships between various demographic groups. These cross-tabulations adjust the raw data to account for the survey design, thus highlighting patterns that might be obscured in unweighted data.

Additionally, I have conducted weighted regressions with control variables to rigorously test the significance of relationships between variables. This method helps us understand whether relationships between variables hold even when other influencing factors are controlled.

For example, it allows us to examine if a relationship between education level and racial identity persists when factors like age are held constant. While I have performed weighted regressions, I primarily present the data as cross-tabulations. This approach is chosen because it visually demonstrates how the distribution of one variable varies among subgroups defined by another variable, making it more accessible and easier to interpret for a wider audience.

In this analysis, I present the educational attainment of respondents by reporting the percentage who have earned at least a bachelor's degree. For income, I detail the percentage of respondents with household incomes below $40,000 as well as those earning more than $200,000 to capture the economic diversity within the community. Additionally, I expand the definition of socioeconomic status to encompass financial stress and security. This includes reporting the percentages of respondents who struggle to meet expenses, those who just manage to meet them, and those who live comfortably.

The findings affirm that American Jews typically represent a highly educated, upper-middle-class demographic predominantly engaged in professional and other high-level occupations.[9] This group often consists of dual-career couples. Moreover, the data suggest an improvement in the standard of living across recent generations among American Jews. Notably, younger Jewish adults under 30 were more likely to report that their families were financially comfortable during their childhood compared to older cohorts. Specifically, 63 percent of those aged 18–29 reported living comfortably, in contrast to 41 percent of those aged 30–49, 46 percent of those aged 50–64, and only 36 percent of those 65 and older who felt the same about their upbringing. This generational difference in perceived financial comfort highlights both socioeconomic progress and changing perceptions of financial security within the community over time.

The following four points illustrate that on common measures of education, income, and economic security, American Jews are faring much better compared to the rest of the U.S. population.[10]

1. **Jews are about twice as likely to have a bachelor's degree (BA) and almost three times as likely to have a postgraduate degree.**
   Nearly six-in-ten Jews are college graduates, including 28 percent

who have obtained a postgraduate degree (e.g., a master's, JD, MD, or PhD). By comparison, among U.S. adults overall, about three in ten are college graduates, and just 11 percent have a postgraduate degree.
2. **Jews are about six times as likely to report household incomes exceeding $200,000.** About one in four Jews report household incomes of $200,000 or more. In contrast, only about 4 percent of all U.S. adults report incomes at this level. At the lower end of the income spectrum, approximately 10 percent of U.S. Jews earn less than $30,000, far fewer than the 26 percent of all U.S. adults below this income threshold. A large proportion of Jews with household incomes under $30,000 are Ḥaredi.
3. **Jews are almost twice as likely to say they are financially comfortable.** When asked to describe their household's financial situation (largely before the COVID-19 pandemic began), roughly half of U.S. Jews said they were living comfortably. By comparison, 29 percent of U.S. adults say they were living comfortably before the pandemic.
4. **About one-quarter of Jews struggle to pay bills, which is half as much as U.S adults overall.** About one-quarter of American Jews had difficulty paying for at least one of the necessities mentioned in the survey (e.g., rent/mortgage, food, medical care) compared to about half of U.S. adults overall (56 percent).

However, there are important differences in socioeconomic status across different demographic measures, including religious affiliation, age, gender, region, race/ethnicity, and immigration status. These heterogeneous patterns are summarized below and explained in greater detail in the rest of the chapter.

- **Religious denomination:** Ḥaredi Jews are half as likely to hold a BA and two to three times more likely to face financial struggles compared to other Jewish denominations.
- **Age:** Jews 65+ have lower education and incomes yet live more comfortably; Jews 30–49 are the most financially insecure age bracket.
- **Gender:** Women's educational attainment is rising among younger cohorts, while men's educational attainment is falling among younger cohorts.

- **Region**: Southern Jews have the lowest education levels and incomes; western and northeastern Jews earn similarly, with western Jews enjoying greater financial comfort.
- **Race/Ethnicity**: Jews of Color have lower education levels and incomes compared to White /non-Hispanic Jews.
- **Immigration status**: Immigrants are just as highly educated and are as likely to earn high incomes, but they are also less financially comfortable than native-born Jews.

Ḥaredi Jews are half as likely to hold a BA and 2–3 times more likely to face financial struggles compared to other Jewish denominations.

Pew grouped respondents by religious denomination based on the following two survey questions: The first asked, "Thinking about Jewish religious denominations, do you consider yourself to be Conservative, Orthodox, Reform, something else, or no particular denomination (which includes 'just Jewish')?"[11] Those who self-identified as Orthodox were then asked a follow-up question: "Do you consider yourself to be 'Modern or Centrist Orthodox,' 'Ḥasidic or Chabad,' 'Yeshivish, Litvish, or Agudah'?" For my analyses, I categorize Jews in the following way: Ḥaredi, Modern/Centrist Orthodox, Conservative, Reform, and no denomination. The Ḥaredi category includes Jews who come from the latter traditions (i.e., not the Modern or Centrist Orthodox).[12]

The data show that Conservative, Reform, Modern/Centrist Orthodox, and nondenominational Jews are substantially more likely than those who are Ḥaredi to complete bachelor's degrees and graduate degrees.[13] As figure 1 shows, more than two-thirds of Reform Jews (68 percent) say they are college graduates, as do 56 percent of Conservative Jews, 56 percent of Modern/Centrist Orthodox Jews, and 64 percent of Jews with no denominational affiliation. However, educational attainment rates among Ḥaredi Jews are much lower, with only 25 percent reporting that they have bachelor's degrees. The differences among Orthodox Jews point to the importance of distinguishing between different branches within Orthodoxy rather than lumping all Orthodox Jews together.

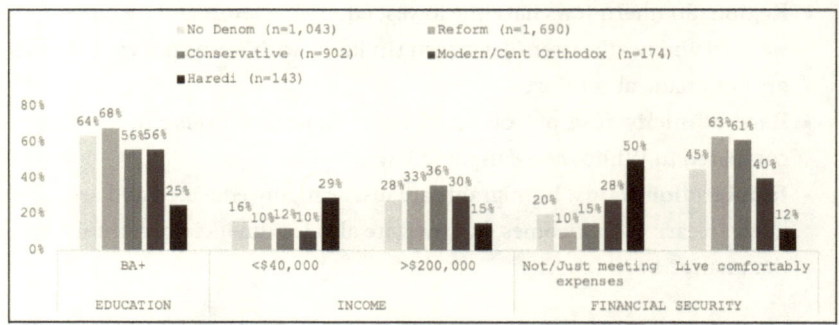

Figure 5.1. Ḥaredi Jews are half as likely to hold a BA and 2–3 times more likely to face financial struggles compared to other Jewish denominations (N = 3, 952).

Ḥaredi Jews also fare much worse economically, which is not surprising, given their low rates of educational attainment. In general, Jews without a college education are more likely to have low household incomes. As figure 5.1 shows, Ḥaredi Jews are about 2–3 times more likely to report an annual household income of less than $40,000 and about 2 times less likely to report an annual income of $200,000 or more. Specifically, about 29 percent of Ḥaredi Jews report incomes of less than $40,000, while only 10–16 percent of Jews from other denominations report such low incomes. While over one-quarter of Reform, Conservative, and Modern/Centrist Orthodox Jews report annual household incomes over $200,000, only 15 percent of Ḥaredi Jews report doing so.

Among Ḥaredi Jews, 50 percent were either not meeting or just meeting their basic expenses compared to 30 percent of Modern/Centrist Orthodox Jews, 14 percent of Conservative Jews, 10 percent of Reform Jews, and 21 percent of Jews of no particular denomination.

Jews 65 and over have lower education and incomes, yet
live more comfortably; Jews 30–49 are the most financially
insecure age bracket.

Educational rates are significantly lower among Jews 65 and over compared to Jews 30–64. Among Jews 65 and over, 51 percent have a bachelor's degree or more, but among 50–64 year-olds, bachelor's degree completion rates are much higher—70 percent. Among 30–49 year olds, the rate of bachelor's degree completion is comparable to 50–64 year-olds at 68 percent.

Older Jews also report lower incomes than do younger Jews. Among Jews 65 and over, 19 percent report an annual household income of less than $40,000 compared to just 10 percent of Jews between 30–49 and 9 percent among those 50–64. Looking at those who report annual incomes over $200,000, Jews 50–64 are faring the best. A little more than one-third (35 percent) of Jews in this late-career stage earn over $200,000, compared with 30 percent of Jews 30–49 and 30 percent of Jews 65+. These trends make sense given that people 50–65 are at the financial peak of their careers, while many people 65+ have already retired.

However, lower incomes do not necessarily mean that Jews 65 and over are experiencing economic insecurity. As figure 5.2 also shows, these Jews are more likely to say they are living comfortably. This may reflect the fact that Jews in the 65+ age bracket are not responsible for high expenses, such as their children's education and mortgages (which they are likely to have paid off). It could also be that Jews 65+ are living off assets rather than income (recall that Pew specifically asked about total family income from all sources before taxes). In fact, it is Jews ages 30–49 who are experiencing the most economic insecurity. Among this younger cohort of Jews, more than one in five (22 percent) are either not meeting expenses or just barely meeting expenses.

Women's educational attainment is rising, while men's is falling.

As mentioned above, educational attainment rates among Jews ages 30–64 are higher than those of Jews 65+. The primary reason why educational attainment rates are rising among younger cohorts is because of women. In the U.S., American women have been outpacing men in educational attainment since around 1982.[14] However, the female advantage in college completion among American Jews specifically is more recent.[15]

As figure 5.2 shows, women's rates of bachelor's degree attainment have skyrocketed. Whereas only 43 percent of women 65 and over have completed college, 72 percent of women ages 30–49 have done

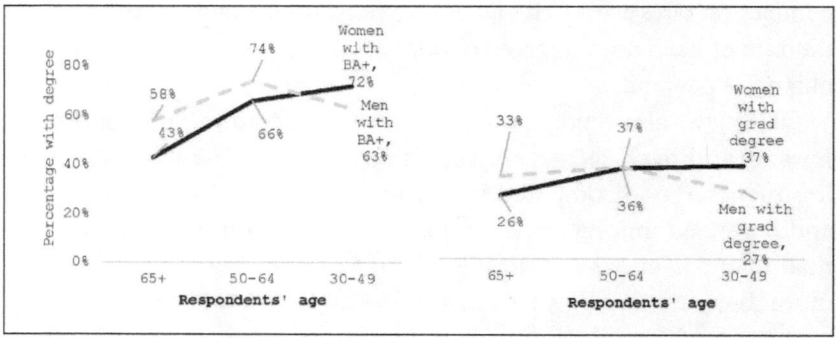

Figure 5.2. Women's educational attainment is rising among younger cohorts, while men's is falling.

so. Meanwhile, men's rates of educational attainment grew but are now falling. Men ages 30–49 are just 5 percentage points more likely to have earned a bachelor's degree than men 65 and over, while women ages 30–49 are 29 percentage points more likely to have earned a bachelor's degree than women 65 and over. The same trend is true when we look at rates of graduate degree completion in figure 5.2. Whereas only 26 percent of women 65 and over completed a graduate degree, 37 percent of women ages 30–49 have done so. And, as with college completion rates, younger cohorts of men are less likely to earn graduate degrees than older cohorts. Men ages 30–49 complete graduate degrees at the same rate as men 65 and over.

The educational accomplishments of recent cohorts of Jewish women align with trends I found in the National Study of Youth and Religion (NSYR). Respondents were 13–17 years old when the NSYR began in 2003, which makes them approximately 30–34 years old in 2020. My analysis of the NSYR showed that this is the first cohort in history in which Jewish women are outpacing Jewish men in educational attainment.[16] The rise of Jewish women reflects several factors. In earlier generations, women were more likely to see their primary roles as mothers, but attitudes of younger cohorts of Jewish women have changed significantly, including a gender egalitarian upbringing where Jewish parents teach their sons *and* their daughters that they can have prominent careers. It is also notable that rates of educational attainment among men in the 30–49 year-old cohort are decreasing, though it is not clear why. People often say that Jews have high rates of educational attainment because they "value education"; however, as I have argued elsewhere, this kind of argument makes it sound like Jews have some inherent cultural values that help them be educationally successful.[17] The fact that Jewish men are now falling behind women provides evidence that there are other structural and social-psychological factors that help explain Jews' educational patterns. In other words, it is probably not the case that Jewish men have just stopped valuing education. Rather, the pattern of Jewish men aligns with a broader pattern in the U.S., where men are dropping out of college in unusually high rates.

Southern Jews have the lowest education levels and incomes; western and northeastern Jews earn similarly, with western Jews enjoying greater financial comfort

Geographic differences in socioeconomic status among Jews reflect broader trends in the U.S., where regional rates of educational attainment and earnings tend to be lower than rates in the Northeast, West, and Midwest. As figure 5.3 shows, Jews living in the South are the least educated, with just over half (52 percent) having earned a bachelor's degree or more. Meanwhile, about one-third of Jews living in the West (65 percent) and in the Northeast (69 percent) have earned a bachelor's degree or more. Jews living in the Midwest are more educated than Jews in the South but less educated than Jews in the West and Northeast.

Although Jews in the South are less educated than Jews in the Northeast and are less likely to earn incomes over $200,000, the differences in reported rates of economic insecurity are not as significant. As figure 5.3 shows, half of Jews in the South report living comfortably, compared to 55 percent of Jews in the Northeast. This likely reflects a lower cost of living in the South. In fact, while Jews in the Northeast are the most educated and most likely to earn over $200,000, they are less financially comfortable than are Jews in the West. This may reflect the exceptionally high cost of living in New York and surrounding towns.[18]

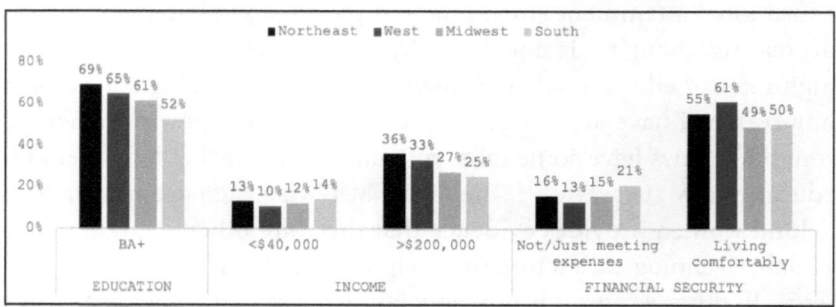

Figure 5.3. Southern Jews have the lowest education levels and incomes; western and northeastern Jews earn similarly, with western Jews enjoying greater financial comfort (N = 4,186).

Jews of Color have lower education levels and incomes compared to White/non-Hispanic Jews.

Pew measures race and ethnicity using categories that mirror the way the U.S. Census Bureau asks about these identities. When given these choices, 93 percent of U.S. Jews describe themselves as White and non-Hispanic, while 7 percent say they belong to another racial or ethnic group. This includes 1 percent who identify as Black and non-Hispanic, 4 percent who identify as Hispanic, and 3 percent who identify with another race or ethnicity, such as Asian, American Indian, or Hawaiian/Pacific Islander, or with more than one race. I refer to these Jews as "Jews of Color," though it is possible that they may not label themselves in that way.

Jews of Color are much less educated than White/non-Hispanic Jews, though Jews of Color still fare better than people of color in America more generally. As figure 5.4 shows, less than half of Jews of Color (48 percent) have completed a bachelor's degree, compared to almost two-thirds of White/non-Hispanic Jews (64 percent).

Jews of Color are also economically worse off. As figure 5.4 shows, they are less likely to report household incomes over $200,000—19 percent compared to 32 percent of White/non-Hispanic Jews. Jews of Color are also much more likely to experience economic hardship. Compared to White/non-Hispanic Jews, Jews of Color are 10 percentage points more likely to say they are just barely meeting expenses or not meeting expenses, and 23 percentage points less likely to say they are living comfortably. Weighted regressions that control for age, region, denomination, and gender confirm that Jews of Color have lower levels of education, earn less, and are more likely to struggle financially than White/non-Hispanic Jews.

Immigrants are just as highly educated and as likely to earn high incomes, but they are also less financially comfortable than native-born Jews.

About 10 percent of Pew respondents identified as immigrants. Although we tend to think of Jewish immigrants as older, Jewish immigrants are fairly evenly distributed among age groups. (12 percent of 30–49 year-olds, 11 percent of 50–64 years-olds, and 11 percent of those 65 and over are immigrants.)

As figure 5.5 shows, Jewish immigrants are just as highly educated as native-born Jews, with about two-thirds of each group earning at least a bachelor's degree. While not shown in this figure, immigrants and native-born Jews also have very similar rates of graduate degree attainment (34 percent of immigrants and 32 percent of native-born Jews have earned a graduate degree). Immigrants are also just as likely as native-born Jews to earn at least $200,000. Weighted regressions that control for age, region, denomination, and gender confirm that being an immigrant is not associated with lower education levels or lower

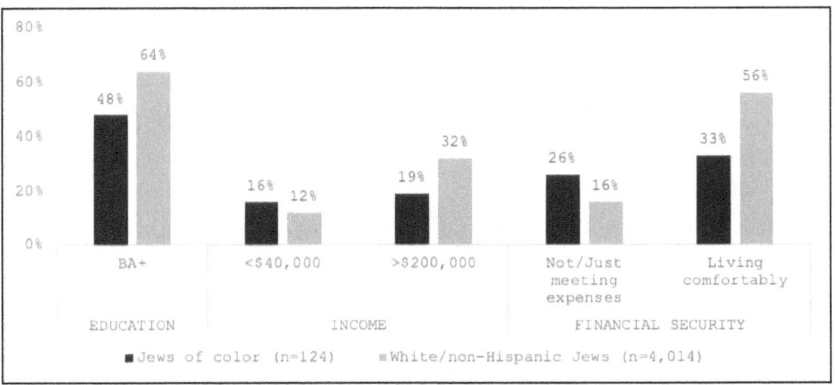

Figure 5.4. Jews of Color have lower education levels and incomes compared to White/non-Hispanic Jews (N = 4, 138).

levels of income. Yet, despite having equally high rates of degree completion and equal chances of earning high incomes, Jewish immigrants are a bit less financially comfortable. Compared to native-born Jews, immigrants are 7 percentage points more likely to report incomes less than $40,000, 13 percentage points less likely to report living comfortably, and 5 percentage points more likely to say they are barely or not able to meet their expenses. This likely has to do with immigrants who came to the U.S. as adults (as opposed to having immigrated as children or as teenagers) and had completed their educational degrees in their former countries. When immigrants come to the U.S., many of them do not have the language skills or correct credentials to continue their work and have to work in lower-paying jobs. For example, many Jews from the former Soviet Union with very high levels of education immigrated to the U.S. in the late 1980s/early 1990s, but took blue-collar jobs when they arrived. Some immigrants were able to secure high paying jobs later on, but many were not. For these immigrants, earnings and savings are lower than their native-born counterparts with comparable education levels.

Conclusion

The chapter opened by contextualizing the socioeconomic ascent of American Jews from the early twentieth century—a period when many Jewish immigrants were engaged in low-wage, blue-collar work—to their current status as one of the most socioeconomically advantaged groups in the U.S. This transformation was facilitated by a significant shift in occupational structures, with more Jews moving into managerial roles and professional fields as the American economy itself evolved from manufacturing to knowledge and service-based industries.

Education has played a crucial role in this socioeconomic journey. The substantial educational attainment of the Jewish community, notably higher than the national average, has been a key driver of their economic success. This chapter has detailed how nearly six in ten Jews are college graduates, with a substantial number holding advanced degrees, which correlates with higher income levels and greater financial security compared to the general U.S. population.

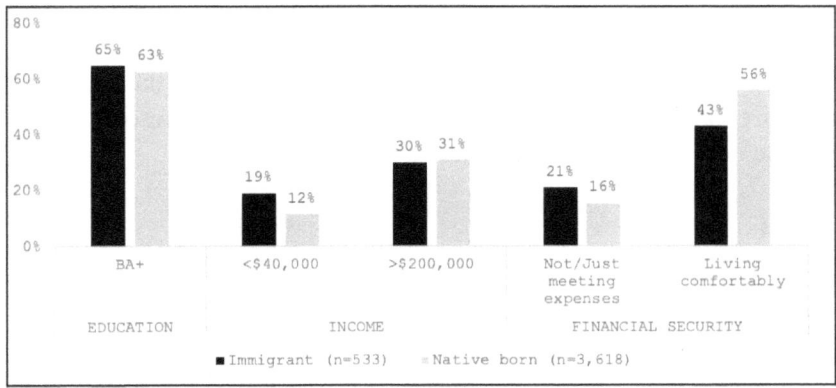

Figure 5.5. Immigrants are just as highly, educated, but less financially comfortable than native-born Jews (N = 4, 151).

However, this narrative is not without its complexities. The analysis has highlighted significant internal diversities and challenges—ranging from the lower socioeconomic standing of Ḥaredi Jews to the financial insecurities faced by younger Jews and regional disparities that mirror national economic trends. These differences within the Jewish community emphasize that socioeconomic status is influenced by a variety of factors, including age, gender, race, and geography.

As younger Jewish adults report higher levels of childhood financial comfort compared to older generations, it suggests generational progress. Yet this is juxtaposed against current challenges such as the rising costs of living and education, which impact younger Jews' perceptions of economic security today. This intergenerational perspective underlines the fluctuating nature of socioeconomic status, shaped by both past legacies and present realities.

Thus, the journey of Jewish Americans serves as a microcosm of the broader American experience, where socioeconomic mobility and challenges coexist. American Jews, while enjoying certain socioeconomic advantages, do not exist in a vacuum. Their experiences are shaped by the same regional, demographic, and economic forces that affect all Americans. However, unique historical and cultural trajectories have influenced their distinct socioeconomic pathways.

Moving forward, it will be crucial to address the unique challenges faced by various subgroups within the Jewish community, ensuring that the gains of past generations provide a foundation rather than a ceiling for future achievements. Future inquiries might explore the causes behind educational declines among young Jewish men and the economic pressures on middle-aged Jews, providing deeper insights into the evolving socioeconomic fabric of American Jewry.

NOTES

1 Socioeconomic status is also commonly measured by occupation, but occupation is not considered in this chapter because of data limitations.
2 Although often conflated with one another, social class and socioeconomic status can be distinguished as separate constructs; see Joan M. Ostrove and Elizabeth R. Cole, "Privileging Class: Toward a Critical Psychology of Social Class in the Context of Education," *Journal of Social Issues* 59 (2003) 677–92; and M. Rubin, N. Denson, S. Kilpatrick, K. E. Matthews, T. Stehlik, and D. Zyngier, "'I Am Working-Class': Subjective Self-Definition as a Missing Measure of Social Class and Socioeconomic Status in Higher Education Research," *Educational Researcher* 43 (2014): 196–200. Social class refers to one's sociocultural background and is more stable, typically remaining static across generations; see S. Jones and M. D. Vagle, "Living Contradictions and Working for Change: Toward a Theory of Social Class-Sensitive Pedagogy," *Educational Researcher* 42 (2013): 129–41. Hence, it is possible for a working-class person to have a relatively high socioeconomic status while remaining in a stereotypically "blue-collar" occupation. Because social class is more stable than socioeconomic status, it is also more likely to be associated with intergroup power and status differences that act as the basis for discrimination and prejudice (Ostrove and Cole, "Privileging Class").
3 Rachel Kranson, *Ambivalent Embrace: Jewish Upward Mobility in Postwar America* (Chapel HillUniversity of North Carolina Press, 2017).
4 Joel Elvery, *Changes in the Occupational Structure of the United States: 1860 to 2015* (Federal Reserve Bank of Cleveland, 2019).
5 Carmel U. Chiswick, *Economics of American Judaism* (New York: Routledge, 2008).
6 Pew surveyed 4,718 U.S. adults who identify as Jewish, including 3,836 Jews by religion and 882 Jews of no religion. The survey was administered online and by mail from November 19, 2019, to June 3, 2020. Respondents were drawn from a national, stratified random sampling of residential mailing addresses, which included addresses from all fifty states and the District of Columbia. No lists of common Jewish names, membership rolls of Jewish organizations, or other indicators of Jewishness were used to draw the initial sample.
7 I exclude respondents whom Pew classifies as having "Jewish background" or "Jewish affinity."
8 Unlike the 2013 Pew Study, the 2020 study didn't ask people for specific ages, but only for their age bracket: 18–29, 30–49, 50–64, and over 65.

9   Among U.S. Jews who were employed at least part-time, about half (48 percent) said they worked at a for-profit company, while one in five (21 percent) were self-employed, 16 percent worked for a nonprofit organization, and 13 percent for the government. When asked what business or industry they work in, 15 percent of Jewish respondents said they work in education, 12 percent said they work in health care, and 11 percent said they work in the arts, entertainment, recreation, travel, accommodations, or food services. An additional 9 percent of employed Jews work in financial services, 8 percent in wholesale or retail trade, and 7 percent in construction, manufacturing, transportation, warehousing, utilities, protective services, or waste management.
10 These insights are derived from the Pew Research Center's 2020 study of Jewish Americans.
11 About 10 percent of respondents provided an answer outside these categories. There is a great amount of variation in the write-in answers—about twenty different write-in categories, none of which is more than about 1.5 percent of the respondents. Therefore, to maintain as large of a sample size as possible, I have reclassified about 3 percent of the write-in answers into one of the five main categories: those who said "a mix of Conservative/Reform" or "Reconstructionist" or "Renewal" are classified as Reform; those who said "a mix of Conservative/Orthodox" are classified as Conservative; those who said "not practicing/not religious," "secular," "liberal/progressive," or "culturally Jewish" are classified as no denomination; those who said "observant" or "traditional" are classified as "Modern or Centrist Orthodox." Because the percentage of people who wrote in answers is so small, the results in the chapter do not change when these write-in respondents are excluded from the sample.
12 Orthodox Jews who said they were "just Orthodox," "other," or who didn't know have been excluded from this analysis.
13 The 2013 Pew data show the same general gap between Ḥaredi and Modern Orthodox Jews, though the question was asked slightly differently. In 2013, which was conducted by phone rather than online, respondents were asked, "Do you consider yourself to be Modern Orthodox, Ḥasidic, Yeshivish, or some other type of Orthodox?" In 2013, the Ḥaredi category included Jews who came from the Ḥasidic and the Yeshivish (or "Lithuanian") traditions. In 2013, 65 percent of Modern Orthodox Jews completed a BA, compared to 25 percent of Ḥaredi Jews. In 2020, Modern and Centrist Orthodox Jews were combined together, which likely explains why the BA attainment rate among "Modern Orthodox" Jews in 2020 is lower than it was in 2013.
14 Claudia Buchmann and Thomas a Diprete, "The Growing Female Advantage in College Completion: The Role of Family Background and Academic Achievement," *American Sociological Review* 71 (2006): 515–41.
15 Ilana M. Horwitz, Kaylee T. Matheny, Krystal Laryea, and Landon Schnabel, "From Bat Mitzvah to the Bar: Religious Habitus, Self-Concept, and Women's Educational Outcomes," *American Sociological Review* 87 (2022): 336–72.

16 For examples of earlier studies when Jewish men outpaced Jewish women, see Harriet Hartman, "The 2013 Pew Report through a Gender Lens" in *American Jewish Year Book*, ed. Arnold Dashefsky and Ira Sheskin (Cham: Springer International, 2015) 41–45; and Harriet Hartman and Moshe Hartman, *Gender and American Jews: Patterns in Work, Education, and Family in Contemporary Life* (Waltham, MA: Brandeis University Press, 2009).

17 Horwitz et al., "Bat Mitzvah to the Bar."

18 New York City and the surrounding region has the largest number of low-income Jewish households in the United States and is an outlier when compared to the ranges included above. According to 2011 data, 20 percent of individuals in Jewish households in New York lived in a household with an income below 150 percent of the federal poverty level, accounting for 361,100 individuals. "Jewish Poverty in the United States: A Summary of Recent Research," Harry and Jeanette Weinberg Foundation, 2019, cdn.fedweb.org.

6

The Liminal Place of Jews in American Society

MARC DOLLINGER

In a landmark 1988 essay, "The Ethics of Jewish Power," Rabbi Irving "Yitz" Greenberg argued that Jews "are at the beginning of a fundamental change in the Jewish condition: the assumption of power."[1] In his essay, Greenberg affirms Lord Acton's famed adage, that power tends to corrupt and absolute power corrupts absolutely, when he writes: "Power corrupts. But there is no other morally tolerable choice. This is the lesson the Jewish people learned from the Holocaust."[2] Centered on the place of Jews within the larger contemporary American society, Greenberg's observation and Acton's warning complicate many of the most basic assumptions about American Jewish history. These two theses challenge the ways history is remembered, especially around the implications for how an ever-more diverse Jewish population understands itself, its commitment to social justice, and its conferred racial privilege. A group that spent most of the last two thousand years in the diaspora, without state power and subject to the political whim of non-Jewish rulers, White American Jews generally live now with access to power and privilege, boasting a social status that counts them as leaders of industry, education, medicine, and the law, among others.

All this while Jews of Color challenge commonly held assumptions about historical causation: How much did racial privilege more than education, culture, or hard work inform the Jew's place within American society?[3] As Jews of all backgrounds wrestle with new and deeper understandings of their place within American society, how can they reconcile an increasing amount of economic, political, and social power without falling victim to Greenberg's and Acton's corruption? Can White American Jews, so widely praised as some of the nation's most important social justice advocates, maintain that distinction even as they enjoy the privileges of resting near the top of the racial hierarchy? Can Jews of

Color, whose experiences are described elsewhere in this volume, enjoy the same communal status as their White coreligionists? As we strive to understand the broad, diverse, and complex place Jews hold in American society, how can we best understand the underlying social dynamics at play and the implications they bear?

Despite a popular narrative that celebrates Jewish exceptionalism—the idea that (in this case) White Jews are different and better than other White Americans because of their Jewishness—Greenberg offers a more pessimistic, if chilling, perspective: Every single person, conferred with social power, lapses into corruption. The very experience of power, under this thinking, undermines the moral authority that Jews and Judaism often claim. As Greenberg opines, moral authority can only be achieved in a state of powerlessness. Jews gained their reputation for social justice, for aiding the oppressed, for empathizing with the marginal as the logical consequence of their structural weakness in the societies in which they lived. From the Passover stories of Jews as slaves in the land of Egypt to the horrors of the attempted genocide of the Jews during World War II to the postwar civil rights allyship with the African American community, White Jews internalized a sense of social justice exceptionalism rooted in their historic experience of marginality.

What happens, then, when Jews attain power? Can they hold on to their historic moral purity? Greenberg creates a cost/benefit analysis with moral purity and weakness on one side and corrupting strength on the other. His answer leaves little to the imagination: "Power corrupts," he writes, "but there is no other morally tolerable choice." Moral innocence, Greenberg holds, ends with the inevitability of power's corruption, regardless of one's status as a Jew. In this sweeping challenge to Jewish exceptionalism, Greenberg calls out the Jewish people's impossible paradox: Power, even if corrupting, remains the most tolerable moral choice for Jews, despite the fact that it is fundamentally flawed. As Greenberg warns, "The alternative is death," a lesson "that the Jewish people learned in the Holocaust." Take your pick, Greenberg challenges. It's either the moral authority of weakness, translated into another Shoah, or the corruption of power that guarantees the very survival of Jews. Under Greenberg's thinking, there's not much to debate when the terms of the question go to the very existence of the Jewish people.[4]

Greenberg's paradox goes to the heart of the Jews' place within American society, over time and especially in the post–World War II era. American Jews, and especially those involved in organized communal life, navigated between self-perceptions of powerlessness informed by a history of oppression and the often awkward and challenging realization that Jews—especially White Jews—have risen to the top of American society. Holding on to one understanding of the Jews' place within American society while a very different reality was unfolding complicated both intra- and intergroup understandings and relationships. Within Jewish communities, White Jews rebuffed suggestions that they could possibly be a part of, much less reinforce, systems of White supremacy even as Jews of Color lived a very different American experience than their White brethren. As White Jews interacted with representatives of marginalized communities, especially in the social justice arena, they often self-identified as a similarly oppressed group, blind to the privilege Whiteness brought them. Jews, it seemed, lived Greenberg's thesis.[5]

Yet, despite this newfound Jewish place of power and privilege within American society, Jewish vulnerability, even powerlessness, remained a feature of American Jewish life. Sadly, the worst incident of antisemitism in all of American Jewish history occurred in the very recent past when a gunman entered the Tree of Life synagogue in Pittsburgh, Pennsylvania, on October 27, 2018, and killed eleven Jews while they prayed during Shabbat morning services.[6] Just months later, another shooter entered a Chabad synagogue in Poway, California, on the last day of the Jewish festival of Passover and killed one parishioner.[7] During Shabbat morning services on January 15, 2022, a gunman held a rabbi and three congregants hostage in Colleyville, Texas, convinced that Jews possessed the power to free a convicted terrorist from a nearby prison.[8] In a contemporary period that would seem to be a time of unqualified success and safety, Jews still suffer violence, discrimination, and persecution from White supremacists who do not consider Jews any part of the White privileged class or, in an ironic flip, consider Jews über-powerful and capable of supernatural social strength.

From the other side of the political aisle, American leftists have taken aim at Jews for leveraging the privilege they did enjoy to bring harm to the very historically marginalized groups with whom Jews once felt a strong sense of kinship. Creation of the State of Israel, viewed by many

Jews as a vital and necessary step to prevent another Shoah, became in the minds of anti-Zionist leftists nothing more than a colonial, imperialist, racist nation intent on aggrandizing Jewish privilege at the expense of Palestinians. As various ethnoracial and religious groups sided together in the recent U.S. past, Jews endured marginalization from marginalized constituencies. Their racial privilege created a barrier that limited White Jewish solidarity with oppressed groups. White Jews, as Zionists, were critiqued as becoming part of the very systems of oppression that they claimed to oppose.

To gain a better and deeper understanding of the Jewish place in America, we must double down on the already challenging conundrum that Greenberg describes. Depending on their social and political location in American life, White Jews presented as both powerful and powerless. Viewed through a binary political lens, they could be an example of a group so powerful that they posed a threat to the right wing's mythical White American past, just as they could be seen by leftwingers as damaging to their social justice causes. And when Jews became the focus of both the right wing and the left wing's ire, they feared physical violence from both sides, whether in their houses of worship as right-wing antisemites attacked or in progressive circles as left-wing antisemites advanced. Even if Jews viewed their place within American society as one defined by their moral purity, people from both sides of the political aisle saw them as oppressors. Caught between a political right that considers them subhuman and a political left that critiques their outsized power, Jews couldn't seem to win for losing in the political culture of contemporary America.

Cultural anthropologists have gifted American Jewry with a term that captures so many of the complexities that animate Jewish power and powerlessness: liminality. As historian Carlo Ginzburg writes in his important 1976 book *The Cheese and the Worms: The Cosmos of a Sixteenth-Century Miller*, there are types of people who enjoy the opportunity to interact with multiple social groups simultaneously.[9] The subject of Ginzburg's study, a medieval Italian miller named Menocchio, enjoyed welcome at the highest levels of Italian society, since even the elites required the skills of a miller. Unlike most anyone else in his highly structured medieval town, though, Menocchio could also interact with the peasant community, who also required his skill set. Millers, then, as liminal people, traversed social divisions that limited most everyone else from this sort of intergroup privilege.

The miller's liminality proved a mixed blessing. On one hand, Menocchio and others like him enjoyed the ability to interact with a wide range of people who traversed many social divides. The peasant class, to be sure, wished it could gain the sort of privileged access enjoyed by millers. For elites otherwise insulated from the day-to-day realities of life outside their rarified quarters, the millers offered a lens into the lived experiences of ordinary people in their society. Liminality, it would seem at first glance, gifted millers with a unique lifestyle that elevated them relative to both sides of the social hierarchy. Everyone else in medieval Italian society, it seemed, wanted the social expanse of the miller.

Yet Ginzburg shows that liminal people lived isolated, lonely lives. While a part of both the elite and the commoners, Menocchio and those like him faced rebuke. Even as the royals conducted business with the millers, they never considered these laborers to be their social equals. At the end of the day, the elites retired to their palatial homes while the millers exited to much more humble lodgings. One might be able to spend time in high society, but the miller's relationship with their social superiors always proved service based. When the day's work ended, so too did their social interaction and their temporal status. No matter how much the peasants viewed millers as elevated due to their elite access, millers always knew the limits of their status.

Peasants erected social barriers against the full inclusion of millers as well. Because of the privilege millers enjoyed with the elites, commoners never considered them a part of their social group. As much as a miller would serve and even socialize with the commoner, they would never enjoy full status and inclusion either. While peasant distrust of those in the middling social ranks may not have been as severe as those of the upper crust, social acceptance and inclusion still proved elusive. Millers as liminal people proved too lowbrow for the elites and too highbrow for the peasants. They lived as a part of two social groups yet a full member of neither.

The social experience of Menocchio and liminal characters like him offer insights and parallels to our understanding of the Jews' place within American society. White American Jews, especially since World War II, have gained access to the nation's elite. Even as sporadic antisemitism continued from 1945 until the early twenty-first century, Jew hatred ceased to limit wide-scale social mobility. Public opinion polling as well as data chronicling discrimination against Jews revealed sharp declines throughout the 1950s, with levels of antisemitism at historic lows by 1960.[10] Thanks in large measure to the expansion of public education and the benefits provided by the GI Bill, young Jews enrolled in universities at disproportionate numbers. Many continued their educations to graduate school, landing impressive faculty appointments and, later, some of the nation's most prestigious university presidencies.[11] While earlier generations of American Jews toiled in low-income small business ventures, their children and grandchildren built impressive companies with high market capitalization or joined existing corporations at the highest levels of leadership. In the postwar religious culture of the United States, Jews enjoyed a one-third share of the nation's faith communities.[12] Like Ginzburg's millers, Jews flirted with those who enjoyed the highest levels of power and privilege in American society.

Still, American Jews continued to experience marginalization from the nation's elite. Even as they moved to the top of the racial hierarchy and enjoyed the benefits that "Whiteness" conferred, Jews suffered unprecedented antisemitic discrimination from the political right. The rise of White supremacists, neo-Nazis, and White nationalists in early twenty-first-century America reminded Jews of their conditional privilege. At its most infamous, in 2017, racist and antisemitic protestors in Charlottesville, Virginia, in full public view, proclaimed, "Jews will not replace us," while President Donald J. Trump, who would continually espouse antisemitic tropes during and after his time in the Oval Office, defended their hatred of Jews by proclaiming that there were "very fine people on both sides" of the rally.[13] National Jewish self-defense agencies reported spikes in anti-Jewish attitudes and actions from a nationalist old guard intent on returning to the "good old days" of an America before Jewish immigration.[14]

The Jews' place within left-wing America proved daunting as well. Despite a well-known history of White Jews standing in solidarity with communities of color, the privilege enjoyed by these social justice–minded Americans resulted in distrust from their one-time allies. The long history of Jewish persecution and strong Jewish electoral support for progressive political candidates met with fierce resistance from leftist activists critical of the choices Jews made when offered White privilege. A Jewish family could not buy a home in an all-White suburb and still expect a warm and unconditional acceptance by Black families still excluded from that segregated neighborhood. For White suburban Jews, the very ability to live next door to White Christians amplified their most basic social, economic, and political differences in American society. Since at least 1960 (or earlier, in some locales), White American Jews lived their lives much more like the White Christian majority than the nation's historically marginalized racial minority groups. All the social justice work in the world did not change the fact that White Jews proved inherently different from those who did not enjoy privileged status in the racial hierarchy. Like the peasants in medieval Italy, America's marginalized communities viewed with suspicion anyone who mingled with the elite.

No matter the level of solidarity White Jews believed they shared, Jewish liminality made for a lonely political and social existence. Whether from the political left or the political right, elite or more ordinary, White Jews could not find an unconditional home. Mediating between these two social ends complicated American Jewish identity for this population of racially privileged Jews. Both insiders and outsiders, empathetic to the plight of the oppressed all while living and functioning in the middle class (and above), White Jews struggled to reconcile their awkward place on the racial and privilege continuum.

For Jews of Color, liminality proved even more challenging. While one's Blackness, for example, would seem to grant equal communal status within different African American communities, one's intersectional (multiple forms of) identity can marginalize those who are both Black and Jewish.[15] To what extent do communities of color react differently upon learning of a person's Jewishness? How do Jews of Color respond to antisemitism, when these sorts of statements are made with the assumption that people of color are not Jewish? Within White Jewish spaces, the assumptions and the questions flip. Why must Jews of Color constantly tell their story to White Jews, forced to prove their membership in the Jewish people? How much of Jewish identity is assumed but not acknowledged to be White identity, reinforcing systemic racism within organized Jewish life?[16]

The dynamics around Jews of Color's liminality become even more complex when engaging Zionism, Israel's treatment of Palestinians, and the intersectional arguments made linking systemic racism in the United States and oppression of people of color in nations around the world.[17] With the politicization of intersectional identities, the State of Israel has been accused of perpetuating similar acts of oppression against ethno/national minorities under its military control. Even more pointed, some anti-racist activists charge Israeli police forces with providing the very training used by U.S. police forces in their suppression of racial minorities, especially Black men. How, then, can a Jew of Color fully identify as a person vulnerable to police abuse while also holding firm to their belief that the Jewish people have the right to national sovereignty and a military able to protect its citizens? In these examples and more, Jews of Color navigate between belonging and alienation on both sides of the religio-racial spectrum.

Flipped on its head, though, the same liminality that prevents Jewish inclusion in different segments of American society also enables Jews to play a leading, perhaps unique, role in bridging those very divides. In this thinking, only individuals with the ability to communicate across social lines can represent the multiple perspectives necessary to bring change. Elites, unable to truly understand the experience of ordinary people, can never gain the knowledge or trust necessary to forge a common path forward. Marginalized folk, victimized by those elites and demanding fundamental changes to the social and political structure, will never ally with the same people who oppress them. Jews, and especially Jews of Color, can give voice to both groups simultaneously. White Jews can leverage their racial privilege to call out inequities against people of color just as they can take advantage of their social status to pressure White Christian elites to listen and to act. Jews of Color can represent their intersectional lived experiences within both fellow communities of color as well as to White Jewish leaders.

Perhaps contemporary American Jewish liminality offers an antidote to Greenberg's pessimistic assumption about power's innate corruption. The inherent, if not frustrating, tension experienced by Jews as both powerful and powerless platforms American Jews as the best hope for undoing corruptive power. What if Jews could urge America's elite to self-reflect on their complicity in systems of oppression and then work for meaningful change? If, as Lord Acton argued, power corrupts and absolute power corrupts absolutely, then the Jews' in-between power status could serve as a check on corruption just as it opens doors to empowering the disenfranchised. With their disproportionate access to higher education, jobs in corporate America, and capital investment funding, White Jews are well positioned to begin the process of dismantling oppressive systems and rebuilding more just and equitable approaches to American democracy. With Jews of Color animating the struggle against White supremacy from within the Jewish community itself, this particular religious minority could gain outsized influence in changing the status quo.

Hopes for a Jewish-inspired movement for positive social change rests in large measure on a long-standing belief in American Jewish exceptionalism. According to the exceptionalist thesis, the United States has offered its Jewish citizens a lived experience different and better than any other country in Jewish history. With a Declaration of Independence that promised natural rights to all the nation's citizens (even as those promises went unrealized for many) and a subsequent Constitution that separated church and state, guaranteeing the right to religious expression, the United States offered a benevolent government committed to the full inclusion of its Jews. The corrupting influence of unchecked power, experienced by the nation's founders in their revolution against Great Britain, led to Articles of Confederation that limited the influence of federal authority. Later, framers at the Philadelphia Constitutional Convention in 1787 instituted mixed and balanced government structures, along with a subsequent Bill of Rights, to head off the threat of tyranny and ensure a nation committed to freedom, liberty, and representative democracy.[18]

Among Jews, the exceptionalist thesis advanced the notion that following the practices and tenets of Judaism (however defined) distinguished America's Jewish population from the rest of the nation's citizenry. For White Jews especially, this meant that the systems of racial oppression present from the beginning of British colonialism did not attract as many Jewish supporters. One's Jewishness, the exceptionalist thesis argued, offered an antidote to the corrupting influence of power. If power corrupts and absolute power corrupt absolutely, then Jews could leverage their Judaism to shield themselves from support or complicity in social evils. Jewishness translated into something special, despite most Jews' privileged racial status, an asterisk that announced a religious minority successful in living by its own elevated sense of justice. While other White Americans would easily fall into the corruption of power trap, Jews would not.[19]

In some ways, these two aspects of the exceptionalist thesis ring true. The United States has offered Jews a different and better experience than most any other time or place, with the modern State of Israel as the obvious possible exception. While more than three and a half centuries of American Jewish life have borne witness to sporadic instants of antisemitic discrimination, the exceptionalist thesis rings true for Jews fortunate to enjoy a U.S. Constitution rooted in religious freedom, federal, state, and local governments largely friendly to their Jewish inhabitants, and an eventual move up the racial hierarchy in the post–World War II era. Compared to the experience of immigrants from Mexico, Central and South America, Japan, China, and other Asian or Pacific island nations, and especially for those from West Africa forced onto American shores by slavery, Jewish immigrants and their descendants climbed the social mobility ladder with impressive speed. Leaving Eastern Europe during an era of intense state-sponsored antisemitism, Jews raised their children and celebrated their grandchildren in a nation where each successive generation outdid its parents on most every educational, economic, and social metric.[20]

White Jews have, as well, separated themselves in disproportionate numbers from the corrupting influence that power brought to other White constituent groups. In the early generations of scholarship as well as popular writings about Jews over time, authors have celebrated White Jews as political actors different from and better than their Christian neighbors. Since 1928, American Jews have voted liberal and Democratic more than any other White ethnic group in the country. Only African Africans voted as more progressive than White Jews in the last century of electoral politics. The ascension of power, it might seem, did not lead White Jews into corruption. If an exceptionalist case could be made for any ethnoreligious minority in the United States, Jews seemed to be best positioned for that distinction.[21]

The roots of American Jewish exceptionalism as well as liminality grew from a centuries-long acculturation process that privileged White

Jews in some times and places while marginalizing them in others. Despite the relative power eventually enjoyed by most American Jews, social marginality defined earlier moments. Regionalism mattered as well, where America's racial binary separating those defined as Black from those defined as White lifted most Jews up the social hierarchy. The urban/rural split also informed the Jewish power/powerless question when city-dwelling Jews surrounded by many of their coreligionists tended to enjoy greater access to power than their brethren who chose small-town living, often as one of a very few Jews in the area. Throughout American Jewish history, the nation's Jewish residents explored their liminal status in differing, complex, and at times seemingly contradictory ways. Pieced together, they created the platform for a better understanding of how Jews came to their unusual place in the contemporary period.

In colonial America, for example, most Jews identified as Sephardic, migrated to port communities such as New York, Newport, and Charlestown, and constituted less than 1 percent of the larger population.[22] As the institution of slavery developed in the South over the seventeenth century, almost all American Jews enjoyed classification as "White" and never faced the dehumanizing experience of those brought to American shores against their will. When southern White Jewish men counted enough money to purchase an African or African American into slavery, some did, affirming Greenberg's corruption thesis. Historical evidence also points to White Jewish men from the North engaging in the transatlantic trade of Africans into slavery as part of their larger mercantile businesses.[23] American Jewish exceptionalism, in this case, translated into a move into Whiteness and support for the system of White supremacy developing on American shores. Perhaps these historical developments reflected Greenberg's corruption, moving Jews away from the social-justice-centered mandates of the prophets. For many of those engaged in these racist practices, though, their ascension to White power and privilege aligned perfectly with Judaism's teachings. They saw their acquisition of power, and its complicity with White supremacy, as anything but corrupting.[24]

Still, colonial Jews experienced liminality, ostracized as Jews, even White Jews, in a dominant Christian society. In several colonies established to protect religious freedom, Jews did not enjoy the right to practice their faith. In the colonial era, religious freedom did not mean what it does today. Puritans, for example, sought the right to practice their own religion after facing backlash from the Church of England. When they settled in the Massachusetts Bay Colony, they wanted an exclusive Puritan community, without any other religious group's presence. At one point, when their own children failed the theological litmus test required for admission to the Puritan church, leaders created a "halfway covenant" loosening the standards of Puritan church admission.[25]

Catholics, similar to Jews, could not find welcome in these religious-freedom colonies. Ironically perhaps, merchant-based colonies such as New York proved most welcoming to religious minorities. Since religious status proved less important and relevant in the business-centered colonies, Jews enjoyed greater religious freedom and economic opportunity. As colonialists and capitalists, they valued an immigrant group's ability to improve the colony's bottom line. Since colonial Jews shared broad transatlantic trade routes with their brethren in Great Britain, Europe, and the Caribbean, they proved essential to trade and enjoyed a warmer welcome and embrace from their non-Jewish neighbors.[26]

The Jews' place within America changed in the mid-nineteenth century when approximately one hundred thousand Jews from German-speaking central Europe immigrated. While colonial-era Jews claimed Sephardic ancestry and ethnicity, the new arrivals brought Ashkenzai Judaism to the United States. Already urban-dwellers, these new American Jews acculturated quickly into East-Coast city life. Identified as White according to the racial hierarchy of the time, the central European American Jews escaped the social marginality experienced by both free Blacks in the North as well as Irish immigrants escaping the economic devastation of the potato famine. In Boston, for example, White-presenting Irish immigrants faced prejudice and discrimination from native-born Bostonians who objected to the new arrivals' Catholicism and called them the "Black Irish."[27]

The central European Jewish immigrants moved quickly into the mainstream, setting up businesses that benefited from massive economic growth fueled by the industrial revolution. In New York City, prominent Jews opened or ran retail establishments, commercial and trade centers, and banks. Even though informal anti-Jewish restrictions limited Jewish engagement in the established White male Protestant hierarchy, the growth of independent Jewish businesses in the northeastern United States created impressive wealth and influence.

As Jewish immigrants of this era moved beyond the northeastern United States, they enjoyed varying levels of welcome moderated by their particular locale and informed by the liminality each experienced as a Jewish minority. In the South, Jewish Whiteness opened doors into the larger White Christian culture. Often beginning as peddlers, Southern Jews built their businesses into regular retail stores. During the Civil War, White Southern Jews sided with the Confederacy even as Jewish merchants distinguished themselves for their more respectful treatment of Black clients. In the post-Reconstruction South, Jews continued to live through the tension of their complex social standing, embracing the conferred White privilege while recognizing their vulnerability as Jews.[28]

In the West, Jews situated themselves on the ground floor of the massive economic boom that followed the 1848 discovery of gold in the Sierra Nevada foothills. Central European Jewish immigrants to San Francisco founded one of the nation's most famous clothing lines, Levi's; created an impressive banking system, Wells Fargo; and, in one particular instance, came to own one-eighth of the San Francisco peninsula when Adolf Sutro, who would later win election as mayor, translated his business success into massive real estate purchases. For California Jews, especially, but also for many who made Oregon their home, three factors accounted for their impressive place within their larger communities. First, Jews in the West migrated in the very early stages of the manifest destiny-inspired military victories that brought new territories, and, later, states, into the Union. Second, these central European immigrants possessed the urban skill sets that would reward them in a rapidly expanding economy. Finally, and most important, these Jews enjoyed racial status as White, marking a fundamentally different West Coast American experience than their fellow immigrants from China and, later, Japan, who suffered xenophobia and racism at every turn.[29]

The economic, political, and social success of these nineteenth-century American Jews dramatized the power and corruption challenges described by Greenberg. Even as so many of these "captains of industry" supported social justice causes and treated marginalized communities with greater respect than their White peers, they also participated in, complied with, and benefited from the system of White supremacy that determined so much of the nation's resource allocation. Their liminality proved exceptional when it translated into White Jewish advocacy for the downtrodden, but it also brought instances far more typical of the rest of White America. As nineteenth-century American Jews navigated their place in American society, they proved Greenberg's corruption thesis to be all too accurate.

In addition to White Southern Jewish men who purchased African Americans in slavery or profited from the "chattel institution," western Jews tended to embrace the dominant anti-Asian sentiments that relegated Chinese, and, later, Japanese, immigrants to inferior status. In San Francisco, for example, Julius Kahn, a Jewish member of the U.S. Congress, took the lead in extending racist anti-Asian federal legislation. In 2019, San Francisco city officials, with support from local Jewish leaders, removed Congressman Kahn's name from a public playground after Chinese Americans expressed concern.[30] Even Julius Rosenwald, the famed CEO and president of Sears Roebuck, who distinguished himself as a leading funder of African American schools in the post-Reconstruction South, operated within the existing segregationist system, refusing to leverage his philanthropy to change the racial status quo. As he wrote, "Equality is furtherest from my mind."[31] Across the country, central European American Jews, upon achieving a level of social acceptance, participated in organizations and businesses that excluded non-Whites. Achieving the American dream, for these Ashkenazi Jewish immigrants, translated into acquiescence to, if not outright support for, the unjust systems that divided the nation's inhabitants by race, gender, and class. Their navigation of their liminality brought both exceptionalism and typicality.

Though the Jewish immigrants arriving from German-speaking central Europe in the mid-nineteenth century enjoyed a warm welcome on American shores, their two million coreligionists arriving half a century later did not. Economically impoverished, politically radical, and religiously traditional, these Jews from Russia, Poland, and other points east faced trying circumstances in a nation whose streets were supposed to be paved with gold. When they arrived, eastern European Jewish immigrants faced a xenophobic political climate that cast even

White-presenting Jews into an inferior racial status. American society proved challenging at best. The dream of assimilation into American life faltered for eastern European Jewish immigrants.[32]

By multiple measures, Jews experienced powerlessness and outsider status. These Yiddish speakers, as so many popular accounts reveal, struggled on the Lower East Side of Manhattan in a challenging environment with little fear of the corruption that power seems to inevitably bring. On the liminality continuum, eastern European American Jews lived more on the "peasant" side even as their central European brethren flirted with the power and influence of a more integrated religious minority. In this American Jewish historical moment, the experience of liminality differed across Jewish groups, with some American Jews powerful and others powerless.[33]

For the eastern European Jewish immigrants who arrived in the United States between 1880 and 1920, a racist and antisemitic eugenics movement punctuated their liminal status, challenged their ability to join larger society, and differentiated their place in America from their central European coreligionists. Rooted in pseudoscientific assertions, eugenicists constructed hierarchies that elevated White, northern European men as those with the greatest inherent abilities, while people of color, as defined by eugenicists, suffered as genetically inferior. In 1899, William Z. Ripley published *Races of Europe: A Sociological Study*, a widely read and university-adopted screed that argued for three distinct European races: the Teutonic, the Alpine, and the Mediterranean, each with its own unique attributes.[34] Other books, including Madison Grant's *The Passing of the Great Race*, affirmed the White supremacist views of the larger movement and placed Jews at the lower end of the racial spectrum.[35]

The popularity of eugenics-based thinking challenged the Jews' place within early twentieth-century American society. Unlike earlier anti-Jewish sentiment rooted in theological differences between Christians and Jews, eugenics' pseudoscientific claims eliminated any sort of remedy for Jews seeking social inclusion. In earlier eras, Christians objected to the Jewish claim that Jesus did not qualify as the Messiah. If Jews wanted acceptance within their larger Christian societies, they could convert, easing Christian concerns. With the advent of eugenics, though, disavowing Judaism would not suffice, since Jews, as a subhuman group, would remain a threat to the future of White Nordic Teutonic America. Under these social conditions, intermarriage between Jews and White native-born Christian Americans would produce tainted, inferior progeny for every generation that followed. In this era, the very existence of Jews posed a never-ending threat to the racial, and therefore social, hierarchy. Jews lost their liminality status because those on the elite end of the continuum would never welcome them, even for a moment. The most efficient means of protecting future generations of superior strain Nordic Americans, eugenicists and lawmakers agreed, would be the restriction of Jewish immigration to the United States.

Even as the large immigration numbers from southern and eastern Europe helped fill needed low-wage factory jobs, local and eventually federal government officials invoked the racist and antisemitic tropes of the eugenics movement to push back against continued Jewish immigration. In 1897, New York City police commissioner Frank Moss blamed Jews for a disproportionate share of the city's vices in his report, *The American Metropolis*.[36] A decade later, then–police commissioner Theodore Bingham argued that "the Jews, while constituting one-fourth the population of Greater New York, supply half its criminals."[37] Throughout the popular press of the era, Jews faced marginalization for their alleged illegal and immoral nature, dramatizing an outsider status that would soon reach the halls of the federal government.

In 1907, Congress passed and President Theodore Roosevelt signed an immigration act that expanded on the race-based restrictions of previous immigration laws, notably the 1882 Chinese Exclusion Act. For Jews, the 1907 law created the Dillingham Commission, which met for four years and created a forty-one-volume report detailing immigrant life in the United States. The massive findings concluded that eastern European Jewish immigrants posed a threat to American life and urged policy makers to institute immigration restriction as a strategy to keep the racial makeup of the United States more "White"—or, as they interpreted that classification, northern European.

In 1911, Congress agreed, sending immigration restriction legislation to the White House, where President Taft vetoed the bill as bad policy at a time of great labor need. Avoiding the risk of alienating voters during an election year, Congress stalled, waiting until 1913 before once again passing legislation to limit Jewish, and other eastern and southern immigration. Presidential vetoes followed in 1913, 1915, and again in 1917. In the wake of the Great War, Congress overturned President Woodrow Wilson's veto, creating the Literacy Test Act of 1917, forcing new arrivals to demonstrate their apparent genetic acumen by showing that they could read and write in their native language as a precondition for admission to the United States.

By 1921, a lame duck session of Congress took immigration restriction even further, calling first for a total cessation of immigration before ultimately voting to institute the nation's first-ever national origins quota system. Under this legislation, the federal government set an annual immigration quota based upon the national origin of Americans during the 1910 census, the most recent available for lawmakers to use. For every one hundred U.S. residents of a particular country, the law stipulated, three new immigrants would be permitted to settle in the United States each year. With passage of this law, the mythical golden door of American immigration, Emma Lazarus's famed call for America to welcome the tired and the poor, closed.

Three years later, Congress revisited the 1921 law. With more time for reflection and analysis, Congress concluded that its first national origins quota system proved too generous to undesirable immigrants seeking refuge. As a result, it penned new legislation that reduced the annual quota from 3 percent to 2 percent. Of greater import, though, it rejected both the recently available 1920 census as well as the previously used 1910 census to create its baseline. Instead, lawmakers looked to the 1890 census as its guide.

With that decision, Congress embraced scientific antisemitism, seeking a national origins quota that counted few eastern European Jews. Faced with the possibility of admitting 3 percent of America's 1910 social landscape or 2 percent of its 1890 "racial" composition, the nation's chief legislative body opted for a census that kept America White, Nordic, and Teutonic, all but eliminating further Jewish (and southern European) immigration to the United States. This restrictive quota later proved a death sentence for European Jews seeking safe haven after the rise of Hitler and the Nazis in the 1930s.

Early twentieth-century eastern European American Jews could not fear Greenberg's corruption because they did not possess significant power. Liminality, for them, proved much more restricted, if present at all. The nation's growing nativism, racism, and antisemitism, articulated so clearly in the eugenics movement, cast Jews as "other" and as a marginalized ethnoreligious group. Their status as non-White placed Jews alongside other American groups of color, even as most Jews reflected a White phenotype. As scientific antisemitism crossed the Atlantic in the decades that followed, only to be reaffirmed in 1920s and 1930s American popular culture, Jews experienced a far more limited sense of racial power and privilege.

The most famous person in the world at that time, aviator Charles Lindbergh, translated his hero status as the first pilot to fly solo across the Atlantic Ocean into an "America First" movement that targeted Jews as anti-American and a threat to the nation. Barnstorming across the American heartland, he gave fiery speeches linking Jews with President Franklin D. Roosevelt and the British government in a tripartite attempt to drag the United States into the European war against Nazism. Father Coughlin leveraged the mass media power of the radio to stretch antisemitic messages across his two million regular listeners. At his height, two million listeners tuned in to his broadcasts. Automaker Henry Ford used the pages of his newspaper, the *Dearborn Independent*, to advance antisemitic tropes first popularized by the Protocols of the Elders of Zion. Domestic polling confirmed that Ford, Coughlin, and Lindbergh's views about Jews enjoyed wide resonance.[38]

Prior to World War II, then, American Jews did not enjoy the full privileges of White racial status. Even though second-generation eastern European American Jews enjoyed some social mobility in the 1920s, the growing strength of nativism at home and the rise of Nazism in Europe during the 1930s placed White-presenting American Jews closer to other marginalized communities than they would be in the decades to come. Especially as we consider the fundamental change in Jewish racial status during the post–World War II years, we can see this interwar period as critical to an understanding of the social construction and malleability of the racial hierarchy in the United States.[39]

In the decade after World War II, White Jews moved into the mainstream, "becoming white," as articulated by anthropologist Karen Brodkin.[40] Even as sporadic acts of antisemitism continued, Jews as a sociological group no longer suffered as they did in earlier decades. The system of White supremacy that Jews did not create and that often targeted them also conferred unearned privilege on them in this period. Jews regained a much more fluid liminality beginning in the 1950s just as they faced, in much more stark ways, the corruption that power brought, as argued by Greenberg.

As Brodkin argues, the U.S. government's G.I. Bill, offering military veterans low-cost student loans, home mortgages, and business loans, lifted White veterans up the economic ladder at a much faster pace than veterans of color. In fact, she calls the massive government funding program the largest affirmative action program in U.S. history, though with the understanding that it was focused on White Americans. As historian Deborah Dash Moore details in her book *GI Jews*, American Jews served in the World War II armed forces in disproportionate numbers, creating wonderful new opportunities for postwar Jews thanks to the GI Bill. An ever-expanding public university system admitted unprecedented numbers of young Jews into the college ranks. Upon completion of their studies, low-interest home mortgages combined with the easing of antisemitic housing covenants opened suburban America to a new generation of young Jewish families. Small business loans afforded Jewish entrepreneurs the opportunity to set up shop in the midst of an expanding Cold War economy.[41]

Jewish ascent into postwar power brought Greenberg's concerns into sharp focus. While the Jews' place in American society improved, so too did the corrupting influence of that newfound status. Welcomed by their non-Jewish suburban neighbors, Jews exercised their liminal status by moving closer to the elites around them, emulating many of the Whites-only structures already in place across the country. A 1951 poll of Jewish community centers conducted by the Anti-Defamation League revealed that half of the Jewish centers willing to admit non-Jews did so on racially exclusive terms: No Blacks allowed. As Jewish Community Relations Council civil rights activist Mike Israel acknowledged about his hometown, Cincinnati, Ohio, "There was a strong feeling that as Jews we had enough trouble, [and so] we should not get involved in black problems."[42] The vulnerability that White Jews still faced mitigated against an uncompromised embrace of racial justice. Mediating between the two social poles, White suburban Jews did all they could to spend time on each side without harming themselves or their sense of what it meant to be successful, an American, and a Jew.[43]

In the South, White Jews faced even more intense liminal pressure, navigating between their status as not Black and their recognition that their businesses, their social life, and certainly their religious standing depended on their acceptance from White neighbors. While northern Jews enjoyed hero status for their journeys to the South in the civil rights movement, that association of Jews with the movement for racial justice focused a Southern Jewish quandary: How can they find ways to defend the social justice mandates of prophetic Judaism while also keeping themselves safe from the violence exacted upon civil rights activists, including White Jews? As the leader of Houston's largest Conservative-movement synagogue defended, "The rabbis have not spoken out, and to have done so would have been to invite resentment and anti-Semitism, if not, indeed, violence towards the Jewish community. Reform Rabbi Moses Landau of Cleveland, Mississippi, explained in a then-confidential interview that his involvement in racial justice work 'would have been limited to twenty-four hours,' after which 'I wouldn't be in the state anymore.'"[44]

Black clergy knew all too well the threat their churches faced from attack. And when Atlanta's Rabbi Jacob Rothschild received word that his temple, the largest in Atlanta, had been rocked by a bombing on October 12, 1958, he acknowledged that the violence occurred in part "because I was so obviously identified with the civil rights movement."[45] Of greatest infamy, two White Jewish civil rights workers, Andrew Goodman and Michael (Mickey) Schwerner, and Black non-Jewish activist James Chaney paid the ultimate price in 1964 when they were murdered by Ku Klux Klan members in Mississippi. For the Southern Jewish community's older generation, the lynching of Leo Frank in 1913 remained within their lived memory as well.

Often criticized for their relative silence during the civil rights movement, southern Jews needed to navigate their powerlessness in contrast to their larger Northern ethnoreligious community that boasted of its oversized commitment to the civil rights movement. Liminality, in this instance, forced White Southern Jewish merchants to do all they could to appease White customers while still keeping their stores, and their credit, available to Black shoppers. Southern rabbis faced pressure not to "preach politics from the pulpit" and, as some scholars have argued, tried nevertheless to do so with "quiet voices."[46] Their liminality typified a historical time and place when Jews, who presented as White, still feared prejudice, retaliation, and violence. For this region's postwar Jewish population, the corrupting influence of power, this time from the White Christians around them, posed a sharp, distinct, and serious threat.

While many observers tend to distinguish Southern Jews from their Northern coreligionists when it comes to participation in the civil rights movement, looking again at the history through a lens of Northern Jewish liminality reveals more similarities than differences. Calls for racial reform in the urban North, making headlines a decade after the Southern-focused movement began, positioned Northern White Jewish liberals in the same awkward place as their Southern compatriots, navigating between two opposing social groups as liminal people. In terms of Greenberg's argument, White Jews in the North navigated their newfound power in the midst of communities of color they claimed to support.

When President John F. Kennedy and, later, President Lyndon Baines Johnson called for the creation of affirmative action programs to achieve greater racial justice, most every national Jewish organization supported them. Jewish leaders understood the limits of liberalism. While there were legal equalities achieved with passage of the 1964 Civil Rights Act and electoral power afforded by the Voting Rights Act of 1965, real racial equality still proved far too elusive. Legislation, no matter how hard fought and important, would not be enough to move the racial justice needle, and Jewish leaders knew it. They supported better outreach efforts to marginalized communities with the recognition that centuries of White supremacy required more than the stroke of a pen to solve. The recognition of systemic oppression opened a door for White liminal Jews to enter. Enjoying a larger measure of power and privilege, they succeeded in moving back and forth between White America and those designated by the federal government as minorities and therefore eligible for more aid. With their support of affirmative action, most White American Jews succeeded in expressing power without corruption.[47]

Yet, at the moment when calls for affirmative action led to judicial rulings for strict quotas, almost every national Jewish organization bolted. Here, and in an ironic social justice moment that revealed the limits of Jewish liberalism, White Jews recalled the antisemitic quotas of the early twentieth century as all the proof they needed to defend their anti-quota position. Jewish leaders claimed that such a radical answer to systemic racism only reinforced historic anti-Jewish discrimination. Jews centered their anti-quota argument on their own history of victimization. Government mandated quotas would undermine, it seemed, the very goal it sought to achieve: equity for non-White Americans. In their minds, a consistent social justice approach demanded an unqualified opposition to quotas.

While they did not acknowledge it at the time, Jewish communal opposition to quotas revealed both the corruption of power as well as the White American Jewish move toward the elite side of the liminality continuum. By centering the Jewish place in American society without recognizing the significant Jewish social mobility they enjoyed in the postwar years, Jewish leaders worked against the very racial justice goals they claimed to support. They failed to recognize the malleability of racial status and the Jewish move into Whiteness, power, and privilege. Their newfound lived experience as social elites blinded White Jews to their own complicity in maintaining the racial status quo.

In the 1920s, when Jews faced victimization from restrictive quotas, White elites had adopted their practice as a way to keep the White old guard in power and prevent marginalized communities, people of color, from accessing influence. When Jews faced quota discrimination, elite institutions such as Harvard University were seeking to maintain their White majorities. Jews faced a quota exclusion because they were not considered White at that time and in that place. In the early twentieth century, White-presenting Jews did not enjoy an embrace from entrenched White Christian powerbrokers. Quotas proved antisemitic because the universities and businesses that instituted them considered Jews an inferior ethnoreligious, if not racial, group. At that moment, Jews shared a common experience with Black Americans as well as other racial minority groups who were also prevented from accessing education, housing, and high-quality jobs.

By the 1960s, though, the entire rationale for quotas flipped. Instead of keeping Whites in power at the expense of marginalized racial groups, President Lyndon Baines Johnson's Great Society sought to leverage court-ordered quotas to finally break down systems of White supremacy so that people of color could finally attain their full citizenship rights.

Quotas only emerged when affirmative action failed. If, for example, a police department or fire department maintained its racist practices of refusing to hire applicants of color, city councils or mayors would institute affirmative action programs to create an employment pipeline of qualified minority applicants. In many cases, these efforts succeeded in reversing long-standing racist hiring practices. Johnson's quotas proved a boon to marginalized people who saw them as a rare opportunity to earn placement in historically all-White spaces. When all-White organizations dug in, refusing still to consider or hire a more diverse workforce, judges instituted strict numerical hiring quotas to force compliance. The very goal of the Great Society era quotas contradicted the intent of the early twentieth-century version. President Johnson and his supporters wanted to empower people of color. Mandatory quotas helped achieve that racial justice goal.

Put another way, a self-interested White Christian would have supported quotas in the early twentieth century because they helped them maintain social power. That same person would reverse their position in the Great Society era since White Christians faced pushback from a quota system designed for marginalized communities. A person of color would have adopted the mirror opposite, rejecting the early version of the quotas while embracing the latter approach. Jews, it appears, emerged as the only ethnoracial group that opposed quotas in both historical moments. The social construction of race translated into status as non-White in the early twentieth century and a newfound status as White in the post–World War II era. While Jewish leaders internalized an argument that claimed logical continuity—quotas are bad for the Jews—they missed the deeper truth at play: Jews, as liminal, simply moved from one end of the social strata to the other. While White Jews ended up on the limiting side of quotas in both cases, their read on the Great Society version of the word revealed a myopic racial justice lens.

Emerging from the social protest movements of the 1960s, Jewish leaders as well as journalists and scholars writing about them built an exceptionalist thesis that located Jews as non-White and marginalized at the very time their power and privilege, ironically, enabled such proclamations. Many White American Jews placed themselves at one end of the liminal spectrum when their actual lived experience placed them at the other. They internalized a sense of themselves as different and better than the rest of White America because Jews, more than any other White-presenting group, voted Democratic, supported liberal candidates, and sent volunteers south to fight for racial equality. New understandings of post–World War II American Jewish history undermined these long-held claims of Jews as powerless, marginalized, and uncontested allies with communities of color. With this historical mythmaking, White American Jews stood on social justice quicksand, undermining their very footing, challenging their accepted truths, and presenting a competing narrative of White Jewish social justice activism far less exceptional than most Jews wanted to believe.

Fault lines across American Jewish historical memory and idealistic notions of exceptionalism revealed another important dynamic in our understanding of the Jew's place in America: the existence, import, and relevance of Jews of Color. Black, Latinx, Asian American, and indigenous Jews, while largely absent from organized Jewish life, navigated intersectional identities that ostracized them both as Jews and people of color. Their lived experiences, as both Jewish and people of color, force White Jews to reexamine commonly held assumptions about American Jewish life. The very question "Are quotas good for the Jews?," for example, assumes Jewish Whiteness, since Jews of Color qualified for inclusion in these legal orders. Whiteness mattered, not only in the postwar Jewish move to the elite side of liminality, but also in the assumptions most White Jews internalized, negating the historical causality of their newfound racial status.[48]

In this moment, we see an important reflection of the Jewish community's internal racial divide, its challenge to much of the shared memory of Jews and the civil rights movement, and an antecedent to the racial reckoning that would come with the murder of George Floyd by Minneapolis police in May 2020. By the twenty-first century, most American Jews had achieved power and racial privilege, sharpening the distinction between them and their allies of color in social justice struggles. Could they remain connected to those on the marginalized side of Jewish liminality? While most White Jews believed so, more and more activists of color disagreed. The lived experiences of most White Jews in America differed so much from those suffering racial oppression that they no longer saw eye to eye. White Jews often held to dated definitions of racism that all but demanded one align with the Ku Klux Klan to be considered a racist while activists of color recognized systemic racism and White supremacy, while seeking structural changes that alienated many White Jews.

White Jewish liberalism faced an internal communal test and failed. In the eyes of many grassroots organizers from communities of color, Jews' conferred privilege of Whiteness had already brought the corrupting influence Greenberg referenced. Worse, the arguments articulated by White Jewish leaders failed to acknowledge the impact of the Jewish community's newfound racial supremacy. By claiming continued victimhood, White Jewish leaders could not see the profound social change that had occurred, nor could they fathom the impact it was having on their interracial relationships. White Jewish ascension to power, the inability to factor racial privilege into their public policy positions, and the invention of an exceptionalist narrative for American Jews defined the place of Jews in contemporary American society, even if few would agree or even understand. From a perspective that understood the systemic nature of racism, White Jews swam in a sea of institutional racism and did not know they were wet.

In the wake of Floyd's murder, some White American Jews opened themselves to the possibility that their social justice constructed narrative and exceptionalist historical memory did not match the evidence. They wanted a better understanding of how the racial reckoning revealed a very different consciousness than they possessed. Faced with a new version of Greenberg's test, White Jewish social justice activists, immersing themselves in new understandings of race, racism, and what constituted anti-racist work, searched for morally tolerable options to their newly acknowledged power. They wanted to know what it looks like for White American Jews to hold themselves as exemplars of social justice activism yet also endure charges that they are complicit in and benefit from a larger system of White supremacy. Perhaps postwar Jewish liberalism did not prove to be the panacea it once portended. The optimistic tones of Cold War anti-Communist liberalism did not translate into systemic change in the racial status quo. Regardless of the dramatic legal victories in the civil rights era and the heroic efforts it took to achieve them, long-standing racial hierarchies remained in place half a century later. Maybe Jews' historic commitment to social justice causes led to a corrupting complacency, as White Jews discounted the harmful impact of their own racial power on the nation's marginalized communities.[49]

The lived experiences of Jews of Color and Black Jews in particular center the racial dynamics of Greenberg's thesis. The moment we consider the actual diversity of American Jews, we must reconsider so many of the most basic assumptions about the Jew's place in contemporary American life. For Black Jews, as well as for Latinx, Asian American, and Indigenous Jews in the United States, Greenberg's supposition never came to be. Jews of Color continued to suffer from systemic racist institutions while their White coreligionists enjoyed a rapid rise up the postwar social mobility ladder, especially in the years after 1945.

Greenberg assumes a Jewish movement from powerlessness to power, from marginalized to White. Yet the acculturation of Jews of Color to American society did not follow Greenberg's thesis. Only White-presenting Jews enjoy the ability to move back and forth across the social spectrum, to live a liminal American existence that offers qualified welcome in White elite America. Unsaid, Greenberg's quotation assumes that all Jews are White and can therefore achieve systemic power in American society. In other words, we can argue that the very existence of Jewish liminality mandates Jewish Whiteness. In this equation, Jews of Color face erasure from the American Jewish experience and our understandings of it.

What happens when protection of Jewish access to society's elites translates, in reality, to expressions of White supremacy among Jews themselves? What would it mean if contemporary Jews opened the conversation about the corrupting influence of power to the experiences of their own racially and ethnically diverse population? This would force a centering of racial privilege in our larger historical understanding of the American Jewish experience and the causal factors responsible for White Jewish social mobility. If, as Greenberg argued, power (and, in this case, the privilege that went with it) led to corruption, then the renewed national interest in the police mistreatment of Black Americans demands a look into White Jewish complicity in the systems of racial hierarchy that created and perpetuated these inequities.

This growing White Jewish awareness of racism within Jewish communal spaces inspired many synagogues and Jewish community centers to reflect on their poor treatment of Jews of Color, who constantly faced micro and macro racist aggressions from White Jews demanding that they prove their standing as Jews, clean up messes in the social hall, or go get congregants another helping of Shabbat dinner. Jews of Color told these sorts of harrowing, pain-filled stories of the outright racial prejudice they routinely experienced in places where promises of a warm, welcoming, and holy community appeared on gigantic signs at building entrances. Applying Greenberg's thesis to these moments, we can see how much conventional understandings of Jewish acquisition of power once again erase Jews of Color from the conversation, if not existence. The history of Jews of Color in communal spaces pierced the thin veneer of an American Jewish historical memory that always, and inaccurately, considered White Jews exceptional to the larger systems of racial oppression operating in twenty-first century America. Once heard and embraced, the experiences of Jews of Color undermine the White Jewish exceptionalist thesis.

We can best understand the Jew's place in America by layering three social tensions that challenge conventional thinking about the American Jewish experience, just as they offer opportunities that are, perhaps, unique to Jews. The first, Greenberg's argument connecting the acquisition of power with the inevitability of corruption, animated White Jews through the twentieth and twenty-first centuries, as social acceptance presented unparalleled opportunities and privileges just as it set the stage for Jewish complicity in larger systems of social inequity. White Jews wrestled with the opportunities and challenges of their own social mobility. Second, and related, White Jewish liminality forced a reckoning with the costs and benefits of flipping back and forth from elite America to its marginalized communities. Jews could not find a home in either, even as their ability to move back and forth positioned them well as agents of positive social change. Finally, the experiences of Jews of Color force a new set of questions on the previous two, as White Jews rethink the import of racial privilege in their own American experience and the ways in which their ascension into Whiteness compromised their ability to support their fellow, if diverse, Jews.

Taken together, American Jews across every sort of intersectional identity marker could create a new form of exceptionalism. This time, they wouldn't be different and better than their White Christian counterparts. They would be, instead, the only American ethnoreligious group holding it all. They would understand the dangers of corrupting power in ways that White Christian America never could. They would hold empathy for marginalized communities because they too continue to experience antisemitism at the hands of some in the radical right. As liminal figures, Jews would traverse long-standing social boundaries, speak to each side even as neither side would offer a full embrace, and then translate that ambiguous social status in positive social change. This would create a new, different, and actual form of American Jewish exceptionalism that everyone could celebrate.

NOTES

1. "The Ethics of Jewish Power," Rabbi Irving (Yitz) Greenberg, rabbiirvinggreenberg.com.
2. Phrase Finder, www.phrases.org.uk.
3. Identified here as Black, Latinx, Asian American, and Indigenous.
4. Irving Greenberg, "The Ethics of Jewish Power," in *Contemporary Jewish Ethics and Morality*, ed. Elliot N. Dorff and Louis E. Newman (Oxford: Oxford University Press, 1995), 403.
5. For more on the debate over Jews' reinforcing a system of white supremacy, see the coverage around the decision of Brandeis University Press to reprint my book, *Black Power, Jewish Politics: Reinventing the Alliance in the 1960s*, without its invited new preface. The initial article— Ari Feldman, "Brandeis U. Press and Historian Split Over how to Talk About Jews and White Supremacy," *Forward*, December 20, 2020, forward.com—brought a series of open letters, the first by a group of nine senior scholars in American Jewish history, and then a reply by Brandeis University Press, See, as well, Marc Dollinger, "Forbidden Words: Academic Freedom, Censorship, and University Presses," *Journal of Academic Freedom* (2021), www.aaup.org.
6. Shelly Bradbury, "Unbroken," *Pittsburgh Post-Gazette*, October 27, 2018, newsinteractive.post-gazette.com.
7. Jill Cowan, "What to Know About the Poway Synagogue Shooting," *New York Times*, April 29, 2019, www.nytimes.com.
8. Jessica Harkay, James Hartley and Domingo Ramirez Jr., "Texas Officials Say All Hostages Safe, Out of Colleyville Synagogue; Hostage-Taker Dead," *Fort Worth Star-Telegram*, January 18, 2022, www.star-telegram.com/.
9. Carlo Ginzburg, *The Cheese and the Worms: The Cosmos of a Sixteenth-Century Miller*, rev. ed. (Baltimore, MD: Johns Hopkins University Press, 2013).
10. See Leonard Dinnerstein, *Antisemitism in America* (New York: Oxford University Press, 1994).

11 See, for example, Karen Brodkin, *How Jews Became White Folks and What That Says about Race in America* (New Brunswick, NJ: Rutgers University Press, 1998).
12 Will Herberg, *Protestant Catholic Jew* (Chicago: University of Chicago Press, 1983).
13 "President Donald Trump on Charlottesville: You Had Very Fine People, on Both Sides," CNBC, August 15, 2017, www.youtube.com.
14 "What We Do," Anti-Defamation Law, www.adl.org.
15 The concept of intersectionality, first described by Kimberle Williams Crenshaw in 1989, examines the ways in which Black women face discrimination because of both their gender and racial status. It is, then, the intersection of Blackness and womanhood that creates a deeper form of oppression than either sexism or racism individually. Applied in a broader context, intersectionality assumes that every person possesses multiple identities, from race to class to gender to any other identity a person claims. The various combinations of these identity markers create unique social experiences. See Kimberle Crenshaw, *On Intersectionality*, (New York: New Press, 2022).
16 For more information on Jews of Color, see the Jews of Color Initiative (jewsofcolorinitiative.org) and B'chol Lashon (globaljews.org), which links to several research projects centering Jews of Color.
17 In this more politicized formulation of intersectionality, people of color, regardless of their country of origin, share a common experience of oppression with one another. Rather than a formulation of the ways in which gender and race intersect, according to Crenshaw's original thesis, or the larger understanding of intersectionality as the existence of multiple identity categories within each one of us, this new transnational definition connects oppressed groups around the world in a common struggle.
18 For more on the debate over Jewish exceptionalism, see Rachel Gordan, "The Sin of American Jewish Exceptionalism," *AJS Review* 45 (2021): 282–301; and Tony Michels, "Is America 'Different?' A Critique of American Jewish Exceptionalism," *American Jewish History* 96 (2010): 201–24.
19 For a monograph that argues a Jewish exceptionalist thesis around the issue of Jews and slavery, see Eli Faber, *Jews, Slaves and the Slave Trade: Setting the Record Straight* (New York University Press, 2000).
20 For an excellent scholarly overview of American Jewish history, see the Johns Hopkins University Press series *Jewish People in America*, edited by Henry L. Feingold and published in five volumes in 1995. A single-volume history is Hasia Diner, *A History of the Jews of the United States* (Berkeley: University of California Press, 2006).
21 See, for example, L. Sandy Maisel and Ira N. Forman, eds., *Jews in American Politics* (Lanham, MD: Rowman & Littlefield, 2001).
22 See for example, Jacob Rader Marcus's classic three-volume *The Colonial American Jew, 1492–1776* (Detroit, MI: Wayne State University Press, 1970).
23 See examples in Gary Zola and Marc Dollinger, *American Jewish History: A Primary Source Reader* (Waltham, MA: Brandeis University Press, 2014).

24 See, especially, Morris Raphall, "'The Bible View of Slavery: A Discourse,' a Defense of Slavery by a Northern Rabbi, January 4, 1861," in Zola and Dollinger, *American Jewish History*, 118.
25 For more on Jewish life in colonial America, see Eli Faber, *A Time for Planting: The First Migration, 1654–1820* (Johns Hopkins University Press, 1995). For more on the halfway covenant, see Robert G. Pope, *The Half-Way Covenant: Church Membership in Puritan New England* (Princeton, NJ: Princeton University Press, 1969).
26 See Faber, *Time for Planting*; as well as Zola and Dollinger, *American Jewish History*, chapter 1.
27 See Hasia Diner, *A Time for Gathering: The Second Migration, 1820–1880* (Baltimore, MD: Johns Hopkins University Press, 1995). For an overview of Irish American life in Boston, see Thomas H. O'Connor, *The Boston Irish: A Political History* (Boston: Northeastern University Press, 1995).
28 See Hasia Diner, *Roads Taken: The Great Migrations to the New World and the Peddlers Who Forged the Way* (New Haven, CT: Yale University Press, 2018). Classic work on the subject includes Eli N. Evans, *The Provincials: A Personal History of Jews in the South* (Chapel Hill:University of North Carolina Press, 2005). Robert N. Rosen covers Civil War–era Southern Jews in *The Jewish Confederates* (Columbia:University of South Carolina Press, 2021).
29 See Ava Kahn, *Jewish Voices of the California Gold Rush: A Documentary History, 1849–1880* (Detroit, MI: Wayne State University Press, 2002); Ellen Eisenberg, Ava Kahn, and William Toll, *Jews of the Pacific Coast: Reinventing Community on America's Edge* (Seattle: University of Washington Press, 2010); and Marc Dollinger and Ava Kahn, *California Jews* (Waltham, MA: Brandeis University Press, 2011).
30 Joe Fitzgerald Rodriguez, "New Name for Julius Kahn Park to Be Unveiled," *San Francisco Examiner*, August 13, 2019, www.sfexaminer.com.
31 "Julius Rosenwald Was Not a Hero" *HistPhil*, June 30, 2017, histphil.org.
32 See Gerald Sorin, *A Time for Building: The Third Migration, 1880–1920* (Baltimore, MD: Johns Hopkins University Press, 1995). An excellent transnational study is Rebecca Kobrin, *Jewish Bialystok and Its Diaspora* (Bloomington: Indiana University Press, 2010).
33 See Hasia R. Diner, *Lower East Side Memories: A Jewish Place in America* (Princeton, NJ: Princeton University Press, 2000).
34 William Z. Ripley, *The Races of Europe: A Sociological Study* (New York: D. Appleton, 1899).
35 Madison Grant, *The Passing of the Great Race or The Racial Basis of European History*, rev. ed. (New York: Charles Scribner's Sons, 1918). See also Edwin Black's *War against the Weak: Eugenics and America's Campaign to Create a Master Race* (Washington, DC: Dialog, 2012).
36 See Gil Ribak, "'The Jew Usually Left Those Crimes to Esau': The Jewish Responses to Accusations about Jewish Criminality in New York, 1908–1913," *AJS*

Review 38 (2014): 1–28. See also Mia Brett, "'Ten Thousand Bigamists In New York': The Criminalization of Jewish Immigrants Using White Slavery Panics," Gotham Center For New York City History, October 27, 2020, www.gothamcenter.org.

37 "The Jews and General Bingham," *New York Times*, September 16, 1908, as quoted in Brett, "Ten Thousand Bigamists."
38 See Max Wallace, *The American Axis: Henry Ford, Charles Lindbergh, and the Rise of the Third Reich* (New York: St. Martin's, 2003); and Donald Warren, *Radio Priest: Charles Coughlin, the Father of Hate Radio* (New York: Free Press, 1996).
39 For a great history of second-generation eastern European Jewish immigrants in Brooklyn, New York, read Deborah Dash Moore's classic *At Home in America: Second Generation New York Jews* (New York: Columbia University Press, 1981).
40 Brodkin, *How Jews Became White Folks*.
41 Deborah Dash Moore, *GI Jews: How World War II Changed a Generation* (Cambridge, MA: Belknap Press of Harvard University Press, 2004).
42 See Marc Dollinger, *Quest for Inclusion: Jews and Liberalism in Modern America* (Princeton, NJ: Princeton University Press, 2000), 184.
43 See Dollinger, *Quest for Inclusion*, 184.
44 Dollinger, 169.
45 Dollinger, 167.
46 See, for example, Mark K. Bauman and Berkley Kalin, *The Quiet Voices: Southern Rabbis and Black Civil Rights, 1880s to 1990s* (Tuscaloosa: University of Alabama Press, 1997).
47 For more, see Dollinger, *Quest for Inclusion*, chapter 8.
48 See, especially, Tobin Belzer, Tory Brundage, Vincent Calvetti, Gage Gorsky, Ari Y. Kelman, and Dalya Perez, eds., *Beyond the Count: Perspectives and Lived Experiences of Jews of Color*, jewsofcolorinitiative.org.
49 For more on how white Jewish liberals reacted to the national reckoning on race, see Yonat Shimron, "He Claimed White Jews Gained from White Supremacy. Now He's More Popular than Ever," Religion News Service, March 12, 2021, religionnews.com.

7

The Changing American Jewish Relationship with Israel

DOV WAXMAN

Introduction

It is widely believed, especially among non-Jews, that American Jews are staunch supporters of Israel. This belief, which often shapes public perceptions and media coverage of the American Jewish community, is understandable, considering how vocal many major American Jewish organizations are in expressing their support for Israel. With prominent groups like the Conference of Presidents of Major American Jewish Organizations frequently expressing their solidarity with Israel and publicly backing the policies and actions of Israeli governments, it is easy to assume that they represent the views of the American Jewish community as a whole and speak on its behalf. Such an assumption might have been true in the past, but nowadays there is a growing gap between the positions that organizations in the so-called American Jewish establishment (which includes the Conference of Presidents, the American Jewish Committee, the Anti-Defamation League, and local Jewish Federations, among others) publicly take in support for Israel and the views and attitudes of American Jews in general. Despite the regular public affirmations of support for Israel made by mainstream Jewish organizations in the United States, behind the scenes there is a lot more discord about Israel within the American Jewish community today.

The American Jewish community's relationship with Israel has become much more ambivalent than it may appear to the casual observer. Although most American Jews still feel connected to Israel and still care about Israel, they are becoming more disillusioned with it and more critical of it.[1] They are now less willing to support Israel's policies and practices, especially regarding Palestinians. In fact, growing numbers of

American Jews are speaking out, criticizing and protesting these policies and practices, and trying to change them. By doing so, they are challenging the terms of the traditional American Jewish relationship with Israel, according to which American Jews were expected to provide political and financial support to Israel and refrain from criticizing it, at least publicly. Hence, the old relationship between American Jews and Israel, marked by deference to Israeli governments and acquiescence with Israeli policies, has become anachronistic.

The central thesis of this chapter, therefore, is that a profound change is taking place in the American Jewish relationship with Israel.[2] The era of unquestioning, uncritical, and unconditional American Jewish support for Israel is over. But this is not because American Jews no longer care about Israel. There is an enduring emotional attachment to Israel, but weakening political support, particularly regarding the Israeli-Palestinian conflict. Support for Israel's actions, including military actions, is no longer automatic or axiomatic. This split between emotional attachment to Israel and political support for its policies and actions is fundamentally reshaping the relationship between American Jews and Israel. Thus, just as American Jewry is changing demographically, economically, religiously, and culturally—as extensively elaborated in the other chapters in this volume—its relationship with Israel is also changing, probably permanently.

The Rise of "Israelolatry"

Before discussing how the American Jewish relationship with Israel is changing, it is first necessary to understand what this relationship was like in the past, particularly during the 1960s and 1970s, when American Jewish support for Israel was generally unconditional and unequivocal. Prior to this era, Israel was actually of little interest and concern to most American Jews during the early years of Israeli statehood from 1948 to 1967. That was a time of upward mobility, suburbanization, and assimilation for American Jews, and the needs of a foreign country thousands of miles away were a lot less pressing to them than their own needs for prosperity, security, and belonging—especially as American Jews still frequently faced domestic discrimination and antisemitism. In the 1950s and early 1960s, most American Jews were simply preoccupied with their own immediate concerns and did not think about Israel very much. They were also concerned about being accused of having "dual loyalties," a concern that was heightened by the prevailing anti-Communist sentiment in the early Cold War period.[3]

More than any other event in Israeli history, the Six-Day War of June 1967 transformed the American Jewish relationship with Israel.[4] Having been largely absent from American Jewish consciousness until 1967, Israel suddenly consumed the thoughts and feelings of American Jewry in the weeks of mounting tension and dread preceding the war and in its euphoric aftermath. The widespread fear of a second Holocaust prior to the war, followed by the relief and jubilation felt after Israel's swift and stunning victory, led to a spontaneous outpouring of support for Israel from American Jews. Lucy Dawidowicz's description at the time captures the collective mood of American Jewry in the wake of the 1967 war: "Israel's military victory brought elation and pride, but, even more, release from tension, gratitude, a sense of deliverance. Of course the pride was one of being victorious, a new kind of pride in being Jewish, in the aura that radiated from General Moshe Dayan, his ruggedness, vigor, determination. Many Jews took pride in the changed image of the Jew, no longer seen as victim or the historic typification of a persecuted people."[5]

In the decade following the 1967 war, support for Israel came to dominate American Jewish public life and politics. (It also became an important part of congregational life and Jewish education.)[6] Indeed, during a time of rapid assimilation and diminishing religious devotion, support for Israel became the one thing that almost all American Jews had in common. As Steven Rosenthal writes, "Israel became the primary focus of Jewish emotion and activity, and its actions became almost sacrosanct in the eyes of most American Jews."[7] Not only was there a huge surge in fundraising and political advocacy for Israel (and a brief surge in emigration to Israel), but also Israel became an "object of secular veneration" for many American Jews,[8] the centerpiece of what Jonathan Woocher termed "the new civil religion of American Jews."[9] So intense was the devotion to Israel among American Jews during this time that it was characterized by Daniel Elazar as "Israelolatry," implying that it was a kind of idolatry.[10] This Israelolatry was marked by unequivocal popular support for Israel, near-total unanimity of opinion concerning the

Arab-Israeli conflict (according to which Israel was the innocent victim of Arab animosity and aggression), and a massive grassroots mobilization on Israel's behalf. As pro-Israelism came to be seen as an essential component of American Jewish identity, and unwavering support for Israel came to occupy a central place in organized Jewish communal life, being a "good Jew" entailed "uncritically supporting, promoting, and defending the Israeli government."[11] Questioning the actions and policies of Israeli governments was generally frowned upon, and criticizing them, especially in public, was forbidden. For a Jew to criticize Israel, especially before a gentile audience, was widely considered to be an act of disloyalty, even heresy. As Rabbi Arthur Hertzberg wrote in 1979: "One can no longer be excommunicated in Modern America for not believing in God, for living totally outside of the tradition, or even for marrying out. Instead, a new heresy has now emerged to mark the boundaries of legitimate Jewish identity, the heresy of opposition to Israel and Zionism."[12] Thus, while there were always some critical voices within the Jewish community, dissent was largely stifled.[13] The vast majority of American Jews abided by the communal prohibition and refrained from any public criticism of Israel. Even in private, criticism was frowned upon because the prevailing belief was that only Israelis had the right to criticize their government, since it was their lives that were at risk.

It was not only the prevailing communal norm governing Jewish public discourse regarding Israel that limited the willingness of American Jews to publicly question and challenge Israel's policies and actions. Most American Jews also adopted—with the encouragement of mainstream American Jewish organizations and institutions—a deferential, even subservient, attitude toward Israeli governments, uncritically accepting and endorsing whatever they did. Instead of questioning or challenging Israeli government policies and actions, most American Jews "saw their roles as providing automatic financial and political support for whatever goals or policies the Jewish state chose to pursue."[14] The uncritical and deferential attitude to Israel held by most American Jews allowed Israeli governments to take American Jewish support for granted, confident in the knowledge that American Jews would overwhelmingly give their backing to whatever they did. As one scholar observed, "Whatever the issue, Israel could count on the enthusiastic, unified support of American Jews almost without exception."[15]

The outpouring of American Jewish emotional, political, and financial support for Israel in the decade from 1967 to 1977 was partly the result of a series of dramatic events involving Israel that occurred over the course of the decade, including three wars (the 1967 war, the War of Attrition with Egypt from 1969 to 1971, and the Yom Kippur War in October 1973); numerous high-profile terrorist attacks (most famously, the seizure and subsequent murder of Israeli athletes at the Munich Olympic games in 1972, and the Entebbe hijacking and rescue in 1976); and the passage of a resolution in the United Nations in 1975 describing Zionism as racism. But the surge of American Jewish support for Israel after 1967 was also the result of a confluence of longer-term processes and developments within the American Jewish community and in American society at large, particularly the growing consciousness of the Holocaust and the rise of identity politics. It was the convergence of Holocaust consciousness and identity politics in the United States, as much as events directly concerning Israel, that turned the American Jewish community from being largely disinterested in Israel to passionately devoted to it.

As the Holocaust became increasingly significant for American Jews, Israel became increasingly important to them.[16] For many, if not most, American Jews, the Holocaust was seen as providing incontestable proof of the need for a Jewish state. Without a state of their own to protect them, European Jewry was powerless in the face of Hitler's genocidal antisemitism. With a state of their own, however, Jews would never again be so weak and defenseless. This became (and still is) the major, and certainly most important, rationale for Israel's existence in the minds of American Jews. Hence, the Holocaust became the definitive reason for American Jews to support Israel. The Holocaust also became discursively linked to Israel in the "Holocaust to rebirth" narrative that became increasingly popular among American Jews. This narrative links the Holocaust and the creation of the State of Israel, depicting the latter as representing the revival (or redemption, in more religious terms) of the Jewish people after its near destruction.[17] The Jewish state came to symbolize the Jewish people, and, as such, its survival was implicitly equated with Jewish survival. Concern for Jewish survival, then, was expressed through supporting Israel.

American Jewish support for Israel intensified, therefore, as consciousness of the Holocaust grew, and it became increasingly symbolically and psychologically associated with Israel. Whether to make amends for their inability to save European Jews, to banish their feeling of impotence during the Holocaust, or to prevent another Holocaust, the ardent pro-Israel activism of many American Jews in the late 1960s and 1970s was motivated in large part by their growing Holocaust consciousness.

Another important development that promoted American Jewish pro-Israel activism in the 1970s was the rise of identity politics in the United States.[18] During an era when women, African Americans, Native Americans, gays and lesbians, and a host of other social groups publicly affirmed and celebrated their difference, it also became acceptable, even fashionable, for Jews to be openly Jewish and publicly affirm their support for Israel. Unlike in the past when American Jews were worried that overt displays of support for Israel might provoke accusations of "dual loyalty," by the 1970s more and more of them felt comfortable and confident about expressing their support for Israel and doing so became a manifestation of their ethnic pride. In this sense, pro-Israel activism became for many American Jews, especially younger ones, what feminism was for women or the Black Power movement was for African Americans—a proud, even defiant, assertion of identity.[19] Moreover, as with the feminist and Black Power movements, supporting Israel gave American Jews a sense of empowerment as well as pride. This new feeling of Jewish pride and power, which arose after 1967, was also a repudiation of the "victim mentality" that diaspora Jews had long been accused of (especially by Zionists) and that allegedly reached its apogee during the Holocaust.[20] Jews would no longer be passive, weak, and helpless victims; instead they would actively and loudly stand up for themselves and for the Jewish state.

For many young American Jews in this period, supporting Israel was also wholly in accordance with their own liberal and leftwing political values and ideals. From afar, they saw Israel as an egalitarian, progressive, and secular society, ruled by Labor governments, with female soldiers and socialist kibbutzim. It appeared to be a country committed to social democracy, to economic and gender equality, and, above all, to peace. As such, it was easy to support, even idolize. Indeed, the popular image of Israel as a progressive's utopia was so alluring to some idealistic young American Jews (and other young Jews in the diaspora) that they went there to work on kibbutzim, join the army, and even live in new Jewish settlements that were being established in the West Bank.[21]

The End of "Israel, Right or Wrong"

American Jews fell in love with Israel during the 1960s and early 1970s, but by the end of the 1970s and throughout the 1980s, the romance was wearing off. "The American Jewish love affair with Israel" was short lived, lasting only about ten years.[22] What followed it, since the late 1970s, was not so much disaffection, but disillusionment among growing numbers of American Jews. Part of the reason for this shift in American Jewish attitudes was that Israel changed in ways that disappointed, disturbed, and even angered many secular, liberal American Jews. Instead of being the secular, social-democratic, egalitarian, idealistic, and peace-seeking country that American Jews once perceived from afar (whether accurately or not), a different, altogether less attractive, Israel appeared from the late 1970s onward. It was more right-wing, more religious, more intolerant, more unequal, and more aggressive and expansionist than the Israel that American Jews had fallen in love with.

This "new" Israel first emerged with the surprise victory of the right-wing Likud party led by Menachem Begin in the 1977 general election. Likud's rise to power, after almost three decades of uninterrupted Mapai/Labor party rule, resulted in significant changes in Israeli government policies toward the Palestinians and the territories that Israel had occupied since the 1967 war. Having long been accustomed to Labor-led governments in Israel with whom they felt a greater affinity, American Jews became increasingly uncomfortable with the hawkish, hardline approach to Israel's conflict with the Palestinians and Arab states taken by the governments of Menachem Begin and his Likud successor Yitzhak Shamir.[23] Of particular concern to American Jews was Likud's settlement policy in the West Bank and Gaza Strip, which seemed aimed at preventing the possibility of any kind of territorial compromise in the future.[24] On July 2, 1980, for instance, fifty-six prominent American

Jews (including three former chairmen of the Conference of Presidents) issued a public statement entitled "Our Way Is Not Theirs," which criticized the Begin government's settlement policy and called for a territorial compromise.[25]

A turning point in American Jewish attitudes to Israel came following Israel's invasion of Lebanon in June, 1982. At first, most American Jews supported the war in Lebanon, much as they had supported Israel's previous wars.[26] But this quickly changed in the wake of the massacre of hundreds of Palestinian civilians in the Sabra and Shatila refugee camps in Beirut by Israel's Lebanese Christian Phalangist allies on September 16–17, 1982.[27] Although Israeli soldiers did not carry out the massacre, most American Jews considered Israel to be at least partially responsible for it (as did most Israelis).[28] The Sabra and Shatila massacre was a watershed in American Jewish attitudes to Israel, as it undermined their idealized image of the country and their long-standing belief that Israel's wars were always just and its wartime conduct morally pure.[29] In response, American Jewish criticism of Israel grew, and with it support for Israeli and American Jewish groups (such as Peace Now and its newly established American offshoot, American Friends of Peace Now) that advocated for major changes in Israeli policies in the Arab-Israeli conflict.[30]

While there was a public outcry from American Jews in reaction to the Sabra and Shatila massacre, the first Palestinian Intifada, which began in December 1987 and lasted until 1991, generated an unprecedented amount of American Jewish criticism of Israel.[31] The mass uprising of Palestinian civilians in the Occupied Territories against Israeli rule and the Israeli army's harsh crackdown in response to it were deeply unsettling for American Jews accustomed to regarding Israel as the innocent victim in the Arab-Israeli conflict. Now that they were being regularly confronted with shocking images of Israeli soldiers shooting and beating Palestinian protestors (including women and children), many American Jews were reluctantly forced to recognize that their view of the conflict and their perception of Israel were inaccurate at best—Israel was not entirely blameless. The Israel that regularly appeared on American television screens during the First Intifada was certainly not the mythic Israel of the American Jewish collective imagination. Thus, the First Intifada further undermined the idealized image of Israel held by American Jews and led to growing disillusionment with Israel among more liberal and progressive Jews.

While Israeli policies and actions were partly responsible for the growing disillusionment with Israel that American Jews experienced in the 1980s, they were not solely responsible for it. An important change that occurred in the nature of the Arab-Israeli conflict also contributed to the process of American Jewish disillusionment with Israel. After Israel's landmark peace treaty with Egypt in 1979, the conflict became largely an Israeli-Palestinian one and less of a conflict between Israel and the Arab states surrounding it. As the Arab-Israeli conflict subsided and the Israeli-Palestinian conflict took center stage, popular perceptions of Israel changed. It was no longer seen as David against the Arab Goliath; instead, in a role reversal, Israel became Goliath and the Palestinians became David—being widely perceived as the weaker, more vulnerable party in the conflict. In stark contrast to the way in which Israel was once perceived as embattled and heroic, from the 1980s onward Israel was increasingly perceived as a dominant military power, an oppressor of Palestinians, and an illegal occupier of their territories. This new, negative image of Israel gained international prominence during the first Intifada and profoundly affected how many American Jews thought of Israel, especially younger ones who had no memory of the country before the 1980s.

In addition to changes in Israel and changes in the Arab-Israeli conflict, changes involving American Jews themselves, specifically their level of engagement with Israel and their knowledge about it, have also affected American Jewish attitudes toward Israel over time. Put simply, more American Jews have been visiting Israel, learning about Israel, and paying closer attention to what's happening there than in the past, when American Jews knew very little about Israeli history, politics, society, and culture.[32] As a result, there is now greater familiarity with Israel and more knowledge about it among American Jews, or at least a significant minority of them, than ever before. To be sure, many American Jews remain quite ignorant about Israel, but more and more of them are gaining some knowledge of Israeli politics and society due to extensive foreign news reporting about Israel and the easy accessibility of English-language versions of major Israeli newspapers on the internet (notably

Ha'aretz, *Yedioth Ahronot*, *Israel Hayom*, and the *Jerusalem Post*).³³ Hence, as American Jews have become more able to regularly read about issues, problems, and debates in Israel, they have gradually become better informed—in a national survey conducted in 2000–2001, 86 percent of American Jews said that they were very or somewhat familiar with the "social and political situation in Israel."³⁴ American Jews are also learning more about Israel by actually going there. There has been a significant increase in travel to Israel, with the number of American Jews who have visited the country at least once rising from just 14 percent in 1970, to 27 percent in 1990, to 35 percent in 2000, to 45 percent in 2020.³⁵

As American Jews read about Israel more often, travel there more, and learn more about it, their views of the country inevitably change—becoming less abstract and idealized, and more realistic.³⁶ And as American Jews have gotten to know Israel better, they have become more critical of those aspects of Israel that conflict with their own values and beliefs. This is especially true for younger American Jews (those between the ages of eighteen and thirty-five, who make up about one-quarter of the total American Jewish population), whose "generational memory" significantly differs from those of older American Jews.³⁷ They have no memory of Israel's early years, of the 1967 and 1973 wars, nor even of the Oslo peace process in the 1990s. Instead, they have grown up during the years of the Second Intifada and Israel's repeated wars with Hamas, and they have only really known center-right or right-wing Israeli governments whose policies toward the Palestinians have often been hawkish and hardline (with the partial exception of the Olmert government from 2006 to 2009). Young American Jews, therefore, tend to look at Israel through a very different lens. Growing up with Israel as a military power and an occupier has given younger American Jews a very different image of the country and its people. While baby boomers may fondly recall images of smiling, suntanned *kibbutznikim* dancing the hora, many younger Jews have images in their minds of stern-faced soldiers manning military checkpoints in the West Bank. Young American Jews are also more inclined to see Israel as powerful, not weak and endangered, and thus less in need of their absolute support.³⁸ Their support for Israel, therefore, is more tentative and less automatic.³⁹ In fact, many young American Jews today believe that Israel deserves their criticism, not their support.⁴⁰ A significant number are even critical of their own government's support for Israel—with four in ten (37 percent) of American Jews aged eighteen to twenty-nine saying in a 2020 survey that the United States supports Israel too much.[41]

Attachment to Israel

Despite the predictions of many experts, growing disillusionment with Israel among American Jews has not yet led to growing alienation from Israel. Since the 1980s, it has often been claimed that American Jews, especially younger ones, were becoming less attached to Israel, and that the American Jewish community and Israel were slowly drifting apart, becoming ever more distant and estranged from each other.[42] This claim has provoked a lot of agonizing within the organized Jewish community.[43] Dozens of seminars, symposia, surveys, and studies have been sponsored by American Jewish organizations addressing the "problem" of American Jewish "distancing" from Israel and trying to answer the questions of whether it is happening, why it is happening, and what can possibly be done to stop it. The allegedly weak commitment of young American Jews to Israel has been the focus of particular concern.[44]

The persistent worry within the American Jewish community for more than two decades about distancing from Israel has, so far at least, been completely unfounded.[45] In survey after survey, around two-thirds of American Jews express an attachment to Israel, and this figure has been roughly the same for the past two decades.[46] Although levels of American Jewish attachment to Israel have fluctuated slightly from year to year, overall, attachment to Israel has been remarkably stable.[47] However much American Jews may have been dismayed by the policies of certain Israeli governments and disturbed by some of their actions, they did not distance themselves from Israel. In fact, American Jews have remained steadfastly attached to Israel, even as they have become more widely critical of its policies.[48]

Despite their disillusionment with Israel and their disagreements with Israeli governments (particularly Likud-led governments), American Jews have not turned away from Israel and become indifferent toward it. This is because caring about Israel does not necessarily mean agreeing with Israeli policies or liking particular Israeli governments. It is thus important to distinguish between emotional attachment to Israel and political support for Israeli governments. Being emotionally distant from Israel entails being apathetic about it—not thinking about it or caring about it. This is very different from being opposed to Israeli government policies, which involves thinking about Israel and, at least for most Jewish critics of Israel's policies, caring about Israel. One can be strongly opposed to Israel's policies and actions, therefore, but still feel strongly attached to the country.[49]

Rather than growing more disconnected from Israel, as many have claimed, American Jews have actually become more actively involved with Israel over the past two decades. They are more engaged with Israel than previous generations whose connection with Israel was largely limited to donating money every year to local American Jewish Federations to pass on to Israel.[50] The big change that is taking place in the American Jewish relationship with Israel is not that American Jews are disengaging from it, but that they are critically engaging with Israel. There is much more public questioning and heated debate about Israel in the American Jewish community today than in the past. This is a manifestation of critical engagement with Israel, not alienation from it. Jack Wertheimer puts it well: "Debate over Israeli policies is a form of engagement and participation, if only from afar. Public silence or conformity in regard to Israel may signal indifference and apathy."[51] As American Jews' critical engagement with Israel has increased, so too has their willingness to challenge those aspects of Israel that they find objectionable (such as its settlement building in the West Bank, its treatment of its Arab citizens, and its ultra-Orthodox-dominated religious establishment). Thus, while American Jews remain emotionally invested in Israel, growing numbers of them have become more critical of its policies and more outspoken in their criticism. Their criticism is not generally driven by hostility to Israel, as it is sometimes depicted to be, but rather by genuine concern for Israel. And as the traditional norm against Jews publicly criticizing Israel has gradually eroded, it is becoming increasingly acceptable, if still controversial, for Jews to openly question, debate, and challenge Israeli government policies and practices. In particular, there is now frequent American Jewish criticism of Israel's occupation of the West Bank, its settlement building, its military conduct, and its treatment of Palestinians.[52] But it is not only liberal and left-wing American Jews who publicly criticize Israel. Right-wing American Jews have been equally vociferous in their criticisms of Israeli governments, albeit generally for very different reasons.[53]

What accounts for this proliferation of dissent is not only greater opposition among American Jews (on both the left and the right) to Israeli government policies, but also a growing sense of assertiveness vis-à-vis Israel. American Jews today are less deferential toward Israeli governments, and more inclined to form their own opinions about what Israel should or shouldn't do.[54] They are also more willing to loudly voice these opinions, believing that they have the right and even the obligation to do so. As Rabbi Arthur Hertzberg wrote during the Second Intifada: "We who love Israel have an obligation to say what we believe. We have for a century or more helped and supported the Zionist endeavor in the state of Israel. We have long lived with the notion that Israeli governments, from right to left, have tried to inculcate in us—that they determine policy, and we are privileged to say amen on cue. This nonsense is now bankrupt."[55] In line with this more assertive attitude, American Jews are no longer prepared to quiescently accept whatever Israeli governments do and to simply send their money to Israel and lobby on its behalf. Instead, they now want to have a bigger say in Israel's future. This greater assertiveness toward Israel is ultimately the product of deeper changes in the collective psychology of American Jews. American Jewry's economic success, political power, and cultural vitality has imbued American Jews with confidence and pride. As such, they are not in the least ashamed of or apologetic about living in the "diaspora" (if, in fact, they see themselves as living in diaspora at all), and they feel that they are completely equal, not inferior, to Jews in Israel.[56] It is from this vantage point that many American Jews now feel entitled to criticize Israel, whereas previous generations did not.

American Jews' relationship with Israel is profoundly changing, therefore, but not in the way that many people believe. Most American Jews still fundamentally support Israel in the sense of wanting it to exist and caring about its welfare and safety. What is different today is not the level of American Jewish support for Israel, but rather its mode of expression—it has become more critical than it was in the past, and it is no longer expressed politically simply through knee-jerk support for whatever Israeli governments do. While supporting Israel continues to be at the top of the American Jewish political agenda, it is no longer widely accepted among American Jews that to be "pro-Israel" requires supporting Israeli governments or that criticizing them is necessarily "anti-Israel."[57] Fewer American Jews are now willing to provide blanket support for Israeli policies and actions, and many now express their support for Israel by opposing, and even lobbying against, the policies of Israeli governments (as demonstrated, for example, by the rise of the liberal "pro-Israel, pro-peace" lobbying group J Street). Consequently, Israeli governments can no longer count on American Jewish political support in the way that they once did.

There is, however, one subset of American Jewry that remains staunchly supportive of Israel and its governments (at least, that is, if they are right-wing governments)—Orthodox Jews, who currently make up 9 percent of the American Jewish population (this figure includes ultra-Orthodox and modern Orthodox Jews).[58] Although Orthodox Jews are just a small minority in the American Jewish community, they are often very vocal and politically mobilized, especially when it comes to issues concerning Israel. They are also disproportionately represented in the organized American Jewish community. Orthodox American Jews tend to be more emotionally attached to Israel than non-Orthodox Jews,[59] and, on most matters concerning Israel, they tend to have very different opinions than non-Orthodox American Jews (the different views of Orthodox and non-Orthodox Jews on issues concerning Israel, and particularly the Israeli-Palestinian conflict, are just one manifestation of a broader political and sociocultural divide between them.)[60] Orthodox American Jews, for instance, are much more hawkish in their views regarding the Israeli-Palestinian conflict. Like their counterparts in Israel, Orthodox American Jews are much more likely than non-Orthodox Jews to oppose Palestinian statehood and any dismantling of Jewish settlements in the West Bank, and they are much less supportive of Israeli territorial compromise with the Palestinians in general than are other American Jews.[61] Hence, in recent years, during which successive right-wing governments have ruled Israel, Orthodox American Jews have been much more supportive of Israeli government policies and actions than non-Orthodox American Jews. While the latter have become increasingly critical of Israeli governments and were highly skeptical of the willingness of Benjamin Netanyahu's governments to make peace with the Palestinians, Orthodox

Jews have staunchly defended Israeli governments and strongly backed Netanyahu's governments in particular.[62] They also enthusiastically supported then–U.S. president Donald Trump, who was deeply unpopular among non-Orthodox American Jews.[63]

Although there has not yet been the feared decline in Jewish attachment to Israel, current trends among non-Orthodox American Jews—particularly the gradual erosion of the ethnic dimension of Jewish identity, the greater emphasis upon Judaism and Jewish identity as a personal choice and source of meaning, and the disengagement of young Jews from Jewish establishment organizations that have played a key role in encouraging American Jewish support for Israel—all suggest that their attachment to Israel is likely to decline in the future (despite the provision of free trips to Israel for young Jewish adults). Above all, the steadily growing secularism of non-Orthodox Jews portends a long-term erosion in their emotional connection to Israel because the more secular Jews are, the less attached they are to Israel. Or, to put it another way, the less important being Jewish is to them, the less important Israel is to them. If non-Orthodox Jews do become increasingly detached from Israel, then Orthodox Jews are almost certain to remain strongly attached. This is bound to have implications for American Jewish support for Israel in the future. Supporting Israel could become merely an Orthodox cause, not one that unites most American Jews. And if Israeli politics and society moves further to the right and the Israeli-Palestinian conflict remains unresolved—as looks likely—then American Jewish criticism of Israeli policies will continue and probably intensify, and growing numbers of non-Orthodox American Jews may well become alienated from Israel and emotionally disengage from it. Ultimately, American Jewish support for Israel, which has historically been so valuable for Israel, might eventually weaken altogether. But, for now, the majority of American Jews continue to support Israel, if not its government, as was most evident in the wake of the horrific attack that Hamas militants carried out in southern Israel on October 7, 2023, during which 1,100 Israelis were brutally killed and over 240 abducted and held captive in the Gaza Strip. The outpouring of grief and the countless expressions of solidarity with Israelis by large numbers of American Jews, young and old, Orthodox and non-Orthodox, testified to the enduring sense of connection that most American Jews feel toward Israel and Israelis, despite the dismay many feel about the direction that the country is going in under Prime Minister Netanyahu's leadership.[64]

NOTES

1. In a large survey of American Jews conducted by the Pew Research Center in 2020, 45 percent of respondents said that caring about Israel is "essential" to what being Jewish means, and a further 37 percent said it is "important, but not essential." Only 16 percent of U.S. Jewish adults said that caring about Israel is "not important" to their Jewish identity. Pew Research Center, "Jewish Americans in 2020," May 2021, www.pewforum.org.
2. For a full elaboration of this change and its implications, see Dov Waxman, *Trouble in the Tribe: The American Jewish Conflict over Israel* (Princeton, NJ: Princeton University Press, 2016).
3. The concern about being accused of having "dual loyalties" may have inhibited American Jews from engaging in political advocacy for Israel. Yossi Shain, *Kinship and Diasporas in International Affairs* (Ann Arbor: University of Michigan Press, 2008), 55.
4. Although most scholars of American Jewry regard the 1967 war as a watershed event in American Jewish relations with Israel, not all scholars share this view. See, for instance, Chaim Waxman, "The Limited Impact of the Six-Day War on American Jews," in Eli Lederhendler, ed., *The Six-Day War and World Jewry* (Bethesda: University Press of Maryland, 2000), 99–116.
5. Lucy Dawidowicz, "American Public Opinion," in *American Jewish Year Book 1968*, ed. Morris Fine and Milton Himmelfarb (New York: American Jewish Committee, 1968), 205.
6. Walter Ackerman, "Israel in American Jewish Education," in *Envisioning Israel: The Changing Ideals and Images of North American Jews*, ed. Allon Gal (Detroit, MI: Wayne State University Press, 1996), 173–90.
7. Steven T. Rosenthal, *Irreconcilable Differences? The Waning of the American Jewish Love Affair with Israel* (Hanover, NH: Brandeis University Press, 2001), 33.
8. Rosenthal, *Irreconcilable Differences?*, xv.
9. Jonathan Woocher, *Sacred Survival: The Civil Religion of American Jews* (Bloomington: Indiana University Press, 1986).
10. Daniel J. Elazar, *Community and Polity: The Organizational Dynamics of American Jewry* (Philadelphia: Jewish Publication Society, 1995), 107. In a similar vein, Rosenthal writes that "worship of Israel became the supreme basis of American Jewish identity" after 1967 (Rosenthal, *Irreconcilable Differences?*, 33).
11. Marla Brettschneider, *Cornerstones of Peace: Jewish Identity Politics and Democratic Theory* (New Brunswick, NJ: Rutgers University Press, 1996), 1.
12. Quoted in Laurence J. Silberstein, "American Jewry's Identification with Israel Problems and Prospects," in *The Wiley-Blackwell History of Jews and Judaism*, ed. Alan T. Levenson (Oxford: Wiley-Blackwell, 2012), 619.

13 Geoffrey Levin, *Our Palestine Question: Israel and American Jewish Dissent, 1948–1978* (New Haven, CT: Yale University Press, 2023).
14 Rosenthal, *Irreconcilable Differences?*, 1.
15 Rosenthal, xiii.
16 Lynn Rapaport, "The Holocaust in American Jewish Life," in *The Cambridge Companion to American Judaism*, ed. Dana Evan Kaplan (New York: Cambridge University Press, 1005), 187–208.
17 This narrative continues to underpin the annual "March of the Living" in which Jewish teenagers from around the world visit the notorious Nazi concentration and death camp Auschwitz-Birkenau and then Israel. The fact that the trip ends in Israel accords with the "Holocaust to rebirth" narrative and evokes the belief that the Jewish state's existence now ensures that Jews are no longer defenseless.
18 Deborah Dash Moore, "Introduction," in *American Jewish Identity Politics*, ed. Deborah D. Moore (Ann Arbor: University of Michigan Press, 2009), 10–29.
19 The increasingly popular campaign to free Soviet Jewry also fulfilled this purpose for American Jews during this time. Shaul Kelner, "Ritualized Protest and Redemptive Politics: Cultural Consequences of the American Mobilization to Free Soviet Jewry," *Jewish Social Studies* 14, no. 3 (Spring–Summer, 2008): 1–37.
20 Michael E. Staub, "Holocaust Consciousness and American Jewish Politics," in *The Columbia History of Jews and Judaism in American*, ed. Marc Lee Raphael (New York: Columbia University Press, 2008), 326.
21 Sara Hirschhorn, *City on a Hilltop: American Jews and the Israeli Settler Movement* (Cambridge, MA: Harvard University Press, 2017).
22 Rosenthal, *Irreconcilable Differences?*
23 In a survey of American Jewish opinion conducted by the American Jewish Committee in 1983, for example, 48 percent of respondents agreed with the statement that they were "often troubled by the policies of the current Israeli government [led by Menachem Begin]," compared to only 29 percent who disagreed. J. J. Goldberg, *Jewish Power: Inside the American Jewish Establishment* (New York: Basic Books, 1996), 216.
24 The Begin government launched a massive settlement drive in the West Bank and Gaza Strip. When it came to power in 1977, there were 24 Jewish settlements in the West Bank and Gaza, inhabited by 3,200 people. By the time of Begin's retirement in 1983, there were 106 settlements (98 in the West Bank and 8 in Gaza) with the number of residents increasing to 28,400. Not only did the number of settlements and settlers increase, but also the type and location of settlements changed during this period, as a large number of settlements were established in central locations in the West Bank and in close proximity to local Palestinian populations—an area that would form the basis of any territorial compromise. Ilan Peleg, *Begin's Foreign Policy, 1977–1983: Israel's Move to the Right* (Westport, CT: Greenwood, 1987), 110–11.
25 Rosenthal, *Irreconcilable Differences?*, 54–55.
26 Rosenthal, 64.

27 Brettschneider, *Cornerstones of Peace*, 30.
28 Rosenthal, *Irreconcilable Differences?*, 73.
29 The Lebanon War, and the Sabra and Shatila massacre in particular, had a similar impact upon Israeli-Jewish attitudes. See, Efraim Inbar, "The 'No Choice War' Debate in Israel," *Journal of Strategic Studies* 12 (1989): 22–37.
30 After the Sabra and Shatila massacre, support grew within American Jewry for the dovish Israeli Peace Now movement, founded in 1979, and "Friends of Peace Now" chapters were formed in many cities across the U.S. Soon after, in 1983, a national organization was established called "American Friends of Peace Now," later renamed Americans for Peace Now (APN). Starting out with just $6,000 in the bank, a decade later, in 1993, APN's annual budget was almost $1.3 million.
31 A majority of American Jews were critical of Israel's response to the Intifada, and a growing number felt that Israel's occupation of the West Bank and Gaza would "erode Israel's democratic and humanitarian character"—by 1990, half of American Jews believed this, up from 30 percent in the spring of 1988, and just 11 percent who felt this way before the first Intifada. Rosenthal, *Irreconcilable Differences?*, 105, 111–12.
32 This widespread ignorance was partly due to the fact that it was prohibitively expensive to visit Israel, and very few American Jews knew enough Hebrew to read Israeli newspapers or books (which were, in any case, hard to obtain).
33 In the 2020 Pew survey of American Jews, 57 percent said they followed news about Israel very or somewhat closely. Pew Research Center, "Jewish Americans in 2020."
34 Jonathon Ament, "Israel Connections and American Jews," Jewish Databank, www.jewishdatabank.org, 41.
35 Uzi Rebhun, "Recent Developments in Jewish Identification in the United States: A Cohort Follow-Up and Facet Analysis," *Papers in Jewish Demography 1997*, ed. Sergio DellaPergola and Judith Even (Jerusalem: Avraham Harman Institute of Contemporary Jewry, Hebrew University of Jerusalem, 2001), 268; Ament, "Israel Connections and American Jews," 41; Pew Research Center, "Jewish Americans in 2020."
36 Theodore Sasson, *The New Realism: American Jewish Views about Israel* (New York: American Jewish Committee, 2009); Theodore Sasson, "Mass Mobilization to Direct Engagement: American Jews' Changing Relationship to Israel," *Israel Studies* 15 (2010): 191.
37 Major national and world events that occur during a person's late childhood, adolescence, or early adulthood leave a lasting impression on people's memories, attitudes, and worldviews. Thus, historians and sociologists refer to "generational memory" to describe how formative events and collective memories differ between generations. See Howard Schuman and Amy Corning, "Generational Memory and the Critical Period: Evidence for National and World Events," *Public Opinion Quarterly* 76 no. 1 (Spring 2012): 1–31.

38 For a detailed analysis of the attitudes of young American Jews toward Israel, see Dov Waxman, "Young American Jews and Israel: Beyond Birthright and BDS," *Israel Studies* 22 (2017): 177–99.
39 This is particularly true for the children of interfaith marriages, who account for almost 50 percent of young American Jewish adults (according to the 2013 Pew survey). For this large proportion of young American Jews, Israel tends to be less important to their Jewish identities, and they are more likely to be critical of Israel or feel ambivalent or apathetic about it than those with two Jewish parents.
40 For expressions of this attitude see Dana Goldstein, "Why Fewer Young American Jews Share Their Parents' View of Israel," *Time*, September 29, 2011; Marc Tracy, "Inside the Unraveling of American Zionism," *New York Times Magazine*, November 2, 2021.
41 Pew Research Center, "Jewish Americans in 2020."
42 The "distancing hypothesis" has been the subject of prolonged debate among scholars of American Jewry. For useful overviews, see Ron Miller and Arnold Dashefsky, "*Brandeis v. Cohen et al.*: The Distancing from Israel Debate," *Contemporary Jewry* 30 (2009): 155–64; and Steven M. Cohen and Ari Y. Kelman, "Thinking about Distancing from Israel," *Contemporary Jewry* 30 (2010): 287–96.
43 For example, the question of whether American Jewry and Israel were "drifting apart" was the subject of a symposium organized by the American Jewish Committee in New York City on November 4, 1989.
44 Shmuel Rosner and Inbal Hakman, *The Challenge of Peoplehood: Strengthening the Attachment of Young American Jews to Israel in the Time of the Distancing Discourse* (Jerusalem: Jewish People Policy Institute, 2011).
45 Theodore Sasson, Charles Kadushin, and Leonard Saxe, "Trends in American Jewish Attachment to Israel: An Assessment of the 'Distancing Hypothesis,'" *Contemporary Jewry* 30 (2010): 297–319. See also Theodore Sasson, *The New American Zionism* (New York: New York University Press, 2013), 138–43.
46 In the National Jewish Population Survey conducted in 2000–2001, 69 percent of American Jews said they felt very (32 percent) or somewhat (37 percent) emotionally attached to Israel (National Jewish Population Survey, "Israel Connections and American Jews," 2005, www.jewishdatabank.org. More than a decade later, in the survey of American Jews conducted by the Pew Research Center in 2013, the same percentage of American Jews (69 percent) said they are very (30 percent) or somewhat (39 percent) emotionally attached to Israel (Pew Research Center, "A Portrait of Jewish Americans," October 2013, www.pewforum.org . Although Pew's survey in 2020 found a decline in attachment to Israel, with 57 percent saying they were very (25 percent) or somewhat (32 percent) emotionally attached to Israel (Pew Research Center, "Jewish Americans in 2020," May 2021, www.pewforum.org. A different survey conducted in 2019 found the same results as those of the 2000–2001 National Jewish Population Survey and the 2013 Pew survey, with two-thirds (67 percent) of American Jews saying they were emotionally attached to Israel. Stuart Winer, "Rather than Drifting Away, Over

Two-Thirds of U.S. Jews Feel Tie to Israel—Poll," *Times of Israel*, February 4, 2020, www.timesofisrael.com.
47 Theodore Sasson, Charles Kadushin and Leonard Saxe, "Trends in American Jewish Attachment to Israel," *Contemporary Jewry* 30 (2010): 297–319.
48 The survey data does consistently indicate that younger American Jews are less attached to Israel than older Jews, but this has always been the case and typically attachment to Israel increases with age.
49 Graham Wright, Leonard Saxe, and Kenneth Wald, "Is Criticism Disloyal? American Jews' Attitudes toward Israel," *Politics and Religion* 15 (2022): 34–60.
50 Sasson, *New American Zionism*.
51 Jack Wertheimer, "American Jews and Israel: A 60-Year Retrospective," in *American Jewish Yearbook 2008* (American Jewish Committee: New York, 2008), 74.
52 For instance, in a 2021 survey of 800 registered Jewish voters by the Jewish Electorate Institute, 58 percent supported restricting U.S. aid to Israel so that it could not be spent on expanding settlements in the West Bank. The most striking findings in the survey were that 25 percent of respondents believed that "Israel is an apartheid state" (among Jews under 40, 38 percent believed this), and 22 percent (and 33 percent of young Jews) believed that "Israel is committing genocide against the Palestinians." Jewish Electorate Institute, "July 2021 National Survey of Jewish Voters," July 13, 2021, www.jewishelectorateinstitute.org.
53 For example, right-wing American Jews fiercely denounced the Rabin government for signing the Oslo Accords with the PLO in the early 1990s, and they assailed the governments of Ehud Barak and Ehud Olmert for their willingness to make concessions to the Palestinians in order to reach a peace agreement. Even Israeli prime minister Ariel Sharon—a longtime hero to many right-wing Jews—was strongly criticized for his government's unilateral disengagement from the Gaza Strip in August 2005.
54 This was clearly evident in the two major surveys of American Jews conducted by the Pew Research Center in 2013 and 2020, both of which revealed widespread skepticism among American Jews concerning Israeli policy towards the Israeli-Palestinian conflict. In both surveys, only a minority of respondents said they believed that the Israeli government, led by then–prime minister Benjamin Netanyahu, had been making a "sincere effort" to reach a peace agreement with the Palestinians. Pew Research Center, "A Portrait of Jewish Americans: Findings from a Pew Research Center Survey of U.S. Jews," October 2013; "Jewish Americans in 2020," May 2021, www.pewforum.org.
55 Arthur Hertzberg, "World Jewry Is Not an Amen Chorus," *Ha'aretz*, January 7, 2004.
56 Caryn S. Aviv and David Shneer, *New Jews: The End of the Jewish Diaspora* (New York: New York University Press, 2005).
57 In the survey conducted by the Jewish Electorate Institute in July 2021, 87 percent of American Jewish adults said that "someone can be critical of Israeli government policies and still be 'pro-Israel.'" Jewish Electorate Institute, "July 2021 National Survey of Jewish Voters."

58 Pew Research Center, "Jewish Americans in 2020."
59 In the Pew Research Center's 2020 survey of American Jews, 82 percent of Orthodox Jews said they were very or somewhat emotionally attached to Israel, compared with 78 percent of Conservative Jews and 58 percent of Reform Jews. Pew Research Center, "Jewish Americans in 2020."
60 Politically, Orthodox Jews have more in common with evangelical Christians and others on the religious right in the United States than they do with non-Orthodox Jews, especially on controversial social issues like abortion and same-sex marriage, and on issues concerning the separation of "church and state" (such as government funding of "parochial"/religious schools).
61 Joel Perlmann, "American Jewish Opinion About the Future of the West Bank: A Reanalysis of American Jewish Committee Surveys," Working Paper No. 526, Levy Economics Institute of Bard College, December 2007, 17–19.
62 In the 2013 Pew survey, for example, three-quarters (76 percent) of modern Orthodox Jews thought that the right-wing Israeli government led by Prime Minister Netanyahu at the time was sincerely trying to make peace with the Palestinians, compared with 51 percent of Conservative Jews, 35 percent of Reform Jews, and only 29 percent of nondenominational Jews.
63 A 2020 survey of Orthodox Jews found substantial support for the Trump administration's policies toward the Israeli-Palestinian conflict. Nishma Research, "A Political Survey of the American Orthodox Jewish Community," 2020, nishmaresearch.com.
64 Michelle Boorstein and Annie Gowen, "American Jews Feel Solidarity about Israel—for the Moment," *Washington Post*, October 8, 2023; Jenna Russell, Eliza Fawcett, Vik Jolly, and Robert Chiarito, "Among American Jews, 'You See a Lot of Broken Spirits' after Attacks," *New York Times*, October 9, 2023.

PART III

Changing Structures within the Jewish Community

8

American Judaism in the Twenty-First Century

ARI Y. KELMAN

American Judaism in the twenty-first century shows little coherence in practice, belief, attitude, connection, or organizational structure. Formal religious authority, if it ever existed, surely does not have a hold on what American Jews do in the name of Judaism, whose variety of expressive forms has metastasized. No longer the domain of synagogues, theologians, and clergy, American Judaism has become profoundly populist with bespoke b'nai mitzvah, one-off spiritual communities, myriad movements dedicated to this or that aspect of Judaism, and even a willingness to identify things as "religious" that may previously have been called "secular" or even "profane." Whatever it is that we talk about when we use the term "American Judaism," it is unclear (a) who "we" are that is doing the talking and (b) whether we are using the term to refer to the same set of dispositions, commitments, activities, beliefs, concepts, or practices.

The same is pretty much true of American Jewish people. Judaism and Jewish communities had, for many generations, predominantly been constituted by people who identified as Jews. That is no longer the case, owing to the relatively high rates of marriages between people who identify as Jews and those who do not. The question "Who is a Jew?" had previously been confined to technical questions of parentage, nationality, or the application of Jewish law. The pathway to becoming Jewish through formal procedures is still governed by religious law, though many people live lives engaged with Jews and ensconced in Jewish communities who do not, themselves, identify as Jews. It is becoming increasingly difficult to draw hard-and-fast lines between those who identify as Jews and those who do not.

Among those who do identify as Jews, the sheer variety of terms to describe their orientations to American Judaism also suggests little in the way of internal coherence. One can be Orthodox, Conservative, Reform, Humanist, Reconstructionist, or Renewal. Ashkenazi, Sephardi, or Mizraḥi. Yeshivish, Ḥaredi, generically frum, Ḥasidic, neo-Ḥasidic, secular, neo-rationalist, humanistic, cultural, intellectual, gastronomic, pediatric, geriatric, or professional. There are self-identified bad Jews and good Jews, traditional Jews, halakhic Jews, post-halakhic Jews, and meta-halakhic Jews. Matrilineal Jews and patrilineal Jews. Neo-Orthodox, Open Orthodox, Modern Orthodox, XO's (ex-Orthodox Jews), and Jews that are OTD (shorthand for "off the derekh").[1] Conservative Jews, though, tend to just be Conservative Jews. There are Jews who are spiritual but not religious, and Jews who are religious but not spiritual. JuBus and HinJews and mystics and hippie Jews. Jews can be heretics, apikoursim, apostates, and agnostics. There are punk Jews and just Jews and one-day-a-year Jews, high holiday Jews, Passover Jews, and film festival Jews. Some of the most devout Jews are those committed to ostensibly secularist ideologies: socialists, communists, democratic socialists, bundists, and so on. We have religious Zionists and religious anti-Zionists, Jews by marriage, Jews by association, Jews by choice, by conversion, by consent, descent, and dissent. People can be Jewish and people can be Jew-ish, and they can (and do) lay claim to any number of these terms in ever-evolving combinations of emphasis and enthusiasm, each one suggesting that it, too, corresponds to some dimension of Judaism.

It is possible to look at this situation and conclude that the variety of ways in which people engage in American Judaism is evidence of a critical failing. After all, how can people do whatever they wish and believe whatever they want and still conclude that they have a stake in a common entity called "Judaism"? Surely, one could conclude that the variety of terms, concepts, and labels indicate a critical failure on the part of Judaism to serve as a gravitational center that might unify or otherwise hold together each of these more particular formulations.

Alternatively, we could look at the variety of expressions of American Judaism and conclude, by contrast, that its diversity is a sign of vitality, albeit without a normative framework. Most of the time, people do not apply the term to everything—there is no specifically Jewish way to go grocery shopping or play soccer—but those who apply the term to some portion of their lives have a concept (latent, occluded, half-formed, or otherwise) that something called "Judaism" exists, and that they are tapping into it. People can do anything without anyone else's permission, drawing connections between their efforts and Judaism, and getting on with it—a million flowers blooming that are still, collectively, called "flowers."

We might, then, think of American Judaism in the twenty-first century as something closer to a creative commons license rather than a strict copyright. People can and do many things, with varying levels of attribution, that draw on, reformulate, or reconfigure Judaism. They can and do draw on certain themes, ignore others, and invent new directions. The Jewish healing movement,[2] Jewish arts initiatives,[3] embodied Judaism, and countless others are examples of syncretic, hybrid, improvisational, and wildly inventive approaches to Judaism in the twenty-first century.[4] For anyone seeking to connect their interests to Judaism, they can almost certainly find some rationale amidst the abundance of podcasts, webinars, prayer-service-simulcasts, sermon recordings, YouTube lectures, blogs, newsletters, or downloadable source sheets. Hybridity and syncretism have long been hallmarks of Judaism, drawing as it had from host cultures and other religions for much of its existence.

Perhaps this trend has been exacerbated by the American emphasis on individual autonomy and the lack of institutional authority providing a gravitational center to Judaism. Some have argued this is the case, most notably in Steven Cohen and Arnold Eisen's 2000 book, *The Jew Within*.[5] Individualism alone might account for some of what's going on in American Judaism but, oddly, it does not account for why or how people sustain their connections to Judaism itself. If people are operating on such individualistic terms, why bother with Judaism at all? Certainly, most American Jews do not feel that they must adhere to an approach to Judaism, its principles, values, ideals, or practices as laid out in a book or institutionalized in a religious movement, but that does not mean that what they are doing is not, somehow, also Judaism. Reinvented, recontextualized, reconfigured, but Judaism nonetheless.

The result is a highly diffuse and wildly varied enterprise lacking in formal authority but still attracting people who call themselves practitioners. American Judaism in the twenty-first century is real and virtual. It is not limited to religious expression and neither is it limited to people who identify themselves as Jews. Attempts to identify it solely as a religion will fall short and frustrate. This does not stop people from doing so, but in the present analysis we will discover that Judaism is not only a religion. It has religious aspects, sure, but so do many other American cultural forms from baseball to Oprah to AI.[6] Even the work of Jewish federations has been sacralized.[7]

In what follows, we will explore American Judaism in greater detail, drawing largely on two sources: one descriptive and one analytical. The first is the data collected by the Pew Research Center for its 2021 report "Jewish Americans in 2020" (hereafter referred to as "Pew 2021").[8] The second source is two recent books about American Judaism, each of which attempts to analyze or explain the current state of affairs. Together, these sources offer a set of rich insights into American Judaism as something both religious and something for which the framework of religion seems conceptually and analytically inadequate.

Jews with and without Judaism

According to Pew 2021, slightly more than one-quarter of American Jews (27 percent) say that they have no religion and still affirm that they are Jewish in some other way: by virtue of their parentage, their ethnicity, or according to some other rationale (like culture). But what does it mean to be a Jew without religion? What does being Jewish mean to the individual who holds a commitment to being Jewish but not to its religious dimensions? Where and how do they draw the line that divides their Jewishness from the religion that they do not have? And what does that possibility mean for American Judaism more generally? Pew 2021 did not answer these questions. Rather, it set out to answer the question "What does it mean to be Jewish in America?," though it did not answer that question either.[9] It couldn't answer that question because the question is impossible to answer in any singular way; "meaning" has so many meanings that it is hard to present in the aggregate. Yet Pew 2021's greatest contribution is not a singular definition of what it means to be Jewish in America but a statistical portrait of a relatively large sample of American Jewry. What emerges in its presentation is not a singular meaning but a strange and sometimes contradictory portrait of American Judaism.

In presenting its findings, Pew provided numerous data tables that laid out survey response frequencies according to an array of sociological variables (gender, household income, educational level, age), as well as variables specific to American Jewry (namely, respondents' affiliations with religious movements: Conservative, Orthodox, and Reform). Respondents' answers to questions posed on the survey were calculated and reproduced to show what percentage of Orthodox-identified Jews believed X or engaged in Y behavior as compared to Jews aged eighteen to thirty-four or those with a college degree.

In addition to standard sociological variables and specifically Jewish ones, the Pew Research Center constructed another variable that highlights religion specifically. This variable resulted from questions designed to screen respondents for inclusion in the study and asked specifically about respondents' relationship to religion. The result, a binary pair of categories: "Jews by religion" and "Jews of no religion." The former category consists of people who indicated that Judaism was their religion. The latter category consisted of people who said that they identified as Jews *and* had no religion at all—neither Judaism nor any other religion.

This variable appeared in most of the data tables in Pew 2021, though it was constructed by Pew and does not necessarily reflect terms or concepts that American Jews might use to describe themselves or their Judaism. While American Jews might define themselves as Orthodox or college educated, they do not, by and large, describe themselves as "Jews of no religion." Along with its opposite, that term is a construct of sociologists and demographers looking for a way to describe American Jews who eschew religion. The necessity for such a term indicates that the relationship between American Jews and religion is already complicated enough that it lacks a vernacular, leaving Pew and others to invent terms, categories, and, ultimately, the people represented by them.[10]

The creation of this binary variable does reveal some interesting patterns in American Jewry. For example, Jews who identified Judaism as their religion engaged in Jewish practices more regularly than did their counterparts who did not have a religion.[11] This is not just limited to obviously "religious" practices, either. They were more likely to read books with Jewish themes or engage in any number of other Jewish practices as well. Yet the variable's constructed nature also obscures some important trends in American Judaism. For example, significant minorities of "Jews of no religion" engage in activities that might otherwise be categorized as "religious." For example, 30 percent of "Jews of no religion" reported participating in a Passover seder in the past year, and 20 percent said that they fasted on Yom Kippur. Twelve percent either "often" or "sometimes" observe Shabbat in some meaningful way (compared to 48 percent of "Jews by religion"). It is unclear if "Jews of no religion" see those activities as "religious" or not, or if they attributed them to culture, family, tradition, or something else.[12]

Pew also found that more than half of "Jews of no religion" (54 percent) eat Jewish foods, and that 41 percent share "Jewish culture/holidays" with non-Jewish friends. Almost one-third of "Jews of no religion" visit historic Jewish sites when traveling, and more than one-quarter read books with Jewish content or consume media (movies, streaming programs) with Jewish content. These are not overwhelming numbers, but they point to the ways in which "Jews of no religion" connect with Judaism, provided we allow for an understanding of it that is not solely congruent with religion.

If we take religion as the appropriate framework for understanding American Judaism, the results are quite confusing. Taking the matter of individual belief, the sine qua non of North American religiosity, we find that nearly half of "Jews of no religion" (48 percent) believe in some other "higher power / spiritual force." The percentage of believers is roughly the same (51 percent) for "Jews by religion." Thus, one's claim on or rejection of Judaism-as-religion appears to have no impact on their willingness to believe in some kind of transcendent force or presence. Looking at a more conservative theological framework does not clarify matters either. In fact, American Jews beliefs tend not to adhere to the Bible. American Jews are among the least likely religious groups in America to believe in the God of the Bible, as only 22 percent of American Jews affirm this position (by comparison, it is held by 94 percent of White evangelicals, 88 percent of Black Protestants, and 71 percent of Catholics). The percentage of Jews who believe in the God of the Bible is only slightly higher than it is for "unaffiliated" Americans (18 percent). Restricting our analysis solely to Jews does not clarify the picture, either. Seven percent of "Jews of no religion" claim to believe in the God of the Bible, while 14 percent of "Jews by religion" do not believe either in the God of the Bible or any other higher power or spiritual force. Thus, while the binary variable of "Jews by religion" and "Jews of no religion" is useful analytically, it does not do much descriptive work with respect to the prevalence of belief in a transcendent being, whether biblical or not.[13]

The binary framework regarding religion does not clarify how people feel about their religion either. Elsewhere, the Pew survey asked respondents to identify elements in their lives that "provide them with a great deal of meaning and fulfillment."[14] Respondents were asked to assess a variety of activities, including spending time with family and friends, their occupations, spending time outdoors, and arts and literature. While nearly three-quarters of American Jews (74 percent) said that they found spending time with family to be "highly meaningful, fulfilling," only 20 percent of American Jews felt similarly about their "faith." By contrast, 43 percent of American Jews felt that spending time with pets was meaningful and fulfilling. Excluding "Jews of no religion," who might be skewing the data on how people feel about religion, does not change matters much either. Looking only at "Jews by religion," we find that 26 percent identified their "religious faith" as a source of fulfillment and meaning. Nearly three-quarters of "Jews by religion" do not.

In fact, of the seven activities that respondents were asked to evaluate, their "religious faith" was the least likely to correlate with meaning and fulfillment. The one exception to this pattern was among Orthodox Jews, 75 percent of whom find their religion fulfilling and meaningful (ranking it below spending time with family and above spending time with friends). That the majority of "Jews by religion" do not find their "religious faith" a source of significant meaning and fulfillment leaves open lots of questions about the meaning of Judaism in the lives of American Jews—and, if nothing else, these findings should give us pause about the stability of the concept of religion in American Jewish life.

Setting aside matters of belief and meaning to focus on questions of self-identification, matters grow still murkier. The survey asked respondents whether or not they attended synagogue and, if they did, how often they did so.[15] Only 20 percent of American Jews said that they attended "at least monthly," indicating that synagogue attendance is not a particularly widespread practice among American Jews. That number climbs only slightly among "Jews by religion" (to 27 percent).

Given that the majority of Jews do not attend synagogue regularly, the survey wanted to know why they stayed away. Fifty-seven percent of self-identified "Jews by religion" responded, "because I'm not religious."

What emerges is a portrait of American Jews among whom religion features in some rather confusing and contradictory ways. Self-identified "Jews by religion" claim to be "not religious," and "Jews of no religion" engage in practices that some might consider to be religious. Outside of Orthodox Jews, most American Jews do not find their "religious faith" to be a source of meaning or fulfillment, leaving a portrait of American Judaism in which affinity is strong but appreciation is weak. What, then, are American Jews holding on to when they hold on to Judaism as a religion? Another way of asking this question: Why are people holding on to "religion" if they are not inclined to describe themselves either as "religious" or as having religion at all?

The answer to that question is clearer for social scientists and demographers than it is for American Jews themselves. In order to qualify for inclusion in what the Pew Research Center calls the "net Jewish population," American Jews can have one religion or none. Owing to the structure of the survey, respondents who claimed to be Jewish *and* Buddhist or Christian, Hindu, or some other religion were categorized as "Jews by affinity" and were not included in the report's main analyses, including the calculation of the overall size and composition of American Jewry. For Pew, Jews who adhere to or practice religious hybridity literally did not count. Demographer Sergio DellaPergola calls this approach the "mutually exclusive identification framework." Religion, for DellaPergola, is an exclusive category, hermetically and statistically sealed.[16] In their meta-analysis of local Jewish population studies, Leonard Saxe and Elizabeth Tighe apply a similar logic, disqualifying from Jewish communal population studies those respondents who claim to belong to "any other religious group."[17] Saxe and Tighe's claim that "the core population should exclude those who currently belong to another religion is non-controversial."[18] Their approach, applied again in Pew 2021, affirms American Jews as a community defined first and foremost as a religious group even though, as illustrated above, there is little coherence to it, either among people identified as Jews or in comparison to other American religious communities.

Of course, American Jews can and do often live religiously hybrid lives.[19] They regularly cobble together practices and commitments that draw not only on other religious sources but new-age wisdom, popular culture, embodied practice, art, music, food, and whatever else they might have access to. Synagogues that offer yoga classes or hopped-up rock-music-driven Friday night services are pretty standard fare among non-Orthodox congregations. So are efforts led by Jewish organizations that are not connected to any of the formal religious movements to enact Jewish practices that focus on food, environmental concerns, or political expression. So-called spiritual communities (non-synagogue entities that basically function like synagogues), film festivals (online and in-person), museums (art and history), retreats (e.g., meditation, eco-themed), wilderness excursions, summer camps (for adults and youth), heritage travel (to Poland, Spain, Israel, Karala, and elsewhere), and one-off online events (often tethered to Jewish holidays like the High Holidays, Passover, or Shavuot) have filled an already packed Jewish calendar with alternative modalities of engagement with Judaism, whether or not one is a "Jew by religion." Perhaps the most powerful hybrid form is the one that emerges between Judaism and nonsectarian secular or cultural forms. American Judaism has long relied on these forms—from educational materials to music to the idea of the "family pew" to newspapers—to sustain and reinvent itself.[20] Even the tripartite structure of religious movements that defined so much of twentieth-century American Judaism (Reform, Conservative, and Orthodox) was adapted from the tendency toward denominationalism in American Protestantism.[21] Thus, some aspects of American Judaism that are now taken for granted and thought of as essential to its overall operation were themselves borrowed from other religious communities. Who is to say that meditation or environmental concerns will not become core aspects of American Judaism in one hundred years?[22] We could ask the same of new technologies like podcasts, webinars, self-paced online classes, virtual gatherings, and so on (there are too many to list here, but a good place to begin is Judaismunbound.com). What once seemed fringe, strange, or innovative may, perhaps, cultivate their own orthodoxies in time.

At present, though, these approaches to Jewish expression have not yet been fully institutionalized. Whether they will or won't is not a question we can answer here, but they point to the ways in which American Judaism has always drawn on secular or nonsectarian cultural forms for its own benefit. This tendency challenges efforts to draw a sharp defining line around American Judaism solely as a religious enterprise and opens up opportunities to appreciate other modes of Jewish engagement that are not entirely religious but are nevertheless aspects of American Judaism. Efforts by demographers and sociologists to distinguish "Jews by religion" and "Jews of no religion" share in this effort, promising clarity but delivering confusion, largely because of their emphasis on religion as a central concern in American Jewish life. While this might be true for Orthodox Jews, it is not true for the 90 percent of American Jews who identify themselves in other ways—and under what conditions does the understanding of 10 percent of a population apply to the remaining 90 percent? The application of religion to American Jews and American Judaism thus casts a long but narrow shadow over the phenomenon, reducing it to a single mode of expression, consideration, and application.

Redefining American Judaism

The tendency to identify American Judaism as a religion runs through other scholarly work as well, even when those works largely disagree on other matters. This discussion will focus on the contributions of two recent books, both of which try to assess the state of American Judaism. One finds American Judaism in remission while the other finds it thriving, though not in the places one might expect to find it. Their differences will become clear, but underlying them is a shared commitment to the religious concerns of American Judaism and an occlusion of its other expressive forms.

The first book is Jack Wertheimer's *The New American Judaism*, a broad survey of the "lived religion of American Jews."[23] Based on interviews with over 160 rabbis and other Jewish leaders, Wertheimer offers a portrait of an American Judaism that has lost its bearings to the effects of individualism, anti-authoritarianism, and personalism. His conclusion is that American Judaism is falling down on the job. Appeals to "peak moments" and what he calls "Golden Rule Judaism" have not only failed to pay off, but they have also resulted in a jumbled, incoherent, appealing-but-shallow set of "vague slogans" that "offer little religious depth of guidance."²⁴ The result is a portrait of American Judaism that is sometimes exciting but ultimately disappointing.²⁵

Wertheimer acknowledges the efforts coming from the margins of American Jewry—at Burning Man, in independent ḥavurot, in independent spiritual communities, and other settings, but he worries that these adaptations cater too much to contemporary culture and do not invest themselves deeply enough (however one might measure "depth") in Judaism as a *religion*.²⁶ Wertheimer grounds his exploration and his argument in a definition of religion borrowed from *Merriam-Webster's* online dictionary: "Religion is an organized system of beliefs, ceremonies, and rules used to worship a god or a group of gods."²⁷ This is an odd choice for a definition of American Judaism because it does not contain a single clause or significant term that applies readily to even a majority of participants in American Judaism.²⁸

Furthermore, and even more strangely, Wertheimer does not apply the definition to his own data; insofar as he is concerned with "worship," it is largely a sociological phenomenon, not a theological one. For Wertheimer, synagogues are places where Jews congregate to engage in shared activities that are often called "worship," but he offers little commentary on whether those activities are oriented toward "god or gods" in any meaningful way. The book's index entry for "God" has four subheadings, none of which indicate anything like the centrality of theological concerns among American Jews (in fact, one is about "skepticism" and another about "doubt"). His description of American Judaism, detailed, wide-ranging, and grounded as it is, does not seem anything like the "organized system" so central to the definition of religion that appears in his introduction. Applying the dictionary definition to American Judaism, it becomes almost impossible to conclude that the religion of Judaism is particularly healthy. Having presented this definition of religion, Wertheimer proceeds to critique American Judaism for not rising to meet it. His conclusions are somber and damning, offering a portrait of American Judaism in sharp decline, with only the Orthodox offering a glimmer of hope for the future.

Rachel Gross reaches a completely different conclusion in her book, *Beyond the Synagogue*, though she, too, advances a perspective on American Judaism that treats it as a religion. Gross shares little of Wertheimer's dour predictions and makes good on her title to find religion in the affective and connective bonds born of genealogical quests, heritage tourism, children's literature, and food, arguing that they constitute a set of sites for the enactment of American Judaism as a religion. The heart of Gross's argument stems from her claim that nostalgia serves as a powerful vector for the expression of Judaism as a religion. She argues that nostalgia "produces personal and communal meaning" and "a way of finding one's place in the world and of laying claim to the past"; "American Jewish nostalgia is a 'structure of feeling,' an emotional reaction to the past that is learned and taught."[29] Gross emphasizes the role of nostalgia as a particularly poignant and powerful register for Jewish religious expression, readily cultivated through material and embodied practices that do not require people to sign on to theological tenets, codes of conduct, or prescribed rituals. She concludes that Wertheimer's worries about the future of American Judaism stem from the fact that he was looking for religion in the wrong places. But, she argues, "if we reorient where we look for American Jewish religion and reconsider how we define it, then we start to find a lot more of it."[30] Wertheimer's definition of religion is too narrow for Gross, focusing as it does on congregational worship, ritual performances, and the perspectives of ordained clergy. Instead, Gross offers a more capacious, flexible, and affectively infused understanding of American Judaism that tries to look beyond that which is theological or synagogue-centered and toward the emotional or affective expressions of American Jews as evidence of their religiosity.

Though Gross effectively disagrees with Wertheimer's conclusions and claims about the state of "American Jewish religion," she shares his understanding that American Judaism is, fundamentally, a religious phenomenon. There is little space in either book for people to engage in Judaism in nonreligious ways. For Wertheimer, this is nearly self-evident, as he is concerned with expressions of American Judaism that would likely be identified by their practitioners as religious. For Gross, this approach leads her to make some unusual claims about American Jews, one-third of whom claim to have no religion whatsoever. Writing that "American Jews are not necessarily very good at articulating and recognizing sacred practices, places, or narratives in their lives," Gross ascribes religious meaning and intent to them, defining their actions, concerns, and desires as religious.[31]

In this strange way, these two books share a common concern that American Judaism is best understood as a religious formation. Yet they both also suggest that it cannot be understood *only* as a religious formation. Both authors acknowledge that defining American Judaism solely as a religion cannot possible capture the complexities of connections, commitments, practices, intentions, behaviors, or orientations that constitute American Judaism. Their terminology reflects this awareness. So, when Gross writes about "American Jewish religion," she is nodding to something that is not precisely congruent with American Judaism. Wertheimer also resorts to similarly clumsy formulations, writing that "Jewish religious identification and participation correlate strongly with all other forms of Jewishness."[32] Their attempts to acknowledge American Judaism as something broader than just religion chafe against their application of religion as the primary analytic lens for the study of American Judaism.

Holding to religion hamstrings both books in their ability to capture the complexities of American Judaism in the twenty-first century. Looking at American Judaism through the lens of religion generates a portrait of decline for Wertheimer and forces Gross to apply religion to people who might not otherwise claim it as their own. Yet both authors clearly understand that Judaism cannot be understood only as a religion, and that the religion and the people who engage with it are fused together, something like a dancer and a dance. Though both authors implicitly acknowledge this tension, neither employs it as a centerpiece of their analysis, retreating instead to religion and leaving the messier (and to my mind more revealing) aspects of American Judaism to others.

How It Looks on the Ground

So, let me share two stories about a more expansive American Judaism that is both religious and not religious and that help illustrate some of the ways in which people experience, share, and contribute to American Judaism in the twenty-first century. They are drawn from my immediate and admittedly partial perspective, but that's the only perspective I have. However, I do hope that they can be illustrative as other fragments of an American Judaism as it is made up by people practicing it.

Story One: On Saturday evening my phone vibrated. It was a message from a friend with a photo of him and his teenage son at an outdoor concert venue. I could make out a stage in the background, but I could not tell who was playing or where exactly they were. The accompanying text read, "Dead and Co. Bar Mitzvah." I don't actually know how my friend identifies, though I know that his son became a bar mitzvah in a synagogue some years before, but the religious framing of the event as a bar mitzvah signaled both a religiously inflected "in joke" among friends, but also a larger sense that for my friend, seeing Dead and Co. (a latter-day offshoot of the Grateful Dead) contained some semblance of religiosity and that taking his son to his first show represented a coming-of-age moment of some significance.

Story Two: Two days later, my wife received a letter from a friend who lives across the country and with whom she has upheld a years-long correspondence via the U.S. Postal Service. They send elaborately decorated envelopes and handwritten letters along with dried flowers, found objects, small pieces of art, and photographs to accompany updates about life, family, and so on. Inside this letter was a clipping from a local newspaper about Black Cat Judaica, a Vermont-based fabric arts studio that has made a name for itself as a producer of handwoven tallitot. The article opens by asking, "How did a Vermonter who grew up atheist come to weave Jewish prayer shawls sold to customers as far away as San Francisco, Denmark, and Australia? The multifaceted answer includes falling in love with an observant Jew." Nelly Wolf, the principal of Black Cat Judaica, explained, "There's a lot of tradition, a lot of cultural expectations that people have for a prayer shawl, but there's not actually a lot of halakhah."

I highlight these two examples not because they're the only ones or because they are unusual, but because they speak to the ways in which American Jews are making American Judaism up as they go along, and how people seeking to live Jewish lives connect Judaism to other aspects of life and find in those other aspects of life the space to summon Judaism within them. Neither my friend's text message nor Ms. Wolf's prayer shawls may be repeated or repeatable. In fact, as Ms. Wolf observed, their efforts were not grounded in Jewish law, but in feelings, expectations, and traditions, all of which are the stuff that people use to construct their Judaism that is both religious and not.

In all likelihood, neither of these would pass muster for Wertheimer, and I have no idea how either Ms. Wolf or my friend would respond to any of the questions posed by Pew in its survey. I am not sure whether or not Gross would see them as nostalgic, though I think she would call them religious. It is clear to me that both are instances of American Judaism as it is lived and experienced, concocted and regularly reimagined. As Robert Orsi has said, "The religious person is the one acting on his or her world in the inherited, improvised, found, constructed idioms of his or her religious culture."[33] I'm less invested in identifying either my friend or Ms. Wolf as a "religious person," but I offer Orsi's insight as a way of thinking about their relationship to their "religious culture," a formulation that leaves open the value of something other than religion within religious narratives. Indeed, neither was tied to a synagogue or other ostensibly "religious" institutions, but both coded their cultural practices as Jewish and used religious terminology. Both are highly idiosyncratic practices; neither weaving nor concert-going can be organized and systematized, but both became channels for the expression of some Jewish sentiment, some feeling, some understanding that what they were doing could be best understood through a Jewish framework.

They were also worth sharing with other people, either in a text message, a tallit, or a newspaper clipping. Whatever those feelings might be that drive someone to text a friend from a concert, to transform an old loom into an instrument for producing sacred garments, to visit an old synagogue while on vacation, to meditate, to breathe deeply while standing atop a vista, to marvel at a rainbow, to celebrate a relationship or a milestone, or to pause before eating to consider the intricacies of the process of producing and ingesting food, the feelings find forms and often encourage people to connect with others by sharing them.

Sometimes we call those forms rituals, and we form rituals around objects: candles, wine, food, incense, water. We might say prescribed words, or we might make them up.[34] We might misremember the words we thought we were supposed to say, or we might recite them from memory even if we don't know precisely what they mean. We might embellish the skeletal frameworks of ritual with additional trappings we adopt to lend gravitas to a situation. The form of the ritual provides a framework for the content, which is to honor whatever it is one is trying to honor at that moment. And the number of rituals and facilitators of ritual have expanded well beyond the range of ordained clergy (though people still like to have access to clergy). Yet, the impulse to honor, to make special, to note or denote always needs a container, and those containers are powerful human products that are sometimes so powerful that they defy the terms and containers designated for representing them.

Virtual Judaism and Virtual Jews

The question of how religion and ethnicity intersect takes on particular poignancy with regard to two developments in American Jewish life. First and most important are the significant numbers of people in intimate relationships with Jewish people as partners, friends, children, grandparents, ex-spouses, co-parents, and others who may not identify as Jewish themselves. The second is the advent of Jewish life online, which emerged powerfully under the conditions of the global pandemic brought on by the spread of the COVID-19 virus. Both challenge the boundaries of the synagogue as the proverbial and practical center of American Jewish life. And both pose important questions about the nature of the relationship between Jews and their Judaisms. How are we to think about or classify people who do not identify as Jews and are in intimate relationships with people who do? How are we to consider religious or ethnic communities largely encountered online?

Returning to Pew 2021, we find that 42 percent of married American Jews are married to someone who does not identify as Jewish. "If one excludes the Orthodox and looks only at non-Orthodox Jews who have gotten married since 2010, 72% are intermarried."[35] Lest we conclude that this is only true among "Jews of no religion," one-third of "Jews by religion" are married to people who do not identify as Jewish.[36] Looking beyond marriage, Pew found that 62 percent of American Jews engage with Jewishness by sharing Jewish culture with non-Jewish friends.[37] The result is an emergent American Judaism constituted by people who identify as Jewish who are in intimate relationships with people who neither grew up as nor currently identify as Jews.

This development, first documented in the 1990 National Jewish Population Study, challenges some fundamental assumptions about the relationship between religion and ethnicity in the lives of American Jews.[38]

The relationship was best captured by a quip attributed to the Jewish sociologist Charles Liebman, who is said to have observed that "Jews go to synagogue to practice their ethnicity." I've not found it in any of Liebman's writings (yet!), but the quip captures two vital truths about American Jews and their religion. First, it suggests that synagogues are not only sites of religious devotion that are oriented heavenward. Second, and perhaps more importantly for the present discussion, it implies that ethnicity has or maybe even requires practices to enact it. To be a "practicing Jew" does not imply a set of beliefs in a supernatural being, but rather a set of actions or activities intended to conjure one's membership in or affinity for something called Judaism. Indeed, to be a "practicing Jew," one does not need to have religion or to be religious at all.

The connection between religion and ethnicity hints at what Judith Weisenfeld calls the "religio-racial" logic of American religion, which holds that race and religion are intertwined, and that each relies on the other as a register for its expression.[39] Religions, in this formulation, are not only spiritual or theological frameworks. They are also sociological, cultural, and political. Religion and race (or ethnicity) are not exclusive spheres of human experience or expression; they are intertwined with one another in ways that can change our understanding of each. American Jews, whether or not they claim to have a religion, approach their ethnicity with religious devotion—and, as Gross and Wertheimer have indicated, religion is a powerful register for the expression of communal bonds. This is not (only) a cheeky observation; it is a profound insight into the ways in which collectivities produce themselves and are produced through engagements with entities imagined to be larger than themselves.

But what of people who do not feel that connection in the abstract, but only in the particular circumstances of their lives? To return to Pew 2021, 85 percent of American Jews feel "some" connection to "the Jewish People," and 48 percent feel "a great deal" of connection.[40] The same cannot be assumed of people who do not identify as Jewish, and yet who are friends or partners, parents, or children of those that do. The particular bonds between people may or may not translate into generalized sentiments and are already reshaping American Judaism from one that can take ethnicity for granted to one that can and does adapt to make space for people who do not identify as Jews.

People have been predicting the impact of this development for decades, though none have panned out.[41] Perhaps it might mean that American Judaism will take a more "religious" turn, as religion is likely a more open access point than ethnicity. Perhaps it might mean the end of certain segments of American Jewry who, in a generation, will find the connection so attenuated as to be meaningless. But the presence of people who do not identify as Jews and their connections to people who do is a characteristic that is shaping American Judaism in the twenty-first century by challenging assumptions about its ethnic foundation and inviting new formulations that might be more accessible to non-Jewish partners than the presumption of an affinity for something called "the Jewish People."

Despite its popularity, "the Jewish People" remains a fairly abstract concept for most American Jews. More immediate measures produce a more complex portrait riven with internal differences and attitudes. As Pew 2021 found, "just 9% of Orthodox Jews say they have a lot in common with Reform Jews, and an identical share of Reform Jews (9%) say they have a lot in common with the Orthodox."[42] Thus, the commitment to "the Jewish People" is not reflected in more immediate instances and might require a kind of commitment or devotion to a concept nearly as abstract as a divinity.

The sense of communal connections among American Jews was challenged further under the pressures of the COVID-19 pandemic. When concerns for public health and safety closed synagogue buildings, communities shifted to provide online services for their members. Zoom services, Torah studies, b'nai mitzvah, weddings, and funerals became common practice, and people rather quickly got comfortable with the idea that they would be "attending" services from the comfort of their own homes.[43] Some, indeed, got a little too comfortable.[44]

Zoom services might have been a pale stand-in for in-person ritual, but the ease and comfort of "attending" events without having to drive or walk, interact with people you might rather not, or even put on shoes gestured toward versions of American Judaism that are already here, if not yet fully developed. In the spring of 2022, the *Forward* reported on a Midwestern synagogue that had purchased virtual reality headsets for its staff and was building a synagogue in the "metaverse."[45] Whether or not the metaverse will be the next best thing or just the next big bust is, at present, unclear. Virtual worlds have come and gone in the past, complete with people spending real money, building real relationships, having life changing experiences, and even attending church or synagogue or concerts or whatever. The construction of a synagogue in the metaverse (of course, Chabad was already there) is, in 2022, something of a novelty, but combining the general success of Zoom and the evolutions of off-the-shelf virtual or augmented reality technologies suggests that virtual participation in Jewish communal life is likely to become a regular occurrence.[46]

Immersive virtual experiences will become more common and more deeply embedded in Americans' everyday lives, so there is little doubt that Zoom Torah studies or services, which served admirably during the COVID-19 pandemic, were really just a beta test for new technologies, new ways of engaging, participating, celebrating, and communing.

American Jews will adapt to these innovations more quickly than will Jewish institutions. For the years of shelter-in-place orders, families have already celebrated achievements and life-cycle events on Zoom, hosted intercontinental Passover seders, and zoomed themselves into High Holiday services around the world. Facilitators of Jewish life have also responded by organizing Jewish events online and broadcasting them worldwide, allowing more people to connect and participate in more ways that previously imagined. In 2020, the star-studded Saturday Night Seder mobilized broadcast technology and the framework of the Passover Seder to entertain and raise money for the CDC Foundation COVID-19 Emergency Response Fund. That same year, the Jewish Emergent Network and Reboot teamed up to host DAWN, an overnight online entertainment and learning opportunity in the spirit of the tradition of staying up all night on Shavuot to study.[47]

These events were notable for their success, but they are really just the beginning of the ways in which digital technologies, devices, and extremely cheap access to extremely large potential audiences are reconfiguring both how and what it means to engage in Jewish holidays. With the advent of even more accessible technologies, new formations will likely emerge that have the power to attract people who might never have hosted their own Passover seders or set foot into a synagogue for Shavuot.

Are non-Jewish members of Jewish families also "virtual Jews"? What happens when the metaverse and virtual reality headsets allow people to participate in Jewish communities without leaving their homes? Or when they participate as avatars rather than flesh-and-blood people? Do they also become "virtual" Jews? Here again the lines are too blurry to be clearly discerned, let alone defined, protected, or defended. Certainly, there is a great deal of porousness in the membrane between religion and not-religion, and between Jews and non-Jews. But the membranes still exist, which means that the categories matter, even if they can be readily transgressed, deconstructed, or evaded. So, too, with the difference between the "real" and the "virtual." After all, what's more "virtual" than the central ritual of the Passover seder (still the most popular ritual for American Jews), when participants are told to imagine themselves as if they had left Egypt? What's more "virtual" than imagining a transcendent being who knows all and who has explained what to eat, whom to marry, and when to work and when to rest? Or does a sense of that transcendent being provide access to a reality that is beyond the everyday, making God realer than real? Both. It is both. And neither. And American Judaism is a framework for holding all of this at once.

The Present and Future

Combined with the prevalence of people who do not identify as Jewish in Jewish communities, we find an American Judaism that is porous, varied, diverse, dynamic, creative, fragmented, and generative in ways that might have been unimaginable one or two generations ago. Given changes in politics, culture, technology, and social life, why would we expect the structures of American Judaism created in the late nineteenth and early twentieth centuries to remain the only options for the expression or institutionalization of Judaism in the twenty-first century? The publication of the *Jewish Catalog* in 1973 may have ushered in a new generation of "do-it-yourself" Judaisms, but even its authors and editors could not have imagined what would be possible a generation later.[48]

American Judaism is increasingly shaped by innovation, access, and new combinations of expression, meaning, and sharing. It is a community of online synagogues, female Orthodox rabbis,[49] online text study,[50] artisanal matzah,[51] eco-friendly Hanukkah candles,[52] "tech Sabbaths,"[53] Jewish witches,[54] Queer Orthodox Jews, rabbis, and rock stars that coexist alongside long-established religious movements.[55] Podcasts and news websites offer unparalleled access to Jewish knowledge and insight, as do platforms dedicated to education like myJewishlearning.com and sefaria.com. It is easier than ever to access sources of Jewish knowledge and wisdom, and it is easier than ever to share knowledge and wisdom if you have it (or even if you think you do). Schools and synagogues, museums and publishers, musicians, clergy, camps, philanthropies, and whoever thinks they have a stake in American Judaism are leveraging whatever they can to weigh in on where things are and shape where they think they ought to go. All of these innovations, those already familiar and those yet to arrive, are changing the ways in which people instantiate American Judaism.

American Judaism only makes sense if we understand it as something not only religious in nature. Somewhere between Judaism everywhere (as Gross suggests) and the Judaism of commandments (as Wertheimer writes) we can find American Judaism in all of its quirky, customized, corporate, idiosyncratic, affective, and concrete forms. American Jews all have a stake in Judaism even as many repudiate its formal definition as a "religion." We know they have a stake in Judaism because 100 percent of those counted as part of the "net Jewish population" have a Jewish identity; it was a prerequisite for participation in the study. Responding to a survey, participating in a Passover seder, eating at a deli, reading a Jewish children's book, or zooming into an online holiday celebration may or may not be religious. That designation would fall to the person taking the action. But they are all still performances of American Judaism *whether they are religious or not*.

The inability of the term "religion" to define American Judaism is not a problem with American Jews; it is a problem with the term and its meanings. Expanding the range of American Judaism to include those practices, orientations, behaviors, and commitments to include those held by Jews who eschew religion offers a more complicated, sometimes contradictory, but nevertheless fuller account of American Judaism as it is lived by people who are themselves Jewish and who are in close relationship to American Jews. It expands our ability to understand and engage with (and maybe even shape) American Judaism that is both real and virtual, both religious and ethnic, both sacred and profane, both traditional and innovative, defined by both what you do and what you believe and what you believe about what you do.

This conclusion might not make things clearer, I know. But that's how it is. Despite the seemingly endless variety of changes, that's how it has always been, to one degree or another.

Welcome.

NOTES

1 Ezra Cappell, Jessica Lang, and Lynn Davidman, "The Embodied Process of Haredi Defection," in *Off the Derech: Leaving Orthodox Judaism* (Albany: State University of New York Press, 2020).
2 Ellen M. Umansky, *From Christian Science to Jewish Science: Spiritual Healing and American Jews* (New York: Oxford University Press, 2005); Nancy Flam, "Healing the Spirit: A Jewish Approach," *CrossCurrents* 46 (1996): 487–96; Laura J. Praglin, "The Jewish Healing Tradition in Historical Perspective," *Reconstructionist* 63, no. 2 (Spring 1999): 6–15.
3 Lena Stanley-Clamp, "Jewish Culture for the Twenty-first Century: An International Seminar," *East European Jewish Affairs* 29 (1999): 147–49.
4 Cia Sautter, *The Miriam Tradition: Teaching Embodied Torah* (Urbana: University of Illinois Press, 2010).
5 Steven M. Cohen and Arnold M. Eisen, *The Jew Within: Self, Family, and Community in America* (Bloomington: Indiana University Press, 2000).
6 David Chidester, *Authentic Fakes: Religion and American Popular Culture* (Berkeley: University of California Press, 2005); Kathryn Lofton, *Oprah: The Gospel of an Icon* (Berkeley: University of California Press, 2011); Kathryn Lofton, *Consuming Religion* (Chicago: University of Chicago Press, 2017); John Lardas Modern, *Neuromatic: Or, A Particular History of Religion and the Brain* (University of Chicago Press, 2021).
7 Jonathan S. Woocher, *Sacred Survival: The Civil Religion of American Jews* (Bloomington: Indiana University Press, 1986).
8 "Jewish Americans in 2020," Pew Research Center, May 11, 2021, www.pewresearch.org.
9 "Jewish Americans in 2020," 8.
10 Ian Hacking, "Biopower and the Avalanche of Printed Numbers," *Humanities in Society* 5 (1982): 279–95; Sarah Igo, *The Averaged American: Surveys, Citizens, and the Making of a Mass Public* (Cambridge, MA: Harvard University Press, 2007).
11 "Jewish Americans in 2020," 26.
12 Ari Y. Kelman, Tobin Belzer, Ilana Horwitz, Ziva Hassenfeld, and Matt Williams, "Traditional Judaism: The Conceptualization of Jewishness in the Lives of American Jewish Post-Boomers," *Jewish Social Studies* 23 (2017): 134–67.
13 "Jewish Americans in 2020," 67.

14 "Jewish Americans in 2020," 69.
15 "Jewish Americans in 2020," 70.
16 Sergio DellaPergola, "World Jewish Population, 2019," *Current Jewish Population Reports* 26, reprinted from the *American Jewish Year Book 2019* (New York: Berman Jewish Databank, 2019), 11.
17 Elizabeth Tighe, Raquel Magidin de Kramer, Xajavion Seabrun, Daniel Parmer, Daniel Kallista, Daniel Nussbaum, and Josh Mandell, "AJPP Technical Report 2020: ZIP Code-Based Jewish Population Estimates" (Waltham, MA: Cohen Center for Modern Jewish Studies, Steinhardt Social Research Instititute Brandeis University, ajpp.brandeis.edu, 36.
18 Tighe et al., "AJPP Technical Report 2020," 36.
19 Emily Sigalow, *American JewBu: Jews, Buddhists, and Religious Change* (Princeton, NJ: Princeton University Press, 2019); Matthew Kassel, "She Could Be the First Jew of Color in Congress," *Jewish Insider*, January 26, 2022.
20 Dianne Ashton, *Rebecca Gratz: Women and Judaism in Antebellum America* (Detroit, MI: Wayne State University Press, 1998); Jonathan D. Sarna, *American Judaism: A History* (New Haven, CT: Yale University Press, 2004); Peggy K. Pearlstein, "Assemblies by the Sea: The Jewish Chautauqua Society in Atlantic City, 1897–1907," *Jewish Political Studies Review* 10 (1998): 5–17; Laura Yares, "Say It with Flowers: Shavuot, Confirmation, and Ritual Reimagination for a Modern American Judaism," *Shofar* 35 (2017): 1–19.
21 Jon Butler, *Awash in a Sea of Faith: Christianizing the American People* (Cambridge, MA: Harvard University Press, 1990); Jonathan D. Sarna, *American Judaism: A History*.
22 Meditation is nearly normative in non-Orthodox American Jewish communities, thanks in no small measure to Aryeh Kaplan, *Jewish Meditation: A Practical Guide* (New York: Schocken, 1995).
23 Jack Wertheimer, *The New American Judaism: How Jews Practice Their Religion Today* (Princeton, NJ: Princeton University Press, 2018), 21.
24 Wertheimer, *New American Judaism*, 42.
25 He holds the emphasis on "healing services" in particularly low regard.
26 Wertheimer, 230–35.
27 Wertheimer, 15.
28 See the discussion above.
29 Rachel B. Gross, *Beyond the Synagogue: Jewish Nostalgia as Religious Practice* (New York: New York University Press, 2021), 28–29.
30 Gross, *Beyond the Synagogue*, 7.
31 Gross, 26.
32 Wertheimer, *New American Judaism*, 21.
33 Robert A. Orsi, "Is the Study of Lived Religion Irrelevant to the World We Live in? Special Presidential Plenary Address, Society for the Scientific Study of Religion, Salt Lake City, November 2, 2002," *Journal for the Scientific Study of Religion* 42 (2003): 169–74.

34. Vanessa L. Ochs, *Inventing Jewish Ritual* (Philadelphia: Jewish Publication Society, 2010).
35. "Jewish Americans in 2020," 93.
36. "Jewish Americans in 2020," 94.
37. "Jewish Americans in 2020," 75.
38. Barry A. Kosmin, Sidney Goldstein, Joseph Waksberg, Nava Lerer, Ariella Keysar, and Jeffrey Shechner, "Highlights of the CJF 1990 National Jewish Population Survey," Council of Jewish Federations, New York, 1991).
39. Judith Weisenfeld, "The House We Live In: Religio-Racial Theories and the Study of Religion," *Journal of the American Academy of Religion* 88 (2020): 440–59.
40. "Jewish Americans in 2020," 110.
41. Steven M. Cohen, "Intermarriage and the Jewish Future," American Jewish Committee, 1997, www.bjpa.org; Steven M. Cohen and Arnold M. Eisen, *The Jew Within: Self, Family, and Community in America* (Bloomington: Indiana University Press, 2000); Steven M. Cohen and Jack Wertheimer, "What Ever Happened to the Jewish People?," *Commentary* 121, no. 6 (June 2006): 33–37; "The Pew Survey Reanalyzed: More Bad News, but a Glimmer of Hope," mosaicmagazine.com; Lila Corwin Berman, Kate Rosenblatt, and Ronit Y. Stahl, "Continuity Crisis: The History and Sexual Politics of an American Jewish Communal Project," *American Jewish History* 104 (2020): 167–94.
42. "Jewish Americans in 2020," 118.
43. Ron Wolfson and Steven Windemueller, "Rise of the Online Jewish Synagogue," *Tablet Magazine*, April 6, 2022, www.tabletmag.com.
44. Jackie Hajdenberg, "Sex Act on Bat Mitzvah Zoom Stream Renews Questions about Online Shabbat Services," *Times of Israel*, June 2, 2022.
45. Andrew Silverstein, "Are Virtual Minyans and Avatar Rabbis the Future of Judaism?," *Forward*, March 21, 2022.
46. Talya Rosen, "Chabad Rabbis Create a Spiritual Space in the Metaverse—Virtual Reality Becomes the Newest Place for Jews to Congregate," Chabad, January 4, 2022, www.chabad.org.
47. "DAWN," Reboot, rebooting.com.
48. Richard Siegel, Michael Strassfeld, and Sharon Strassfeld, *The Jewish Catalog: A Do-It-Yourself Kit* (Philadelphia: Jewish Publication Society, 1973).
49. Julie Zauzmer, "In a Break with Tradition, Orthodox Jewish Women Are Leading Synagogues," *Washington Post*, July 28, 2017.
50. projectzug.org.
51. Justine Sterling, "5 Artisanal Matzos for Passover," *Food and Wine*, May 23, 2017, www.foodandwine.com.
52. "8 Ways to Make Your Hanukkah More Eco-Friendly," My Jewish Learning, www.myjewishlearning.com.
53. Tiffany Shlain, *24/6: The Power of Unplugging One Day a Week* (New York: Simon & Schuster, 2019).

54 Rachel Roman, "The Season of the Jewitch: Meet the Occultists Who Blend Witchcraft and Jewish Folklore," *Jewish Telegraphic Agency*, October 27, 202, www.jta.org.
55 Condé Nast, "Queer Orthodox Jews Want More Than Tolerance," Them, October 24, 201, www.them.us; Miriam Schweiger, "With a Dress and Tzitzit, Ezra Furman Reminds Me Why I Love My Judaism," Hey Alma, April 24, 2020, www.heyalma.com; Sam Sokol, "First Openly Gay Orthodox Rabbi Ordained in Jerusalem—Detroit Jewish News," *Jewish Telegraphic Agency*, May 31, 2019, thejewishnews.com.

9

Orthodox Judaism in the United States

ZEV ELEFF

Orthodox Jews represent 10 percent of the American Jewish population which, since the postwar period, has numbered around five and a half million in total.¹ The Orthodox proportion has been more or less constant since Jewish agencies started conducting population studies in the 1970s, defying the earlier prognosticators who had prophesied that this group was a "case study of institutional decay."² The sociologist Peter Berger was one of the pessimists about the long-term sustainability of the Orthodox—and all other tradition-bound faiths—and its capacity to persist in modern society. Berger, initially anyway, doubted whether this group could continue to pull its adherents along a path of all-or-nothing strict observance of Shabbat, ritual purity for married women, and kosher dietary laws, to list the most well-known strictures of halakhah (Jewish law). He was skeptical that Orthodoxy would hold its adherents against the push of technology, secularism, and other social forces.³ In a word, Orthodox Judaism was perceived as too countercultural to survive.

These prognostications were not altogether wrong. An uncountable number left the Orthodox fold, part of a "winnowing" process in which, so suggests the chaff-and-grain analogy, the most committed Orthodox remained while others departed to more liberal religious movements or altogether secular lives.⁴ But the Orthodox Jewish community managed to persevere due to its high birthrate, low intermarriage rate, and the increase in ba'alei teshuva, so-called returnees to traditional Jewish life.⁵ Owing to this, thirty-five years after he first opined on the subject, Peter Berger admitted that the "aggressiveness" of those Orthodox Jews who "chose" to remain had fortified their "vulnerable" faith community.⁶

The Pew Research Center's "Jewish Americans in 2020" report suggests that Orthodox Judaism in the United States is not just surviving—it's thriving. Among Jews ages eighteen to twenty-nine, according to Pew's tallies, 17 percent self-identify as Orthodox.[7] Even before this, Pew's earlier study of American Jews, conducted in 2013, convinced a new generation of sociologists that "over two generations, the Orthodox pretty much quadrupled in size," and that their "market share" will in short order "soar."[8] This is particularly the case in New York City, home to 1.75 million Jews, according to the UJA-Federation of New York's 2011 population study. About a half million of these Gothamites are Orthodox, and 61 percent of Jewish children are raised in Orthodox households. The highest concentration resides in Brooklyn and, to get more granular about these figures, identify as part of the "right-wing" Orthodox Yeshiva World ("yeshiva" is the Hebrew word for an all-male Talmud academy) and ḥasidic communities.[9] The triumphant Yeshiva World is also densely populated in Lakewood, New Jersey, and Monsey, New York. Other major Orthodox hubs include Baltimore, Chicago, Cleveland, Detroit, Los Angeles, and South Florida. This chapter explores how America's Orthodox Jewish communities have "bargained" with modernity to position themselves for unprecedented social stability and significant growth.[10]

Heterogeneous Orthodoxy

There is no single constellation of schools, seminaries, or synagogues that represent the whole of Orthodox Judaism in the United States. Unlike, say, the Conservative or Reform movements, Orthodox Judaism did not develop from a close-knit cluster of rabbinical seminaries and likeminded organizations. The latter movements borrowed bishopric-like organizational infrastructures from their Mainline Protestant neighbors. In the case of Reform Judaism, its flagships—Union of American Hebrew Congregations (1873), Hebrew Union College (1875), and Central Conference of American Rabbis (1889)—were all formed, as their names suggest, to centralize the movement around particular agencies.[11] Likewise, Conservative Judaism emerged out of the close association of the Jewish Theological Seminary (1886), United Synagogue (1913), and Rabbinical Assembly (1918).[12] As Jewish heterodox groups took root and separated themselves from traditionalists, the remnant people and institutions adjusted and, in time, reactively claimed the mantle of "Orthodoxy."[13]

For that reason, Orthodox Judaism functions more like a federation of loosely connected Congregationalists.[14] There exists no single establishment or small circle of organizations that can account for the hearts and minds of all—or most—Orthodox Jews. This doesn't mean that no one has tried to unite all groups. To the contrary, written in a certain way, the history of American Orthodox Jews reads like a series of failed attempts to establish a centralized chief rabbinate, rabbinical guilds, kosher certification agencies, private school systems, and rabbinical seminaries.[15] Yet, over time, Orthodox Jews have filtered into subgroups. Each shares a basic commitment to traditional Jewish observance. To differentiate from one another, synagogue groups and rabbinical schools have developed hyphenated monikers and splintered themselves into Orthodox subcommunities. Some are European imports while others were made in America. To account for this, Pew researchers in 2013 asked all self-identified Orthodox interviewees whether they considered themselves Modern Orthodox, Ḥasidic, or Yeshivish. For the 2020 population study, Pew added further nuance to its Orthodox groups: Ḥasidic or Chabad; Modern or Centrist Orthodox; and Yeshivish, Litvish (Lithuanian), and Agudah. I suggest a slight but important realignment of the Pew Research Center's categories, since there exist profound differences between Chabad-Lubavitch Ḥasidim and other Ḥasidic sects such as Satmar and Skver.

What links these subgroups, to draw from historian Sidney Mead's definition and American Protestant denominationalism, is an "underlying unity" that "prevented any true denomination from making . . . absolutistic claim[s]."[16] Notwithstanding crucial and contentious points of disagreement and preference for their own theological path over the others, members of each Orthodox denomination believe that tradition-abiding adherents of other Orthodox communities are heaven bound. Each abides by, at least in theory, the essential components of Jewish law (and that they are, at some very significant level, derived from Sinai) and basic observances. It's just that they much prefer their religious route over other Orthodox coreligionists.

The three major movements—Mead would have called them "sects"—within American Judaism do not function in this way.[17] The Conservative, Orthodox, and Reform rabbinates have their own particular standards in conversion (i.e., the ability to create a new Jew),

Jewish identity, and approach to halakhah.[18] Important distinctions in marriage ceremonies and divorce rites have also created massive incongruities. For instance, the Reform Movement does not require a couple divorced in a civil court to obtain a religious writ of divorce. The Conservative Movement does not consider this sufficient and, at least officially, would consider children born to someone who was previously divorced without a religious writ a bastard, born out of wedlock. Meanwhile, Orthodox rabbis do not acknowledge the divorce rituals of either their Conservative or Reform counterparts. No Jewish religious movement, then, agrees with the others on who is actually single, married, or divorced. Among the "denominations" of Orthodox Judaism, though, there is consensus on core aspects of Jewish life. What each subgroup disagrees about on religious, educational, cultural and socioeconomic levels is the focus of this chapter.

A final note concerns America's traditional-minded Sephardic communities. As the sociologist Mijal Bitton notes, the Sephardic communities that emigrated from the Levant region since World War II defy "denominational" categories. These groups arrived to the United States with different customs and religious behaviors than the dominant Ashkenazic (European) community and, at times, varying practices among one another within the Sephardic fold. Over time, these Sephardic groups have started their own "bargaining" with American culture. Sephardic Jews have also found their way into preexisting Ashkenazic Orthodox communities. Accordingly, Persian Jews attend Modern Orthodox schools in Brooklyn, Los Angeles, and Manhattan. Other Sephardic Jews have matriculated to Yeshiva World schools and synagogues and currently comprise a large cluster of Chabad communities.[19]

The Yeshiva World

Scholars of American Jewish life have tended, and much too narrowly, to define the so-called Yeshiva World by focusing on its oppositional attitudes and its men-only Talmud study halls.[20] Jeffrey Gurock described this group as "resisters" who "reject acculturation and disdained cooperation with other American Jewish elements" out of fear of diluting "traditional faith and practice."[21] Samuel Heilman preferred the "Rejectionist" who "denies and hence conceptually rejects the legitimacy of his non-Orthodox contemporary" and "remains within the shelter of the traditional Orthodox world."²² Charles Liebman typically labeled it "Sectarian Orthodox" and dwelled on this group's separatist tendencies, although he did acknowledge their constructive commitment to traditional Talmud study (for men) and moralistic teachings.²³ Borrowing from a vocabulary already in circulation among America's Orthodox Right, Liebman was the first to introduce "Yeshiva World" into the scholarly lexicon.²⁴

More than anyone else, Rabbi Aharon Kotler was responsible for the emergence of the Yeshiva World. In 1943, he founded his Beth Medrash Govoha in Lakewood, New Jersey, with a handful of students. Lakewood was a small "resort town" with a basic Orthodox infrastructure: it had a few synagogues, a mikveh (a ritual bath for married women to immerse after their menstruation), and a cemetery. Kotler chose Lakewood because it contained all this—it didn't hurt that potential Jewish donors still vacationed there—but was far away from the major hubs of Orthodox Jewish life in New York.²⁵

Before Kotler emigrated from Eastern Europe in 1941, the Agudath Ha-Rabbonim had been the leading rabbinical organization representing the Orthodox Right in the United States. Since its founding in 1902, this rabbinical organization had ratcheted up kosher standards, protected the interest of synagogue rabbis, and advocated, within limits, Religious Zionism.²⁶ Kotler, on the other hand, believed that the future of Orthodox rabbinic leadership belonged to yeshiva heads who presided over academies that taught Talmud, the medieval digest of rabbinic codes written in terse Judeo-Aramaic; he did not pay much mind to congregational rabbis, nor did he support Zionism. The yeshiva, the all-male study space, was central to Kotler's vision. The separate girls' Bais Yaakov schools were a crucial component of the Yeshiva World's educational system, but the focus was always on the boys' schools.²⁷ One either studied in a yeshiva or worked to support it. This focal emphasis was something new. Kotler's forebears in Eastern Europe preached intensive Torah study as an ideal, but they were "comfortable with the idea that God's original plan was to have only a minority of full-time yeshiva students."²⁸ In contrast, Kotler's sermons, argued historian Yoel Finkelman, displayed "discomfort with the very idea of Orthodox businessmen."²⁹

The latter matter is important to make a crucial distinction between the culture of Torah study in Eastern Europe and the later types in Israel and the United States. The term "Yeshiva World" does not appear, at least with any regularity, in Lithuanian rabbinic literature, neither in its Yiddish (*yeshiva velt*) or its Hebrew (*olam ha-yeshiva*) incarnations. This designation would have had too far-reaching implications for the Orthodox rank-and-file. In Eastern Europe, most boys received a rudimentary religious education in *ḥeder*. The bulk of these young men concluded their formal studies at thirteen to work and help their families. "The majority of Jews," wrote Shaul Stampfer, "such as the peddlers, shoemakers, and tailors, could not study a page of Talmud on their own. They were pious, they said their psalms, they went to hear the midrashic sermons on Saturday afternoons in the synagogues, but they were not themselves learned."[30]

The situation was different in the United States. Here, the rabbinic newcomers in the postwar era championed Jewish education for all young people.[31] This was part of a larger effort, conscious or not, to revise the past to suit modern needs.[32] This is how Kotler and others figured they could ensure the "continuation of Israel's Torah tradition, brutally interrupted by Nazi tyranny."[33] It worked. From 1947 to 1963, the number of Orthodox girls attending the Orthodox Right's all-female Bais Yaakov schools, brought to the United States by Vichna Kaplan, increased from 1,200 to 5,000 students.[34] The yeshivas swelled, as well. The United States was host to a handful of these half-filled schools in the 1930s. By 1976, there existed 40 advanced yeshivas and a total enrollment that hovered around 6,500 students.[35] Kotler's Beth Medrash Govoha, Mesivta Rabbi Chaim Berlin, Ner Israel, Rabbi Jacob Joseph School, Telshe Yeshiva, Tifereth Jerusalem, Torah Vodaath, and Yeshivas Chofetz Chaim all took significant steps to attract young men to their yeshivas.[36] Today, Beth Medrash Govoha in Lakewood enrolls more than 7,000 students.

The leaders of the Orthodox Right reimagined their communities through their own Yeshiva World perspective rather than through the routine and more common lives of, to borrow from Stampfer, the unlearned "peddlers, shoemakers and tailors." As the Yeshiva World symbolized, these schools became the essential cultural anchor for the Orthodox Right. As the community's lifeblood, the yeshiva was the nucleus for social networks, a reference point for shared experiences and the seat of the most powerful leaders in this faith-based enclave. The Yeshiva World moniker caught on as more of its male adherents could claim stature and experience studying in these academies. It is also common for women to identify with this designation even though the traditional yeshiva is an exclusively male space. Women, just as much as men, identify as "yeshivish." In addition to particular modes of dress, language, and other behaviors linked to this religious group, women's efforts to earn a living to support their husbands engage in full-time Torah study and to raise sons who will one day enroll in advanced yeshivas make these women integral—not just honorary—members of the Yeshiva World.[37]

Recall Peter Berger's initial pessimism about Orthodox Judaism's sustainability in modern climes. The Yeshiva World has relied on expanded notions of rabbinic authority to control external forces from destabilizing it. The Yeshiva World designated its extra-halakhic proclamations as "Da'as Torah," literally the "knowledge of Torah"—though, ironically, stated quite deliberately without basis from the Bible or the Talmud.[38] In April 1979, Rabbi Henoch Leibowitz of New York's Yeshiva Chofetz Chaim spoke about the supreme role of rabbinic intuition to help guide members of the Orthodox Right and negotiate the choices of everyday modern life. A Jew, explained Leibowitz, "if he is attached so to speak to that chain of communication, and he accepts *da'as Torah*, and he is willing and understanding to consult superior judgment in Torah and all its aspects in relation to the world, then it's additional insurance for the world for greater protection from the depraved pressures that may be exerted upon him."[39] The heightened religious authority endowed certain rabbinic personalities with the power to identify who and what was "in" and "out" in Orthodox Judaism.

This did not jibe with the moods of more malleable American faiths. Yet the Yeshiva World was in a different place, overcome by a wave of religious triumphalism, and energized with an invigorated devotion to clericalism.[40] Perhaps more than in any prior period, a wider but incalculable swath of Yeshiva World Jews accepted a form of increased rabbinic authority that extended well beyond regular matters of Jewish law and ritual and helped bracket and police the boundaries of this faith-based group. On a communal level, this includes decisions on how to vote in presidential elections (lately, Republican candidates, in contrast to most liberal-minded American Jews) and how to negotiate the use of the Internet, television, and other technologies. On personal levels, many members of this community seek rabbinic direction on employment, courtship, and medical decisions.[41]

The same empowered rabbinic authority has standardized certain behaviors and expectations. This includes dress codes for men (white shirts, dark pants, and Borsalino hats) and women (modest, understated clothing, pleated skirts, and wigs upon marriage). Young women and men court one another through a matchmaker who vets "*shidduch* [matchmaking] résumés" beforehand. The Yeshiva World also produces its own books, newspapers, music, and even toys.[42]

The Yeshiva World boasts systems that reinforce and celebrate its particular lifestyle.[43] Foremost is a constellation of social welfare agencies. Founded in the 1960s, Hatzalah is a volunteer-based emergency medical service (EMS) organization that operates in no fewer than ten states: California, Connecticut, Florida, Illinois, Maryland, Michigan, New Jersey, New York, and Pennsylvania. Equipped with trained paramedics, volunteers, and fleets of ambulances, Hatzalah is designed to offer urgent medical care to its Orthodox constituencies (and anyone else who has its emergency contact numbers). A related organization, Chaverim, provides advanced roadside assistance in more than thirty Orthodox locales, while Shomrim provides security and patrol protection. In addition, philanthropists within the Yeshiva World provide special "Shabbos apartments" and resources to support families with ailing relatives in hospitals. These communities also operate "gamach" systems for Orthodox Jews to borrow wedding dresses, tablecloths, and other items (for all occasions) to ease financial burdens.

The Yeshiva World has also worked hard to address education. Due to the high costs of private schooling (and the unacceptability of public schools for this group), the Yeshiva World is active in the political arena to secure government funding for Orthodox day schools, from bussing subvention to vouchers. The Yeshiva World strongly discourages most traditional private and public colleges. Instead, young people often seek out business opportunities that are not linked to college training or enroll in preapproved college programs. For instance, in 2001 the Orthodox Right partnered with Fairleigh Dickinson University to start a gender-separate adult degree completion program that converts several years of yeshiva (for men) and seminary (for women) learning into multiple years of college credit. Other efforts include leveraging the discounted, expedient College-Level Examination Program (CLEP) tests that can, in many cases, take the place of formal courses and classes, a point made clear in Reuven Frankel's *The Bochur's Guide to College*. Frankel wrote his manual for "yeshiva or Bais Yaakov student[s] and graduate[s] in search of a collegiate journey" that could "alleviate some concerns" of traditional college life.[44] The two-hundred-page guidebook provides a rundown of distance learning options, nontraditional credit testing centers, and a catalog of colleges and universities—most prominently, Charter Oaks State College, Excelsior College, Thomas Edison State College—that have developed collaborations (and obtained the hard-earned trust) of the Yeshiva World.[45]

Is the Yeshiva World fully isolated? Certainly not. A few examples of cultural secretion from mainstream America will suffice. Despite Rabbi Kotler's warnings about this, the Yeshiva World has found curious ways to indulge in American materialism and modernism. In 2021, census tabulations suggested about three-quarters of Lakewood's population of 140,000 is part of the Yeshiva World.[46] As of 2023, some insiders count 150,000 Jews living in Lakewood and nearby Toms River, Manchester, and Howell townships.[47] In other words, Lakewood's Yeshiva World community adds up to the most conservative estimates of the entire American Modern Orthodox population. Lakewood is teeming with religiously modest (but often expensive) dress shops, kosher supermarkets, and varieties of stores that serve a large Orthodox community, far bigger than Kotler had ever hoped for (or approved of). Another example: In 2020 the Agudath Israel sponsored a special event to celebrate the completion of the seven-year cycle of daily Talmud study (called "Daf Yomi") at MetLife Stadium. Over 90,000 women and men filled the stadium, received glossy programs, watched state-of-the-art videos and music, and bought merchandise and food from vendors. In March 2021, the Yeshiva World News website claimed that 100,000 Orthodox Jews descended on Orlando to stay in resorts and hotels for the Passover holiday.[48] These "Pesach programs" function like landed cruises, featuring gourmet food, musical guests, and comedians. Fashionable folks have managed to find ways to express themselves within the rigid dress code. Some men wear stylish slim dark pants and designer shoes while a large number of married women adorn expensive wigs that, frankly, appear better than most people's hair.

Finally, on the political level, the Yeshiva World's embrace of political conservatism has posed problems for this community's categorical obedience to Da'as Torah. In April 2020, Rabbi Yaakov Perlow, the so-described Novominsker Rebbe and head of the Agudath Israel's Council of Torah Sages (Moetzes Gedolei HaTorah) pleaded on his deathbed, stricken with the coronavirus, for his followers to "listen to doctors," adorn masks, and practice social distancing.[49] Government officials had already singled out the Yeshiva World for its dereliction of COVID protocols. Despite Perlow's remonstrations, many within the Yeshiva World continued to flout physicians' policies during the balance of the pandemic.[50] With the pandemic and his community's political proclivities in mind, the Orthodox singer Yaakov Shwekey grabbed headlines in the Jewish press when a YouTube recording surfaced of him singing "Four More Years" at an Orthodox Jewish camp accompanied by lyrics that described president Donald Trump as God's messenger.[51]

Modern Orthodox

The Modern Orthodox were once the most oft-discussed American Orthodox subgroup. In the 1960s, Rabbi Norman Lamm emerged as the leading champion of this community, one that saw itself as "Halachically legitimate, philosophically persuasive, religiously inspiring, and personally convincing."[52] The New York rabbi and future president of Yeshiva University (YU), Lamm supported a brand of Orthodoxy that was unabashedly committed to Religious Zionism and the State of Israel, liberal education, and dialogue (so long as it did not compromise Orthodoxy's interpretation of Jewish law) with their Conservative and Reform counterparts. Lamm derived religious confidence from his teacher, Rabbi Joseph B. Soloveitchik. At YU, Soloveitchik trained multiple generations of Modern Orthodox rabbis—although he rarely used that phrase.[53] That was Lamm's province. Lamm's Modern Orthodoxy encouraged its adherents to "maintain our undiminished loyalty to the Halakhah" while completely engaged in the societal currents that flowed around them, leaving behind any and all "antagonistic attitudes."[54] Lamm was helped along by a cadre of committed young people—many of them trained in the rising number of Orthodox private schools, camps, and youth groups—who likewise proved Orthodox Judaism's compatibility with postwar American culture.[55] This rising generation observed the Six-Day War in June 1967 and interpreted Israel's unprecedented victories as an act of God and a harbinger for the coming of the Messiah. Since the 1980s, the Modern Orthodox–aligned Rabbinical Council of America's official prayer book contains a ritual read aloud on the Shabbat that calls for "Our Father in heaven, Protector and Redeemer of Israel, bless the State of Israel, the first flowering of our redemption."[56] Several rabbinic elites and female voices added religious leadership and advanced Torah education for women to the Modern Orthodox agenda, with mixed success.[57]

Modern Orthodox Judaism flourished in the 1970s under the leadership of Lamm and its flagship, Yeshiva University, in Upper Manhattan. YU is part of an unofficial triumvirate that includes the Orthodox Union and the Rabbinical Council of America mentioned above. From schools to synagogues, publications and programs, the Modern Orthodox emerged as the most prominent sector of the Orthodox community. In the 1980s, Lamm and others were upset over criticism that theirs was too "modern" for a tradition-bound faith enclave. It was time for a rebrand. Lamm wrote in 1986 that "modern" somehow started in many people's minds to connote religious compromise, which was never his intention. Drawing from Maimonides's (and Aristotle's) "golden mean," Lamm preached Centrist Orthodoxy's belief in moderation and nuance in the areas of higher learning and Western culture. Centrist Orthodoxy, like Modern Orthodoxy before it, valued Religious Zionism.[58] But right-wing critics took just as much advantage of the new religious taxonomy, and Lamm reverted back to Modern Orthodox by the end of the 1990s.[59]

Whatever the moniker in vogue, in the late 1980s sociologists Samuel Heilman and Steven Cohen referred to this group as the "mainstream."[60] That is no longer the case. According to the 2013 Pew report, the Modern Orthodox hold a 30 percent share of the overall American Orthodox population, or about 150,000–200,000 women and men. Part of the reason for the decline is what Heilman termed the "slide to the right" (as well as relatively lower birthrates compared with families belonging to other sectors of American Orthodoxy) that increased the numbers of erstwhile Modern Orthodox–educated young people who now identify as part of the Yeshiva World.[61]

To be sure, there are still bustling Orthodox strongholds. In Bergen County in Northern New Jersey, Modern Orthodox communities in Bergenfield, Englewood, Fair Lawn, and Teaneck are thriving. Modern Orthodox schools are full; synagogue sanctuaries fill (with men, not usually women) each morning before the workday; and thousands of families spend Shabbat morning praying in formalized children's groups, junior congregations, and, after services, socializing beside trays of food and snacks. There are multiple baseball leagues for Modern Orthodox children, women-only aerobic centers, restaurants (even a kosher bar), and other amenities in Teaneck's commercial sector. Teaneck's Modern Orthodox Jews have also borrowed from the Yeshiva World playbook, establishing Chaverim of Bergen County in 2009; the nonmedical emergency organization had, as of 2023, 100 volunteers.[62] Recognizing that many of its constituents live across the George Washington Bridge, Yeshiva University leases billboards to advertise its programs and fundraising campaigns on Route 4 to catch the attention of the Modern Orthodox Jews of Teaneck, New Jersey.[63]

But this, and perhaps Modern Orthodox communities on Long Island, are the exceptions that prove the rule. In other locales, Modern Orthodoxy struggles. Many Modern Orthodox communities, as a result of their Religious Zionist beliefs, have lost members due to migration to Israel. Another major reason is that the tenets of Modern Orthodoxy are no longer all that distinguishable from the Yeshiva World. First, the latter has softened its stance on Israel; the erstwhile anti-Zionists are by and large non-Zionists. The Yeshiva World visits Israel, champions it, and votes for American politicians whom they believe best serve Israel's interests.

Second, the Modern Orthodox and the Yeshiva World are much closer aligned in terms of education. It is most apparent within the private school orbit: Orthodox Union and Agudath Israel officials spend much time, in partnership, to advocate for government tuition subvention and funding. There is also increased parity in the realm of higher education. The Yeshiva World has developed partnerships with universities to help its sons and daughters earn degrees in "practical" fields such as accounting and the health sciences. Their children enroll in top medical schools and elite law schools. Meanwhile, the Modern Orthodox have cooled to the liberal arts and the traditional nonvocational undergraduate experience. It is very expensive to live a Modern Orthodox lifestyle. The cost of education is particularly painful. Private school and college are very expensive.[64] Tuition for families, say, with four children enrolled in private school and summer camp can run, easily, about $120,000. Some Modern Orthodox Jews worry about how their children will do on a secular college campus amid BDS (the Boycott, Divestment, and Sanctions movement against Israel) and rising antisemitism. Even before these developments, though, in 2003, two recent college graduates, Gil Perl and Yaakov Weinstein, published a widely disseminated *Parent's Guide to Orthodox Assimilation on University Campuses*. The coauthors warned that "many Orthodox Jewish students at secular colleges are questioning and finding only unorthodox answers."[65] The short tract with a Modern Orthodox audience in mind warned about the perils of the campus quad. It received significant attention; it was passed around in yeshivas and seminaries in Israel and discussed at many Hillels throughout the United States.

It's not just the social and cultural aspects of college life. The Modern Orthodox—like so many Americans—have counseled their youngsters to forsake "impractical" degrees in the humanities in favor of business programs, computer science, and other professional-minded tracks. Consider the case of Yeshiva University. In 1987, YU opened the Sy Syms School of Business in response to student requests for "new areas of interest." President Norman Lamm anticipated the criticism. Even as a minority of students pleaded for business programs, he was adamant that Yeshiva remain a liberal arts school. YU's business school, therefore, trumpeted Rabbi Lamm, "insists on a liberal dose of the liberal arts." He remained resolutely opposed to total vocationalism and intended for the business school to retain a small portion of the university's total undergraduate offerings. This was in contradistinction to Touro College (now Touro University), which founded undergraduate programs limited to majors and pathways that emphasized employability.[66] Today, YU has borrowed from the Touro "playbook." Sy Syms's male student body is larger than (the all-male) Yeshiva College's. (Stern College for Women is still much larger than the women's cohort at Sy Syms.)

Third, the Modern Orthodox voting patterns seem to be moving in line with their Yeshiva World counterparts. In truth, Modern Orthodox Jews probably vote somewhere in between the GOP-leaning Orthodox Right and the majority of American Jews who have, since Franklin Roosevelt, voted for Democrats.[67] Yet it is also the case that in recent years Modern Orthodox groups have taken public steps to align with conservative America. For example, in November 2016, the Rabbinical Council of America purchased a full page advertisement in the *New York Times* to "wish President-elect Trump the greatest success in making every effort to heal a divided country" and to reverse "anti-Israel" resolutions adopted by the United Nations with the support of President Barack Obama.[68] Two years later, the Orthodox Union honored Trump-appointed attorney general Jeff Sessions at its annual conference even though Sessions was at that time embroiled in a major immigration crisis that centered on the administration's protocol that led to the indefinite separation of parents and children entering the United States at the southern border.[69] Neither notable instance was the same as the decision of Yeshiva World leader Rabbi Shmuel Kamenetsky to formally endorse Donald Trump before the 2020 election.[70] However, all this demonstrates the increasing proximity of the two American Orthodox subgroups and the decreased capacities of the Modern Orthodox to distinguish itself from the balance of the Orthodox community.

Modern Orthodox Judaism is also facing a cultural public relations crisis. Concomitant to all the above is the reluctance of the Modern Orthodox to embrace liberal calls to elevate women's leadership and take determined steps to include members of the LGBTQ community. The numbers of those affected by these politicized issues has become far less important than their import in public discourse. Modern Orthodoxy has struggled to articulate a clear position on both. As a result, this group has suffered from an identity crisis on the public relations front. In February 2017, the Orthodox Union (OU) released a statement that banned women from serving as clergy but granted them other leadership roles outside of the pulpit.[71] The OU's policy was backed by a decision of a seven-member rabbinic panel—most of its members were YU rabbinic faculty—that acknowledged the importance of female community educators and other nonrabbinic positions, much to the chagrin of more liberal elements.

Perhaps a greater tumult erupted in April 2023, in response to a report that YU had cancelled three Talmud courses at Stern College for Women due to low enrollment. The decision was met by a firestorm of complaints that questioned YU's commitment to women's advanced Talmud study. More than 1,400 people signed a petition that urged the university to reinstate the Talmud classes, a request that was, in short order, granted by Yeshiva's administration.[72] These episodes betoken the fragility of women's leadership and advanced learning within the Modern Orthodox orbit.

LGBTQ represents another important but divisive issue. Given the Bible's explicit condemnation of homosexuality (Lev. 18:22), the Modern Orthodox rabbinate—like other tradition-bound faith leaders—have sensed that theirs was a no-win proposition. In the 1980s, one Orthodox rabbi preached resolute fidelity to the biblical text to withstand the "media's continuing portrayal of homosexuals as positive role models and the increasing acceptance of the homosexual as a minority group with 'legitimate' civil rights."[73] Others were more congenial about the predicament. In December 1992, an Orthodox rabbinic writer expressed "sympathy" with homosexuals who wished to live an Orthodox life. On the other hand, Reuven Bulka was incorrigible about the halakhic implications. To him, the plain meaning of the Bible's view on homosexual relations was immutable.[74]

Most Modern Orthodox rabbis just preferred to stay silent. When the YU-trained rabbi Steven Greenberg recalled publicly acknowledging his sexuality in the late 1990s, he wrote that "my coming out was largely ignored by the organized Orthodox community."[75] Most public discussion within the Orthodox fold was concentrated on muting the conversation. In December 2009, YU students held a panel on "Being Gay in the Modern Orthodox World." Leading members of the YU faculty disapproved, reprimanding that "publicizing or seeking legitimization even for the homosexual orientation one feels, runs contrary to Torah."[76] However, their call went by and large unheeded. The event attracted eight hundred students and interested listeners, but Modern Orthodox organizations and leaders remained, on the whole, mostly silent.

In 2021, YU refused to recognize a Pride Alliance of undergraduate LGBTQ students and their allies. In turn, the Pride Alliance successfully sued to overturn the decision, and the university has rigorously appealed to higher courts to defend its decision on "religious" grounds. The controversy has sparked interest throughout the Jewish community, compelling faculty and donors to criticize YU's efforts to bar the Pride Alliance from its listing of approved and funded student organizations.[77]

These cultural controversies have splintered the fragile Modern Orthodox community into smaller factions. In some circles, they break down, albeit unofficially, into three small camps: Centrist Orthodox, Modern Orthodox, and Open Orthodox. According to sociologist Sylvia Fishman, Centrist Orthodox "have deep misgivings about many elements of contemporary American culture and try to keep their distance from anything that symbolizes them."[78] To Fishman, the Modern Orthodox—while their "lifestyles are similar in many particulars to those of Centrist Orthodox Jews"—are more willing to embrace modern mores such as coeducation and feminism. To the leftward flank of the Modern Orthodox are the Open Orthodox, a group that has pushed for women's Orthodox ordination and several ritual items that are unacceptable to those on the relative religious right. The Open Orthodox operate their own small organizations such as Yeshivat Chovevei Torah (for men) and Yeshivat Maharat (for women) and the International Rabbinic Fellowship (for male and female clergy).[79] It has at times been energized by short-lived grassroots organizations such as Edah and PORAT (People for Orthodox Renaissance and Torah).[80] Notwithstanding these decided differences, these nomenclatures are by no means official designations, especially given the relative tininess of each Modern Orthodox subgroup.

More than anything else, the Modern Orthodox have lacked leadership. Rabbi Lamm retired from Yeshiva University in 2003, and few others have emerged as champions of the Modern Orthodox movement. In October 2017, Rabbi Jonathan Sacks, former chief rabbi of the British Commonwealth, publicly pleaded with YU's newest president, Rabbi Ari Berman (in between Lamm and Berman, YU was led by Richard Joel), to "find another label" since the "phrase Modern Orthodoxy was overrated to the nth degree."[81]

Instead, America's Modern Orthodox community has drawn strength from their Dati Le'umi counterparts in Israel. The Dati Le'umi hold Religious Zionism at the center of their movement, a far greater emphasis than the Modern Orthodox in the diaspora. In Israel, writes one sociologist, the religious Zionists desire to "leave nothing outside the boundaries of religion."[82] Perhaps something of an overstatement, it is certainly the case that Dati Le'umi Jews are prone to create an integrated religious culture in Israel that does its best to transform somewhat secular elements like politics and business into religious experiences.[83] In keeping with the teachings of Rabbi Avraham Yitzhak Kook and his son, Rabbi Zvi Yehudah Kook, they do all this for the sake of a fervent messianic Zionist agenda.[84] Modern Orthodox Jews in America are comfortable with a far more "compartmentalized" lifestyle.[85] True, religiously observant Jews accept the dictates of halakhah in all areas of life, but this hardly rivals the sort of religious pathos achieved in Israel. In the Holy Land, there is much and recurring discussion about Judaism's responsibility to govern public policy, legislation, and Shabbat bus schedules.

The spirit of Religious Zionism and the dense concentration of tradition-abiding Jews in Israel animates a strong cultural current that has, to a significant degree, washed onto American shores. The Dati Le'umi leaders have inspired new and more advanced forms of learning for America's Modern Orthodox women and introduced new thinkers and ideas, thanks in large part to Koren Publishers.[86] For decades, Religious Zionist summer overnight camps have attracted hundreds of Modern Orthodox young people; to a certain extent, their success is responsible for the steady stream of migration of U.S.-born Modern Orthodox Jews to Israel since the 1970s.[87] The Israel-based yeshivas and educational institutions have furnished education technology and multimedia that are in wide use in Modern Orthodox day schools.[88] These invaluable imports are critical to the vitality of American Modern Orthodoxy as it searches for stronger, indigenous footholds.

Ḥasidim Come to America

In September 1946, Rabbi Yoel Teitelbaum, the Satmar Rebbe, arrived in the United States. Political connections had rescued Teitelbaum from the horrors of the Nazi Holocaust and Bergen-Belsen death camp, but the Satmar Rebbe had been unable to save the majority of his Hungarian Ḥasidic followers. Teitelbaum was determined to rebuild his ḥasidic court. After struggling to accomplish this in Palestine (the State of Israel wasn't established until 1948), a small group convinced Teitelbaum that he could resurrect Satmar in New York.[89]

Teitelbaum was demanding. He vociferously opposed Zionism as a kind of heresy and insisted that his community speak Yiddish rather than adopt (for many, forcibly "forget") the English language. Fearful of the influences of liberal education, Teitelbaum built separate schools for boys and girls that offered limited secular studies. Satmar's educational system did not prepare its young people for college. College was emblematic of Teitelbaum's deep anxieties about liberal learning. As a result, most Satmar Ḥasidim live very modestly, if not, to be frank, in poverty. Teitelbaum also enforced a uniform for his followers. Even amid New York's summer heat, Satmar men dress in dark three-piece suits, light but lengthy coats, long socks, and furred black hats. Women adorn long-sleeved blouses and ankle-length skirts, and a small hat atop wigs.[90]

Satmar, like most ḥasidic imports to the United States, placed a high value on insularity. The exception is the Chabad-Lubavitch group, which is why I address Chabad in its own section. Satmar started to flourish as a separatist enclave in Brooklyn's Williamsburg neighborhood. In the 1960s, amid so-called White flight, Teitelbaum and his close-knit circle decided to remain in Williamsburg and lean into the policies produced by president Lyndon Johnson's war on poverty legislation. Satmar helped steward the formation of the United Jewish Organizations advocacy group to work with lawmakers to support needy Jewish families. Satmar worked with government officials and ethnic groups to move families into two housing projects, Independence Tower and the Jonathan Williams Houses. In this way, Satmar embraced their new political climes.[91]

All the while, the Satmar Rebbe was in search of a place to call his own. He had in mind Rabbi Aharon Kotler's settlement in Lakewood, New Jersey. In addition, Teitelbaum aspired to build what Rabbi Yaakov Yosef Twersky, the Skever Rebbe, had accomplished in 1954 when he purchased a 130-acre dairy farm along Route 45 in Rockland County, New York. The small group of Skever Ḥasidim were ill prepared to handle the opposition from zoning boards but eventually established New Square as a haven apart from the American mainstream.[92] Teitelbaum and his Satmar community learned from the Skever experience and were otherwise better prepared to negotiate the legal aspects of incorporating their own separatist village. In 1977, after significant lobbying and several false starts, Teitelbaum moved with many of his Satmar Ḥasidim from Williamsburg to Orange County, New York. Satmar named their newly established village after their leader, calling it Kiryas Joel.[93]

Today, Satmar is the largest ḥasidic group in the United States, totaling about 125,000 of the 300,000 ḥasidim (200,000 in New York).[94] Other reconstituted ḥasidic courts include Bobov, Klausenburg, and Vizhnitz. In a few cases, leaders such as Rabbi Pinchas David Horowitz, the Boston Rebbe, established American-made ḥasidic courts.

Da'as Torah, that powerful current of rabbinic authority, is even more important within ḥasidic circles than it is among the Yeshiva World. Almost every ḥasidic sect is led by a rebbe who enjoys unparalleled clout and decision-making for his followers. Accordingly, succession upon the death (rarely, upon abdication) of a rebbe has the capacity to create massive upheaval. When Rabbi Yoel Teitelbaum died, there was major discord between Teitelbaum's childless widow and his nephew, Rabbi Moshe Teitelbaum. In 2006, Rabbi Moshe Teitelbaum died, and two of his sons splintered Satmar into combative factions: Rabbi Aaron Teitelbaum in Kiryas Joel and Rabbi Zalman Teitelbaum in the older Williamsburg neighborhood. Various and troublesome challenges of transition of succession have also plagued ḥasidim belonging to Bobov, Boyan, Kopyczynitz, and Munkács.[95]

Withal, ḥasidic communities have a knack for stabilizing—even at the cost of irrevocable division, as in the case of Satmar. The result has been the formation of communal blocs that have leveraged America's political system. In general, ḥasidic groups have voted for Democratic candidates who have promised welfare and government systems to support low-income families with limited employment opportunities. The exception is presidential elections; ḥasidim have tended to vote for Republican candidates. Overall, politicians have taken significant notice because of these communities' high voter-turnout and allegiance to the prevailing authority. In 2006, for example, the *New York Post* covered Hillary Clinton's condolence visit—the paper described it as "The Senator and the Satmars"—to the Teitelbaum family upon the death of Rabbi Moshe Teitelbaum.[96]

Political know-how and connections have their limits. For instance, the American ḥasidic machine backfired in a very public front page story in the *New York Times* in September 2022. The newspaper reported that ḥasidic private schools had taken federal and state aid—perhaps as much as a billion dollars from 2018 to 2022—but had provided inadequate general studies instruction. In 2019, the story reported, a thousand students at the Satmar-affiliated Central United Talmudical Academy sat for standardized tests in reading and math, and each of them failed. The journalists examined records of ḥasidic schools that enroll about fifty thousand boys and found that less than 1 percent of the pupils scored at grade level. Among ḥasidic girls' schools, just 20 percent of students scored at passable benchmarks in standardized exams. Some ḥasidic schools find teachers on Craigslist and other websites. The exposé reported that teachers in these New York schools are poorly paid and lack significant teaching experience (and most cannot speak Yiddish, the pupils' primary language).[97]

Chabad-Lubavitch

In March 1940, Rabbi Yosef Yitzchak Schneersohn transplanted his Chabad-Lubavitch court from Warsaw, Poland, to New York. Schneersohn was the sixth Lubavitcher Rebbe, the head of the ḥasidic group founded in the late eighteenth century that traces its roots to a small village, Lyubavichi, in Belarus. Upon arrival, Schneersohn declared that "America is no different," an indication that Chabad intended to operate along the same lines that it had done in Europe rather than adapt to the entrenched rhythm of American Jewish life.[98] Schneersohn established his headquarters in the Crown Heights neighborhood in Brooklyn, already home to a large Orthodox enclave. After his death in 1950, Schneersohn's cousin and son-in-law, Rabbi Menachem Schneerson, took the reins of the Chabad movement. The seventh (and last) Lubavitcher Rebbe doubled down on his predecessor's vision, expanding the Chabad rabbinic emissary network throughout the United States (with a focus on college campuses, like Berkeley) and outreach to America's unaffiliated Jews.[99]

By the 1980s, a member of the Chabad inner circle, owing to major fundraising and the establishment of "Chabad houses" on two hundred college campuses, declared that "Lubavitch has become an empire."[100] The Chabad house became an all-in-one religious center for the Chabad rabbinic family and its constituencies. It served as a synagogue, social space, learning site, and pastoral station. Chabad attracted significant attention. In 1985, the *New Yorker* published a lengthy three-part story on Chabad "counterculture."[101] This and other media coverage of Chabad seized on a common theme: As Rabbi Schneersohn had pledged, Chabad did not feel beholden to the social and institutional conventions of American Jewish life. Chabad's embrace of alcohol and aggressive outreach programs are two examples of this, points that frustrated even some Orthodox leaders with whom Chabad shared a common set of religious practices.

Chabad was a polarizing force. In the 1980s, some vocal Jewish parents in Boston objected to Chabad's "cult-like practices" that drew in their children.[102] At Yale University, the rabbi in charge of the Hillel campus organization complained that the local Chabad rabbi arrested the attention of the Jewish undergraduates with, according to him, shallow forms of spirituality and party games. Whatever the reasons, the positive reception of the upstart Chabad in New Haven had significant fundraising implications. According to Yale's campus rabbi, "The Lubavitchers rented a space that cost more than the entire yearly budget for Hillel."[103] In Southern California, Chabad reportedly took root in the 1970s and grew "from a garage in West Los Angeles to a network of institutions, up and down the state, in little more than a decade."[104]

In 2017, Chabad organized a Chabad house in South Dakota (a community of fewer than four hundred Jews), ensuring that the movement had satellites in all fifty American states.[105] Chabad's rabbis (and their wives) are trained to cultivate relationships. To that end, the Chabad rabbinate is fundamentally pastoral, despite the fact that its students receive minimal professional training. Chabad coaches their young rabbis, called *shlichim* (messengers of the Rebbe), to go about their work in an easygoing and nonjudgmental demeanor. This style suits the women and men with whom Chabad interacts. These mostly nonobservant Jews much prefer a Judaism that can be understood without extensive Jewish literacy and offered to them by a warm and indulgent rabbinic pastor. It is also conceivable that the many unaffiliated Jews who enter Chabad houses also enjoy that their local rabbi is a Lubavitch ḥasid with the otherworldly trappings of a long beard and coat rather than a well-groomed Orthodox rabbi dressed in a standard suit and tie. This contrasted with the typical Orthodox rabbi, who preferred a "formal look" and was content with "in-reach," appealing to the steadfast Orthodox Jews.[106]

The other key to the Chabad rabbinate is the rabbi's wife, or "rebbetzin." In 1990, Fay Kranz declared the Chabad rebbetzin a "minor miracle." She surmised that the Chabad rabbi's wife had become "an integral part of the organization and her husband could not function without her."[107] The position of the Chabad rebbetzin cannot be overstated. At the minimum, she runs the preschools and other educational activities which help bring children and their parents into the Chabad fold. In truth, though, her position is far more essential to the Chabad cause. Paired with her unshaven, unmodern-seeming husband, the standard Chabad rebbetzin is sure to appear in public covered with heavy doses of makeup and clothed in stylish outfits. For many Orthodox and non-Orthodox Jews, it is the Chabad woman who is far more approachable and relatable to their modern senses. The rebbetzin, therefore, is more than a vital component of the Chabad organization: she is a full-partner in the Chabad enterprise. For sure, there are limits. In concert with traditional Jewish practice, the rebbetzin does not lead prayer services. Yet, cloaked in a traditional role, the female emissary heads many of the Chabad events and functions in areas that her husband is too socially limited to properly access.[108]

One tabulation of Chabad's population in the United States totals thirty thousand women and men.[109] But Chabad's reach is far wider, since its Shabbat services, programs, and preschools are attended by other Orthodox Jews and, in some cases primarily, marginally affiliated American Jews. Chabad's outreach program breaks from the all-or-nothing position of most Orthodox communities. The Yeshiva World expects full obedience of its members to all its religious and social strictures, and for that its constituents obtain access to its community resources and philanthropic support and the Modern Orthodox, in theory, prescribe a particular way of life that is both "modern" and "Orthodox." Chabad, on the other hand, led by the Lubavitcher Rebbe's vision, articulates a "mitzvah campaign" that asks Jews to accrue behaviors (e.g., giving charity, purchasing Jewish books) and acceptance of rituals (kindling Shabbat candles, laying tefillin) one at a time. Rather than enforce a rigid religious system, Chabad asks its followers to thicken their Jewishness over time. While those within the inner circles of Chabad punctiliously observe the gamut of Jewish law, no individual or family is shunned for honoring the majority of Jewish observance in the breach.[110]

Chabad has not operated without controversies. First and foremost, an uncountable number of Chabad rabbis and community members believe that the Rabbi Menachem Schneerson, who died in 1994, is the Messiah. The movement to crown Schneerson began at the end of his lifetime, when he was unwell, likely unable to fully comprehend and squash the burgeoning messianic movement emerging around him. Today, there exist Chabad members who wave yellow flags with Schneerson's picture and Hebrew or English wording that anticipate his return to the world as the fateful messiah and future king of Israel. One of Chabad's most virulent critics is the Orthodox historian David Berger of Yeshiva University. Berger authored a book to challenge what he perceived as the "Scandal of Orthodox Indifference" to Chabad messianism, replete with sources and accounts of the Orthodox leaders who, despite the claim, were publicly critical of Schneerson and his most radical followers. Berger feared that the continued momentum gained by this movement would mean that the "difference between the Christian and Sabbatian redemption and that of Lubavitch messianists blurs to the point of vanishing."[111]

Chabad has also pushed the envelope on First Amendment policies by advocating for public menorah lightings on government grounds and urging for the reintroduction of formalized prayer in public schools.[112] These episodes have rankled the liberal American Jewish public and their community organizers. However, like the perceived "indifference" about Chabad's eschatological vision, most Jews—Orthodox or otherwise—seem to provide Chabad a high degree of freedom because of the group's value in providing outreach and a Jewish lifeline to Jews (and sometimes non-Jews) wherever they may be.

Conclusion

In the postpandemic religious ecosystem, Orthodox Judaism is an outlier. While most synagogues and churches adapted to the coronavirus epidemic by pivoting to remote services, Orthodox Jews, since they prohibit the use of electronic devices on Shabbat, were one of the few that refused to modify their stance. As a result, the Orthodox—of all above-discussed persuasions—are one of the very few faith communities that are not grappling with how to attract worshipers back to in-person religious services.[113]

This is one of the more profound ways in which all sectors of the American Orthodox community, no matter how disparate in other ways, remain profoundly linked. It's part of the thick social network that, at some degree or another, "summons" Orthodox Jews to remain and flourish in their religious communities.[114] Owing to the need to live within walking distance of a synagogue (since driving is prohibited on Shabbat), Orthodox Jews live in geographically close-knit communities. Since they attend the same synagogues, enroll their children in the same schools, and participate in the same organizations, Orthodox Jews develop strong relationships to each other, and this makes it worth the high costs of living an Orthodox lifestyle. Put simply, unless Orthodox Jewish families earn upward of $200,000–$300,000 per year (depending on family size and choices of schools, etc.), every cent of their post-tax paychecks, on the whole, will be spent on education, synagogue dues, and the high costs of kosher food for Shabbat and holidays. Yet, given that value—social networks, babysitting/education groups on Shabbat morning, communal meals ("kiddush"), and social services that vary from medical support to private school scholarships—Orthodox Jews believe that is a worthy return on investment.

The Internet and the broader impact of the digital age is another binding force for the Orthodox precisely because cyberspace poses a challenge to the compelling social network of Orthodox Jewish life. In May 2012, Yeshiva World leaders convened a major gathering at Citi Field in Queens, New York, to warn about the dangers of the Internet.[115] Yet, despite threats of shunning and other social censures, members of the Yeshiva World have found a space within social media such as Twitter—they call it Frum Twitter (now X)—to share and learn ideas. Ḥasidic heads are also fearful of social media's impact by disrupting their control over adherents. Albeit in small number, some ḥasidic women and men have taken to social media and other digital forums, armed with covert aliases, to learn about taboo subjects in their local environs. These "hidden heretics" share their findings with one another and those outside of their ḥasidic communities.[116]

The Modern Orthodox are the most comfortable with the digital age. With this freedom, Modern Orthodox Jews have, in subtle ways, disrupted some of the social hierarchy of their community. This is particularly poignant for Modern Orthodox women. Unlike their synagogue, at which men lead the prayers and the rabbinate is (in most instances) a male profession, Modern Orthodox women have the same access as men to post about their religious communities and opine on matters that are important to them. This ranges from the April 2023 controversy over Talmud study at Stern College to sharing recipes and images of Shabbat and holiday cuisines. Even beyond the Modern Orthodox realm, Orthodox women leverage social media and create podcast content to address fertility issues and mental health.[117] In a very real way, then, social media has generated another close-knit space for the Orthodox Jewish community that parallels, complements, and sometimes disrupts the in-person communities that have survived and thrived for the past decades. America's Orthodox Jewish communities, then, are better prepared than most faith groups to tackle the myriad technological, economic, and social issues that stand, presumably, to confront and challenge them.

NOTES

1 For a useful table with numbers on the American Jewish population, see Jonathan D. Sarna, *American Judaism: A History*, 2nd ed. (New Haven, CT: Yale University Press, 2019), 391–92. I dutifully acknowledge my gratitude to Rabbi Jay Goldmitz and Dovi Safier for their helpful comments that improved an earlier draft of this chapter.
2 Marshall Sklare, *Conservative Judaism: An American Religious Movement* (Glencoe, IL: Free Press, 1955), 42.
3 Peter L. Berger, *The Heretical Imperative: Contemporary Possibilities of Religious Affirmation* (Garden City, NJ: Anchor, 1979), 27.
4 Jeffrey S. Gurock, "The Winnowing of American Orthodoxy," in *Approaches to Modern Judaism*, vol. 2, ed. Marc Lee Raphael (Chico, CA: Scholars Press, 1984), 41–53.
5 M. Herbert Danzger, *Returning to Tradition: The Contemporary Revival of Orthodox Judaism* (New Haven, CT: Yale University Press, 1989), 71–95. On how these returnees socialize into Orthodox norms, see Sarah Bunin Benor, *Becoming Frum: How Newcomers Learn the Language and Culture of Orthodox Judaism* (New Brunswick, NJ: Rutgers University Press, 2012).

6   Peter L. Berger, *The Many Altars of Modernity: Toward a Paradigm for Religion in a Pluralist Age* (Boston: De Gruyter, 2014), 10.
7   Alan Cooperman and Becka A. Alper, *Jewish Americans in 2020* (Washington, DC: Pew Research Center, 2021), 8.
8   Steven M. Cohen, "The Irresistible Numeric Rise of the Orthodox," *Forward*, December 30, 2016, 16. For the first Pew report on American Jews, see Luis Lugo et al., *A Portrait of Jewish Americans* (Washington, DC: Pew Research Center, 2013).
9   J. J. Goldberg, "It's Time to Rethink Who Is a New York Jew," *Forward*, June 22, 2012, forward.com.
10 I borrow "bargain" from scholars of the American Amish. See Donald B. Kraybill, *The Riddle of Amish Culture* (Baltimore, MD: Johns Hopkins University Press, 1989), 186.
11 See Michael A. Meyer, *Response to Modernity: A History of the Reform Movement in Judaism* (New York: Oxford University Press, 1988), 235–63. Preceding these institutions (and afterward), there was ample controversy among Reform leaders on how to unite their movement. See Zev Eleff, *Who Rules the Synagogue? Religious Authority and the Formation of American Judaism* (New York: Oxford University Press, 2016).
12 See Michael R. Cohen, *The Birth of Conservative Judaism: Solomon Schechter's Disciples and the Creation of an American Religious Movement* (New York: Columbia University Press, 2012), 44–68.
13 As late as 1898, it was not at all clear to traditional Jewish leaders that the term "Orthodox" was the very best nomenclature. See summary of minutes and meetings that led to the founding of the Union of Orthodox Jewish Congregations of America in Zev Eleff, *Modern Orthodox Judaism: A Documentary History* (Lincoln: University of Nebraska Press/Jewish Publication Society, 2016), 94–96.
14 In fact, in the very first known declaration of Jewish Orthodox in the United States, an essay authored by Jacob Mordecai, describes this community as a "congregationalists." For this text, see Eleff, *Modern Orthodox Judaism*, 10. See also Roger Horowitz, *Kosher U.S.A: How Coke Became Kosher and Other Tales of Modern Food* (New York: Columbia University Press, 2016).
15 See, for example, Jeffrey S. Gurock, *Orthodox Jews in America* (Bloomington: Indiana University Press, 2009), 255–72.
16 Sidney E. Mead, "The Fact of Pluralism and the Persistence of Sectarianism," in *The Religion of the Republic*, ed. Elwyn A. Smith (Philadelphia: Fortress, 1971), 261.
17 See Sidney E. Mead, "Denominationalism: The Shape of Protestantism in America," *Church History* 23 (December 1954): 291–320.
18 See David Ellenson and Daniel Gordis, *Pledges of Jewish Allegiance: Conversion, Law, and Policymaking in Nineteenth- and Twentieth-Century Orthodox Responsa* (Stanford, CA: Stanford University Press, 2012), 90–120.
19 See Mijal Bitton, "Liberal Grammar and the Construction of American Jewish Identity," *American Sociologist* 53 (November 2022): 1–19.

20 See Michal Raucher, "Ultra-Orthodox Jews from the 'Margins': Revisiting Book Tradition," *AJS Review* 46 (April 2022): 38–62.
21 Jeffrey S. Gurock, "Resisters and Accommodators: Varieties of Orthodox Rabbis in America, 1886–1983," *American Jewish Archives Journal* 35 (November 1983): 109.
22 Samuel C. Heilman, "The Many Faces of Orthodoxy, Part I," *Modern Judaism* 2 (February 1982): 27.
23 Charles S. Liebman, "Orthodoxy in American Jewish Life," *American Jewish Year Book* 66 (1965): 91. This feature was on par with America's Protestant fundamentalists, who possessed antimodernist proclivities but also due to the small but important positivistic aspects of their faith. See Joel A. Carpenter, *Revive Us Again: The Reawakening of American Fundamentalism* (Oxford: Oxford University Press, 1997), 88.
24 Liebman, "Orthodoxy in American Jewish Life," 33.
25 See Yoel Finkelman, "Ḥaredi Isolation in Changing Environments: A Case Study in Yeshiva Immigration," *Modern Judaism* 22 (February 2002): 61–82.
26 See Jeffrey S. Gurock, "American Orthodox Organizations in Support of Zionism, 1880–1930," in *Zionism and Religion*, ed. Shmuel Almog, Jehuda Reinharz, and Anita Shapira (Hanover, NH: Brandeis University Press, 1998), 219–34.
27 See Leslie Ginsparg Klein, "'No Candy Store, No Pizza Shops, No Maxi-Skirts, No Makeup': Socializing Orthodox Jewish Girls through Schooling," *Journal of the History of Childhood and Youth* 9 (Winter 2016): 140–58.
28 Yoel Finkelman, "An Ideology for American Yeshiva Students: The Sermons of R. Aharon Kotler, 1942–1962," *Journal of Jewish Studies* 58 (Autumn 2007): 319. See also Zev Eleff, "Rabbi Hayim of Volozhin, Rabbi Aharon Kotler, and the Remaking of an American Jewish Prophecy," *American Jewish Archives Journal* 72 (2020): 87–114.
29 Finkelman, "Ideology for American Yeshiva Students," 320.
30 See Shaul Stampfer, "*Heder* Study, Knowledge of Torah, and the Maintenance of Social Stratification in Traditional East European Jewish Society," *Studies in Jewish Education* 3 (1988): 283.
31 See Doniel Zvi Kramer, *The Day Schools and Torah Umesorah: The Seeding of Traditional Judaism in America* (New York: Yeshiva University Press, 1984), 13.
32 See Marc B. Shapiro, *Changing the Immutable: How Orthodox Judaism Rewrites Its History* (Oxford: Littman Library, 2015), 1–55.
33 Cited in Doniel Zvi Kramer, "The History and Impact of Torah Umesorah and Hebrew Day Schools in America" (PhD diss., Yeshiva University, 1976), 30.
34 Leslie M. Ginsparg, "Defining Bais Yaakov: A Historical Study of Yeshivish Orthodox Girls High School Education in America, 1963–1984" (PhD diss., New York University, 2009), 12–13.
35 See David Singer, "The Yeshivah World," *Commentary* 62 (October 1976): 72.
36 See Alvin Irwin Schiff, *The Jewish Day School in America* (New York: Jewish Education Committee, 1966), 61–62, 237–39.

37 See Sarah Bunin Benor, *Becoming Frum: How Newcomers Learn the Language and Culture of Orthodox Judaism* (New Brunswick, NJ: Rutgers University Press, 2012), 111–17; and Laura Shaw Frank, "Yeshivish Women Clergy: The Secular State and Changing Roles for Women in 'Haredi' Orthodoxy," in *You Arose, a Mother in Israel: A Festschrift in Honor of Blu Greenberg*, ed. Devorah Zlochower (New York: Jewish Orthodox Feminist Alliance, 2017), 103–9.
38 See Zev Eleff and Seth Farber, "Antimodernism and Orthodox Judaism's Heretical Imperative: An American Religious Counterpoint," *Religion and American Culture* 30 (Summer 2020): 237–72.
39 William B. Helmreich and Henoch Leibowitz Interview Transcript, April 6, 1979, Mendel Gottesman Library, Yeshiva University, MS-1230.
40 See Zev Eleff, "The Jewish Observer: Champion of the Orthodox Right," *Jewish Action* 78 (Winter 2017): 43–45; and Zev Eleff, "The Jewish Center, Herman Wouk, and the Origins of Orthodox Triumphalism," in *A Century at the Center: Orthodox Judaism and the Jewish Center*, ed. Zev Eleff (New Milford, CT: Toby, 2017), 279–99.
41 See Lawrence Kaplan, "Daas Torah: A Modern Conception of Rabbinic Authority," in *Rabbinic Authority and Personal Autonomy*, ed. Moshe Sokol (Northvale, NJ: Jason Aronson, 1992), 1–60.
42 See Zev Eleff, *Authentically Orthodox: A Tradition-Bound Faith in American Life* (Detroit, MI: Wayne State University Press, 2020), 104–23; and Yoel Finkelman, *Strictly Kosher Reading: Popular Literature and the Condition of Contemporary Orthodoxy* (Boston: Academic Studies Press, 2011).
43 See Jonathan Boyarin, *Yeshiva Days: Learning on the Lower East Side* (Princeton, NJ: Princeton University Press, 2020).
44 Reuven Frankel, *The Bochur's Guide to College: The Authoritative Guide to Da'as College* (Tallman, NY: Forshay, 2009), 10 and 13.
45 Francisco Parra, "A Qualitative Study of the Yeshiva Program at Fairleigh Dickinson University and the Educational Outcomes of Orthodox Jewish Students in the Northeastern United States" (Ed.D diss., Northcentral University, 2018), 27–28.
46 Alex N. Gecan, "Growth Spurt: Lakewood's Population Has Exploded in 10 Years," *Asbury Park Press*, August 22, 2021. A1.
47 My thanks to Shlomo Schorr and Dovi Safier for sharing their tabulations.
48 "Hundreds of Homes 'Double-Booked' in Orlando, Many Left without Place for Yom Tov," *Yeshiva World News*, March 23, 2021, www.theyeshivaworld.com. The same figure was tabulated for 2023, see "Over 100,000 Yidden to Spend Pesach in Orlando This Year," *Matzav*, April 5, 2023, matzav.com.
49 Sam Roberts, "Rabbi Yaakov Perlow, 89," *New York Times*, April 15, 2020, B12.
50 See Mark L. Trencher, "The Orthodox Jewish Community and the Coronavirus: Halacha Grapples with the Pandemic," *Contemporary Jewry* 41 (March 2021): 123–39.
51 See Harry Baumgarten, "Something Foul Grows in Brooklyn," *Jerusalem Post*, January 14, 2021, 10.

52　Norman Lamm, "Modern Orthodoxy's Identity Crisis," *Jewish Life* 36 (May–June 1969): 6.
53　For an earlier iteration of "Modern Orthodoxy," see Zev Eleff, "The Origins of the Young Israel of Brookline and the Contest for 'Modern Orthodoxy,'" *Me'orei Ha'eish* (2017): 141–63.
54　Eleff, *Modern Orthodox Judaism*, xxxi.
55　See Benny Kraut, *The Greening of American Orthodox Judaism: Yavneh in the 1960s* (Cincinnati, OH: Hebrew Union College Press, 2011), 20–34.
56　*The Rabbinical Council of America Edition of the ArtScroll Siddur*, ed. Nosson Scherman (Brooklyn, NY: Mesorah, 1984), 450–51.
57　Eleff, *Authentically Orthodox*, 165–84.
58　Norman Lamm, "Some Comments on Centrist Orthodoxy," *Tradition* 22 (Fall 1986), 1–12.
59　See Norman Lamm, *Seventy Faces: Articles of Faith*, vol. 1 (Hoboken, NJ: Ktav, 2002), 1.
60　See Samuel C. Heilman and Steven M. Cohen, *Cosmopolitans and Parochials: Modern Orthodox Jews in America* (Chicago: University of Chicago Press, 1989), 160.
61　See Samuel C. Heilman, *Sliding to the Right: The Contest for the Future of American Jewish Orthodoxy* (Berkeley: University of California Press, 2006). On Orthodox birthrates and use of birth control, see Zev Eleff, "Piety and the Pill: Orthodox Judaism and Contraception in the Postwar Era," *American Jewish History* 104 (December 2020): 533–52.
62　Eitan Nissel, "Chaverim's Sol Itzkowitz Named 'Hometown Hero,'" *Jewish Link*, August 3, 2023, 16.
63　See Adam S. Ferziger, *Beyond Sectarianism: The Realignment of American Orthodox Judaism* (Detroit, MI: Wayne State University Press, 2015), 221–23.
64　For an important survey of the costs of Jewish living and education, for the Orthodox and other American Jews, see Carmel U. Chiswick, *Judaism in Transition: How Economic Choices Shape Religious Tradition* (Stanford, CA: Stanford University Press, 2014), 53–102.
65　See Gil Perl and Yaakov Weinstein, *A Parent's Guide to Orthodox Assimilation on University Campuses* (Boston: self-published, 2003) 1. See also Alan L. Mittleman, "Fretful Orthodoxy," *First Things* 136 (October 2003): 23–25.
66　See Zev Eleff and Menachem Butler, "Papering over an Era of American Orthodox Pragmatism: The Case of College," in *Emet le-Ya'akov: Facing the Truths of History—Essays in Honor of Jacob J. Schacter*, ed. Zev Eleff and Shaul Seidler-Feller (Boston: Academic Studies Press, 2023), 298–318.
67　See Kenneth D. Wald, *The Foundations of American Jewish Liberalism* (Cambridge: Cambridge University Press, 2019), 202–8.
68　The advertisement appeared in the *New York Times*, November 17, 2016, A11.
69　"Orthodox Union Says It Raised Immigration Issue While Honoring AG Sessions," *Times of Israel*, June 14, 2018.

70 Avital Chizhik-Goldschmidt, "Leading Ultra-Orthodox Rabbi Shmuel Kamenetsky Endorses Trump, in Rare Move," *Forward*, July 30, 2020.
71 See Adam S. Ferziger, "Sanctuary for the Specialist: Gender and the Reconceptualization of the American Orthodox Rabbinate," *Jewish Social Studies* 23 (Spring–Summer, 2018): 1–37.
72 Jackie Hajdenberg, "Citing 'Outpouring of Interest,' Yeshiva U Restores Women's Talmud Classes Whose Cancellation Incited an Uproar," Jewish Telegraphic Agency, April 25, 2023.
73 Barry Freundel, "Homosexuality and Judaism," *Journal of Halacha and Contemporary Society* 11 (Spring 1986): 87.
74 Reuven P. Bulka, "Is Homosexuality Religiously Legitimate?," *Midstream* 38 (December 1992): 26.
75 Steven Greenberg, *Wrestling with God and Men: Homosexuality in the Jewish Tradition* (Madison, WI: University of Wisconsin Press, 2004), 12.
76 Zvi Schachter, Meir Eliyahu Twersky, Yaakov Neuburger, and Michael Rosensweig, Public Letter, December 22, 2009, a copy in the possession of the author.
77 See Zvika Klein and Sarah Ben-Nun, "Yeshiva U. to Get LGBTQ Club," *Jerusalem Post*, June 16, 2022.
78 Sylvia Barack Fishman, *The Way into the Varieties of Jewishness* (Woodstock, VT: Jewish Lights, 2007), 132.
79 See Jack Wertheimer, "Can Modern Orthodoxy Survive?," in *Yitz Greenberg and Modern Orthodoxy: The Road Not Taken*, ed. Adam Ferziger, Miri Freud-Kandel, and Steven Bayme (Boston: Academic Studies Press, 2019), 193–210.
80 See Steven Bayme, "A New Voice for Modern Orthodoxy Comes to Washington," *Washington Jewish Week*, October 13, 2016, 22–23. For a selection of sources and commentaries on this phenomenon, see Eleff, *Modern Orthodox Judaism*, 348–96.
81 Sacks' remarks took place in the opening session of the YU and the World of Tomorrow conference held on October 22, 2017. For a video recording, see www.youtube.com.
82 Gideon Aran, "Jewish Zionist Fundamentalism: The Bloc of the Faithful in Israel (Gush Emunim)," in *Fundamentalisms Observed* (Chicago: University of Chicago Press, 1991), 296.
83 See Yoel Finkelman, "On the Irrelevance of Religious-Zionism," *Tradition* 39 (Spring 2005): 21–44.
84 On this, see Yehudah Mirsky, *Rav Kook: Mystic in a Time of Revolution* (New Haven, CT: Yale University Press, 2014), 218–39.
85 See Charles S. Liebman, "Orthodox Judaism Today," *Midstream* 25 (August–September 1979): 24.
86 Abigail Klein Leichman, "Koren Publishers Celebrates 60," *Jerusalem Post*, July 1, 2022, 40.
87 See Sharon Flatto, "The Modern Orthodox Brain Drain," *Jewish Week*, May 1, 2015, 24.

88 See, for example, Alex Pomson and Jack Wertheimer, *Inside Jewish Day Schools: Leadership, Learning, and Community* (Waltham, MA: Brandeis University Press, 2022), 17–42.
89 A great survey of the arrival of Satmar and other ḥasidim to the United States is found in David Biale, David Assaf, Benjamin Brown, Uriel Gellman, Samuel Heilman, Moshe Rosman, Gadi Sagiv, and Marcin Wodziński, *Ḥasidism: A New History* (Princeton, NJ: Princeton University Press, 2018), 677–705.
90 Joseph Berger, "Dressing with Faith, Not Heat, in Mind," *New York Times*, June 29, 2012, A19.
91 See Nathaniel Deutsch and Michael Casper, *A Fortress in Brooklyn: Race, Real Estate, and the Making of Ḥasidic Williamsburg* (New Haven, CT: Yale University Press, 2021), 74–97.
92 See Jerome R. Mintz, *Ḥasidic People: A Place in the New World* (Cambridge, MA: Harvard University Press, 1992), 198–205.
93 See Nomi M. Stolzenberg and David N. Myers, *American Shtetl: The Making of Kiryas Joel, a Ḥasidic Village in Upstate New York* (Princeton, NJ: Princeton University Press, 2021), 115–62.
94 Marcin Wodziński, *Historical Atlas of Hasidism* (Princeton, NJ: Princeton University Press, 2018), 191–92. On the methodological challenges of tabulating the ḥasidic population, see Joshua Comenetz, "Census-Based Estimation of the Ḥasidic Jewish Population," *Contemporary Jewry* 26 (2006): 35–74.
95 See Samuel C. Heilman, *Who Will Lead Us? The Story of Five Ḥasidic Dynasties in America* (Berkeley: University of California Press, 2017).
96 Patrick Gallahue and Philip Messing, "The Senator and the Satmars," *New York Post*, April 29, 2006, 3.
97 Eliza Shapiro and Brian M. Rosenthal, "In Ḥasidic Enclaves, Failing Private Schools Flush with Public Money," *New York Times*, September 11, 2022, 1.
98 See Shaul Magid, "'America Is No Different,' 'America Is Different'—Is There an American Jewish Fundamentalism? Part I: American Habad," in *Fundamentalism: Perspectives on a Contested History*, ed. Simon A. Wood and David Harrington Watt (Charleston: University of South Carolina Press, 2014), 70–91.
99 There are several biographies of Rabbi Menachem Schneerson. See, for example, Samuel Heilman and Menachem Friedman, *The Rebbe: The Life and Afterlife of Menachem Mendel Schneerson* (Princeton, NJ: Princeton University Press, 2010); and Joseph Telushkin, *Rebbe: The Life and Teachings of Menachem M. Schneerson, the Most Influential Rabbi in Modern History* (New York: HarperWave, 2014).
100 Ray Kestenbaum, "Lubavitch Becomes an Empire," *Jewish Week*, April 4, 1982, 36.
101 For this first segment, see Lis Harris, "Holy Days," *New Yorker*, September 16, 1985, 41–101.
102 Todd Singer, "Lubavitch Recruitment Methods Worry Some Jewish Parents," *Jewish Advocate*, November 15, 1984, 8.
103 Arnold Jacob Wolf, "Chabad," *Jewish Spectator* 45 (Fall 1980): 61.
104 Stephen J. Sass, "Southern California," *Present Tense* 9 (Spring 1982): 33.

105 Danielle Ziri, "Chabad Center to Open in South Dakota—the Only U.S. State without One," *Jerusalem Post*, November 29, 2016.
106 On this Chabad phenomenon and its eventual impact on the broader Orthodox rabbinate, see Zev Eleff, "The Orthodox Rabbinate and its Chabad Revolution," *Looking Forward: The Aspen Center for Social Values Journal* 2 (2014): 39–48.
107 Fay Kranz, "The Super Shlicha," in *Shlichus: Meeting the Outreach Challenge*, ed. Chana Piekarski (Brooklyn, NY: Nshei Chabad, 1990), 19.
108 See Naftali Loewenthal, "From 'Ladies' Auxiliary' to 'Shluhot Network': Women's Activism in Twentieth Century Habad," in *A Touch of Grace: Studies in Ashkenazi Culture, Women's History, and the Languages of the Jews Presented to Chava Turniansky*, ed. Israel Bartal, Galit Hasan-Rokem, Ada Rapoport-Albert, Claudia Rosenzweig, Vicky Shifriss, and Erika Timm (Jerusalem: Zalman Shazar Center for Jewish History, 2013), 69–93. See also Bonnie J. Morris, *Lubavitcher Women in America: Identity and Activism in the Postwar Era* (Albany: State University of New York Press, 1998), 105; and Elite Ben-Yosef, "Literacy and Power: The Shiyour as a Site of Subordination and Empowerment for Chabad Women," *Journal of Feminist Studies in Religion* 27 (Spring 2011): 53–74.
109 Wodziński, *Historical Atlas of Hasidism*, 194.
110 I owe this insight to Elliot Cosgrove, "A Choosing People," *Sources* 5 (Spring 2023): 11–19.
111 David Berger, *The Rebbe, the Messiah, and the Scandal of Orthodox Indifference* (Oxford: Littman Library, 2008), 55.
112 See Sue Fishkoff, *The Rebbe's Army: Inside the World of Chabad-Lubavitch* (New York: Schocken, 2003), 184–200, 285–300.
113 See Christopher J. Jacobi, Maria Andronicou, and Brandon Vaidyanathan, "Looking Beyond the COVID-19 Pandemic: Congregants' Expectations of Future Online Religious Service Attendance," *Religions* 13 (2022): 559.
114 See Iddo Tavory, *Summoned: Identification and Religious Life in a Jewish Neighborhood* (Chicago: University of Chicago Press, 2016), 1–19.
115 Michael M. Grynbaum, "Ultra-Orthodox Jews Rally to Discuss Risks of Internet," *New York Times*, May 21, 2012, A17.
116 Ayala Fader, *Hidden Heretics: Jewish Doubt in the Digital Age* (Princeton, NJ: Princeton University Press, 2020), 1–27.
117 Shira Hanau, "A New Lens on Orthodox Women," *Jewish Week*, September 8, 2017, 3.

10

Continuity and Change in the American Jewish Organizational Ecosystem

THEODORE SASSON

When political scientist Daniel Elazar published his treatise on the Jewish nonprofit system in 1976 and then again in a revised edition in 1995, the book reflected the professional character of the field it sought to describe. Clocking in at nearly five hundred pages, the book, entitled *Community and Polity: The Organizational Dynamics of American Jewry*, included historical chapters on Jewish society in the United States and Canada, theoretical analyses of Jewish and American political structures, typologies of Jewish communal organizations, and numerous lengthy tables. It was a book meant to be read and discussed and became mandatory reading for at least two generations of graduate students enrolled in training programs for the burgeoning field of Jewish communal service. I'd hazard to guess that the book with the big red cover is still on the shelves of most senior executives of federations, Jewish community centers, and other mainstays of the Jewish nonprofit sector.[1]

In the revised edition, Elazar described a nonprofit ecosystem comprised of robust networks of congregations, denominationally linked educational systems, cradle-to-grave human service agencies, and consensus-oriented local and national advocacy organizations. Undergirding the system as a whole was a network of 176 professionally staffed Jewish community federations that raised funds, identified community priorities, and initiated new projects. "American Jews have created an unanticipated polity fully within the framework of American society," Elazar observed, "as Jewish in its commitments as any Jewish community in the past, yet as American as any other segment of the mosaic that is present-day America."[2]

At the time Elazar wrote, the Jewish polity had largely shifted from a social welfare focus to a focus on education and advocacy, reflecting the rising affluence of North American Jewish communities and a growing concern over assimilation and the fate of the state of Israel. The Jewish communal system had also extended its capacity to serve the needs of the Jewish community, growing more structured and integrated around "government-like" institutions, and with increasing power to raise funds, coordinate action, and exercise political influence. Looking ahead, Elazar prognosticated that the centralizing, structuring, and integrating tendencies would continue to unfold.

In retrospect, Elazar's 1995 edition represented a kind of high-water mark. Over the quarter-century that followed, the processes of consolidation and integration that he described slipped into reverse. Rank and file participation in Jewish communal life among the liberal majority declined, with synagogues and Jewish community centers shedding members, day schools and Hebrew schools shrinking, and donor pools to federations' annual campaigns contracting. At the same time, private foundations joined federations as philanthropic engines of Jewish communal innovation by funding engagement-oriented start-ups that spread throughout the landscape. The consensus-oriented national advocacy frameworks, no longer able to consistently communicate a unified message on Israel or antisemitism, weakened. By the onset of the COVID-19 pandemic in 2020, the ecosystem coming into focus reflected the contours of the changing Jewish community. In an era of secularization, Jewish communal organizations were increasingly oriented around outreach and innovation; in an era of rising inequality, they were increasingly funded by the elite; and in an era of growing polarization, they were increasingly divided among rival partisan voices.

When the pandemic struck, knowledgeable observers wondered whether the once powerful Jewish communal apparatus could mount an effective response and sustain Jewish communal organizations through the crisis. This chapter draws on Daniel Elazar's classic book to describe the Jewish organizational ecosystem that developed during the period between the end of World War II and the mid-1990s. Building upon more recent research, it then traces the trendlines up until the onset of the pandemic, concluding with a preliminary assessment of how the Jewish organizational system navigated the pandemic and then the October 7, 2023, attack on Israel by Ḥamas, and what those actions might indicate regarding future developments.

Emergence of an Integrated Polity: 1945–1995

American Jews never established centralized and authoritative organizational structures at the national level, and, indeed, efforts to fully integrate communal organizations city wide have generally been short-lived. One notable example was the American Jewish Committee's attempt in 1906 to establish a unitary structure for New York's Jewish organizations, the Kehillah. Animated by progressive ideology and emphasizing efficiency and professional administration, the organization established bureaus of industry, social morals, philanthropy, and Jewish education. The effort failed to achieve a sound financial basis and collapsed after a decade, leaving only New York's Bureau of Jewish Education as its legacy.[3]

The community federation proved a more enduring model. Beginning in Boston in 1895 and Cleveland in 1903, Jewish human services and social welfare organizations, including hospitals, nursing homes, community centers, and vocational training programs, joined forces in joint fundraising campaigns. Spurred by the need to provide comprehensive social welfare and educational support for masses of Eastern European Jewish immigrants that were arriving on American shores, additional cities adopted the model. By the beginning of World War I, 23 federations had been established; by 1950, there were 125.[4] Continent-wide, federations in the United States and Canada established the Council of Jewish Federations as an umbrella organization.

After World War II, Jews joined other Americans in a wave of migration to the suburbs. As new suburbanites, "Jews who once maintained their Jewishness through organic relationships had to seek more formal associational ties."[5] Synagogue building and congregational membership skyrocketed, and "Jewish life in the United States became synagogue-centered to an unprecedented degree."[6] Jews established large suburban synagogue facilities with social halls and school wings. Congregationally based supplementary Hebrew school replaced the independent Talmud Torahs as the mainstays of formal Jewish education. Nationally, four large religious denominations (Reform, Reconstructionist, Conservative, and Orthodox) established national offices, summer camps, youth movements, departments of education, seminaries, and rabbinical associations. Together, the large synagogue confederations established the Synagogue Council of America as an umbrella organization.

By the 1960s, the core mission of the Jewish community federations had begun to shift. As government institutions began serving needs previously met by church-based nonprofits—and as Jewish hospitals, nursing homes, and welfare agencies increasingly served non-Jewish clients—federations sharpened their focus on fundraising for Israel and Jewish education.[7] Federations coordinated annual drives and emergency campaigns for Israel under the banner of the United Jewish Appeal. The sums raised for global Jewish needs were generally allocated to the Jewish Agency for Israel, which funded refugee resettlement and economic development, and the American Jewish Joint Distribution Committee, which funded humanitarian projects in Europe and Israel. Broad consensus around the need to rally financial and political support for the fledgling Jewish state, particularly in the years that straddled the 1967 Six-Day War and the 1973 Yom Kippur War, fueled annual and emergency campaigns of increasing scope and scale. Overall, Elazar reports that between 1939 and 1974 federations raised approximately $5.7 billion—including approximately $2.6 billion between the Six Day and Yom Kippur wars—mostly for use in Israel.[8]

Concern about assimilation, particularly after publication of surveys in the 1980s and 1990s reporting intermarriage rates in the United States of about 50 percent, animated federations' increasing focus on Jewish education and identity building.[9] The national federation movement established the Jewish Educational Service of North America (JESNA) to professionalize supplementary education and increased its support for the Foundation for Jewish Culture to promote the arts. Local federations stepped up support for bureaus of Jewish education and campus-based Hillel organizations that served university students, and increased investment in Israel experience tourism. Federations also extended support to Jewish day schools, including the Solomon Schechter (Conservative) and Torah U'Mesora (Orthodox) networks.

Broad Jewish consensus on support for Israel and, in the United States, civil rights, also enabled deeper investment in communal advocacy organizations. Locally, Jewish community relations councils—incorporated within federations or funded as separate federation-supported agencies—promoted liberal causes and represented Jewish communities in interfaith and metropolitan contexts. Nationally, advocacy organizations grew in size, scope, and influence. The network of Jewish community relations councils supported a national umbrella organization, the National Jewish Community Relations Advisory Council (NJCRAC). The American Israel Public Affairs Committee (AIPAC) and the Conference of Presidents of Major American Jewish Organizations lobbied Congress and the White House on Israel-related issues, generally adopting the talking points of successive Israeli governments. The National Conference on Soviet Jewry and Union of Councils for Soviet Jews coordinated mobilization efforts to assist Jews trying to leave America's cold war rival and build new lives in the West. Other large advocacy organizations, including the American Jewish Committee and the Anti-Defamation League, developed advocacy programs on Israel, antisemitism, and civil rights.

In the mid-1990s, Elazar described the Jewish organizational ecosystem as "a mosaic, a multidimensional matrix of institutions and organizations that interact with each other in their attempts to cover the range of communal concerns, while preserving their respective integrities."[10] It was an ecosystem, moreover, that was becoming more integrated with a growing number of "government-like" structures at the local and national levels:

> The most clear-cut examples of government-like institutions in the American Jewish community are to be found on the local plane: the Jewish federations, which provide comprehensive services to the community either directly or through their constituent agencies. They reach virtually all Jews in the community through their central fundraising activities. . . . Indeed, the federations are in the process of becoming the comprehensive-representative organizations of the community, its framing institutions.
>
> On the countrywide plane, the Council of Jewish Federations is the closest to being a single framing institution. The Conference of Presidents of Major Jewish Organizations, the Synagogue Council of America, the Jewish Community Centers Association of North America, the National Community Relations Advisory Council and the Jewish Educational

Service of North America also fill special countywide tasks as associations of organizations.[11]

At the time, Elazar estimated that federations and federation-supported agencies controlled roughly half of all communal expenditures, with synagogues and organizations fundraising for Israel controlling most of the rest.[12] Taking in the long view, Elazar described a "generally tightening matrix" of Jewish communal organizations; looking ahead, he prognosticated further consolidation and centralization of the American Jewish polity.

The Next Quarter-Century: 1995–2020

Over the quarter-century that followed publication of the revised edition of *Community and Polity*, changes that swept through American society as a whole also shaped American Jewish communities. Secularization—in particular, disaffiliation from religious denominations and institutions—was one such trend. Overall rates of religious affiliation declined, as Americans switched away from the religions in which they were raised to join the ranks of the religiously unaffiliated. Whereas in 1972 just 5 percent of Americans responded "none" when asked about their religious affiliation, the figure climbed to 12 percent in 1996 and 29 percent in 2022. The decline in religious affiliation has been sharpest among Protestants and has been driven, according to the Pew Research Center, by improving health and longevity, intermarriage, and the association of Christianity with conservative politics and clergy scandals.[13]

The process of religious disaffiliation has also played out among American Jews. According to the Pew Research Center's 2020 survey, 27 percent of U.S. Jewish adults identify as Jewish by culture, ethnicity, or family background, but do not identify Judaism as their religion. Instead, when asked about their religion, they respond "atheist," "agnostic," or "nothing in particular." The unaffiliated share of the Jewish population skews young: among respondents sixty-five and older, just 16 percent are Jews of no religion; among respondents ages eighteen to twenty-nine, the number increases to 40 percent.

Whereas researchers identify many causes of disaffiliation in the general population, among Jews the primary driver appears to be the rising rate of intermarriage. In the Pew survey, among Jews who married before 1980 just 18 percent were married to a non-Jewish spouse; among Jews who married during 2010–20 that figure rose to 61 percent. At the same time, the Pew survey finds that interfaith parents are much less likely than their Jewish-only counterparts to raise their children as Jewish by religion (28 percent vs. 93 percent) and much more likely to raise them as "Jewish, not by religion" (29 percent vs. 3 percent).[14] In adulthood, the offspring of intermarriage are, as one might expect, more likely to identify as Jews of no religion.[15]

Although the adult offspring of intermarriage are more likely to be religiously unaffiliated, most continue to identify as Jewish in other ways, including by culture, ethnicity, and family background. As a result, the rising rate of intermarriage did not depress the overall size of the Jewish population, which continued to grow in proportion to the broader U.S. population, from 5.2 million in 2000–01, to 6.7 million in 2013, and 7.5 million in 2020.[16]

Another development in American society that has shaped American Jewry is the general trend toward political polarization. In American society, beginning in the 1980s, political party identification became an ever more important point of cleavage, encompassing other sources of identity, including race, region, and religion. Americans divided into Republican and Democratic political "tribes" or "mega-identities" that both reflected and shaped class differences, cultural preferences, and political views across an expanding array of issues.[17] Rooted in divergent responses to the civil rights, feminist, and antiwar movements of the 1960s, political polarization has amplified in recent decades within the echo chambers of social media. A month before the U.S. 2020 presidential election, the Pew Research Center reported that eight in ten voters in both political camps viewed their differences with the other side as "about core American values," and roughly nine in ten worried that a victory of the other side would cause "lasting harm" to the United States.[18]

Among American Jews, political polarization increasingly mapped onto the denominational landscape. In 2020, 71 percent of American Jewish adults identified with or leaned toward the Democratic party, including 70 percent of Conservative, 80 percent of Reform, and 75 percent of unaffiliated Jews. Among Orthodox Jews, however, just 20 percent identified with or leaned toward the Democratic party, compared to 75 percent who identified or leaned Republican. The partisan gap had grown mainly because of dynamics among Orthodox Jews. In Pew's 2013 survey, Orthodox Jews were more evenly split, with just 57 percent favoring the Republican party, compared to 36 percent who favored the Democrats.[19]

Finally, over the decades since the mid-1990s, American society has become more economically divided, with a growing concentration of wealth at the top of the economic distribution. Driven by globalization, automation, and the weakening of unions, income inequality—measured as a ratio of income earned by the top ninetieth percentile compared to the bottom tenth percentile—grew from 10.1 in 1990 to 11.7 in 2010 and 12.6 in 2018. The income and wealth of the richest families grew even more rapidly, particularly in the years following the Great Recession. Between the years 2009 and 2022, the share of wealth held by the top 0.1 percent of U.S. households increased from just below six percent to more than 18 percent.[20] Although robust data on income and wealth among American Jews, particularly the wealthiest, is unavailable, trends in fundraising and philanthropic behavior suggest a similar pattern.

Overall, the societal trends of secularization, polarization, and wealth concentration have influenced patterns of participation in Jewish communal organizations and the purposes those organizations identified as paramount, as we shall see in the sections that follow.

Synagogues and Schools

The ongoing secularization of American Jewry has affected liberal (non-Orthodox) congregations and schools. Self-identification in national surveys with a liberal denomination declined overall, largely because of a drop in identification with Conservative Judaism from 35 percent in 1990 to 27 percent in 2000–2001 to 17 percent in 2020.[21] The number of Conservative-affiliated synagogues declined by about one-third, from more than 800 congregations to about 560, and the number of large congregations (with more than 900 members) declined by half, from about 60 to about 30.[22] Identification with the Reform movement held steady at between 35 and 37 percent, whereas the number of synagogues overall—and the number of very large congregations—declined during the 2010s.[23] At the metropolitan level, most federations that conducted community surveys at regular intervals during the 2000s and 2010s reported declining synagogue membership.[24] Taking in the scene of non-Orthodox Jewish religious life as a whole, Jewish Theological Seminary historian Jack Wertheimer describes "declining numbers of adherents and flagging observance—even as pockets of strength are evident."[25]

Reflecting the challenge of maintaining membership, liberal synagogues of all varieties experimented with new revenue structures, including tiered membership and voluntary donations rather than fixed dues.[26] Although synagogue movements continue to support national associations, some scaled back their activities, and the national umbrella organization, the Synagogue Council of America, closed down in 2014 and was not replaced.

The liberal denominations' supplementary schools and day schools have also struggled. Supplementary schools, which served the vast majority of American Jewish school-age children during the second half of the twentieth century, experienced steep retrenchment. Enrollments in Hebrew schools and Sunday schools of Reform, Conservative, and other non-Orthodox synagogues declined year over year.[27] The three-day-per-week (Reform) and four-day-per-week (Conservative) formats for supplementary education were overhauled, with most congregations switching to one or two days per week, or a tutorial format. National capacity-building organizations for congregational education, including JESNA, were shut down and not replaced.[28] Meanwhile, day schools serving non-Orthodox students—including the Conservative movement's Schechter network, the Reform movement's Rashi network, and an independent network of community day schools—also experienced declining enrollments.[29] At the encouragement of funders, the national umbrella organizations serving those networks consolidated to form a single capacity-building entity, Prizmah.[30]

In contrast to these trends, informal or "experiential" Jewish education, supported by robust philanthropic investment, has flourished. Jewish summer camps, with support from the Foundation for Jewish Camp and the Grinspoon Foundation, have maintained their enrollments and improved the quality of their educational programs. Among older teenagers and young adults, Israel-based educational programs, such as Birthright Israel and university-based Hillel and Chabad programs, have achieved enormous reach. Indeed, for many non-Orthodox American Jewish children, teens, and young adults, summer camps, Jewish community center (JCC) programs, Israel-based educational tourism, and campus-based experiences have replaced Hebrew school as core frameworks for Jewish education.[31]

At the other end of the religious spectrum, Orthodox congregations and schools have thrived. The portion of American Jews who self-identify as Orthodox in national surveys held steady at 9 or 10 percent between 2000–2001 and 2020.[32] Virtually all Orthodox Jews belong to congregations, but tabulating and tracking their numbers is difficult due to their enormous diversity—including Ḥasidic courts, Ḥaredi "yeshiva world" institutions, Chabad Lubavitch congregations, and synagogues of centrist and modern Orthodoxy. The Orthodox Union, an umbrella organization, has 360 affiliates (about half the number of the Reform movement) but reports ongoing interaction with 2,500 congregations.[33]

The data on Orthodox day schools and yeshivas is more comprehensive. In 2018–19, the AVI CHAI Foundation's census identified 906 full-time schools—the vast majority Orthodox—up from 802 in 2009 and 676 in 1998.[34] In 2018–19, day schools and yeshivas enrolled 292,172 students, about 65 percent at Ḥasidic and Ḥaredi institutions, and about 17 percent at other Orthodox institutions. Overall, day school and yeshiva enrollments increased by about 108,000 or 60 percent compared to the 1998 census.[35] Thus, among Orthodox Jews, day schools and yeshivot continue to serve as core frameworks of Jewish education, and are indeed rapidly expanding.

Federations and Foundations

As Jewish demography changed and the wealth of the richest families surged, federations shifted their fundraising priorities. Many federations deemphasized their annual campaigns, which courted small and large donors alike, and expanded their efforts with the largest givers.

Federations adopted greater flexibility to accommodate donors' particular interests, allowing more designated gifts rather than limiting donations to the general fund. At the same time, federations expanded their platforms for donor advised funds and created endowments to provide for community needs in perpetuity.[36] As a result of these shifts, federations have continued to raise an estimated $2 billion annually, albeit through a variety of fundraising vehicles rather than just the annual campaign—those campaigns held steady at less than $1 billion a year and declined in inflation-adjusted dollars.[37]

One clear result of federations' decisions to focus greater fundraising resources on large donors is a dramatic drop in the number of donor households, from about 900,000 in 1989 to about 800,000 in 1994, 500,000 in 2009, and 400,000 in 2013.[38] The shrinking donor pool may also reflect a growing preference for rank-and-file donors to give to particular organizations or narrow causes rather than community-wide campaigns.[39] Notably, the number of donors to United Way, which operates community-wide fundraising campaigns on behalf of partner nonprofits across the United States, also declined.

Alongside shifts in how federations raised money, many also changed their approach to allocations. In place of generally routine allocations to partner agencies, such as JCCs, Jewish family services, and bureaus of Jewish education, many federations adopted grantmaking models akin to private foundations. Federations increasingly required program proposals from partner agencies and extensive reporting on agreed-upon metrics and measures of impact. This approach aligned well with the need to court larger donors who had their own priorities as well as the cultural shift toward more strategic rather than expressive philanthropy.[40]

Finally, federations expanded their involvement in the direct delivery of services. Rather than exclusively raising funds for Jewish communal organizations that provide services, federations began operating more of their own programs, including, for example, programs for teens, Israel experience programs, public affairs and advocacy initiatives, and programs for interfaith families.[41]

Federation-supported agencies, such as JCCs, Hillels, museums, and community relations councils, responded to these changing dynamics—including contingent federation dollars and occasional direct competition in the delivery of programs—by expanding their own fundraising activities. U.S.-based affiliates of Israeli nonprofit and educational organizations also proliferated and stepped up their direct fundraising. By 2010, the number of "American Friends" organizations had increased to 667 (up from 265 in 1984), and they were collectively raising more than one billion dollars annually for causes in Israel, independently of the United Jewish Appeal-Jewish Agency framework.[42] In Jewish communities throughout the United States, competition for donors, particularly among local wealthy families, strained the federation movement's historical model of collective fundraising.

In parallel to these developments, the number of private foundations active in support of the Jewish nonprofit enterprise increased. By 2018, more than 250 private foundations were donating more than a half-million dollars each annually to Jewish causes, and 100 of those foundations employed professional staff.[43] Several large foundations also operated their own programs, particularly in the field of leadership development.[44] Although the total allocated by foundations still lagged behind the total allocated by the federation movement, the sums steadily grew.[45] Overall, on the eve of the pandemic, foundation funding accounted for about one-fifth of all Jewish-focused philanthropy and 10 percent of all revenue for Jewish nonprofits.[46]

Notably, many foundations that prioritize Jewish life give a portion of their funds to federations, as do wealthy donors who give through donor advised funds. Taken together, federations' growing focus on fundraising among the wealthy and the increasing role of private foundations in Jewish life signaled a shift toward greater elite control over the Jewish nonprofit sector. Although elite control is not a new phenomenon in Jewish life, it has become more pronounced in an era of mounting inequality and increased concentration of wealth.[47]

Outreach and Innovation

As liberal synagogues and schools retrenched, Jewish nonprofit entrepreneurs launched hundreds of new start-ups.[48] Such initiatives reflected the founders' sense of urgency about the need to engage population segments that were seemingly disengaged or underserved. For many, accomplishing those purposes necessitated inventing new forms of Jewish practice and new platforms for participation in Jewish life.[49] The start-ups they created differed from more established communal organizations in that they tended to serve particular constituencies (e.g., young adults and LGBTQ+ Jews) or promote particular purposes (e.g., social action and spiritual life). Many also operated at the national or continental levels rather than serving specific localities.

Funded mainly by the growing number of Jewishly oriented private foundations, the "innovation sector," as it came to be known, breathed new excitement into the American Jewish scene.[50] The start-ups tended to convene people outside of conventional Jewish spaces—for example, in participants' homes, at retreat centers, or in public parks rather than in synagogues, JCCs, and school buildings. These organizations also tended to emphasize elements of Jewish renewal, grassroots empowerment, and member-led activities. The proliferation of innovation-sector organizations introduced new forms of competition, as start-ups jostled with more traditional synagogues and federation-supported agencies for the attention of American Jews.

Although initially funded by private foundations, many innovation-sector organizations eventually attracted support from federations and individual donors.[51] Many of the organizations also developed revenue streams from tuition and user fees. During the 2010s, as the sector became better integrated into the national ecosystem, leaders moved easily between jobs at innovation sector and establishment organizations, and many start-ups transitioned into mature nonprofits. (See this chapter's appendix for a typology and illustrative list of innovation sector organizations.)

At the ecosystem level, one notable consequence of the growth of the innovation sector has been a diminished division of labor among organizations. During the postwar period, as Elazar described, a fairly clear division of labor existed between organizations that raised funds and organizations that delivered services in the religious, educational, advocacy, and social welfare arenas. In more recent decades, as population-specific and single-purpose start-ups have come to coexist with local multipurpose organizations, competition for funds and rank-and-file participants has increased and organizational missions and purposes have overlapped.

Advocacy and Activism

During the postwar period that Elazar wrote about, American Jews fielded national advocacy organizations that sought to communicate consensus views about support for Israel and civil rights. In the decades that followed the publication of *Community and Polity*, the "big three" advocacy organizations, AIPAC, American Jewish Committee, and the Anti-Defamation League, grew their budgets and professional staffs.[52] At the same time, organizations championing positions to their left and right entered the fray, effectively ending the establishment groups' quasi-monopoly role as spokespersons for American Jewry.[53]

Although the process unfolded over many years, the Oslo Peace Accords were the catalyst for the fracturing of the pro-Israel lobby. Signed in 1993 by Israeli prime minister Yitzhak Rabin and Palestine Liberation Organization chairman Yasser Arafat, the framework included mutual recognition between Israel and the PLO and phased Israeli withdrawal from the Gaza Strip and West Bank. The ultimate aim, although not explicit in the agreement, was the eventual establishment of a Palestinian state.

Deeply controversial in Israel, the Oslo Accords divided American Jews as well. Although the major organizations of the pro-Israel lobby, including AIPAC, eventually embraced the Israeli government's position, the right-wing Zionist Organization of America (ZOA) and the Orthodox Union joined forces with the Israeli opposition Likud Party to organize against the accords. From that point forward, the pro-Israel lobby split into camps. The large establishment organizations continued to support the positions of successive Israeli governments, swinging to the right when Likud wielded power and then to the left when various center-left coalitions gained the Israeli helm. The ZOA and other right-wing organizations, however, consistently advocated for Jews' right to settle throughout the West Bank and Gaza Strip and to promote militant responses to regional threats, particularly from Ḥamas and Iran. Left-wing organizations, including Brit Tzedek v'Shalom and its successor organization, J Street, lobbied against Jewish settlements and in favor of a two-state solution to the Israeli-Palestinian conflict as well as diplomatic approaches to the Iranian nuclear threat.

The case of J Street is particularly instructive. Launched in 2007, J Street advocates for a two-state solution to the Israeli-Palestinian conflict, a purpose it describes as "pro-Israel and pro-peace." J Street holds that a two-state solution is necessary for Israel's flourishing as a Jewish and democratic state, and that achieving a deal has been hampered by AIPAC's lobbying, which prevents the United States from pressuring Israel. By providing an alternative Jewish voice, J Street has demonstrated that AIPAC does not speak on behalf of all American Jews and thereby has neutralized its political influence to some degree. When Barack Obama launched an initiative to secure an Israeli-Palestinian accord, J Street pledged to "act as the president's blocking back" in Congress, protecting his policies from AIPAC's criticism.[54]

The pluralization of Israel-related advocacy reflected a deepening polarization in American Jewish opinion. According to the 2013 Pew survey, 44 percent of American Jews believed that Jewish settlements in the West Bank hurt Israel's security compared to 46 percent who believed they helped or made no difference. Forty-eight percent doubted the Israeli government was making a sincere effort to achieve a peace agreement with the Palestinians compared to thirty-eight percent that trusted the government's sincerity.[55] Thus, more wide-ranging advocacy accurately captured the growing diversity of American Jewish opinion and ensured that all voices and perspectives would be represented in the halls of power.

At the same time, the cacophony of voices on the right, center, and left tended to cancel each other out, weakening the capacity of American Jews to exercise political power. Perhaps the deepest rupture of the Israel lobby—and the surest evidence of its diminished influence—unfolded over the course of the 2015 congressional vote on the Iran nuclear accord. Hewing closely to Israel's position, AIPAC and other centrist advocacy organizations mobilized all of their resources to persuade Congress to reject the accord, which had been negotiated by President Obama alongside other world leaders. But J Street, together with advocacy organizations on the left, came out strongly in favor of the deal. The Obama administration quite persuasively argued that it had kept the faith with a segment of the American Jewish community but that pleasing all American Jews would be impossible. By pushing through the Iran nuclear accord despite AIPAC's no-holds-barred opposition, the administration proved that the once unassailable Israel lobby could be defeated.

During the Trump years, political differences among American Jews extended to the U.S. political arena. Whereas most American Jews voted against Trump and expressed an unfavorable view of his performance throughout his presidency, the opposite was true among Orthodox Jews. Trump's policies on Israel, including moving the U.S. embassy to Jerusalem and recognizing Israeli sovereignty in the Golan Heights, earned the president increased support among Orthodox American Jews. In New York City, moreover, ultra-Orthodox Jews rallied to the president's policies on the COVID-19 pandemic, particularly his insistence that schools and synagogues should remain open despite the orders of local authorities.[56]

More broadly, by the waning years of the Trump presidency, much of the liberal, pro–civil rights consensus among American Jews had frayed. Although Jewish community relations councils throughout the country continued to join local coalitions on issues such as racial justice, LGBTQ+ rights, criminal justice reform, and immigration, agreement on such issues at the national level proved elusive. Disputes flared over whether antisemitism on the left or the right posed a graver threat and whether Jewish organizations should join coalitions with those that were perceived as anti-Zionist. The task of seeking consensus on such issues belonged to the Jewish Council of Public Affairs (JCPA), the successor organization to the National Jewish Community Relations Advisory Council (NJCRAC). When, in 2020, in the wake of the murder of George Floyd, JCPA signed onto a letter supporting the Black Lives Matter movement, many donors denounced it, claiming the movement is anti-Israel.[57] A few years later, recognizing that the need for consensus had stymied the organization's capacity for action, JCPA reconstituted itself as an independent advocacy organization with an expressly liberal agenda.[58]

The Ecosystem circa 2020

In the decades running up to 2020, the Jewish community grew in size even as the share of Jews that participate in communal life declined.

Like the rest of U.S. society, American Jews also became more politically and religiously polarized, as Orthodox Jews grew more politically conservative and apt to identify as Republican, and non-Orthodox Reform, Conservative, and Reconstructionist Jews continued to lean liberal and support the Democratic party.

As we have seen, the Jewish nonprofit ecosystem changed in ways that reflect these trends. Rank and file membership in synagogues and donations to legacy organizations such as federations declined. New start-ups, funded by private foundations and oriented toward innovation and underserved populations, flourished. The ecosystem as a whole became more localized, fragmented, and primed for outreach, engagement, and inclusion. Competition for funders and participants intensified, the division of labor among organizations declined, and the system-wide capacity for planning, coordination, and collective action diminished. Moreover, American Jews' capacity to exercise political influence on issues related to Israel and U.S. domestic policies weakened, as they could no longer identify consensus views and positions.

The Impact of the Pandemic

During the first quarter of 2020, the global COVID-19 pandemic unfolded, bringing enormous pressure on the Jewish communal system. As with most religious and voluntary activity, Jewish communal life had been organized around face-to-face gatherings. During the first year of the pandemic those kinds of gatherings ground to a halt. Synagogues, schools, and JCCs closed their physical doors and transitioned to Zoom. Summer camps were canceled or convened as truncated virtual events. As most Jewish organizations are supported primarily by membership dues, tuition, and user fees, funding streams threatened to dry up, and the entire Jewish communal venture seemed fragile and vulnerable in a way that had been previously unimaginable.

As the pandemic unfolded, some observers prognosticated an impending disaster for Jewish communal organizations. After decades of erosion, they predicted the Jewish communal system no longer had the wherewithal for crisis management and might collapse under the pressure of rising needs and diminishing resources. Writing in an online publication geared to funders and communal professionals, Yehuda

Kurtzer, president of the Shalom Hartman Institute of North America, offered the following prognostication:

> Leaders of institutions in today's Jewish community are operating in relative isolation from one another . . . because we no longer have a strong enough system of umbrella organizations and collective mobilization. This means we are likely to see huge duplication of creative efforts, probably a good bit of implicit competition among Jewish organizations today in their pivots for resources and attention, and a whole host of missed opportunities. . . . The simple reason is that the process of atomization of Jewish identity and community in America away from collectivism and towards institutional idiosyncrasy has been good for caring for particular, micro-communal interests and needs; but it has eviscerated our ability to do something big when it comes to collective concerns.[59]

In Kurtzer's view, the weakening of umbrella organizations, the proliferation of specialized institutions, and the increased competition for resources and attention had sapped American Jewish organizations of their capacity to mount an effective response to the pandemic.

A few months later, teaching at a seminar for leaders of federations and Jewish community centers, Hebrew College historian Daniel Judson offered a contrasting assessment. Looking back a full century, Judson noted that the Spanish flu pandemic of 1918 caused Jewish organizations, particularly federations, to double down on their mission as catalysts for collective action among disparate organizations:

> What comes out of the [Spanish Flu] pandemic is in some way the federation feeling the sense of what they can do and for all of their capacities, monetarily, physical buildings, human resources in terms of their having constituent agencies, orphan homes and hospitals, and bringing them together to have a coherent response to the pandemic. And the outcome of all of that is the sense of the federations' mission as being a uniter amongst all of these disparate agencies, and responding so strongly to the problem that was on the table. . . . The pandemic of 1918 allowed federations to come out stronger and more confident of their mission. I wouldn't be surprised if synagogues, day schools, and federations come out [of the 2020 COVID-19] pandemic stronger and more confident as well.[60]

Judson predicted that establishment Jewish institutions, such as synagogues, day schools, and federations, would find their footing, provide much needed and valued services to the Jewish community, and emerge from the COVID-19 pandemic stronger and with a renewed sense of purpose.

Based on the evidence available after just a few years, Judson's historical perspective seems to have captured the dynamics that ensued. Almost immediately following the first lockdowns, in spring 2020, synagogues and day schools moved their programs online. Synagogues reported higher levels of attendance, and several institutions with especially charismatic leadership extended their geographic range to attract worshippers from across the United States and around the world.[61] Day schools were among the first educational institutions to transition to online teaching; they were also among the first to subsequently reopen to in-person instruction under restrictive pandemic guidelines. In the fall of 2020, schools in the Prizmah network that had for years experienced declining enrollment began reporting enrollment increases. A year later, network wide, enrollments remained several percentage points above prepandemic levels.[62] The innovation sector also showed its dynamism, with the introduction of a flurry of new platforms for online Jewish learning, arts and culture, and educational programs for children.

Legacy organizations such as federations, Jewish family services agencies, and Jewish community centers showcased their capacity to act strategically in a time of crisis. Federations convened local nonprofits and raised emergency funds, keeping local Jewish agencies afloat and contributing to broader community relief projects.[63] Jewish family services agencies provided frontline responses to spiraling financial and mental health needs. Jewish community centers launched online programs and summer camps, and then, after reopening for preschools, established "J all day" programs for children who were enrolled in public schools that had shifted to remote learning. National umbrella organizations of the legacy networks also leaned into the crisis. The Jewish Federations of North America (JFNA, the successor to the Council of Jewish Federations) lobbied for government assistance to nonprofits, created a Personal Protective Equipment (PPE) purchasing platform, and provided technical support to federations and federation-supported agencies to apply for "payroll protection" and other emergency funds.[64] JCC

Association of North America convened webinars and disseminated guidance on how to reopen community preschools, fitness centers, and summer camps under changing public safety guidelines and promoted collaboration among JCCs to offer alternative programming via online platforms. Prizmah convened school leaders, collected and shared strategies for virtual education, and provided technical assistance for return to in-person instruction.[65]

The national organizations also forged a web of emergency planning roundtables, coalitions, and joint projects that seemed to override the ecosystem's fragmentation. JFNA and JCC Association of North America convened an Emergency Pandemic Coalition via Zoom. The group began as eight national organizations meeting twice monthly; it rapidly expanded to include representatives from private foundations, engagement organizations, human services organizations, and the religious denominations. The national organizations also helped establish and scaffold planning roundtables for particular fields—for example, mental health, Israel travel, human services, and outreach organizations. A group of private foundations established the Jewish Community Relief Fund (JCRIF), which awarded $91 million in grants and no-interest loans during the pandemic's first year. (Subsequently, JCRIF created a $50 million fund for "moonshot" initiatives that promised to recalibrate Jewish communal life for a postpandemic future.) As a result of these disparate responses, the Jewish nonprofit ecosystem grew more capable of deliberation, information sharing, and collective action than it had been in decades.

The system's renewed capacity for consensus-building and collective action was put to the test following Hamas's October 7, 2023, attack on Israel. During the immediate aftermath, liberal Zionist organizations that had previously opposed Israel's right-wing government declared their support for the country's war aims, joining with the establishment advocacy organizations.[66] Then, in November, JFNA assembled a broad coalition of organizations extending from the right wing Zionist Organization of America to liberal Zionist groups such as J Street and T'ruah (a rabbinic human rights group) to plan a solidarity rally. In November, the partner organizations staged a "march for Israel" in Washington, DC. The rally drew nearly three hundred thousand demonstrators to the national mall, making it the largest demonstration ever organized by American Jews.[67] Further to the left, however, anti-Zionist groups such as Jewish Voice for Peace also gained momentum in the aftermath of October 7, suggesting that new forms of polarization will continue, notwithstanding the overall centripetal forces of change.

Conclusion

The Jewish communal enterprise faces significant challenges. Orthodox and non-Orthodox networks have little connective tissue between them, and the communal gaps are overlayed by increasing political polarization. The still-unfolding trends of secularization and assimilation have proven deeply challenging for liberal Jewish congregations and organizations, which struggle to attract and retain the rank-and-file. And, despite very recent developments, Israel and antisemitism will likely continue to spark discord in the Jewish community.

Still, as we have seen, the ecosystem has demonstrated a capacity to adapt. Innovation-sector organizations are reaching many disconnected, underserved, and previously excluded populations. Experiential education is expanding where supplementary school education is falling off, particularly through camping and Israel-based educational tourism. Federation, JCC, and other legacy networks are collaborating more effectively as a consequence of the pandemic. Day schools that earned substantial credit from families for their pandemic responses are experiencing enrollment increases. And there are new causes that galvanize organizations and grassroots activists, from combating antisemitism and climate change to shoring up democratic institutions. These signs of vitality reveal an ecosystem responding to the changing character of the Jewish community and the changing contours of American society.

Appendix

Typology and Examples of Innovation Sector Start-ups

YOUNG ADULT
- **Moishe House**, launched in 2006, supports young adults in forming residential communities and reaches tens of thousands of young adults through its residentially based programming.

- **One Table**, established in 2015, provides subsidies and other support to young adults to host Shabbat meals in their homes with more than 250,000 participants during its first seven years.
- **Birthright Israel**, launched in 1999, brings tens of thousands of young adults to Israel annually for ten-day educational tours.

ADULT EDUCATION

- **Limmud** convenes multiday festivals of Jewish learning in cities around the world, beginning in England in the 1980s and the United States in 2004.
- **Svara**, launched in 2003, promotes Talmud learning through a lens of queer Jewish experience, seeking to promote Jewish renewal in a multilevel, "traditionally radical" yeshiva.
- **Hadar**, founded in 2006, seeks to empower Jews to create egalitarian communities of Torah (learning), Avodah (worship) and Ḥesed (deeds of lovingkindness). The organization hosts immersive learning opportunities and reaches an expanding following through online and print offerings.

SOCIAL ACTION

- **Repair the World**, established in 2009, mobilizes Jewish young adults to address community needs through learning and service opportunities. Core tenets of the organization include *tikkun olam* (repairing the world) and *tzedek* (justice).
- **American Jewish World Service**, an international development organization formed in 1985, advocates for human rights and combats poverty across Africa, Asia, Latin America, and the Caribbean.
- **Avodah**, developed in 1988, inspires Jewish leadership grounded in social justice and community engagement. The organization focuses on social action initiatives, notably the Jewish Service Corps, pairing young Jewish adults with a host nonprofit organization for a year of service work.

DIVERSITY, EQUITY AND INCLUSION

- **18Doors**, launched in 1998, supports interfaith couples and families in developing their relationship with Judaism by providing a series of resources and trainings.

- **Jews of Color Initiative**, launched in 2017, works to advance the professional, organizational, and communal field for Jews of Color through community education, research, and grantmaking.
- **RespectAbility**, established in 2013, advocates for Jews with disabilities by strengthening policies and practices that fight stigmas, encourage inclusion, and foster opportunities.

ENVIRONMENTAL AND OUTDOORS

- **Hazon**, founded in 2000, emphasizes integrating sustainability into everyday Jewish life to promote a healthy, sustainable, and equitable world.
- **Wilderness Torah**, created in 2007, fosters healing, belonging, and resilience through community building and education programs that are informed by earth-based Jewish traditions.
- **Dayenu: A Jewish Call to Climate Action**, launched in 2019, creates opportunities for local Jewish communities to act on the climate crisis. The organization is rooted in three core pillars: bold action, movement building, and spiritual adaption.

SPIRITUAL LIFE

- **Institute for Jewish Spirituality**, established in 1999, creates and teaches a variety of Jewish spiritual practices rooted in Jewish wisdom, including meditation, prayer, and Torah study.
- **Romemu**, developed in 2006, is a holistic Jewish spiritual community dedicated to reinvigorating the mind, body, and spirit through worship and learning.
- **Ikar** is a dynamic Jewish congregation and spiritual community based in Los Angeles that strives to inspire Jews across the religious spectrum since its founding in 2014.

ISRAEL ADVOCACY

- **IfNotNow**, formed in 2014, is a movement of American Jews engaged in community organizing to protect and promote equality and justice for all Palestinians and Israelis.
- **J Street**, an American grassroots organization established in 2007, advocates for pro-Israel, pro-peace, and pro-democracy through policy support, political campaigns, and campus engagement.

- **Stand With Us**, an international nonpartisan organization founded in 2001, combats antisemitism and supports Israel through trainings, education, social media, and missions to Israel.

NOTES

1 Many thanks to Roy Buchler and Hanna Paris for research assistance. Thanks also to Jonah Hassenfeld for coauthoring a working paper about the Jewish nonprofit ecosystem that explored many similar themes (on file with the author) and to Jack Wertheimer, Shaul Kelner, and Seymour Kopelowitz for comments on a previous draft.
2 Daniel Judah Elazar, *Community and Polity: The Organizational Dynamics of American Jewry* (Philadelphia: Jewish Publication Society, 1995), 43.
3 The Bureau of Social Morals was meant to address the problem of Jewish crime, following the accusation by Police Commissioner Theodore A. Bingham that 50 percent of all New York City criminals were Jews (Elazar, *Community and Polity*, 205).
4 Lila Corwin Berman, "How Americans Give: The Financialization of American Jewish Philanthropy," *American Historical Review* 122 (2017): 1459–89.
5 Elazar, *Community and Polity*, 231.
6 Elazar, 118; see also Jonathan Sarna, *American Judaism* (New Haven, CT: Yale University Press, 2004), 279; and Lance Sussman, "The Suburbanization of American Judaism as Reflected in Synagogue Building and Architecture," *Journal of American Jewish History* 75 (1985): 31–47.
7 Lila Corwin Berman, "Donor Advised Funds in Historical Perspective," *Boston College Law Forum on Philanthropy and the Public Good* (October 2015): 1472. See also Ann Pava, *Redefining Jewish Education: Federations' Goals for a New Century*, eJewish Philanthropy, January 29, 2019, ejewishphilanthropy.com.
8 Elazar, *Community and Polity*, 220.
9 Elazar, 95.
10 Elazar, 8.
11 Elazar, 246–48.
12 Elazar, 220.
13 Reem Nadeem, "Modeling the Future of Religion in America—How U.S. Religious Composition Has Changed in Recent Decades," Pew Research Center's Religion & Public Life Project, September 13, 2022, www.pewresearch.org. See also Robert D. Putnam and David E. Campbell, *American Grace: How Religion Divides and Unites Us* (New York: Simon & Schuster, 2012).
14 "Jewish Americans in 2020," Pew Research Center, May 21, 2021, www.pewresearch.org.
15 Theodore Sasson, "New Analysis of Pew Data: Children of Intermarriage Increasingly Identify as Jewish," *Tablet Magazine*, November 11, 2013. See also Elizabeth Tighe, Leonard Saxe, Daniel Parmer, Daniel Nussenbaum, and Raquel

Magidan deKramer, "According to their Numbers: Assessing the Pew Research Center's Estimate of 7.5 Million Jewish Americans," *Contemporary Jewry* 43, no. 2 (2023): 201–24.

16 Jonothon Ament, *American Jewish Religious Denominations. Report Series on National Jewish Population Survey 2000–01* (New York: United Jewish Communities, 2005); see also "Jewish Americans in 2020."

17 Amy Chua, *Political Tribes: Group Instinct and the Fate of Nations* (London: Bloomsbury, 2019); see also Ezra Klein, *Why We're Polarized* (London: Profile, 2020).

18 Michael Dimock and Richard Wike, "America Is Exceptional in Its Political Divide," Pew Charitable Trusts, March 29, 2021, www.pewresearch.org.

19 "Jewish Americans in 2020"; see also "A Portrait of Jewish Americans," Pew Research Center, October 1, 2013, www.pewresearch.org.

20 Board of Governors of the Federal Reserve System, "Distribution of Household Wealth in the U.S. Since 1989," December 16, 2022, www.federalreserve.gov.

21 Sidney Goldstein. *Profile of American Jewry: Insights from the 1990 National Jewish Population Survey* (New York: North American Jewish Data Bank, 1993), 129; Ament, *American Jewish Religious Denominations (Report Series on National Jewish Population Survey 2000–01)*; see also "Jewish Americans in 2020."

22 Jennifer Stofman, Director of Synagogue Consulting, United Synagogues of Conservative Judaism, interview with author, April 2022. According to one source, the number of paying members of Conservative synagogues nationwide dropped 14 percent between 2001 and 2011; see Josh Nathan-Kazis, "Liberal Denominations Face Crisis as Rabbis Rebel, Numbers Shrink," *Forward*, February 10, 2011, forward.com.

23 The number of Reform synagogues declined during the 2010s from a number in the "900s" to a number in the "800s." Esther Lederman, Director of Congregational Innovation, Union of Reform Judaism, interview with author, April 2022).

24 For example, the share of households reporting synagogue membership in Baltimore dropped from 46 percent in 2010 to 33 percent in 2020; in Boston from 42 percent in 2005 to 39 percent in 2015; in Chicago from 36 percent in 2010 to 26 percent in 2020; in Denver from 32 percent in 2007 to 16 percent in 2018; in Miami from 39 percent in 2004 to 36 percent in 2014; in Pittsburgh from 53 percent in 2002 to 38 percent in 2017; and, in Greater Washington, DC, from 37 percent in 2003 to 26 percent in 2017. Some communities such as Los Angeles, Atlanta, and Palm Beach County report no significant changes; Seattle reported increases. Community studies can be accessed through the Berman Jewish Policy Archives, www.bjpa.org.

25 Jack Wertheimer, *The New American Judaism: How Jews Practice Their Religion Today* (Princeton, NJ: Princeton University Press, 2018), 2.

26 Paul Kipnes and David Weisz, "Synagogue Dues Are Dead," Clergy Leadership Incubator, February 28, 2022; www.cliforum.org. See also Kerry M. Olitzky and Avi S. Olitzky, *New Membership and Financial Alternatives for the American*

Synagogue: From Traditional Dues to Fair Share to Gifts from the Heart (Woodstock, VT: Jewish Lights, 2015); and Daniel Judson, *Pennies for Heaven: The History of American Synagogues and Money* (Waltham, MA: Brandeis University Press, 2018).

27 A comprehensive census of supplementary schools in the United States conducted by the Jewish Education Project for the year 2019–20 estimated total enrollment of 135,087 students in 1,398 schools. A comparable census conducted in 2006–7 estimated total enrollment of 230,000 in about 2,000 schools. These data suggest a decline in enrollment of 45 percent over a period of 13 years. See "A Census of Jewish Supplementary Schools in North America, 2019–2020," Jewish Education Project, 2023: pathways.jewishedproject.org. Additional evidence of declining participation in supplementary education can be gleaned from federation-sponsored community surveys. For example, in Denver, the share of Jewish children enrolled in supplementary education dropped from 41 percent in 2007 to 21 percent in 2018; in Chicago, from 35 percent in 2010 to 19 percent in 2020; in Cincinnati from 52 percent in 2008 to 21 percent in 2018. Community surveys can be accessed through the Berman Jewish Policy Archives, www.bjpa.org.

28 Another national capacity building initiative in supplementary Jewish education, the Conference for Advancement of Jewish Education (CAJE), was also closed in 2009 after operating continuously since 1976.

29 According to a day school census conducted by the Avi Chai Foundation in 2019, enrollment in non-Orthodox day schools had declined 16.6 percent over the previous 20 years. See Mordechai Besser, "A Census of Jewish Day Schools, 2018–2019," AVI CHAI Foundation, August 2020, avichai.org.

30 Prizmah also serves a number of Modern Orthodox day schools previously networked with Yeshiva University.

31 Shaul Kelner, *Tours That Bind: Diaspora, Pilgrimage, and Israeli Birthright Tourism* (New York University Press, 2010); see also Leonard Saxe and Barry Chazan, *Ten Days of Birthright Israel* (Waltham, MA: Brandeis University Press, 2008); Amy L. Sales and Leonard Saxe, *"How Goodly Are Thy Tents": Summer Camps as Jewish Socializing Experiences* (Waltham, MA: Brandeis University Press, 2004); and Joseph Reimer, *Making Shabbat: Celebrating and Learning at American Jewish Summer Camps* (Waltham, MA: Brandeis University Press, 2022).

32 Ament, *American Jewish Religious Denominations*; see also "Jewish Americans in 2020."

33 Mark Gurvis, "Business Continuity Analysis of Major Jewish Communal Networks 3.0" (internal report), Jewish Federations of North America, May 6, 2021.

34 Besser, *Census of Jewish Day Schools*.

35 Besser.

36 Lila Corwin Berman, *The American Jewish Philanthropic Complex* (Princeton, NJ: Princeton University Press, 2020); see also Robert Hyfler, "The Rise of the Mega-Donor and the Privatization of Organized Jewish Life," eJewish Philanthropy, July 10, 2017, ejewishphilanthropy.com.

37 Between 2012 and 2015, 138 federations raised a combined $5.7 billion and distributed $3.6 billion in the United States and Israel. Collectively, they held $16 billion in assets. See Maayan Hoffman, "Federation and Its Future: Floundering or Flourishing?," eJewish Philanthropy, November 12, 2017, ejewishphilanthropy.com. See also Uri Blau, "Special Report: What the Jewish Federations Do with Your Money," *Haaretz*, October 30, 2017, www.haaretz.com.

38 Jack Wertheimer, "Current Trends in American Jewish Philanthropy," *American Jewish Year Book* 97 (1997): 3–92; Abny Santicola, "All For One," NonProfit PRO, October 1, 2009, www.nonprofitpro.com; see also "Oral Testimony of William C. Daroff, Vice President for Public Policy, Jewish Federations of North America," United States House of Representatives Committee on Ways & Means, Hearing on Charitable Contribution Deduction, 113th Congress, 2013, docs.house.gov.

39 Jack Wertheimer, *Giving Jewish: How Big Funders Have Transformed American Jewish Philanthropy* (AVI CHAI Foundation, March 27, 2018).

40 Wertheimer, *Giving Jewish*.

41 Hoffman, "Federation and Its Future."

42 Theodore Sasson, "The Politics of Israel: Relations with the American Jewish Community," in *Contemporary Israel: New Insights and Scholarship*, ed. Frederick E. Greenspahn (New York University Press, 2016); see also Eric Fleisch and Theodore Sasson, *The New Philanthropy: American Jewish Giving to Israeli Organizations* (Waltham, MA: Cohen Center for Modern Jewish Studies, Brandeis University, 2012).

43 Wertheimer, *Giving Jewish*.

44 Shaul Kelner, "In Its Own Image: Independent Philanthropy and the Cultivation of Young Jewish Leadership," in *The New Jewish Leaders: Reshaping the American Jewish Landscape*, ed. Jack Wertheimer (Waltham, MA: Brandeis University Press, 2011), 261–321.

45 In 2014, Jewish nonprofits received $1.55 billion from federations, $1 billion from 250 private foundations, and $400 million from donor-advised funds; see Wertheimer, *Giving Jewish*, 3.

46 Wertheimer.

47 Alongside the deepening control of the financial elite, men continue to occupy most top leadership positions in Jewish communal organizations. Although the number of women in top executive positions is rising, the broader gender gap in organizational leadership remains entrenched. Men are more likely to lead larger nonprofits compared to women. For example, according to a 2019 report from Leading Edge, men lead 65 percent or more of organizations with a budget over 10 million and 92 percent of organizations with a budget of 60 million or more. Conversely, women who hold top executive positions tend to lead smaller organizations with leaner budgets. Leading Edge, "The Gender Gap in Jewish Nonprofit Leadership: An Ecosystem View," 2021, www.leadingedge.org.

48 The research institute Jumpstart surveyed the field and identified 305 start-ups launched between 2000 and 2010. See *The Jewish Innovation Economy: An Emerging Market for Knowledge and Social Capital* (New York: Jumpstart, the Natan Fund, the Samuel Bronfman Foundation, 2011), *The Innovation Ecosystem: Emergence of a New Jewish Landscape* (Jumpstart, the Natan Fund, and the Samuel Bronfman Foundation, 2009); and Steven Windmueller, "The Jewish Marketplace: Introducing the New American Jew," eJewish Philanthropy, August 16, 2017, ejewishphilanthropy.com.
49 Sarah Bunin Benor, "Young Jewish Leaders in Los Angeles: Strengthening the Jewish People in Conventional and Unconventional Ways," in Wertheimer, *New Jewish Leaders*, 112–58.
50 Kelner, "In Its Own Image."
51 Wertheimer, *Giving Jewish*.
52 Sasson, "Politics of Israel."
53 Theodore Sasson, *The New American Zionism* (New York University Press, 2014); see also Dov Waxman, *Trouble in the Tribe: The American Jewish Conflict over Israel* (Princeton, NJ: Princeton University Press, 2016).
54 Sasson, *New American Zionism*, 42.
55 "Portrait of Jewish Americans."
56 Liam Stack and Joseph Goldstein, "Inspired by Trump, Ḥasidic Backlash Grows Over Virus Rules," *New York Times*, October 22, 2020.
57 Ron Kampeas and Asaf Elia-Shalev, "This Organization Was Supposed to Unite Jews. A Debate over Black Lives Matter May Fuel Its Demise," Jewish Telegraphic Agency, June 23, 2021.
58 Arno Rosenfeld, "Pressed over Liberal Politics, Jewish Public Affairs Group Declares Independence," *Forward*, December 22, 2022, forward.com.
59 Yehuda Kurtzer, "Courageous Leadership Now: An Urgent Agenda for the Jewish Community and its Institutions," eJewish Philanthropy, March 23, 2020, ejewishphilanthropy.com.
60 Daniel Judson, "History of the Federation Movement," lecture to the fellows of the Mandel Executive Leadership Program, August 5, 2020.
61 One Reform congregation, Central Synagogue in New York City, reports six hundred thousand worshipers across all platforms for Yom Kippur, 2021. See Ron Wolfson and Steven Windmueller, "The Rise of the Online Synagogue," *Tablet Magazine*, April 6, 2022, www.tabletmag.com.
62 Two-thirds of the schools in the Prizmah network reported enrollment increases between 2019 and 2022; overall, enrollments across the network increased by 3.7 percent. Elliot Rabin, *A Year in Review: Data and Reflections on Jewish Day Schools and Yeshivas: 2022* (New York: Prizmah, 2022).
63 During the first year of the pandemic, federations and private Jewish foundations raised more than $1 billion, with two-thirds of funding directed to general rather than Jewish community needs. Hanna Bar Nissim, "Jewish Philanthropy during

COVID-19 Focuses on Need, Not Affinity," Inside Philanthropy, February 22, 2021, www.insidephilanthropy.com.
64   Ron Kampeas, "Get Ready to Apply, Again: Jewish Nonprofits to Get Advice about Security Slices of $284 Billion Pandemic Relief Bill," Jewish Telegraphic Agency, December 22, 2020, www.jta.org.
65   Faygie Holt, "Amid the Pandemic, Jewish Day Schools Survive (and Even Thrive)," *Jewish Journal*, June 21, 2020, jewishjournal.com.
66   Yehuda Kurtzer, "How October 7 Is Reshaping the Zionist—and Anti-Zionist—Left in the U.S.," *Forward*, November 30, 2023.
67   Andrew Silow-Carroll, "In Washington, Jews Manage to Rally around an Intentionally Murky Message. Will It Last?," Jewish Telegraphic Agency, November 15, 2023, www.jta.org.

Conclusion

The Ever-Changing People

HASIA DINER

In 1986, a posthumously published essay by the Polish-born historian Simon Rawidowicz (1896–1957) rocked the world of Jewish thought. Originally written in the 1950s, this often cited and deeply provocative piece came to occupy a singular place in the field of modern Jewish history. In "Israel: The Ever-Dying People," Rawidowicz observed that the Jewish people, in its long history, has always seen itself "on the verge of ceasing to be, of disappearing." But "our incessant dying," he continued as a follow-up, "means uninterrupted living, rising, standing up, and beginning anew."[1] All announcements of dying, he argued, generated not just gloom and foreboding, but a sense of urgency that then spawned bursts of creativity, innovation, and positive responses to change. Those responses varied and took multiple forms, but statements about the imminent end of Jewish life inspired Jews worried about the future to slow down, and then look at the facts on the ground, see glimmers of hope, and experiment with new forms as seeds for innovation.

The concept of the ever dying people offers a way to put into context the original chapters of this volume, focusing on the discernible trends of the early twenty-first century. The book itself, and the research that fed into each one of the pieces, emerges at a moment in time when the American Jewish world has found itself awash in studies and discussion galore about the future of Jewish life in the United States. Those discussions take place in synagogues, communal bodies, the Jewish press, and beyond, and for the most part echo the jeremiahs of Rawidowicz, who predicted that the end of Jewish life, as known, lay close at hand. Academics joined the conversation as well, often commissioned by Jewish agencies to examine the data, confirm or complicate the dire predictions, and make suggestions about possible solutions to stave off what to many seemed inevitable. Other scholars, not in the employ of Jewish foundations and federations, acting, rather, as critical analysts, also pored over the troves of information collected about the state of America's Jews and came to their own conclusions. Either way, they responded to the discourse swirling around the Jewish world that told a story of decline, decay, and death set amid the mountains of data collected.

Hardly a new subject of conversation and scholarship, the 2013 report "A Portrait of Jewish Americans: Findings from a Pew Research Center Survey of U.S. Jews," however, hit a nerve and served as the launch pad for many scholars, often funded by Jewish communal agencies, to ponder what it meant that "Pew," as it is commonly called, highlighted the dwindling numbers of American Jews, their dropping proportion of the American population, and the steep decline in religious identification and observance among them.[2] The report pointed to increasing and seemingly unending intermarriages between Jews and non-Jews, and the fact that a majority of Jews affiliate with and participate formally in no organized Jewish institutions and activities.

Being Jewish for most has become, Pew concluded, a personal matter, something to be proud of but not something that generated sustained communal involvement. They increasingly defined "Jewish" as a function of individual preference and not communal obligation. The younger the respondent, the lower the level of actual affiliation and even of any kind of consistent engagement beyond enjoying a limited set of activities, such as attending a Hanukkah party or Passover seder, eating some iconic Ashkenazi food, and the like. Few respondents felt that their Jewishness held them back or stigmatized them in the public sphere. They just did not invest much in it or consider themselves responsible for what community leaders labeled "the Jewish future."

If ever there was a moment in which Rawidowicz's insights might be marshaled to think about the present and, by extension, the future, the post-Pew era might be it. Jewish communal leaders, whether from the religious sphere or the organizational sector, read Pew as nearly a death sentence, a grim prognosis for an utterly transformed future, one in which the only generative element in American Jewish life comes from Orthodoxy, and the rest of American Jewry would fall by the wayside, swallowed up by secularism. The publication of the Pew report not only became the fodder for sermons and follow up studies, community discussions, and articles in the Jewish press, but it also made it to the front pages of major American newspapers. It became American news.

But, in fact, issuing such dire predictions pre-dated Pew. Moving backward in time, in 1997 Harvard professor Alan Dershowitz published *The Vanishing American Jew*, a widely reviewed book that caught the attention of most major news outlets.[3] Further back in time, in 1970, the National Jewish Population Survey sounded the alarm as well.[4] It focused particularly on exogamy and the fact that more and more younger Jews chose marriage partners from outside the Jewish world, and that the number of households which included a Jewish and non-Jewish member would grow with time. More and more children would grow up with both Jewish and non-Jewish—presumably Christian—relatives and extended families. The *New York Times* and the *Washington Post* carried news of the survey and quoted at length from Jewish community leaders shocked by the findings. How, they asked, might they address this trend? What could they do to stem the tide? And, as far back as 1964, the nationally circulating glossy news magazine *Look* published an article whose title may have inspired Dershowitz three decades later.[5] Also entitled "The Vanishing American Jew," the article became the grist for sermons and commentary within the Jewish world, spurring on jittery conversations that the piece spoke the truth about an inevitable future.

So much commentary had swirled around the American Jewish world on this subject, a good deal of it coming even before the *Look* article. It would be no exaggeration to say that grim prognoses of the American Jewish future have run throughout the several centuries of their history on these shores. At any point in time, whether when the mass migration of relatively poor Jews from the German-speaking lands of Central Europe inundated the small Sephardi-run communities of the early nineteenth century or the dramatically larger migrations from eastern Europe starting in the 1870s, community leaders, well situated and economically comfortable American Jews, spoke out and wrote about the dire consequences that the changes engulfing the Jewish population would bring about.

In the 1910s, for example, reports decried the dreadful state of Jewish education and the fact that so few boys—as only they mattered—received any Jewish instruction. Other reports lamented the dysfunction of Jewish families. Some focused on low levels of synagogue attendance by the children of the immigrants and indeed of the immigrants themselves. Others worried that the increasing "diversity"—a word that they did not use—of the Jewish population of America, made up of people from the German-speaking world as well as from Ukraine, Lithuania, Galicia, Romania, Hungary, and various parts of the Ottoman Empire, meant that there could never be Jewish unity in the United States. They had much to say about the allure of American culture, its glittery entertainments, and the pernicious spread of such values as independence and personal preference that undermined Jewish solidarity. Commentators noted that as the children of the immigrants swam in the waters of American culture they became ashamed and alienated from their foreign-born antecedents and inevitably opted for the American rather than their parents' ethos.

For the most part such reports declared that under present conditions, whenever that might have been, the next generation of Jews would drift away, become disinterested, and feel alienated from Jewish culture. The doomsayers, whether rabbis who preached about this in their sermons, journalists who filled the pages of the Jewish press, either in English or Yiddish, or deeply concerned Jewish activists, all pondered the dismal future that lay in store for America's Jews. A perusal of the volumes of *The American Jewish Yearbook*, launched in 1898, for example, provides a yearly repertoire of Cassandra-like statements as to the insolvable internal problem facing the Jews, betokening a dismal future.

Yet amid the vast corpus of statements about the dissolution of Jewish life under American conditions, a counterargument emerged. Those who voiced it contended that not all had been lost, that one can look at the trends, whether embodied in numbers or qualitative anecdotal evidence, and discern that all is not lost. They, whether religious leaders, educational innovators, crusading journalists, or partisans for new political movements, argued that they did have the power to create new ways of being Jewish, could reconstruct Judaism to breathe life into it, and find ways to harness what already existed, using those trends as forces for life, not death.

For sure, many commentators who predicted a dwindling future for Jewish life in America set their predictions in the reality that because of antisemitism Jews faced limitations in their access to resources, and if not in blatant, violent, and state-based form, just a pervasive feeling on the part of many Americans that Jews were somehow different and did not quite fit in. If being Jewish kept one from, for example, attending the school of her choice or joining a club or getting a job in a particular office, then maybe being Jewish was not worth it. After all, the prophets of gloom and doom said, young American Jews received so little from their Jewishness and, instead, because of their Jewishness found themselves excluded from that which they yearned for. The obstacles Jews faced, the rhetoric declared, exacerbated but did not actually cause the decline of Jewish intensity in America. Except for a few of the commentators, most argued indirectly that the antisemites could not be blamed for the bleak prospects of Jewish life. The Jews had only themselves to hold accountable.

That essentially brings us back to Rawidowicz. His point, relevant to the chapters in this volume, points to a long-lived and ongoing Jewish reality that resonates into the twenty-first century. As a people with a history that stretches over millennia, who constantly moved from place to place, Jews always faced the challenges and opportunities of having to reinvent themselves. Over that great arc of time they pondered in one form or another such linked questions as where have we been, what does it mean that we find ourselves here—wherever that was—and can we actually sustain what we had been back there, in the past, under such new and unknown circumstances.

Mostly, as Rawidowicz so powerfully argued, they found themselves wanting as they looked at their own behaviors in the present, no matter where and when, considering themselves weak and altered versions of the Jewish vitality and authenticity of those who came before. They held up times and places where Jewish commitments had really mattered, unlike their own present. They rarely pondered the reality that those past generations had also gone through the same processes. But, as he so cogently argued, as did the Columbia University historian Salo Baron (1895–1989), the first scholar to hold a chair in Jewish history at an American university, the Jews had persevered, regrouped, reinvented, and adapted themselves to create new markers of Jewishness in new places, which their real or fictive heirs would consider traditional. Those heirs rarely understood that the practices of their parents, real or metaphoric, had once been new, controversial, and, in the eyes of some, poor iterations of what Jews ought to do.

But the cycle kept going, testament to Rawidowicz's "beginning anew." In this way, he could have also titled his article "Israel, the Ever-Changing People." After all, the changes never came without an array of criticism of the new. Jews and Jewish communal leaders expressed worries that the new practices and innovative formulations would make Judaism and Jewish life unsustainable in the future. They considered that some of the new practices seemed imitative of the cultures of the people around them, non-Jews.

The concern felt by some, whom we might consider the defenders of the old order, inspired extensive writing and oratory, and, starting in the later part of the nineteenth century, they turned to the newly born social sciences, conducting sociological studies based on the highest levels of contemporary methodological sophistication.

At key moments, including now at the beginning of the twenty-first century, in the shadow of Pew, Jewish communal leaders, teachers, writers, intellectuals, rabbis, and others surveyed present realities, mostly defined them as problems, and proposed solutions to try to stem the tide. How, they asked, could they prevent the slow or rapid slide toward extinction? What could they do now, given the gravity of the situation, to make sure that levels of Jewish participation and practice did not deteriorate further? What strategies could they employ to stave off what seemed like an inevitable decline? What signs of hope could they discern that might calm them down, quelling their predictions of the death of Judaism and the Jewish people?

At no point in time did the jeremiahs of Jewish life, the predictors of death, provide the sole voice in communal discussions about the present and the future. At every point, someone offered a counternarrative, pointing out signs of vibrancy and continued commitment. Those who saw positive developments on their local Jewish scene noted continuities between past and present and sought to temper the statements of doom and gloom. Essentially, they asked the naysayers to look beyond all the negative data and behold how Jews, the people or, as often articulated in Hebrew, *amcha*, remained committed, albeit in forms unrecognizable to ancestors in some distant past. They suggested, again in a tone captured by Rawidowicz, that changes taking place could be potentially forces for life. They also strongly suggested that the power to harness new trends in order to breathe life into the dying body of Jewish life lay in the hands of the Jews themselves. Thought leaders and communal activists could, with effort, organization, and funding, create new institutions and spread new ideas that could inject vitality and reverse course.

It may be accurate to say that the innovations in diaspora Jewish life, from the Middle Ages and onward, adopted this stance, one that essentially said that we can never go back to what had been, and, to live, we as custodians of the Jewish future must figure out how to go forward. Only by innovating can we do so. Even movements and ideas that justified their actions as traditional and as returns to the authentic and old have been seen by historians as radical and revolutionary as they redefined Judaism to fit new circumstances, to keep it from expiring. Mysticism, Ḥasidism, the Musar movement, Reform, the Positive-Historical school that fed into Conservative Judaism, Modern Orthodoxy, Zionism, and the Yiddish cultural movements associated with diaspora nationalism and elements of the Jewish Left, all posited the existence of a problem, the need and ability to address it, and the reality that large reservoirs of Jews cared about the Jewish future, but just needed new ways to express their loyalties. One American-born denomination of Judaism even called itself Reconstructionism, declaring itself in both name and ideology as an effort to rebuild that which had been shattered.

Even those who predicted the inevitable end of Jewish life and culture still felt called upon to act and do something to slow down what they predicted as inevitable. As one of many possible examples, community leaders bitterly decried the low levels of Jewish knowledge among the masses and the inadequacy of Jewish educational opportunities, realities that they predicted would certainly lead to the Jews' disappearance. But they did not advocate then closing the schools that existed. Instead, here they became innovators, suggesting new pedagogic models, training new cadres of teachers, and creating local boards of Jewish education to set standards for schools. They conducted campaigns to convince parents who had not done so to send their children to the newly fashioned Jewish schools that would presumably address the deficiencies of the ones that had come before.

Those problems that Jewish leaders identified have been, variously, the crises of migration and the disruptions of community life, the lack of unity. They lamented the absence of a common culture among Jews, doing so repeatedly and, in many places, as a consequence of their incessant movements around the world. Those who scanned the clouds hovering over the Jewish people commented upon changed family patterns, shifting gender relations, and class matters, including tensions surrounding intra-Jewish economic inequality. Commentators, regardless of how they defined an ideal and solid Jewish education and how to achieve it, decried the landscape of learning. They also worried that, as they saw it, once fixed relations between men and women, parents and children had come undone, putting great stress upon Jewish families. The practice of Judaism as a religious system, on both a communal and a home level, also agitated these conversations. What has happened to observance and piety, including Sabbath observance and keeping the dietary laws, posed as at one time utterly universal and agreed upon?

Additionally, throughout this history, as Jewish communal leaders articulated their worries about the future, whether they perceived great threats or ripe opportunities for positive growth, they pondered how much of the outside culture had crept into Jewish practice. For the doomsayers, those outside forces threatened to pollute the once pure Jewish tradition, robbing it of its unchanged essence. They also asked if Jews today, whenever, had been learning too much from the non-Jews around them, aping their ways, following their lead, overassociating with them, and in the process losing the core of their Jewishness.

The inner Jewish discourse about death and life has resembled the proverbial "glass half empty" and "glass half full" dichotomy. In this continuous inner-Jewish discussion, partisans arrayed on multiple sides of such questions as how dire are the circumstances, can they be fixed, how, and who will do it, required knowledge of the facts on the ground. All involved had to make their case, which in turn required information, gleaned from whatever sources happened to be available at the time and, indeed, what, given the historic era under consideration, constituted knowledge. The questions changed somewhat, with language, names, and exact formulation specific to time and place, but the methodologies that both the worriers and the hopeful employed to solve the problems at hand transformed profoundly.

The age of "modernity," a slippery term whose meaning historians and other analysts debate with no consensus in sight, provides an important point of departure to ponder how knowledge changed. In the premodern era, the community leaders who wrote and spoke about the Jewish crisis at hand relied on their own observations of life around them. They heard from travelers who had seen Jewish life in other places, and through relatively slow mail service received letters from Jews in other places describing the woeful state of Jewish affairs. But the nineteenth century changed all this. Innovations in transportation and communication technologies, the rise of the Jewish press, the vast migrations that began in mid-century and then skyrocketed in the twentieth century, and, perhaps most importantly here, the late nineteenth-century development of the social sciences and in particular the field of statistics, all converged, equipping Jewish religious and communal authorities with hard data, information that allowed them to be more concrete in terms of what they said about the Jews in the present and the trends which they saw for the future.

Armed with numbers and percentages, referring to proportions, to trends of change over time, and talking in the language of representative samples, averages, mean, median, and mode, those presenting their case about the state of the Jews in the present spoke with a new confidence, greater than those who came before them. But they asked very similar questions about religious practice, education, communal involvement, and origins as well as class, gender, and family that had been heard decades, indeed centuries, earlier. These kinds of questions could be heard for millennia. True everywhere and at all times, the American scene, past and present, provides a fascinating setting from which to think of this history.

Certain characteristics of American life shaped the discourses about the Jewish future in the nineteenth and twentieth centuries, and into the twenty-first. Commentators then, and now, noted the ability in America for people to transform themselves in whatever ways they wanted, and they pointed out, then as now, that Jews had access to a great array of resources that allowed them as individuals to chart their own course. American culture celebrated the individual as the key unit for decision-making, and, given the absence of state support, Jewish communal institutions had no power to enforce conformity. Everyone in essence operated as a Jew of choice. When Jews, for example, did not like the religious options available, they just went out and created new ones that fit their tastes and sensibilities. If they wanted to associate with other Jews but did not want to belong to synagogues, they founded whatever kind of clubs and associations that appealed to them. Perhaps not surprisingly, in the nineteenth century the most popular Jewish organization was the B'nai B'rith, a fraternal order disconnected from religious or synagogue life. American Jews did not need anyone's permission to form new iterations of Judaism, including Reform, Conservative, Reconstructionism, Secular, Humanistic, New Age, and so on. They had the ability to pick and choose, to do as they wanted—or, as the phrase went in the 1960s, to "do their own thing."

The chapters in this book all make a point about twenty-first-century America, a place of fluid identities and open opportunities. In this world, which celebrates hybridity, individuals can change whatever they want about themselves with no obligation to stick to the categories of affiliation inherited from the past. They can call themselves what they want and expect to be respected for what they are, no matter how it may deviate from what preceded it.

While the worlds in which American Jews function now show some similarities to the worlds of their parents and grandparents, the pace of change and the nature of the changes have made it not just a matter of differences in degree but differences in kind. The chapters in this volume capture this dynamic moment, one of great change. They clearly represent a scholarly engagement with the American Jewish world as documented by Pew and its predecessors, but while none cite Rawidowicz, they reflect his thinking. No matter how dire the predictions of death and decay, change creates innovation, and innovation offers the greatest evidence of life. That evidence, they declare, needs to be collected, analyzed, and presented so that the harbingers of doom and destruction can be systematically staved off to promise a more robust Jewish future.

NOTES

1 Simon Rawidowicz, *Israel, The Ever-Dying People and Other Essays*, ed. Benjamin C. I. Ravid (Rutherford, NJ: Fairleigh Dickinson University Press, 1986), 53–63.
2 Berman Archive at Stanford University, www.bjpa.org.
3 Alan M. Dershowitz, *The Vanishing American Jew: In Search of Jewish Identity for the Next Century* (New York: Simon & Schuster, 1997).
4 Fred Massarik and Alvin Chenkin, "United States National Jewish Populations Study, A First Report," *American Jewish Yearbook* 74 (1973): 264–66.
5 Thomas B. Morgan "The Vanishing American Jew," *Look*, May 5, 1964, 42–46.

ABOUT THE CONTRIBUTORS

HASIA DINER is Professor Emerita at New York University, where she had been the Paul and Sylvia Steinberg Professor of American Jewish History. She is the author of numerous books in that field, as well as in American immigration and ethnic history and modern Jewish History. She won the National Jewish Book Award and held a Guggenheim Fellowship.

MARC DOLLINGER, Richard and Rhoda Goldman Chair in Jewish Studies and Social Responsibility at San Francisco State University, is the author of four scholarly books, most recently *Black Power, Jewish Politics: Reinventing The Alliance in the 1960s* (Waltham, MA: Brandeis University Press, 2018). Dr. Dollinger's work appears in the *Encyclopedia Judaica*, the *Encyclopedia of Antisemitism*, and the *Encyclopedia of African American Education*. He has appeared on the NBC Primetime TV Show *Who Do You Think You Are?*, CNN Don Lemon's podcast, *Silence Is Not an Option*, and the PBS American Experience documentary *American Jerusalem*.

ZEV ELEFF is President of Gratz College and professor of American Jewish history. He is the author or editor of ten books and more than sixty scholarly articles.

STEVEN J. GOLD is Professor and Graduate Program Director in the Department of Sociology at Michigan State University. Gold is the author, coauthor, or coeditor of nine books, including *The Israeli Diaspora* (Routledge/University of Washington Press, 2002) which won the Thomas and Znaniecki Award from the American Sociology Association's International Migration Section for the best book on international migration in 2003.

ABOUT THE CONTRIBUTORS

FREDERICK E. GREENSPAHN is the Gimelstob Eminent Scholar of Judaica Emeritus at Florida Atlantic University. He is the author/editor of numerous other titles and past president of the National Association of Professors of Hebrew and editor of its journal *Hebrew Studies*.

BRUCE HAYNES is Professor of Sociology at the University of California, Davis, where he holds affiliations in Geography, Community Development, African American Studies, Religious Studies, and Jewish Studies. His research focuses on racialization, spatial segregation, suburbanization, community organization, the Black middle class, and Jews of African descent. His publications include *The Ghetto: Contemporary Issues and Global Controversies* (co-editor, R. Hutchison, Routledge, 2011); *Red Lines, Black Spaces: The Politics of Race and Space in a Black Middle-Class Suburb* (Yale University Press, 2006); *Down the Up Staircase: Three Generations of a Harlem Family* (co-author, S. Solovitch, Columbia University Press, 2017); and his most recent study of race and religion, *The Soul of Judaism; Jews of African Descent in America* (New York University Press, 2018).

ILANA M. HORWITZ serves as an Assistant Professor and chair of Contemporary American Jewry at the Stuart and Suzanne Grant Center for the American Jewish Experience at Tulane University.

SARAH IMHOFF is Associate Professor in the Department of Religious Studies and the Borns Jewish Studies Program at Indiana University. She is author of *Masculinity and the Making of American Judaism* (Indiana University Press, 2017) and *The Lives of Jessie Sampter: Queer, Disabled, Zionist* (Duke University Press, 2022), and she is a founding editor of the journal *American Religion*.

ARI Y. KELMAN is the inaugural holder of the Jim Joseph Professorship in Education and Jewish Studies in the Stanford Graduate School of Education, where he is the director of the Concentration in Education and Jewish Studies and serves as the Director of the Berman Jewish Policy Archive at Stanford.

THEODORE SASSON is Director of Programs of the Jack, Joseph, and Morton Mandel Foundation and a professor of Jewish Studies (on leave) at Middlebury College. He is author most recently of *The New American Zionism* (New York University Press, 2014).

JENNIFER A. THOMPSON is Maurice Amado Professor of Applied Jewish Ethics and Civic Engagement and Director of the Jewish Studies Interdisciplinary Program at California State University, Northridge. She is the author of *Jewish on Their Own Terms: How Intermarried Couples Are Changing American Judaism* (Rutgers University Press, 2014).

DOV WAXMAN is the Rosalinde and Arthur Gilbert Foundation Professor of Israel Studies at the University of California, Los Angeles (UCLA). He is the author of four books, including *Trouble in the Tribe: The American Jewish Conflict over Israel* (Princeton University Press, 2016).

INDEX

Page numbers in italics indicate Figures.

Abayudaya (Ugandan movement), 68
Acton, Lord, 131, 139
Adler, Rachel, 44
adoptees, 89, 90
advocacy, 144, 242–43, 245–46; for Israel, 164, 169, 177n3, 255–57, 264–65; JCPA, 257; for Jews of Color, 68, 77; LGBTQ+, 52; for low-income Jews, 227
affirmative action, 151–53
Africa/Africans, 58; Egypt, 68, 166, 170; Ethiopian Jews, 67; Igbo in, 68; JIMENA, 73; Mizraḥim, 59, 66, 186; Uganda, 68, 74
African American Museum, Los Angeles, 68
African Americans, 2, 132, 154, 155, 257; slavery, 59, 140–41. *See also* Black Jews
Agudah Jews, 212
Agudath Ha-Rabbonim, 214
Agudath Israel, 42, 218–19, 221
AIPAC. *See* American Israel Public Affairs Committee
aliyah, 93–94
Allen, Theodore W., 67
Alliance of Black Jews, 68
alternative action, 151
Altshul, Brooklyn, New York, 106–7
amcha (the people), 276
Ameinu, 51
America First, 148
American Constitution, 58

American Israel Public Affairs Committee (AIPAC), 246, 255–57
American Jewish Committee, 1, 162, 244, 246, 255
American Jewish Congress, 1
American Jewish Historical Society, 1
American Jewish Joint Distribution Committee, 245
American Jewish World Service, 263
American Jewish Yearbook, 79, 274
AMMUD Jews of Color Torah Academy, 73
Am Tikva, Boston, Massachusetts, 51
androginos (person with dual genitalia), 39, 50
Anti-Defamation League, 1, 149, 162, 246, 255
antisemitism, 63, 135, 138, 158, 163, 257; activism against, 243, 246, 262, 265; Black Jews racial discrimination with, 78; corruption of power and, 152; eugenics movement and scientific, 145–46, 147–48; Ford and, 148; genocidal, 166; increase in, 4, 78, 136, 222; Jews of Color and, 137; limited access relation to, 274–75; mixed-religion families and, 99–100, 108; quotas, 151–52; Soviet Jews and, 13, 16; state-sponsored, 140; Trump and, 136; violent, 3, 68, 133, 134
antiwar movement, 248
anti-Zionists, 134, 186, 221, 257, 261–62
anusim (forced ones), 73

285

apartheid, 181n52
apikoursim, 186
Arafat, Yasser, 255
Archdeacon, Thomas, 11
Aristotle, 220
Arkansas, 62
Articles of Confederation, 139
Ashkenazi, 1, 58–59, 89, 142, 144, 186, 213, 272
Asian people, 2
Assimilation, 243, 245, 262
Association for Jewish Studies, 5
Atlanta, Georgia, 150
AVI CHAI foundation, 251
Avodah, 263
Ayecha Resource Center, 69, 73
Azoulay, Katya Gibel. *See* Mevorach, Katya Gibel

ba'alei teshuvah (return to Judaism), 72, 210
Babylonian Talmud, 4, 44
Bais Yaakov (schools), 214–15, 218
Baltimore, Maryland, 211
Barak, Ehud, 181n52
bar mitzvah, 85, 94, 198
Baron, Salo, 275
bat mitzvah, 85, 94
Bay Area Multicultural Jewish Family Connection, 69
BDS movement. *See* Boycott, Divestment, and Sanctions movement
Bechol Lashon, 68, 69, 70, 73
Begin, Menachem, 168, 178nn23–24
Beit Simchat Torah, 51
Bejarano, Margalit, 26, 27
Belzer, Tobin, 77
Bergen-Belsen (death camp), 226
Bergen County, New Jersey, 217, 221
Bergenfield, New Jersey, 221
Berger, David, 232
Berger, Peter, 210, 216
Berman, Ari, 225

Berman, Lila Corwin, 64
Beta Israel, 68
Beth Chayim Chadashim, 51
Beth Hillel Temple, Kenosha, Wisconsin, 106
Beth Medrash Govoha, 215
Bialik, Mayim, 47–48
the Bible, 190
Big Tent Judaism, 98
Bill of Rights, U.S. Constitution, 139
bimah (platform where Torah is read), 85, 94
Bingham, Theodore A., 146, 265n3
birth control, 238n61
birthrate, 210, 238n61
Birthright Israel, 251, 263
Bitton, Mijal, 213
Black, Nissim, 74
Black Cat Judaica, 198
Black Jewish Liberation Collective, 68
Black Jews, 68, 74, 78, 156
Black Lives Matter, 257
Black Power, 167
Black Protestants, 190
Blumenbach, Johann Friedrich, 62
B'nai B'rith (fraternal order), 280
b'nai mitzvah, 92–93, 185
Bobov (ḥasidic community), 228
Bochur's Guide to College (Frankel), 218
Boston, Massachusetts, 51, 142, 244
Boston Rebbe (Pinchas David Horowitz), 228
Boyan (ḥasidic community), 228
Boycott, Divestment, and Sanctions (BDS) movement, 222
Brandeis, Louis, 2
breaking a glass (at wedding), 94
Breyer, Stephen, 2
Bridges (journal), 69
Bridges and Boundaries Conference, 68
Brit Ger Toshav (Covenant of a Resident Stranger), 96
Brit Nissuin (Covenant of Marriage), 96

Brit Tzedek v'Shalom (left-wing organization), 255–56
Brodkin (Sacks), Karen, 3, 67, 148–49
Brooklyn, New York, 210; Altshul in, 106–7; Crown Heights neighborhood in, 229; House of David and Jonathan in, 56n59; Williamsburg neighborhood in, 227–28
Bruder, Edith, 70
Buchdahl, Angela, 73
Buddhists, 192
Bulka, Reuven, 224
Bundists, 186
Bureau of Social Morals, 265n3
bureaus of Jewish education, 244–45, 252
Burning Man (event), 195
Bush, George H. W., 16

CAJE. *See* Conference for Advancement of Jewish Education
California: Los Angeles, 23, 29, 68; Poway, 3, 133; San Diego, 29; San Francisco, 69, 143, 144
Campbell, David E., 86
Cardozo, Benjamin, 2
Carlebach, Shlomo, 47
Castro, Fidel, 24–25
Catholics, 142, 190
cemeteries, 103
Census, U.S. (2000), 15, 19–20, 32n20
Central Conference of American Rabbis, 103, 211
Central United Talmudic Academy, 229
Centrist Orthodoxy. *See* Modern/Centrist Orthodoxy
Chabad-Lubavitch, 19, 119, 203, 212–13, 227, 229–32, 251
Chaney, James, 150
Charles and Lynn Schusterman Family Philanthropies, 70
Charlottesville, Virginia, 3, 136
Charter Oaks State College, 218
Chaverim of Bergen County, 217, 221

Chefets, Zev, 74
Chicago, Illinois, 63, 210
China, 143–44
Chinese Exclusion Act (1882), 146
Christian Phalangist, 169
Christians, 9, 192, 232; Black Protestant, 190; fundamentalist, 236n23; Pentecostal, 72, 73; Puritan, 142
church ladies, 37
Church of England, 142
Cincinnati, Ohio, 149
circumcision, 88; *mohel* performing, 90
civil rights, 246, 248
Civil Rights Act of 1964, 151
CLEP. *See* College-Level Examination Program
Cleveland, Ohio, 105–6, 210, 244
Clinton, Hillary, 228
Cohen, Steven, 76, 187, 220
College-Level Examination Program (CLEP), 218
colleges. *See* education; universities
Colleyville, Texas, 3, 133
colonial Jews, 139–42
Commandment Keepers, 75
communal meals (kiddush), 233
community centers, 1, 149, 243, 246, 251–52, 260, 262
Confederacy, 143
Conference for Advancement of Jewish Education (CAJE), 267n28
Conference of Presidents of Major American Jewish Organizations, 162, 169, 246
Congregationalists, 212
Conservative Judaism, 22, 37–38, 40, 51, 88–89, 186, 210–13, 219, 244, 248–49, 258, 277, 280; decline in membership, 266n22; education and income levels, 119–20, *120*; United Synagogue of Conservative Judaism, 104, 211
Constitution, U.S., 12, 139, 232
Constitutional Convention, 139
Contemporary Jewry (journal), 76

conversion, 3, 88, 98–99, 109n12
corruption, of power: antisemitic quotas and, 152; exceptionalist thesis and, 139–40; Greenberg, I., on, 131–34, 138, 141, 143–44, 147, 149, 151, 155–57; Jews of Color and, 156
Costa, Rose, 98
Coughlin, Father Charles, 148
Council of Jewish Federations, 244, 246, 260
Council of Torah Sages, 219
Cousin, Glynis, 70
Covenant of a Resident Stranger (Brit Ger Toshav), 96
Covenant of Marriage (Brit Nissuin), 96
COVID-19, 202, 203, 219, 232–33, 243, 257–58; Jewish fundraising during, 269n63
Craigslist, 229
Crenshaw, Kimberle Williams, 159n15, 159n17
Crown Heights neighborhood, Brooklyn, 229
Cuban Jews, 24–28, 30, 73
cultural pluralism, 64

Da'as Torah, 216, 219, 228
Daf Yomi (daily Talmud study), 38, 218
Dashefsky, Arnold, 77
Dati Le'umi, 225–26
Davidman, Lynn, 65
Davis, Erika, 99
Davis, Thomas J., 62
Dawidowicz, Lucy, 164
DAWN, 203
Dayan, Moshe, 164
Dayenu (environmental startup), 264
day schools, 243, 245, 251, 260
Dead and Co., 198
Declaration of Independence, 139
DellaPergola, Sergio, 9, 192
Democratic party, 249, 258
denominationalism, 193

denominations, 1, 2, 19
Dershowitz, Alan, 273
Detroit, Michigan, 210
diaspora, 277
dietary laws, 21, 99
Dillingham Commission, 146
disabilities, Jews with, 264
distancing hypothesis, 172, 180n42
diversity, equity, and inclusion initiatives, 79
divider between men and women (*mechitza/meḥitza*), 38, 52
Dorman, Jacob, 72
Dorshei Tzedek congregation, West Newton, Massachusetts, 105–7
dual loyalties, 164, 167, 177n3
Du Bois, W. E. B., 67

Edah (grassroots organization), 225
education: Bais Yaakov, 214–15, 218; bureaus of Jewish, 244–45, 252; Central United Talmudic Academy, 229; for children, 267nn27–29; Conservative Jews and level of, 119–20, *120*; day schools, 243, 245, 251, 260; gender relation to attainment of, 121–23, *122*; Hebrew schools, 243–44, 250–51; JESNA and, 245–47, 250; Jewish immigrants levels of, 125–26, *127*; of Jews by region, 123, *124*; Jews of Color and level of, 124–25, *125*; Nishmat Orthodox, for women, 42–43; Sy Syms School of Business, 222; Talmud Torahs, 244; Torah, for women, 41–42, 44, 220; Ziegler School of Rabbinic Studies, 74. *See also* universities/colleges; *specific yeshivas*
Egypt, 68, 166, 170
Eichmann, Adolph, 1
18Doors (website), 95–96, 98, 102, 263
Eisen, Arnold, 187
Eisner, Jane, 46
Elazar, Daniel, 164, 242–43, 245–47, 254–55

elite, 243, 253
employment: affirmative action and, 153; industry for, 129n9; rabbinic, 40–41; self, 18, 21. *See also* income
Englewood, New Jersey, 221
English language, 227
Entebbe, 166
environmental concerns, 193, 264
Eshel, 52
"The Ethics of Jewish Power" (Greenberg, I.), 131
Ethiopian Jews, 67
ethnicity, 1, 64, 176, 200–202. *See also* Jews of Color; people of color
ethnic studies, 79
eugenics, 145–46, 147–48
evangelicals, 190
"evil inclination" (*yetzer hara*), 49
Excelsior College, 218
exceptionalism, 139–41, 144, 153, 157
ex-Orthodox, 186

Fair Lawn, New Jersey, 221
Fairleigh Dickinson University, 217
federations, 1, 162, 188, 242–43, 245, 247, 250–54, 258, 262; Council of Jewish Federations, 244, 246, 260; JFNA, 260–61; money raised by, 268n37
feminism, 44, 167, 248
Fernheimer, Janice W., 75
Fine, Robert, 71
Finkelman, Yoel, 214
First Amendment, U.S. Constitution, 232
Fishman, Sylvia, 102, 225
Florida, 210; Jewish Community Services of South Florida, 29; Miami, 11, 23, 25–29; Orlando, 218
Floyd, George, 154, 155, 257
forced ones (*anusim*), 73
Ford, Henry, 148
Fortas, Abe, 2
Foundation for Jewish Camp, 250
Foundation for Jewish Culture, 245

foundations, 243, 253–54
Frank, Leo, 150
Frankel, Reuven, 218
Frankenberg, Ruth, 67
Frankfurter, Felix, 2
frum, 186
Frum Twitter, 233
Fugitive Slave Acts of 1793 and 1850, 59
fundamentalists, 236n23
Funnye, Capers, 72, 74

gamach, 217
GamAni, 46
gastronomic (Judaism), 186
Gaza Strip, 168, 176, 255; settlement drive, 178n24
Geller, Laura, 40
gender, 20; *androginos* and *ṭumṭum*, 39, 50; co-creation, 50; education attainment by, 121–23, *122*; non-binary, 38, 50; non-conforming, 50; Torah and, 38, 41–42; trans people and, 38, 39, 49–52. *See also* men; women
genderqueer, 38–39, 44, 50
generational memory, 171, 179n37
genocide, 132, 166, 181n52
Georgia, 150
ger toshav, 92, 98, 107
G.I. Bill, 136, 149
Gilman, Sander L., 70
Ginsburg, Ruth Bader, 2, 45
Ginzburg, Carlo, 134–35
God, 190, 204
Golan Heights, 257
Goldberg, Arthur, 2
Goldberg, J. J., 16
Golden Rule Judaism, 194
Gonyu, Shannon, 99
Goodman, Andrew, 150
Gordon, Lewis R., 70, 79
Grant, Madison, 145
Great Society, 152, 153
Greenberg, Cheryl, 70

Greenberg, Irving "Yitz," 131–34, 138, 141, 143–44, 147, 149, 151, 155–57
Greenberg, Steven, 224
Grinspoon Foundation, 250
Gross, Rachel, 195–97, 199, 201, 205
Gurock, Jeffrey, 213

Hadar, 263
Hadassah, 1
Haddish, Tiffany, 74
halakhah (Jewish religious law), 87–88, 106, 210, 213, 219, 226
Ḥamas, 171, 176, 243, 255, 261
Hammer, Jill, 45
Hanukkah, 205, 272
Ḥaredi, 38, 42, 118, 127, 186, 251
Harlem Renaissance, 63
Harris, Cheryl, 59, 67
Harris, Maurice, 101
Harvard University, 152
Ḥasidim, 38, 44, 47, 119, 210, 251, 277; neo-Ḥasidic, 186; Satmar community, 43, 212, 226–28; Skever, 212, 227
Hatza'ad Harishon, 74
Hatzalah, 217
ḥavurot, 195
Haynes, Bruce D., 70
Hazon, 264
healing movement, 187
Hebrew College, 259
Hebrew Immigration Aid Society (HIAS), 11, 13
Hebrew Israelite, 71, 74
Hebrew language, 63
Hebrew schools, 243–44, 250–51
Hebrew Union College, 47, 211
Heeb (magazine), 69
Heilman, Samuel, 213, 220
heritage tourism, 196
Hertzberg, Arthur, 165, 174
HIAS. *See* Hebrew Immigration Aid Society
High Holidays, 193

Hillel, 1, 222, 252–53; college campus-based, 70, 230, 245, 251
Hindu, 192
HinJews, 186
Hitler, Adolf, 147
Holocaust, 1, 65, 108, 131–32, 164, 166–67; death camps, 226; "March of the Living" and, 178n17
Homestead Act (1862), 61
homosexuality, 224
Horowitz, Pinchas David, 228
hospitals, 245
House of David and Jonathan (organization), 56n59
housing projects, 227
Houston, Texas, 150
Howell township, 218
Humanistic Judaism, 186, 280
ḥuppah (wedding canopy), 94, 96
Hurwitz, Sara, 41–42
Husbands-Hankin, Yitzhak, 92, 101
hybridity, 187
hypodescent, 61

identity, intersectionality, 137, 159n15, 159n17
identity building, 245
identity politics, 166–67
IfNotNow, 264
Igbo people (in Nigeria), 68
Ignatiev, Noel, 67
Ikar, 264
Illinois, 63, 210
immigrants: Irish, 142; Italian, 11; Japanese, 144; Russian, 11, 12, 13–14
immigrants, Jewish, 1, 3, 115; *aliyah*, 93–94; census data in 2000 on, 15, 19–20, 32n20; education and income levels for, 125–26, *127*; Johnson-Reed Act and, 11; restrictions during 1920s to 1940s on, 31n7
Immigration Act of 1965, 65
income: Conservative Judaism, 119–20, *120*; Jewish immigrants, 125–26, *127*; for Jews

by region, 123, *124*; Jews of Color, 124–25, *125*. *See also* low-income Jews
Independence Tower (housing project), 227
individualism, 187
inequality, 243
innovation sector, 254, 260–65
Institute for Jewish Spirituality, 264
Interfaithfamily.com, 95, 98
interfaith marriages, 95, 98, 108n2; children from, 180n39
intermarriage, 64, 94, 103, 210, 245, 247–48; term defined, 108n2
International Israelite Board of Rabbis of the Ethiopian Hebrews, 74
International Rabbinic Fellowship, 225
Internet: Craigslist and, 229; social media communities on, 233–34; Zoom and, 202–3, 205, 258
intersectionality, 137, 159n15, 159n17
Intifada, 169–71, 279
Iran, 255–56
Iranian Jews, 2
Irish immigrants, 142
Israel, 1–4, 10, 19, 28, 89, 133, 138, 140, 215, 219–23, 225–26, 243, 245–46, 252, 258, 262; advocacy for, 164, 169, 177n3, 255–57, 264–65; American Jews views on, 173–77, 177n1, 178n23, 180n46, 181n48, 181n57, 181nn52–53; Birthright Israel and, 251, 263; Jerusalem, 257; Likud Party in, 172, 255; Peace Now movement, 169, 179n30; settlements in, 168, 173, 178n24, 181n52; visiting, 179n32. *See also* West Bank
Israel, Mike, 149
Israeli Jews, 2, 11, 16–18, 19–24, 30, 66
Israeli-Palestinian conflict, 134, 163; American Jews views on, 168–69, 175–76, 181nn52–54; history, 169–70; Trump policies on, 182n63
Israelolatry, 163–68
Italian immigrants, 11

Jackson, John L., 72
Jacobson, Matthew Frye, 67
Japan, 143
Japanese immigrants, 144
JCC Association of North America, 260–61
JCPA. *See* Jewish Council of Public Affairs
JCRIF. *See* Jewish Community Relief Fund
Jerusalem, 257
Jerusalem Talmud, 4
JESNA. *See* Jewish Educational Service of North American
Jesus, 96, 99–100, 145
Jewish Agency for Israel, 245, 253
Jewish Catalog (Siegel, Strassfeld, Michael, and Strassfeld, S.), 204
Jewish cemeteries, 103
Jewish community centers, 1, 149, 243, 246, 251–52, 260, 262
Jewish Community Centers Association of North America, 246
Jewish Community Relations Councils, 149, 245, 252, 257
Jewish Community Relief Fund (JCRIF), 261
Jewish Community Services of South Florida, 29
Jewish Council of Public Affairs (JCPA), 257
Jewish Educational Service of North American (JESNA), 245–47, 250
Jewish Education Project, 267n27
Jewish Emergent Network, 203
Jewish Family Services, 252, 260
Jewish Federations of North America (JFNA), 260–61
Jewish healing movement, 187
Jewish Multiracial Network, 68, 73
Jewish Orthodox Feminist Alliance, 41
Jewish people, 202; of no religion, 189, 190, 191, 194; by religion, 189, 191, 194. *See also specific topics*

Jewish Publication Society, 1
Jewish Renewal, 186
Jewish Studies, 4, 5
Jewish Theological Seminary, 211, 250
Jewish Voice for Peace, 262
Jewish Week, 74
Jewish Welfare Board, 1
Jews in All Hues, 73
Jews Indigenous to the Middle East and North Africa (JIMENA), 73
Jews of Color, 119, 131–33, 138–39, 154, 157; advocacy for, 68, 77; antisemitism and, 137; corruption of power and, 156; education and income levels, 124–25, *125*; Jews of Color Initiative, 70, 73, 77, 264. *See also* Black Jews
Jewtina y Co., 73
JFNA. *See* Jewish Federations of North America
JIMENA. *See* Jews Indigenous to the Middle East and North Africa
Jim Joseph Foundation, 70
Joel, Richard, 225
Johnson, Lyndon Baines, 151–53, 227
Johnson-Reed Act, 11
Jonathan Williams Houses (housing project), 227
J Street (grassroots organization), 175, 256, 261, 264
JuBus, 186
Judson, Daniel, 259–60

Kaddish, 99, 106
Kagan, Elena, 2, 45
Kahn, Julius, 144
Kallen, Horace M., 63–64
Kamenetsky, Shmuel, 223
Kamochah, 73–74
Kaplan, Steven, 68, 70
Kaplan, Vichna, 215
Kapor, Aviva, 51
Kaufman, Ilana, 73
Kehillah, 244

Kelman, Ari Y., 75–76
Kennedy, John F., 151
Kenosha, Wisconsin, 106
ketubah (marriage contract), 94, 96
kiddush (communal meals), 233
Kinberg, Myron, 92, 96
Kiryas Joel neighborhood, New York, 228
Klausenburg (ḥasidic community), 228
Kohenet Hebrew Priestess Institute, 44–45
Kol HaLev congregation, Cleveland, Ohio, 105–6
Kook, Avraham Yitzhak, 226
Kook, Zvi Yehudah, 226
Kopyczynitz (ḥasidic community), 228
Koren Publishers, 226
kosher, 210, 212, 214
Kotler, Aharon, 214–15, 218, 227
Kranz, Fay, 231
Kukla, Elliot, 50
Ku Klux Klan, 150, 154
Kulanu, 73
Kurtzer, Yehuda, 258–59

Lakewood, New Jersey, 210, 214–15, 218, 227
Lamm, Norman, 219, 222, 225
LAMP. *See* Latin American Migration Program
Landau, Rabbi Moses, 150
Landing, James, 71
Latin America, 3, 11, 27
Latin American Jews, 24–28, 30; population growth, 35n67
Latin American Migration Program (LAMP), 28
Latinx, 2, 154
Lau-Lavie, Amichai, 92
Law of Return, 89
Lawson, Sandra, 73–74
Lazarus, Emma, 147
leftists, 133–34
left-wing organizations, 175, 255–56, 261, 264

Leibowitz, Henoch, 216
Lester, Julius, 67, 98
Levi's, 143
LGBTQ+, 51, 52, 95, 205, 223–24, 257. *See also* trans people
liberalism, 155, 257
Liebman, Charles, 201, 214
Likud Party, 172, 255
liminality, 4, 87, 89–90, 134–35, 138, 140–42, 144–47, 149–54, 157
Limmud, 263
Lindbergh, Charles, 148
Lipsitz, George, 67
Litvish, 212
Liwerant, Bokser, 27
Locke, Alain, 63
Longevity, 247
Look magazine, 79, 273
Los Angeles, 23, 29, 35n67, 76, 211, 213; African American Museum in, 68; Black Jews in, 74
Loving v. Virginia (1967), 66
low-income Jews: Cuban refugees and, 26–27; in New York City, 130n18; Satmar Ḥasidim and, 227
loyalties, dual, 164, 167, 177n3
Lubavitch, 230–31. *See also* Chabad-Lubavitch
LUNAR Collective, 73
Lyubavichi, Belarus, 229

Magida, Arthur J., 97
maharat (ordained women), 41
Maimonides, 220
Manchester township, New Jersey, 218
Mandel, Maud, 5
Manhattan, New York, 145, 213, 220
MaNishtana (Rabbi Shais Rishon), 74
Mapai (Labor party), 168
"March of the Living" (event), 178n17
Marder, Janet, 100
marginality, 132, 141
Markoe, Lauren, 100

Markowitz, Fran, 17, 70
marriages, 94; children from interfaith, 180n39; mixed, 86, 103. *See also* intermarriage; weddings
Maryland, 211
masculinity, 38, 48–49
Massachusetts, 5; Boston, 51, 142, 244; West Newton, 105–7
Massachusetts Bay Colony, 142
matchmaking (*shidduch*), 217
Matlins, Stuart M., 97
matrilineal descent, 89, 104
matzah, 205
Mayyim Ḥayyim, 51
McCoy, Yavilah, 69
McGinity, Keren, 91
Mead, Sidney, 212
mechitza/meḥitza (divider between men and women), 38, 52
meditation, 193, 207n22
Mehta, Samira, 101–2
memory, generational, 171, 179n37
men, 115, 118; educational attainment for, 121–23, *122*; leadership compared with women, 268n47; *mechitza* divider between women, 38, 52
Menocchio, 134–35
Mesivta Rabbi Chaim Berlin, 215
messianism, 220, 232
metaverse, 202, 203, 204
MetLife Stadium, 218
#MeToo movement, 38–39, 45–46, 48
Mevorach, Katya Gibel, 70
Miami, 11, 23, 25–29
Michigan, 210
midwestern Jews, education and income levels, 123, *124*
mikveh (ritual bath), 51, 88, 214
millers, 134–35
Mills, Charles W., 60
minyan, 106
mitzvah campaign, 231
mixed marriages, 86, 103

Mizraḥim (Jews from northern Africa), 59, 66, 186
Modern/Centrist Orthodoxy, 119, 120, 186, 212–13, 219–23, 225, 231, 234, 251, 277
modesty, 48
mohel (Jew performing ritual circumcision), 90
Moishe House, 262
Monsey, New York, 210
Moore, Deborah Dash, 149
Mordecai, Jacob, 235n14
Moss, Frank, 146
Mothers Circle, 98
Munich Olympics (1972), 166
Munkács (ḥasidic community), 228
Munro, Patricia, 92–94, 104, 108
Musar movement, 277
Muslims, 9
mysticism, 277

National Conference on Soviet Jewry, 246
National Council of Jewish Women, 1
National Jewish Community Relations Advisory Council (NJCRAC), 246, 257
National Jewish Population Study, 12, 76, 200, 273
Naturalization Act, 60
Nazism, 136, 148, 215; Jewish immigrants seeking refuge from, 31n7. *See also* Holocaust
neo-Ḥasidic, 186
Neo-Orthodox, 186
neo-rationalist, 186
Ner Israel, 215
Netanyahu, Benjamin, 175–77, 182n62
New Age, 280
New Amsterdam, 59
New Jersey, 211; Bergen County, 217, 221; Englewood, 221; Lakewood, 210, 214–15, 218, 227; Teaneck, 221
New Square (ḥasidic community), 227
New York, 11, 23, 29, 142, 146, 211; Harlem Renaissance, 63; ḥasidim succession in, 228; Kehillah in, 244; low-income Jews in, 130n18; Manhattan, 145, 213, 220; Monsey, 210; Rockland County, 227. *See also* Brooklyn, New York
New Yorker, 230
New York Times, 223, 273
Nishmat, 42–43
NJCRAC. *See* National Jewish Community Relations Advisory Council
non-binary, 38–39
non-denominational, 2
non-Jewish woman (shiksa), 91
non-Jews, 2–3
nonprofits, funds to, 268n45
northeastern Jews, education and income levels, 123, *124*
nostalgia, 196
Nuremberg Laws, 63
nursing homes, 245

Obama, Barack, 223, 256
off the derekh (OTD), 186
Ohio: Cincinnati, 149; Cleveland, 105–6, 210, 244
Olamim, 73
Oleinick, Barbara, 98–99
Olmert, Ehud, 171, 181n53
Olympics in Munich (1972), 166
One Table, 263
Open Orthodoxy, 41–42, 186, 225
Operation Moses, 67
Operation Solomon, 67
ordained women (maharat), 41
Oregon, 143
Orlando, Florida, 218
Orsi, Robert, 199
Orthodox, 1, 4, 37, 39, 48, 52, 88–89, 93–94, 175–76, 191–92, 194–95, 202, 210, 245, 248–49, 257–58, 262; birthrates, 238n61; education for women, 42–43; Modern/Centrist, 119, 120, 186, 212–13, 219–23, 225, 231, 234, 251, 277; Open Orthodoxy and, 41–42, 186, 225;

terminology and history, 235nn13–14; ultra-Orthodox, 38
Orthodox Union, 220–21, 223, 251, 255
Orthodykes, 52
Oslo Peace Accords, 171, 181n53, 255
OTD. *See* off the derekh

Pale of Settlement, 11
Palestinians, 134, 138, 162, 168–71, 175–76, 182n62, 256. *See also* Israeli-Palestinian conflict
Palm tights, 43
Parent's Guide to Orthodox Assimilation on University Campuses (Perl and Weinstein, Y.), 222
Parfitt, Tudor, 38, 68, 72, 86, 132, 190, 193, 204–5, 272
Passover seder, 106, 203, 204
patrilineal descent, 88, 105
Peace Now movement, 169, 179n30
peasants, 135, 137
Pennsylvania, 3, 78, 133
Pentecostal Christianity, 72, 73
the people (*amcha*), 276
People for Orthodox Renaissance and Torah (PORAT), 225
people of color, 89–90. *See also* Jews of Color
Perl, Gil, 222
Perlow, Yaakov, 219
Perry, Yonason, 74
Persian Jews, 213
Pew Research Center, 9, 66, 76–77, 116, 177n1, 181n54, 188–89, 191, 200, 210, 212, 220, 247–48, 256, 272, 276
Phillips, Bruce A., 76, 86, 95
Pittsburgh, Pennsylvania, 3, 78, 133
Plaskow, Judith, 44
Plessy v. Ferguson, 62
polarization, 230, 243, 248–49, 262
Pomson, Alex, 86
PORAT. *See* People for Orthodox Renaissance and Torah

Portes, Alejandro, 25
Positive-Historical Judaism, 277
Poway, California, 3, 133
prayer shawls (ṭallit), 45, 93, 198–99
Pride Alliance, 224–25
Priesand, Sally, 39
Prizmah, 250, 260
prophetic Judaism, 150
Protestants, Black, 190
Protocols of the Elders of Zion, 148
Puritans, 142
Putnam, Robert D., 86

Queer Orthodox Jews, 205
Quirin, James, 68
quotas, 151–53

RA. *See* Rabbinical Assembly
rabba (rabbinical title), 41–42
rabbanit (rabbinical title), 41
Rabbi Jacob Joseph School, 215
Rabbinical Assembly (RA), 37, 94, 103–4, 211
Rabbinical Council of America, 41–42, 220, 223
Rabin, Yitzhak, 255; American Jews views on, 181n52
race, 201. *See also* Jews of Color; people of color
racism, 143, 146, 156
Raphael, Geela Rayzel, 92
Rashi network, 250
Raucher, Michal, 43
Rawidowicz, Simon, 271–72, 275–76, 280
Rebbetzin, 39, 231
Reboot, 203
Reconstructing Judaism, 38, 73, 88, 94, 104, 186, 244, 258, 277, 280
Reform Judaism, 1, 22, 38–40, 51, 88, 94, 103, 186, 202, 210–13, 219, 244, 248–49, 258, 277, 280; decline during 2010s, 266n23; education and income levels, 119–20, *120*; online, 269n61; rabbis, 95

refuseniks, 17
religion, 195–97, 200, 202, 205; Jewish people by, 189, 191, 194; Jewish people of no, 189, 190, 191, 194. *See also specific religions*
Religion News Service, 100
Religious Zionism, 214, 219–21, 225–26
Repair the World, 263
Republican Party, 18, 249
RespectAbility, 264
return to Judaism (*ba'alei teshuvah*), 72, 210
Ripley, William Z., 145
Rishon, Rabbi Shais (MaNishtana), 74
rituals, 100
Robinson, Isaiah, 74
Rockland County, New York, 227
Rock-Singer, Cara, 44
Roediger, David, 67
Romemu, 264
Roosevelt, Franklin D., 148, 223
Roosevelt, Theodore, 146
Rosenthal, Steven, 164
Rosenwald, Julius, 144
Rosh Ḥodesh, 44
Rosichan, Arthur, 26
Rothschild, Jacob, 150
Rubin Schwartz, Shuly, 39
Russian immigrants, 11, 12, 13–14
Russian Jews, 2. *See also* Soviet Jewry

Sabbatianism, 232
Sabra and Shatila massacre, 169
Sacks, Jonathan, 225
same-sex relationships, 95. *See also* LGBTQ+
San Diego, California, 29
San Francisco, California, 69, 143, 144
Sapperstein, Aliya, 75
Satmar (ḥasidic community), 43, 212, 226–28
Saturday Night Seder (event), 203
Saxe, Leonard, 192

Schechter network, 250
Schindler, Alexander, 97
Schneersohn, Yosef Yitzchak, 229–30
Schneerson, Menachem, 229, 232
Schnoor, Randal F., 86
schools. *See* education; universities/colleges; *specific yeshivas*
Schulweis, Harold, 97
Schwerner, Michael "Mickey," 150
Sears Roebuck, 144
secularization, 243, 247, 249, 262, 280
seder, 106, 203–4
Semite, as linguistic term, 63
Sephardic, 141–42, 186, 213, 273
Sessions, Jeff, 223
settlements, 175; in Israel, 168, 173, 178n24, 181n52
sexual abuse, 47. *See also* #MeToo movement
Shabbat, 85–86, 190, 210, 221
Shalom Hartman Institute of North America, 259
Shamir, Yitzhak, 168
Sharon, Ariel, 181n52
Shavuot, 193, 203
Sheskin, Ira, 77, 79
shidduch (matchmaking), 217
shiksa (non-Jewish woman), 91
Shoah, 133
Shomrim, 217
Shulḥan Aruch, 4
Shwekey, Yaakov, 219
Sicher, Efraim, 70
Siegel, Richard, 204
Sinai Academy, 29
Six Day War, 1, 66, 164, 220, 245
Sizomu, Rabbi Gershom, 74
Skever Ḥasidim, 212, 227
slavery, 59, 140–41
social class, defined, 128n2
Social Darwinism, 63
social media, 233–34
social mobility, 140

social welfare, 243
socioeconomic status, defined, 128n2
Solomon Schechter (day school), 245
Soloveitchik, Joseph B., 219
South Dakota, 230
southern Jews, 119, 150; education and income levels for, 123, *124*
Southern Poverty Law Center, 72, 78
South Florida, 29, 210
Soviet Jewry, 3, 21, 27, 29, 126, 178n19, 246; antisemitism and, 13, 16
Soviet Union, former, 13–19
Spanish flu, 259
Sperber, Daniel, 41
Spielberg, Steven, 73
spiritual beliefs and communities (in Judaism), 186, 193, 264
Spitzer, Toba, 100
Stampfer, Shaul, 215–16
Stand With Us, 265
Stanton, Alysa, 73
startups, 263–65, 269n48
Stern College for Women, 222, 224, 234
Strassfeld, Max, 50
Strassfeld, Michael, 204
Strassfeld, Sharon, 204
suburbs, 244
summer camp, 49
Sun Belt region, 25
Sunday schools, 250
Supreme Court, 2, 4; *Loving v. Virginia* (1967), 66; *Plessy v. Ferguson*, 62
Sutro, Adolf, 143
SVARA, 38, 44, 263
Synagogue Council of America, 245–46, 259
synagogues, 191–92, 195, 200–202, 244, 260; membership decline, 266nn22–24
syncretism, 187
Sy Syms School of Business, 222

Taft, William Howard, 146
ṭallit (prayer shawls), 45, 93, 198–99
Talmud, 44, 214, 224; Daf Yomi of, 38, 218; Jerusalem, 4
Talmud Torahs (schools), 244
Tapper, Aaron Hahn, 75
Teaneck, New Jersey, 221
tefillin, 232
Teitelbaum, Aaron, 228
Teitelbaum, Moshe, 228
Teitelbaum, Yoel, 43, 226–28
Teitelbaum, Zalman, 228
Telshe Yeshiva, 215
Tennenbaum, Shelly, 65
Texas: Colleyville, 3, 133; Houston, 150
Thomas, Laurence M., 70
Thomas Edison State College, 218
Tifereth Jerusalem, 215
Tighe, Elizabeth, 192
Toms River, 218
Torah, 216; *aliyah* honor and, 93–94; bar mitzvah and, 85; *bimah* and, 85, 94; blessing, 100–101; education for women, 41–42, 44, 220; gender and, 38, 41–42; service, 105–6; studies online, 203; study in Europe, 214–15; Talmud, 244
Torah U'Mesora, 245
Torah Vodaath, 215
tourism, heritage, 196
Touro College/University, 222
trans people, 3, 38, 49; Jewish, 39, 50–52; theology, 50
Tree of Life synagogue, Pittsburgh, 78, 133
T'ruah, 261
Trump, Donald J., 176, 219, 223, 257; antisemitism and, 136; on Israeli-Palestinian conflict, 182n63
ṭumṭum (person with ambiguous genitalia), 39, 50
Twersky, Yaakov Yosef, 227
Twitter (X), 233
Twitty, Michael, 74

Uganda, 68, 74
UJA-Federation of New York, 210

ultra-Orthodox, 38
Union for Reform Judaism, 48, 100
Union of American Hebrew Congregations, 211
Union of Councils for Soviet Jews, 246
United Jewish Appeal, 1, 245, 253
United Jewish Organizations, 227
United Nations, 223
United States: Articles of Confederation, 139; Census (2000), 15, 19–20, 32n20; colonial Jews and slavery in, 141; Constitution, 12, 139, 232
United Synagogue of Conservative Judaism, 104, 211
United Way, 252
universities/colleges: in *Bochur's Guide to College*, 218; CLEP and, 218; Fairleigh Dickinson University, 217; Harvard University, 152; Hebrew College, 259; Hebrew Union College, 47, 211; Hillel in, 70, 230, 245, 251; *Parent's Guide to Orthodox Assimilation on University Campuses*, 222; Stern College for Women, 222, 224, 234; Touro College/University, 222; University of Chicago, 63; Williams College, 5; Yale University, 230; Yeshiva University, 74, 219–22, 224, 232

Viñas, Rabbi "Manny," 73
Virginia, 66; Charlottesville, 3, 136
Vizhnitz (ḥasidic community), 228
Voting Rights Act of 1965, 151

Warner, R. Stephen, 58
War of Attrition (1969 to 1971), 166
Washington Post, 100, 273
wealth concentration, 249
weddings, 94; Brit Ger Toshav and Brit Nissuim covenants at, 96
Weinstein, Harvey, 46
Weinstein, Yaakov, 222
Weisenfeld, Judith, 72, 201

Weiss, Avi, 41
welfare agencies, 245
Wells Fargo, 143
Wertheimer, Jack, 173, 194–96, 199, 201, 205, 250
West Bank, Israel: American Jewish views on, 173, 179n31, 256; military checkpoints in, 171; settlements, 168, 173, 178n24, 181n52; ZOA and, 255
western Jews, education and income levels for, 123, *124*
West Newton, Massachusetts, 105–7
WhatsApp, 44
white Americans, 140
white Jews, 131–34, 139–40; Jews of Color education and income levels contrasted with, 124–25, *125*
white nationalists, 136
whiteness, 136, 141
white supremacy, 133, 136, 139, 148
Wilderness Torah, 264
Williamsburg neighborhood, Brooklyn, 227–28
Williams College, Williamstown, Massachusetts, 5
Williamstown, Massachusetts, 5
Wilson, Woodrow, 147
Wirth, Louis, 63
Wisconsin, 106
Wolf, Nelly, 198
women, 2–3, 115, 118, 221, 223, 226–27, 233; church ladies, 37; educational attainment for, 121–23, *122*; leadership compared with men, 268n47; maharat title for ordained, 41; *mechitza* divider between men, 38, 52; #MeToo movement, 38–39, 45–46, 48; Nishmat Orthodox education for, 42–43; shiksa term for non-Jewish, 91; Stern College for Women, 222, 224, 234; Torah education for, 41–42, 44, 220; Yoetzot.org for, 42–43. *See also* feminism

Women's Halakhic Hotline, 42
Woocher, Jonathan, 164

X. *See* Twitter
xenophobia, 143–44

Yale University, 230
Yeshiva Chofetz Chaim, 216
yeshivas, 251
Yeshivas Chofetz Chaim, 215
Yeshivat Chovevei Torah, 225
Yeshivat Maharat, 41–42, 225
Yeshiva University, 74, 219–22, 224, 232
Yeshiva World, 210, 213–19, 221, 223, 228, 231, 233
Yeshiva World News, 218
yeshivish, 186, 212, 216

yetzer hara ("evil inclination"), 49
Yiddishkeit, 65
Yiddish language, 11, 145, 227, 229
yoetzet halakhah, 42–43
Yoetzot.org, 42–43
Yom Kippur, 190
Yom Kippur War, 166, 245
yordim, 21
young adult organizations, 262–63

Zack, Naomi, 70
Ziegler School of Rabbinic Studies, 74
Zionism, 1, 16, 138, 186, 214, 226–27, 277. *See also* anti-Zionists
Zionist Organization of America (ZOA), 255
Zoom, 202–3, 205, 258

www.ingramcontent.com/pod-product-compliance
Lightning Source LLC
Chambersburg PA
CBHW020356080526
44584CB00014B/1047